COLLECTED PERSPECTIVES

Choosing and Using Books
For the Classroom

COLLECTED PERSPECTIVES

Choosing and Using Books For the Classroom

Edited by
Hughes Moir
Melissa Cain
Leslie Prosak-Beres

Christopher-Gordon Publishers, Inc., Boston

In association with
Cooperative Services for Children's Literature
The University of Toledo

ISBN 0-926842-03-X

Christopher-Gordon Publishers, Inc.
480 Washington Street
Norwood, MA 02062

Collected Perspectives was prepared on a Macintosh Plus computer using WriteNow 2.0 and ReadySetGo! 3.0, Times and Helvetica fonts, and printed camera-ready on a LaserWriter II printer at The University of Toledo. Printed in the United States of America by Capital City Press in Berlin, Vermont.

CONTENTS

FOREWORD by Lee Bennett Hopkins.. vii

INTRODUCTION by Hughes Moir... ix

REVIEWERS.. xii

PICTURE STORY BOOKS.. 1

FICTION FOR YOUNGER READERS (Ages 6-12).. 71

FICTION FOR OLDER READERS (Ages 12-up)... 127

POETRY (all ages).. 181

NONFICTION (all ages).. 205

AUTHOR–TITLE INDEX... 275

SUBJECT INDEX.. 279

PUBLISHERS' ADDRESSES.. 280

"This is one of the pleasures of reading—you may make any pictures out of the words you can and will; and a poem may have as many different meanings as there are different minds…"

Walter de la Mare

FOREWORD

In a welcome era where books for children and young adults are speedily entering the mainstream of the total curriculum, it is a delight to have *Collected Perspectives: Choosing and Using Books for the Classroom*. Since 1984, Hughes Moir, and a dedicated staff at the Cooperative Services for Children's Literature at The University of Toledo, have published the unique journal, *PERSPECTIVES*, aiming to promote literature in elementary and secondary school programs.

Collected Perspectives is packed with information on bringing children and books together in classrooms, school and public libraries, and in homes.

A salient feature of this volume is that the reviews are written by practicing, working day-to-day educators who are *using* books *with* children and young adults. More than just another review media source, *Collected Perspectives* offers tried and tested suggestions for integrating children's books into various areas of the curriculum—from music to mathematics, social studies to spelling.

It is very exciting to view the many creative possibilities of using one specific title with others of the same theme. The review lead prose to poetry, fiction into nonfiction, and suggest numerous ways to enhance literature programs to the fullest.

Far too often guides to children's books come across my desk filled with a plethora of questions, monotonous sets of worksheets, tests, and endless lists of activities that only serve to beat a specific title to its inevitable demise. You will not find this type of mindless didacticism in this volume. Take, for example, the brief notation of *The Jolly Postman and Other People's Letters* by Janet and Allan Ahlberg (page 2), a book that all ages have taken tinto their hearts, where the reviewer *suggests* not *dictates* how this ingenious volume can be used to spark both real and imagined letter writing projects—a far cry from a pedantic workbook page suggesting children write to an unknown, ficticious "friend!"

Astute parents and educators know there is no one book; that one title should lead to another and another, enabling readers of all ages, whether they are in kindergarten or senior high school, to become critical, thoughtful, proficient readers—to foster a lifelong habit to encourage the *love* of reading.

Whether you are currently using children's books as part of a literature-based reading program, whole language approaches to literacy development, extending programs beyond basal materials, or just using books with children to have a good time, *Collected Perspectives: Choosing and Using Books for the Classroom* is a volume you will want to dip into again and again.

I know I will.

Lee Bennett Hopkins
Scarborough, New York

INTRODUCTION

PERSPECTIVES is a book review journal written by teachers and librarians and published by Cooperative Services for Children's Literature at The University of Toledo. CSCL set out to bring a new approach to looking at children's and young adult literature, a point of view we thought was missing in other review journals: a point of view about how to use new books in schools and libraries by professionals who work with young people. In addition to alerting our readers to the best new materials as they are published, our fundamental goal has always been to offer realistic and creative approaches to integrating literature in all areas of the curriculum, thereby promoting literacy, the wider use of books, and a lifetime of enjoyment from reading.

Five years have passed and thousands of new books have been published since our first issue in the fall of 1984. *PERSPECTIVES* has printed nearly two thousand reviews and teaching suggestions. By bringing together these selected reviews in this special volume, we hope to remind teachers and librarians of some of the best books of 1984–88 and how they might effectively help young readers discover the pleasures of reading and the satisfaction of learning through interesting books.

Collected Perspectives is organized into five sections: *Picture Story Books, Fiction for Younger Readers* (elementary grades), *Fiction for Older Readers* (junior and senior high school), *Poetry* (all grades), and *Nonfiction* (all grades). These sections are based upon the publisher's recommended age range and the grade levels where we think the book is likely to have its broadest appeal. Our approach is to realistically seek out the widest possible audience for each book. Many books in picture book format, for example, are better suited to an older audience of intermediate or junior high school students; stories intended to be read by older children often can also be enjoyed by a group of younger listeners. In some cases we have listed books from the same series in different sections to call attention to the breadth of the books' audience. Therefore, in seeking materials for a particular grade level, be sure to look through all sections for books and teaching ideas for your particular age group(s). Although a book might not fit your specific needs, perhaps a teaching idea will suggest some resource you already use.

Each review looks at the book from one of two points of view. One approach is to try to look at a book from the point of view of the young reader. Based upon experience with children and adolescents, what are the likeliest areas of response? Which aspects of the book are more likely to spark interest after the book is finished, as well as while it is being read? What might a reader wonder about or want to do after reading a particular book? Will the book likely evoke a strong emotional response? Will a young reader learn something interesting or useful? Will it make the reader laugh? Is this book likely to make the reader want another by the same author? These are some of the questions that a reviewer might consider while preparing the review.

A second point of view is that of the teacher or librarian—a literate adult and experienced reader who is looking at a piece of literature with an interested and open mind ready to be stimulated, to be delighted, to laugh or cry, or to learn about the world of people and things. Our own enthusiasm, we know, can motivate young people to share our responses to the same piece of literature. We also take the position that literature enhances learning in any curricular area. Therefore, some reviews focus on how a specific book can effectively serve the goals of instruction.

Each book review is presented in two paragraphs: a brief summary and evaluation in the first paragraph, and a second paragraph describing an activity intended to extend a reader's response to the book. In an effort to present as many books and teaching suggestions as possible in a limited format, each review is intended to be about 200 words. The first paragraph of the review, therefore, must be concise, provide information about the book's content, and a qualitative assessment.

The suggested teaching activity discussed in the second paragraph of each review is intended to encourage interest in some aspect of the plot, or about a character, an episode, the setting, or about some other facet of the story, poem, or topic. We recognize that there are a myriad of possible follow-up activities that could be suggested; we try to describe one in sufficient depth to be clear and specific. The close interrelationship between literature and reading/English language arts makes many instructional suggestions focus on these areas. However, teachers in all areas will find many examples of literature that also support instruction in the sciences, the social studies, and the arts.

It is clear from what is known about response theory and from regular contact with young people, that response to literature is highly individualistic and specifically unpredictable. However, experience with young people helps a teacher or librarian to anticipate the areas or ways in which many children are most likely to respond. Imperfect as it may be, without the capacity and wisdom to judge and anticipate, we could not plan effective instruction and experience would fail to teach us anything. Your judgment is crucial in the end. You must assess each idea in light of your instructional context—your curriculum and facilities, your interests and talents, and your students' needs and their abilities.

In addition to discussing how books might be used, the reviews often suggest "companion books" which can extend a reader's interest, or that a teacher will find useful in an instructional setting. Though some few titles may now be out of print, most are probably part of a school or public library collection. Experienced teachers and librarians will certainly be able to suggest others. They are worth seeking out.

Each review is further annotated to indicate potential curriculum areas or topics for which the book might be applicable. Also noted are the range of potential audiences and occasionally other information about the book (e.g., an award, part of a series or a sequel, etc.). The books are numbered sequentially for quicker reference and indexing. Bibliographic data is provided for each entry. Appendices include a title-author index, a subject index, and a listing of publishers' addresses and toll free numbers for ordering books.

The reviews included in this volume of **Collected Perspectives** were chosen because we believe the books are interesting and worth a young reader's time to read them. They can offer readers a high return on their investment of time, and each has the potential for encouraging the reader to take another book off the shelf. They hold many possibilities for creative teachers and librarians who know that an integrated curriculum where literature is truly basic and fundamental to an educated mind. Finally, after reading thousands of books over the past five years, we included books that we liked and were excited about. We hope you find our enthusiasm catching.

We created **Collected Perspectives** to help teachers and librarians find their best ways to bring young people together with the fine works of literature they deserve. The insights and suggestions presented reflect our experience with children, our responses to literature, and our understanding of curriculum. Ultimately, the responsibility for selecting and using books in a classroom or library is in your hands. You must decide how literature can best help you achieve the intructional aims of your programs. You must decide, along with your students, the route to finding the pleasures and satisfactions we know literaure can provide.

Hughes Moir
Cooperative Services for Children's Literature
The University of Toledo
September, 1989

CONTRIBUTING REVIEWERS

D.M.A.	Denise Adamski, The University of Toledo
J.F.A.	Dr. John Ahern, Professor of Education, The University of Toledo
L.B.	Lorraine Beeker, Coordinator of Gifted and Talented Education, Fremont, OH
L.A.B.	Lori Beverage, Elementary Teacher, Perrysburg, OH
L.P.B.	Dr. Leslie Prosak-Beres, Professor of Education, Xavier University
N.J.B.	Nancy Bertsche, Elementary Teacher, Pandora, Ohio
K.B.B.	Katherine Bishop-Brassell, Elementary Teacher, Rossford, OH
B.B.	Barbara Britsch, Instructor, Lourdes College, Sylvania, OH
G.B.	Dr. Greg Brownell, Professor of Education, Bowling Green State University
M.A.C.	Dr. Melissa Cain, Editor of PERSPECTIVES
M.B.C.	Marge Cater, High School Teacher, Whitehouse, OH
B.C.	Dr. Bonnie Chambers, Professor of Education, Bowling Green State University
G.E.C.	Dr. Gary Cooke, Professor of Education, The University of Toledo
W.J.C.	Dr. William Curtis, Visiting Professor of Speech, Brunswick (GA) College
E.M.F.	Edith Fetter, Elementary Teacher, Toledo, OH
H.A.F.	Hollee Frick, Elementary Teacher, Monroe, MI
R.M.G.	Rose Mary Galoosis, Junior High School Teacher, Sylvania, OH
G.G.	Gretchen Good, Doctoral Student, The University of Toledo
K.J.G.	Kate Gundy, Assistant Director, The Lion and the Lamb Peace Arts Center, Bluffton, OH
L.M.H.	Dr. Lola Haller, Professor of Education, Houghton (NY) College
F.M.H.	Marilynn Hazard, School Librarian, Toledo, OH
A.H.	Alice Henning, School Librarian, Toledo, OH
M.J.H.	Dr. Mary Jo Henning, Professor of Education, The University of Toledo
E.A.H.	Dr. Elizabeth Hostetler, Professor of Education, Bluffton (OH) College
K.I.	Kay Ingle, Elementary Teacher, Sylvania, OH
R.K.J.	Robin Jolly, Elementary Teacher, Perrysburg, OH
C.E.L.	Cheryl LaFave, High School Teacher, Whitehouse, OH
J.E.M.	Johanna Mack, Elementary Teacher, Defiance, OH
K.L.M.	Kelley McConnaughy, Elementary Teacher, Prince Georges County, MD
M.M.	Marriane McCreight, Elementary Teacher, Ottawa Hills, OH
A.M.M.	Ann Marie Minnick, Special Education Teacher, Toledo, OH
H.M.	Dr. Hughes Moir, Professor of Education, The University of Toledo
M.E.M.	Martha Mollenkopf, Director of School Library Services, Ida, MI
A.P.N.	Dr. Alice Naylor, Professor of Education, Appalachian State University
E.N.	Dr. Elmer Neufeld, President, Bluffton (OH) College
J.P.	Joan Page, Elementary Teacher, Swanton, OH
N.S.R.	Nita Randolph, Elementary Teacher, Toledo, OH
J.B.R.	Jennifer Boney Reynolds, Elementary Teachers, Monroe, MI
B.S.J.	Dr. Barbara St. John, Professor of English, Bowling Green State University
M.M.S.	Michiale Schneider, Graduate Assistant, The University of Toledo
A.S.	Anne Shimojima, IMC Director, Highland Park, IL
L.S.	Linda Shreve, Middle School Teacher, Jacksonville, FL
S.J.S.	Sue Snow, Elementary Teacher, Sylvania, OH
J.J.S.	Jeannine Jordan-Squire, High School Teacher, Lima, OH
V.H.S.	Virginia Stelk, Middle School Teacher, Lakeland Schools, Shrub Oak, NY
M.A.S.	Dr. Mary Ann Stibbe, Director of Learning Development, Adrian (MI) College
C.S.	Cynthia Stilley, Public Librarian, Flint, MI
C.G.T.	Cindy Tedrow, Elementary Teacher, Swanton, OH
J.T.	Judy Thomaswick, Elementary Teacher, Toledo, OH
M.O.T.	Dr. Michael Tunnell, Professor of Education, Northern Illinois University
K.W.	Kathy Wachtman, Elementary Teacher, Toledo, OH
J.R.W.	Dr. J. Richard Weaver, Professor of Education, Bluffton (OH) College
S.L.W.	Sarah Widman, School Librarian, Toledo, OH
C.A.Y.	Carol Yates, School Librarian, Toledo, OH

PICTURE
STORY
BOOKS

PICTURE STORY BOOKS

1. Aardema, Verna. *Oh, Kojo! How Could You!* Illustrated by Marc Brown. Dial, 1984. ISBN 0-8037-0006-7, $10.95. Ages 4-8.

In Ashantiland, beside the River-That-Gurgles-PonponponPonsa, lived Ananse the trickster and Tutuola, a lonely, childless woman. The River Spirit grants Tutuola her wish for a son, but warns her that he will not like to work and will like to spend money, though he will someday repay her. Kojo is and does exactly that! As in *Why Mosquitoes Buzz in People's Ears* (Dial 1975), Verna Aardema has incorporated a variety of onomatopoeia that contributes significantly to the West African flavor of this new story. Marc Brown did that too: influenced by his study of West African cave paintings, he wove curving linear motifs into the illustrations.

Related Source

Without the works of Verna Aardema, it is quite likely that American children would have less exposure to the wealth of fine stories that have been passed along by means of the oral tradition on the African continent. They have been additionally blessed by her lively writing style and obvious love of the sounds of language. Older students might like to write to Verna Aardema c/o Dial Books, 2 Park Avenue, New York, NY 10016 to ask her about how she came to be interested in the folklore of Africa and how she researches her stories. M.A.C.

*Author Study
Primary
Intermediate*

2. Ackerman, Karen. *Song and Dance Man.* Illustrated by Stephen Gammell. Knopf, 1988. ISBN 0-394-99330-6, $11.99. Ages 3-7.

The 1989 Caldecott winner, *Song and Dance Man,* tells of a retired vaudeville performer who ventures up the rickety attic steps, grandchildren in tow, to put on a stage show for them. Included in his act is a bit of soft shoe, a corny joke or two, and plenty of clowning around. Told in the voice of a grandchild, the book's strength lies in the endearing song and dance man. Ackerman has done justice to grandfathers, developing a character free from traditional stereotypes. Though he holds tight to the staircase rail on the trip downstairs and is a bit out of breath from singing and dancing, this is a grandfather with unique talents and a host of memories. Gammell has enlivened his face with jubilant expressions. His colored pencil techniques transform attic to stage, lighted with floods, spots, and colorful gels.

*Caldecott Award Winner
ALA Notable Book*

Music, Drama, Art
Primary
Intermediate

From the cedar smells of an old leather-trimmed trunk appear Grandpa's props: bowlers and top hats, striped vests with matching bow ties, tap shoes, and gold-tipped canes. A trunk full of old stage items and clothing stored in the classroom can open up a world of imaginative delights. Many such items sell cheaply at flea markets and second hand stores. Introduce students to the old song and dance days, putting their unique talents to work creating a vaudeville show to perform for each other or other classes.   K.L.M.

3.   Ahlberg, Janet and Allan. *The Jolly Postman and Other People's Letters*. Illustrated by the authors. Little, Brown, 1986. ISBN 0-316-02036-2, $9.95. Ages 4-up.

The jolly postman delivers letters to fairy tale characters such as Cinderella, The Three Bears, Goldilocks, and others. The story is told in simple rhyme, but the unique feature and strength of this book is the inclusion of the letters themselves, complete with envelopes, stamps, and, where appropriate, invented spellings—e.g., by Goldilocks in her letter of apology to The Three Bears. The witch receives a flyer advertising "witch" supplies, the giant receives a postcard from Jack, Cinderella receives a business letter, and the wolf receives a letter from Little Red Riding Hood's lawyer. The letters are placed in envelopes and are easily removed for reading. This is a very clever and enjoyable book for children of all ages, one that will be appreciated by teachers.

Language Arts
Primary
Intermediate

The Jolly Postman and Other People's Letters can be used to introduce children to letter writing for various purposes. Children could develop a class book by writing letters to characters from their literary readings or from the content areas (scientists, politicians, explorers; e.g., what types of letters might Madame Curie have received before and after her discovery?) This shows transfer of learning in a creative way as the children must understand the situation before they can write the letter. Older children could also compare this type of text with that of Cleary's *Dear Mr. Henshaw* (Morrow, 1983).   B.C.

Related Source

4.   Allard, Harry. *Miss Nelson Has a Field Day*. Illustrated by James Marshall. Houghton Mifflin, 1985. ISBN 0-395-36690-9, $12.95. Ages 6-9.

Third in series of
Miss Nelson books

The Smedley School Tornadoes were the worst football team anyone had ever seen. Coach Armstrong couldn't handle them. When the principal, Mr. Blandsworth, tried to get them ready for the big game against the Central Werewolves, they laughed him off the field. Only Miss Viola Swamp could do the job—and she does, in this third hilarious adventure featuring "the meanest substitute in the whole wide world." Fans are in for a puzzle, however, when both Miss Nelson and Miss Viola Swamp are seen in pictures at the same time, and the explanation is an enjoyable surprise. Allard and Marshall have again created a sure winner to delight their many fans, old and young alike.

The illustrations in this book humorously and effectively show feelings. What can you tell about Miss Viola Swamp even before you read about her? How can you tell that she's a no-nonsense person? What can you tell about the players on the Smedley football team by looking at their pictures on pages 6-7? Discussion can follow about how illustrations help the reader learn more about the story. Teachers can explore other books and illustrations to see how other artists show emotion.   M.E.M.

5. Anno, Mitsumasa. *Anno's Flea Market*. Illustrated by the author. Philomel, 1984. ISBN 0-399-21031-8, $11.95. All ages.

The fair sets up early within the town walls, allowing us to wander to our heart's content through an amazing, nostalgic array of wares. Anno believes men are best understood by what they make with their hands. So, he has assembled a wealth of evidence, from household objects and strange musical instruments to tombstones. Entertainers, musicians, and food sellers mingle with ordinary and famous browsers—literary and real (Laurel and Hardy, Alice in Wonderland). Anno teases us to find jokes and little dramas on each double page spread. The total impression is one of historical mingling: people haven't changed much although things are changing all the time.

Since Anno believes in the integrity of handmade objects, this picture book offers an excellent chance to develop respect for our ancestors' ingenuity and artistry. Ask students to bring something old or beautiful for sharing. Visit an historical museum, such as the Henry Ford Museum in Dearborn, Michigan, or the Smithsonian Museum to further explore the evolution of artifacts and costuming. Collect some "whatzits" for students to speculate about and research.   B.B.

6. Anno, Mitsumasa. *In Shadowland*. Illustrated by the author. Orchard, 1988 (1st Am. ed.). ISBN 0-531-05741-0, $14.95. Ages 4-7.

With the release in America of *In Shadowland*, Anno reasserts his claim as one of the most imaginative book illustrators in the world. The simple story of the watchman of Shadowland who helped the young match-seller in the village, and of their flight back to Shadowland, is enhanced by Anno's use of contrasting illustrations on facing pages. The muted watercolors of the small village and black paper cut silhouettes that create Shadowland are striking and effective in representing the textures and hues of the real world and the weightless, two-dimensional world of shadows. Though the story is slight, the illustrations make this an irresistible selection for an elementary library and a welcome addition to other books by this remarkable artist.

Silhouettes can be created in a variety of ways, from using cut paper shapes on an overhead projector or in a shadow theater, to paper cutting and drawing with black ink. Younger children can draw each other's shadows using chalk on the playground and compare their similarities and differences. Among the books for younger readers that

Literature, Art
Primary

Social Studies
Primary
Intermediate
Middle School

Art, Drama
Primary
Intermediate

effectively use silhouettes or paper cut techniques are Elizabeth Cleaver's **The Enchanted Caribou** (Atheneum, 1985), Cheng Houtien's version of **Six Chinese Brothers** (Holt, 1979), and Jane Yolen's **The Emperor and the Kite** (World, 1967) which features Ed Young's paper cut illustrations.   H.M./N.J.B.

7.   Aruego, Jose and Ariane Dewey. **Rockabye Crocodile**. Illustrated by the authors. Greenwillow, 1988. ISBN 0-688-06739-5, $11.88. Ages 4-up.

Amabel, a kindhearted elderly bear, is a neighbor to Nettie, a mean, selfish boar. Amabel is polite when a bamboo tree drops fish into her basket and is rewarded when she kindly soothes a crocodile's howling baby. Nettie is eager to fill her own basket with fish, but her rude, impatient behavior brings her very different results. All ends well, however, when Nettie learns her lesson and is ready to earn her rewards justly. Aruego and Dewey, illustrators of over three dozen picture story books, have used bright, clear watercolors and gouache to illustrate this gentle story and create two especially appealing characters.

This retelling of a Philippine folk tale is a variation of a familiar theme: a good character is rewarded and an evil character punished. Some other traditional tales that portray this theme include the Grimms' "Mother Holle," **The Tongue-Cut Sparrow** by Momoko Ishii (Dutton, 1987), and **Chen Ping and His Magic Ax** by Demi (Dodd, Mead, 1987). Students can compare these on a chart or on the chalkboard. This comparison should include such story elements as good and bad characters, plot, setting, theme, resolution, and the supporting detail that reflects the various cultures.   A.S.

Literature Primary Intermediate

Related Source

8.   Aylesworth, Jim. **Hanna's Hog**. Illustrated by Glen Rounds. Atheneum, 1988. ISBN 0-689-31367-5, $13.95. Ages 5-8.

How do you keep a wild hog tame? Well, you feed it "things that hogs are partial to...like melon rinds and cobs from roastin' ears, and such." That was Hanna's secret, anyway. When she called out, "Soowee!" her pig would come running home—until the day it was stolen by that devil Kenny Jackson. Hanna's clever plan to retrieve her pig and cure Kenny of his cheating ways will tickle plenty of funny bones. An easy-flowing, conversational narrative, accompanied by Rounds's typically expressive and bold drawings, makes this sprightly and humorous yarn one that children could return to again and again.

Both the story and the illustrations have many similarities to Wright's **The Old Woman and the Willy Nilly Man** (Putnam, 1987). Students could read them side by side and discuss how they are the same and where they differ. For example, both have strong-willed and clever female characters, and both are set in the country. However, Wright's story is written in dialect, Aylesworth's is not. These sorts of comparisons can be presented as enjoyable "puzzles" that can become the foundation for developing more literate readers.   L.B.

Related Source

Literature Primary

9. Baker, Jeannie. *Home in the Sky*. Illustrated by the author. Greenwillow, 1984. ISBN 0-688-03841-7, $13.00. All ages.

Mike calls his flock of pigeons home to eat, but one of the pigeons, Light, flies away. Light meets street pigeons who fight him for food, he gets wet from the rain, and he becomes "trapped" in a subway train. The young boy who rescues him wants to keep him. When she sees the bird, his mother says it belongs to someone else, and he must let it go. The story is accompanied by extraordinary three-dimensional art which incorporates ceramics, grasses, leaves, pigeon feathers, clay, fabric, and pieces of real hair, as well as original paintings. Jeannie Baker, an Australian artist, spent ten months in New York doing research and two years completing this incredible picture book. Children and adults alike will relish the art work as they try to determine how she accomplished it.

Home in the Sky typifies the kind of picture book that deserves study and appreciation by art students and art teachers. While the story may be limited to the interests of very young children, older students can study this as a model for how collage can be used to achieve artistic heights. Baker's technique can also be compared to the successful use of collage achieved by Eric Carle, Elizabeth Cleaver, Marcia Brown, Ezra Jack Keats, and Leo Lionni, to mention but a few artists who work in this medium.   B.C.

ALA Notable Book

Art
All Grades

10. Baker, Jeannie. *Where the Forest Meets the Sea*. Illustrated by the author. Greenwillow, 1988 (1st Am. ed.). ISBN 0-688-06364-0, $11.88. All ages.

This certainly must be one of the most beautiful ecology books ever written. Using the same three dimensional collage constructions she introduced to American audiences in *Home in the Sky* (Greenwillow, 1984), Jeannie Baker tells us about the endangered tropical rain forest wilderness that meets the ocean waters of the Great Barrier Reef of Australia. She does this through following a boy and his dad on a day's adventure into this untouched area. As the boy explores the forest, we see shadows superimposed upon his reality, shadows of the people and animals that might have lived there, and of the way the area may look in the future if it is not protected. The text is powerful in its simplicity, told from the child's point of view and reflecting the child's concerns. The pictures are superb: their three dimensions lure the viewer to stroke the glossy pages seeking texture and make him/her feel as if he/she could walk right into the rain forest via the book as well. If there could only be one picture story book purchased for the school or public library for 1988, *Where the Forest Meets the Sea* would be a top contender.

An obvious use for this book would be to interest students in doing three dimensional collage. Use *Home in the Sky* for that. *Where the Forest Meets the Sea* can be used to stimulate students to research wilderness areas of the world that are shrinking and efforts that are being made to save them. Students might want to debate the diverse viewpoints of land developers versus the concerns of conservationists. Such issues could be raised as whether the needs of the human popu-

Related Source

Science,
Social Studies
Intermediate
Middle School
Junior High School

lation should take precedence over the needs of wildlife, whether private landowners should have total control over the use of their land, and what role governments should take in conservation. Students could search newspapers for related stories. The recent national debate between the Toledo Zoo and The National Wildlife Federation about the display of two pandas is an example of differing opinions people have about the best way to protect an endangered species.   M.A.C.

11.   Bang, Molly. *The Paper Crane*. Illustrated by the author. Greenwillow, 1985. ISBN 0-688-04109-4, $12.88. Ages 5-8.

ALA Notable Book

The Paper Crane is a remarkable visual experience for readers of a wide age range. The spare style in which this engrossing tale is told and the textured illustrations, both by Molly Bang, work well together, but it is the art that is outstanding. Bang creates meticulously detailed, three-dimensional collages that extend the reader's interest and deepen the simple story of a restaurant owner whose act of kindness to a stranger results in a revival of his once failing business. There is magic in the story: the stranger leaves a paper napkin folded into a crane which comes to life and dances when the owner claps his hands. But Molly Bang's collage technique is magical in itself. The characterizations are most striking: people of many cultures are depicted as experiencing that awed *joie de vivre* that only such things as dancing cranes can stimulate. Yet for the owner's son, the experience stimulates even more. The last page reveals him practicing the flute, the instrument the stranger played so beautifully.

*Art
Primary*

This is a book to be used in art classes. Students can examine the detail in the collage to see how Molly Bang created certain effects, notably the rich characterizations. Careful scrutiny may give them some insights, and experimentation with three-dimensional techniques should yield others. Students might also enjoy comparing Bang's technique

Related Source

with that of Leo Lionni in his *Frederick's Fables* (Pantheon, 1985), that uses collage effectively also.   M.A.C.

12.   Berger, Barbara. *Grandfather Twilight*. Illustrated by the author. Philomel, 1984. ISBN 0-399-20996-4, $11.95. Ages 5-9.

This beautifully illustrated story describes that time of day, just before nightfall, when leaves begin to whisper and little birds hush. Grandfather Twilight offers a pearl to the sky which gets larger and brighter as he moves along and which eventually becomes the moon. The text is simple and is accompanied by lovely "twilight-like" pictures, including three double-page wordless illustrations. There is a overriding feeling of peace and serenity throughout the book which could make *Grandfather Twilight* become, like Margaret Wise Brown's *Goodnight Moon* (Harper & Row, 1947), a favorite bedtime story.

Related Source

There is a musical quality to both the story and the illustrations in *Grandfather Twilight*. A challenging, yet satisfying, class or group project would be to prepare either a slide-tape or videotape presentation of the book with appropriate music to complement the mood, tone, and imagery of the story. Primary age children could work in small groups with middle school students on this project for presentation to students in both grade groups.   B.C.

13.   Birch, David. *The King's Chessboard.* Illustrated by Devis Grebu. Dial, 1988. ISBN 0-8037-0365-1, $10.95. Ages 5-up.

A king of the East tries to repay a wise man for a certain service and promises a greater reward than he is able to deliver. Though he first mocks the wise man, who has simply asked for one grain of rice to be doubled each day for as many days as there are squares on a chessboard, the king is soon forced to swallow his pride and retract his offer. Through the character of the proud king, Birch points out the danger of rash promises. The generosity of the gentle wise man forms a powerful contrast to the arrogance of the king. The illustrations, carefully rendered in ink, watercolor, and colored pencils, expand effectively upon the text and reflect an Eastern cultural setting.

Birch's book would make an excellent springboard for a math discovery lesson for upper primary or intermediate levels. Students could be asked to find the daily amount of rice if one more grain was added each day, if two more grains were added, and if five more were added. Once they have arrived at daily figures, they can search for patterns recurring among the numbers. Older children might be able to generalize these patterns into a mathematical formula. Younger children may find recognition of the patterns to be a sufficient task .   E.M.F.

14.   Birdseye, Tom. *Airmail to the Moon.* Illustrated by Stephen Gammell. Holiday House, 1988. ISBN 0-8234-0683-0, $13.95. Ages 5-8.

In a perfect union of text and illustration, Birdseye and Gammell have created one of the most memorable characters since Pippi Longstocking. When Ora Mae Cotton loses her tooth and cannot find it or any money the next morning, she is convinced someone "so crooked they screw their socks on every morning" has stolen her tooth. Narrated by Ora Mae, the story is told with the emotions and suspicions of a six- to seven-year-old interspersed with delightful expressions such as "I was popcorn-in-the-pan excited," "as ornery as a bull in a beehive," and her repeated phrase "Somebody stole my tooth, and when I catch'em I'm gonna open up a can of gotcha and send'em airmail to the moon." Gammell uses colored pencil illustrations to create unforgettable characters and scenery to make the story come alive with humor and whimsy.

The picture book is useful to teach artistic style to children. Using this book, as well as some of Gammell's other books, such as *The Relatives Came* by Cynthia Rylant (Bradbury, 1985), *Old Henry* by Joan Blos (Morrow, 1987) and *Where the Buffaloes Begin* by Olaf Baker (Warne, 1981), discuss Gammell's techniques. Younger

Art, Author Studies
Primary
Intermediate

children can become aware of different types of media as well. Gammell's colored pencil illustrations can be compared to other artists' different uses of media, such as Leo Lionni's collage, Ed Young's pastels, or Thomas Locker's oils. Older children can discuss how Gammell uses color and line to portray mood and setting, or how his illustrations have changed from his first books to his latest.   K.B.B.

15.   Birrer, Cynthia and William. *Song to Demeter*. Illustrated by the authors. Lothrop, Lee & Shepard, 1987. ISBN 0-688-04041-1, $11.88. Ages 5-8.

The first thing most readers will be apt to notice about *Song to Demeter* are the book's unusual illustrations. All are machine-stitched applique and embroidery on fabric with the same border connecting each page, conveying a continuity similar to a mural or stone frieze. The story is the straightforward retelling of the Greek myth about Demeter, the goddess of the harvest, and her daughter, Persephone. Pluto, the god of Hades and Demeter's brother, loves Persephone and wishes to make her queen of the Kingdom of the Dead. When Pluto whisks Persephone off to the underworld, it brings grief and then anger to Demeter, causing the earth to turn cold. Zeus resolves the conflict by allowing Persephone to return to Hades for four months, when the earth turns cold and dreary. This is the explanation of the seasons according to the Greek myth.

Science,
Language Arts
Primary
Intermediate

Besides being used in a study of mythology at any age, this would be an excellent resource in a classroom which is studying the seasons or cycles in nature. The last nine pages clearly show the changing of the seasons. Students can study these pages and tell what changes they can see taking place, including the clothing, background, and colors of each season. Older children can speculate about the possibility of seasons not changing, or changing only slightly, as they do in warmer climates. Young children can dictate, and older children write, their own explanation of why the seasons change—either mythical or scientific. Then share a book with students that explains the true reason that seasons change. For youngsters, Branley's *Sunshine Makes the Seasons*

Related Sources

(Crowell, 1985) is an appealing and effective introductory source. Older children can find a wealth of entertaining and informative projects and activities from Linda Allison's *The Reason for Seasons: The Great Cosmic Megagalactic Trip Without Moving From Your Chair* (Little, Brown, 1975).   V.H.S./L.S.

16.   Blake, Quentin. *Mrs. Armitage on Wheels*. Illustrated by the author. Knopf, 1988 (1st Am. ed.). ISBN 0-394-99498-1, $11.99. Ages 5-8.

Quixotic Mrs. Armitage is out for a ride on her bicycle when she discovers that her bell won't even stop a hedgehog from crossing the road in front of her. "What this bike needs is a really loud horn," she says, thus beginning a chain of improvements that eventually leads to disaster—and a new pair of roller skates! Blake's cartoon-style pen-

and-ink and watercolor drawings are truly comical, showing Mrs. Armitage at her zaniest. Children should also enjoy watching the antics of Breakspear the dog, who appears on each page. This is an excellent example of honest humor that younger children can understand and appreciate. Quentin Blake has created a character in Mrs. Armitage that has the potential for many more adventures.

Mrs. Armitage on Wheels is an appealing book that could stimulate children to think about how to "improve" some of the ordinary things around them. To become an inventor, one must also be a divergent thinker, something not always fostered by our schools as they are presently structured. Ask students to select something that has already been invented—a scooter, a car, a blender, a saw, a toy, a coffee maker, etc. Encourage them to think about ways they could improve it. Urge them to stretch their thinking to come up with more ways after they think they are tapped out. Then trade objects to see if others in the class can come up with even more ideas. Finally, have them look back over all of the ideas to decide which ones are feasible and which might be too much, like the sail on Mrs. Armitage's bike.   M.A.C.

*Science,
Social Studies
Primary
Intermediate*

17.   Brown, Ruth. *The Big Sneeze*. Illustrated by the author. Lothrop, Lee & Shepard, 1985. ISBN 0-688-04666-5, $11.88. Ages 3-6.

Atishooooo! A single sneeze is the catalyst for a series of events in this beautifully illustrated cumulative tale. A farmer's sneeze blows a fly into a spider's web, disturbing the spider, which wakes a sparrow, and so on, until the farmer's wife comes into the barnyard to find out why the donkey is braying. The lush, full-page illustrations depict the ambiance of lazy summer afternoon: one can almost feel the heat of a still afternoon in mid-July. While there may be other books that relate a more unusual chain of events or characters, few have illustrations as rich and evocative as Ruth Brown's.

This book presents an excellent opportunity to teach children about cause and effect. After the class has shared this short story and been introduced to the concept of cause and effect, build a "cause and effect machine," where one thing happening triggers another, which triggers another. One possibility: drop a marble into a tube, which would move a lever at the bottom of the tube when the marble lands. The lever that is moved would release fish food into the class aquarium. Audrey and Don Woods' *Elbert's Bad Word* (Harcourt Brace Jovanovich, 1988) demonstrates a much more implausible sequence of events that lead, ultimately, to the escape of "the bad word."   J.J.S.

*Science, Math
Primary*

Related Source

18.   Bunting, Eve. *Ghost's Hour, Spook's Hour*. Illustrated by Donald Carrick. Clarion, 1987. ISBN 0-89919-484-2, $12.95. Ages 3-6.

Waking in the middle of the night to a storm can be scary when you are a child like Jake or a big white dog named Biff. Even more scary is finding that the lights don't work and that Mom and Dad are not in their room. Where can they be in this darkened and noise-filled night? When the clock strikes midnight—"Ghost's Hour, Spook's Hour"—both boys are terrified, but continue looking for Mom and Dad. When they are finally found, Jake confesses that Biff was very frightened of the storm and afraid that they had been left alone. Biff and Jake get their necessary reassurance as the family all settles in on the sleeper sofa downstairs. Carrick's haunting watercolor illustrations adjust to the changing moods throughout this nighttime tale: they are at first cool and dark and a bit unsettling, and then change to warmer colors to match the mood as Biff and Jake find security in Dad's arms. This comforting ending to a scary beginning should appeal to those who have been frightened at night.

Jake's fear throughout the story is evident, but he never admits to his parents that he was scared. Instead, he talks reassuringly to his dog, pretending that only Biff was scared. Young children can use this same manner to discuss something that frightens them. Each child in the class could be provided with a puppet, or everyone in the class could make puppets following the steps in Gates's *Easy-to-Make-Puppets* (Treehouse, 1981), a very useful resource. Encourage each child to tell about a time when their puppet was scared and what he/she did to alleviate that fear. This activity could allowing the children to discuss other emotions—e.g., anger, joy, and sadness—while still using their puppet to do all the talking. Students too shy to participate in a group could work with a partner or alone with the teacher. L.S.

Drama, Social Studies
Primary

Related Source

19. Bunting, Eve. *How Many Days to America?* Illustrated by Beth Peck. Clarion, 1988. ISBN 0-89919-521-0, $14.95. Ages 5-9.

Eve Bunting has written a touching story that is much more than a Thanksgiving story, for it relates what is happening today as many people are forced to become refugees searching for freedom in a new land. Told from a young boy's perspective, the story begins in a pleasant Caribbean island village from which he and his family flee to avoid persecution. They face numerous hardships as they and other refugees travel by boat to America. As they struggle with adversity, they always remember their hope of being free. The muted oil pastel drawings extend the feelings created in the text, the shadowy colors of escaping into the night moving to brighter colors as the refugees give thanks after reaching the new land.

Many children have moved, but only a few will understand being *forced* to move. Begin with brainstorming on why people choose to move, including reasons they think some people are forced to relocate. Discuss various ways to travel and list what could be brought along considering the restrictions of the modes of travel. Compare and contrast other historic and modern stories of people leaving their homes, such as Riki Levinson's *Watch the Stars Come Out* (Dutton, 1985), Alice Fleming's *The King of Prussia and a Peanut Butter Sandwich* (Scribner's, 1988), and Eleanor Coerr's *The Josephina Story Quilt* (Harper & Row, 1986). K.J.G.

Multicultural Studies,
U.S. History
Primary
Intermediate

Related Sources

20. Bunting, Eve. *The Man Who Could Call Down Owls*. Illustrated by Charles Mikolaycak. Macmillan, 1984. ISBN 0-02-715380-0, $9.95. Ages 5-8.

A wise, gentle old man calls down owls every night in the woods, accompanied by Con, a village boy. By day he tends their hurts in his owl barn and teaches Con to love and respect them. When a stranger destroys the old man and attempts to take his place, the owls' revenge is swift and fitting. In classic folklore tradition, this picture book tells much with spare detail. Strength from love is a powerful theme. Black and white pencil illustrations bordered in light blue have strong highlights, which contrast with the owls' feathery textures and enrich the text with dramatic perspectives. The story is excellent on its own, but it is made more meaningful because of the art. There is the feeling of enchantment in this charming, thoughtful tale.

Primarily for reading aloud with children for the story and sound of the language, there is such rich meaning beyond the plot that it would be excellent for extending children's inferring skills (e.g., What does Con feel about the stranger?) and for helping them understand metaphors and story structure. As several types of owls are named and described and the illustrations of the birds are detailed, this book could also be a fine adjunct to a nature study. The style, compositions, and medium of artwork are worthy of study and comparison with other forms of art and illustrations.   B.B.

Science, Art
Primary
Intermediate

21. Caseley, Judith. *Apple Pie and Onions*. Illustrated by the author. Greenwillow, 1987. ISBN 0-688-06763-8, $11.88. Ages 6-9.

A story within a story, *Apple Pie and Onions* is a poignant, yet telling, commentary on how easily we can forget our roots or traditions in this melting pot we call America. Young Rebecca loves to visit Grandmother's little apartment in the big city. Together they shop, like Grandma did in the old country, visiting each little store, filling their mesh bag and chatting with the merchants. But Rebecca finds herself embarrassed when her grandmother runs into a friend from the old country and boisterously breaks into her native Yiddish language. Grandma helps Rebecca with these feelings by telling a touching story of herself, her father, and his bag of onions. The colorful bordered illustrations will capture the viewer with wonderful little details. Our country continues to grow in the number of people from foreign lands, and books like this highlight not only the differences in human cultures, but wisely, the similarities.

Although this story is in picture book format, older children could surely enjoy it as well, though for different reasons. Teachers might have the children try to determine their national or cultural origins and collect family traditions or special stories that may have been passed down through the family. The children might focus upon a holiday tradition and compile a class booklet which would reflect all of the different cultures they represent.   L.A.B.

Multicultural Studies,
U.S. History
Primary
Intermediate

---

22.   Cleaver, Elizabeth. *The Enchanted Caribou*. Illustrated by the author. Atheneum, 1985. ISBN 0-689-31170-2. $9.95. Ages 5-9.

ALA Notable Book

Tyya, a young Inuit girl, becomes lost in the fog and is rescued by Etosack, a hunter of caribou. Etosack and his brothers care for her and tell her to let no one into their tent while they are out hunting the next day. Tyya is tricked, however, by an evil shaman who turns her into a white caribou. The solution to her problem comes to Etosack in a dream and he is able to rescue her. White caribou, however, are still protected by Inuit hunters to this day just in case history repeats itself. Elizabeth Cleaver retold this traditional story using a storyteller's fluid language, rich with imagery. The shadow puppet pictures are a perfect visual extension of the text. Their stark black and white forms evoke images of snow and the bleak environment of the tundra, and reflect the essential simplicity of the culture.

Drama, Art
Primary
Intermediate

Elizabeth Cleaver has provided instructions at the back of the book for making shadow puppets and for producing shadow theater plays. She even gives the basic shapes necessary to make the characters in *The Enchanted Caribou*. Thus, a class or small group can start right in with little preparation. In this way, children can begin to see for themselves how shape and movement brings shadow theater to life. Once they have been successful learning shadow theater techniques using the shapes from *The Enchanted Caribou*, they can discover other stories to present using this form of puppetry.   M.A.C.

23.   Climo, Shirley. *King of the Birds*. Illustrated by Ruth Heller. Crowell, 1988. ISBN 0-690-04623-5, $12.89. Ages 4-8.

In this pourquois tale, Climo masterfully retells one of the world's oldest and most widely dispersed legends. When the birds' ceaseless squawks and squabbles keep Old Mother Owl from a good day's sleep, she ends the rumpus by announcing a contest to appoint a ruler: "Whoever flies highest and longest shall be king." The tiny wren wins through strength of wing and mind. He then spreads his subjects over different habitats on the earth so that all may live peacefully. The story also explains why various birds have unique characteristics. Their chatter can be heard in the text as well. Heller's vibrant illustrations give colorful wing to the tale, beautifully detailing the variety of birds. The end product is a worthy addition to any folklore collection.

Science, Social Studies
Primary
Intermediate

Though the book's suggested age range is four to eight, share it with intermediate students in an integrated science and social studies unit. Students can be introduced to field guides to identify the birds shown in the accurate and dynamic illustrations. They can also chart the various geographic regions different species inhabit and, where appropriate, their migration patterns. Finally, each student may want to select a bird, research how its physical characteristics are appropriate for its habitat, and report findings back to the class.   K.L.M.

24. Cohn, Janice, D.S.W. *I Had a Friend Named Peter.* Illustrated by Gail Owens. Morrow, 1987. ISBN 0-688-06686-0, $12.88. Ages 4-7.

I Had a Friend Named Peter begins with a five page introduction that uses a question and answer format to explain the child's understanding of death. The story, which reflects the information given in the introduction, consists of Betsy's coping with the death of a classmate who has been a good friend. The responses of her parents to Betsy's questions and the teacher's discussion with her students provide adult readers with excellent models. Cohn has very sensitively and simply described the kinds of things that children wonder about when they are confronted with death. Gail Owens's soft pastel illustrations on blue paper complement the somber, questioning mood of the text.

It is a rare teacher who completes a career without experiencing the grief all suffer when a child in an elementary school building dies. This is the book a librarian needs when there is the emergency faculty meeting to discuss: "What do we do/say?" Teachers, as well as administrators, are taught little about this subject. This is a children's book that adults need to read for guidance to meet such an emergency.   J.F.A.

Family Life, Social Studies Primary

25. Conover, Chris. *The Wizard's Daughter.* Illustrated by the author. Little, Brown, 1984. ISBN 0-316-15314-1, $12.95. Ages 6-9.

This Viking legend describes a cruel and greedy wizard who controls the luck of farmers and hunters, steals their crops and game, and extracts huge ransoms for food. His daughter, imprisoned at the bottom of the sea, assists Boots, the poor farmer's son, in destroying the wizard. Evil is defeated, good triumphs, and Boots and the wizard's daughter live happily ever after in a land of plenty. Although Conover's retelling is very well written, it almost pales beside her large format, detailed, and fanciful illustrations. In addition to the four double-page spreads, the single-page paintings extend to the opposing pages of text and unite the story, text, and illustration.

Although the story's content is geared to the elementary student, this would be an excellent example to use with older students in a writing class to teach (1) story structure; (2) criteria for writing in this genre; (3) active, descriptive word choices; (4) mature, tightly constructed sentences; and (5) sentence variety. However, as valuable as a study of the text might be, the enjoyment of the story and of the imaginative paintings should have first priority.   M.A.S.

Language Arts Primary Intermediate

26. Crews, Donald. *School Bus.* Illustrated by the author. Greenwillow, 1984. ISBN 0-688-02808-X, $9.55. Ages 4-7.

With his customary verve, Donald Crews has given younger audiences another fine picture book with simple, short explanatory captions and bold, bright illustrations. This time the subject is the yellow school bus, so familiar and important in a child's small world. Every page is of a different scene as the bus makes its way from the parking garage to school and back again. Faceless students with backpacks, purses, notebooks, and guitar, board the bus, disembark at school, and go home again at the end of the day. There is enough detail for a child to peruse with pleasure.

Teaching topics or situations emerge easily from the detailed pictures: (1) safe street crossing; (2) bus stop safety rules; (3) bus boarding conducted in orderly fashion; (4) traffic signals; (5) friendships with schoolmates; and (6) parental love and concern. Art projects relating to the book would include safety posters, traffic signals of colored paper, and drawings of school buses. Teachers can discuss writing of poems or essays on school bus experiences.   F.M.H.

*Art, Language Arts
Primary*

27.   de Beaumont, Mme. Leprince. *Beauty and the Beast*. Illustrated by Binette Schroeder. Potter, 1986. ISBN 0-517-56173-5, $12.95. Ages 7-9.

The romantic tale of virtuous love that develops between the innocent Beauty and the prince transformed into the hideous Beast is one of the oldest and most beautiful fairy tales to come from the French. This version, and Anne Carter's lyrical and readable translation, retains the power of the "old magic" to uplift and to inspire. While the lush illustrations maintain the dread-like quality of the narrative and depict a beast who is truly monstrous in appearance, credit for the success of this presentation must go to the author and translator. Children who hear this beautiful story read aloud will be transported to a time and place where love seeks the heart and spiritual goodness of others.

Creating images and meaning from written language is basic to becoming a proficient reader. Pre-readers and beginning readers can practice this mental/psycholinguistic skill by hearing stories read without seeing the illustrations. Because the beast is not described in the text of the story, try reading this book aloud to children and ask them to draw or describe the beast they envisioned as they heard the story. Be careful not to show them the illustrator's vision of the beast. Later they can compare their interpretation with Schroeder's.   H.M.

*Language Arts
Primary*

28.   de Gerez, Toni. *Louhi, Witch of North Farm*. Illustrated by Barbara Cooney. Viking Kestrel, 1986. ISBN 0-670-80556-4, $12.95. Ages 3-8.

This retelling of a Finnish tale—taken from their national epic, the Kalevala—portrays the story of Witch Louhi's stealing of the sun and the moon. The responsibility of ridding the land of darkness falls to Vainamoinen, the Great Knower, who asks Seppo, the smith, to forge a new sun and moon. While Seppo successfully accomplishes this, they will not shine and so another solution must be sought. Louhi, proud to have stolen these great lights, is curious about what Vainamoinen and Seppo are up to. Changing herself into a hawk, she visits Seppo and finds him preparing "an iron collar and nine terrible iron chains to wrap around the skinny gray neck of a certain witch!" Seized by fear, Louhi returns the sun and moon to the sky, making all things right again. Caldecott Medal-winner Cooney's use of color and medium appropriately complement this well-told story.

While this story could easily be read or told to young children, it could also be used with older children when studying the culture of Finland. The "Author's Notes" on the last page of the text give some background information on the source of this story. Students could explore their library to find other information about Finland. Some sources to look for include Erick Berry's *The Land & People of Finland* (Lippincott, 1972), Ursula Synge's *Land of Heroes: Re-Telling of the Kalevala* (McElderry, 1978), and Aini Rajanen's *Of Finnish Ways* (Dillion, 1981).   L.S.

Storytelling, Social Studies Primary Intermediate

Related Sources

29. Dragonwagon, Crescent. *Half a Moon and One Whole Star*. Illustrated by Jerry Pinkney. Macmillan, 1986. ISBN 0-02-733120-2, $12.95. Ages 5-8.

Many children wonder what happens when they are asleep at night. This book's combination of gorgeous watercolors and a quiet, reassuring story written in verse gives the reader a peaceful feeling that all is well when we sleep. Each event that takes place is written and illustrated in an expressive way that makes it come alive to the reader.

Kindergarten teachers and parents of pre-school children will find using this book at nap time is very relaxing. Then, upon waking, the children may draw pictures of what might have happened while they slept. The book could also be used with Cynthia Rylant's *Night in the Country* (Bradbury, 1986) and Mauri Kunna's *The Nighttime Book* (Crown, 1985) to stimulate discussion about what they think goes on in the world at night.   C.A.Y.

Art, Language Arts Primary

Related Sources

30. Esbensen, Barbara Juster, reteller. *The Star Maiden*. Illustrated by Helen K. Davie. Little, Brown, 1988. ISBN 0-316-24951-3, $14.95. Ages 4-8.

This retelling of an Ojibway (Chippewa) tale explains the creation of water lilies. A star maiden tires of wandering across the sky and becomes part of the land and its people. She is transformed, along with all her sky-sisters, into the water lilies we so frequently see floating on lakes and ponds. Davie's uniquely designed and beautifully executed paintings focus attention upon the legend by framing the larger portion of each illustration with Indian designs and upon the environment and wildlife in the smaller section beneath. The combination of stunning illustration and a beautifully retold tale make this an outstanding example of the art of the picture story book.

This would be a welcome addition to a collection of Native American tales that are available for younger and older readers in picture story book format. Students can use them to study tribal designs from

Native American Studies
Primary
Intermediate
Middle School

Related Sources

different cultural traditions. There are many contrasting styles of illustrating Native American stories that can be enjoyed, including those in such books as John Bierhorst's *The Ring in the Prairie* (Dial, 1970); all of Paul Goble's books, especially *The Girl Who Loved Wild Horses* (Bradbury, 1979); Margaret Hodges's *The Fire Bringer* (Little, Brown, 1972); Elizabeth Cleaver's *The Enchanted Caribou* (Atheneum, 1985); and the *Legend of the Bluebonnet* by Tomie de Paola (Putnam, 1983).   M.G.C.

31.   Euvremer, Teryl. *Sun's Up*. Illustrated by the author. Crown, 1987. ISBN 0-517-56432-7, $9.95. Ages 3-7.

This delightful wordless picture story book personifying the sun is a welcome first effort by a very talented artist. Using impressionistic watercolors, Euvremer skillfully shows not only what the sun is doing all day and evening, but also the activities of two families living on earth below. Thus, there are really three stories to tell and there is plenty of extra detail to provoke comment as well.

The personification of natural phenomena often occurs in folklore and recently has been the subject of other picture story books. Most notable are Caldecott Medal winner *Arrow to the Sun* by McDermott (Viking, 1974), Berger's gentle *Grandfather Twilight* (Philomel, 1984), and Ungerer's strangely wonderful *Moon Man* (Harper & Row, 1967). *Claude and Sun* by Matt Novak (Bradbury, 1987), though it does not personify the sun, still leaves readers wondering if Claude is somehow a keeper of the sun and invites comparison. After studying these books students may want to think about a natural phenomenon, such as the tides, cycles of the moon, or a tornado and how it could be personified or explained through human connection. The resulting ideas could be worked into stories either in writing, in illustration, or both.   M.A.C.

Related Sources

Literature, Art, Science, Language Arts
Primary

32.   Faulkner, Matt. *The Amazing Voyage of Jackie Grace*. Illustrated by the author. Scholastic, 1987. ISBN 0-590-40713-9, $13.95. Ages 5-8.

A wonderful old Victorian bathtub is the setting for young Jackie's adventure into the imagination. His peaceful bath is shattered when a cast of lively seafaring characters appear tubside and draws him into a raging ocean storm and a battle with pirates. Victory is theirs when Jackie accidentally knocks out the head pirate, scaring off his cronies. Faulkner has designed this book so that it appears to be a cross between a wordless picture book and a cartoon strip. Pen and ink cross-hatching adds texture and depth to the already exciting pictures. The perspectives are also intriguing, especially those with the tumultuous ocean and the personified stormy wind. This is a resounding affirmation of the delights of the imagination.

An excellent companion to *The Amazing Voyage of Jackie Grace* would be *King Bidgood's in the Bathtub*, by Don and

Related Sources

Audrey Wood (Harcourt Brace Jovanovich, 1985), in which a king refuses to leave his tub so that his court is forced to fish, dine, battle, and dance with him in the tub. Students might enjoy creating their own "tub tales" in illustration and text, perhaps as a further adventure for Jackie Grace. These could be placed in a large paper tub on a bulletin board in the school library. Students visiting the library could then select a story to read or share with younger children. This could be just one of many activities in a schoolwide "imagination celebration."   M.A.C.

*Language Arts
Primary
Intermediate*

33.   Fleischman, Paul. *Rondo in C*. Illustrated by Janet Wentworth. Harper & Row, 1988. ISBN 0-06-021857-6, $13.89. Ages 5-8.

Paul Fleischman's latest work offers a thoughtful, brief introduction to classical music for children. His spare text combines with Janet Wentworth's pastel illustrations to show a number of people listening to a girl's rendition of Beethoven's "Rondo in C." As they listen to the piece, each is reminded of a particular feeling, place, or event. Wentworth illustrates these on double pages: one side is a portrait of the person listening, the other is a photograph of their memory. Just as the "Rondo in C" leaves a different impression with each person, Wentworth uses her pastels in an impressionistic style, recreating a mood and memory for the reader. While Fleischman's talents as an author may be understated in this book, it leaves the reader with an image of the power which music invokes upon the listener. Combined with Wentworth's illustrations, few words are needed to stir the feelings and impressions which the book creates.

Most children are not familiar with classical music, let alone musical terms. Children can be informed before reading this book what a rondo is. It would be especially helpful to have a recording of Beethoven's "Rondo in C" for children to listen to before, during, or after reading the book; teachers who play piano should find a copy of the score at a local library or music store. Discuss how certain instruments can create moods. Children can then compare a symphony by Hayden with one by Rachmaninoff, and then discuss how the music made them feel or what it reminds them of. Students could also draw their own renditions of what the music brings to their minds.   K.B.B.

*Music, Art
Primary
Intermediate*

34.   Fox, Mem. *Hattie and the Fox*. Illustrated by Patricia Mullins. Bradbury, 1987 (1st Am. ed.). ISBN 0-02-735470-9, $12.95. Ages 4-7.

Author Mem Fox was stimulated to write *Hattie and the Fox* by a session at an International Reading Association conference on making reading easy for little children. This cumulative tale succeeded: it is full of the repetitive, exciting language that makes good early readers. The story is simple: while Hattie Hen continues to warn the rest of the barnyard animals about the danger she spies in the bush, they disregard her plea with "Good grief!" said the goose. "Well, well!" said the pig.

"Who cares?" said the sheep. "So what!" said the horse. "What next?" said the cow. Lively and humorous illustrations made of tissue paper collage and conte crayon accompany this suspenseful story with its surprise ending. The delightful characters of Patricia Mullins, with their expressive eyes, are not to be missed.

Emerging Readers, Art
Primary
Intermediate

Working with tissue paper collage can be a challenging art project for students of all ages, with results depending upon individual development. The tissue paper can be torn or cut into shapes to make blurred or distinct lines and can be affixed to a background paper with liquid starch applied with a Q-tip. Students will discover through working with this medium that interesting effects can be achieved by applying water to create bleeds and runs, by applying multiple layers to create shading, and by applying other media—conte crayon, markers, colored pencils, sponge printing, etc.—after the collage has dried. C.A.Y./M.A.C./K.B.B.

35.   Galdone, Paul. *The Teeny-Tiny Woman*. Illustrated by the author. Clarion, 1984. ISBN 0-89919-270-X, $11.95. Ages 4-7

This is an appealing retelling of the mild ghost story involving a teeny-tiny woman who finds a teeny-tiny bone and takes it home, only to be plagued all night by a voice demanding its return. The story builds to a jump-story climax, beautifully illustrated with eerie hidden faces vaguely hinted at throughout the drawings. It has just the right amount of tingling for a small child's spine, and the illustrations lend a somberness necessary to a ghost story.

Storytelling,
Emerging Readers
Primary

This book would be excellent for reading aloud to the very young as the repetition aids in recognizing the words on the pages. However, it is best as a story to tell, preferably on a gray day, with the lights low, and with the class huddled close together in anticipation. The sudden ending should not nor need not be too dramatic or shouted for young audiences to enjoy the surprise. The performance can easily be evaluated if there are surprised looks, giggles all around, followed by requests to "Tell it again."   H.A.F.

36.   Gardner, Beau. *The Look Again...and Again, and Again, and Again Book*. Illustrated by the author. Lothrop, Lee & Shepard, 1984. ISBN 0-688-03806-9, $10.08. All ages.

This is an unusual, clever, and appealing sequence of visual puzzles that should delight readers of a wide age range. Each picture becomes a different object when viewed upside down, becomes a third object when the page is turned ninety degrees, and becomes even a fourth object on another ninety degree turn of the page. It might be called a book of optical illusions. Colors are vivid: basic primary and secondary colors only. Younger children will enjoy the sight jokes and will look forward to guessing what is coming next as the page is revolved.

One obvious class project using this format would be creating similar two-, three-, or four-viewpoint constructions and writing accompanying captions. The secret is to keep the pictures very simple and basic in their design. Perhaps an art teacher would like to help in the early planning. It is also a great book to share aloud with a class, as they will enjoy the variety of captions on one page.   F.M.H.

Art, Language Arts
Primary
Intermediate

37.   Geisel, Theodore (Dr. Seuss). *The Butter Battle Book*. Illustrated by the author. Random House, 1984. ISBN 0-394-96580-9, $7.99. All ages.

In language and rhymes that are typically playful and inventive, Dr. Seuss tells readers of all ages how two irrational and arrogant countries arrived at the very brink of mutual annihilation as each sought to build bigger and more destructive weapons of warfare. This fanciful allegory brings the reader face to face with the stakes involved in the global arms race and with a clearer understanding of the current status of the world military situation. The ending should be viewed as hopeful—if cautionary, and unfinished.

The image of the wall that separates the Yooks and the Zooks provides a rich opportunity for exploration by intermediate grade students and older. Seuss's wall has had its historical counterparts with their own unique origins and consequences: The Great Wall of China, The Berlin Wall, Hadrian's Wall, and others. Students may also identify such symbolic walls as the Iron Curtain and the Bamboo Curtain, as well as social factors that divide people: racism, sex discrimination, school rivalries, and handicaps. Students of all ages may be encouraged to create a sequel to *The Butter Battle Book* (either in prose or in verse, like Dr. Seuss's) showing what happened and why.   H.M.

Peace Studies
Intermediate
Middle School
Junior High School
High School

38.   Geisel, Theodore (Dr. Seuss). *You're Only Old Once! A Book for Obsolete Children*. Illustrated by the author. Random House, 1986. ISBN 0-394-55190-7, $9.95. All ages.

With characteristic rhythms, invented words, and fanciful pictures, Dr. Seuss entertains his audience with a light-hearted, yet satirical look at the consequences of aging—an odyssey through the Golden Years Clinic. Milestones in the journey include a judgment of solvency, followed by multiple, detailed examinations, a collection of pills, and, finally, myriad bills. Happily, our hero leaves the clinic in "pretty good shape for the shape you are in." *You're Only Old Once* as social commentary is both humorous and thought-provoking. However, only more mature readers are likely to appreciate its various dimensions.

Although elementary students may enjoy its cadences and rhymes, *You're Only Old Once* is, according to the publisher, most appropriate for the "obsolete child of 70" or more. Despite the "tongue in cheek" recommendation, this book provides an excellent introduction to the mock epic poem for English classes. In addition to studying versification (foot, meter, meter change for effect, rhyme scheme, and alliteration), the allusions to contemporary social issues can provoke much discussion. By comparing *You're Only Old Once* to Sendak's

Language Arts,
Social Studies
Middle School
Junior High School
High School

Where the Wild Things Are (Harper & Row, 1963), older students can discriminate between epic and mock epic genres.   M.A.S.

Related Source

39. Gerstein, Mordicai. *The Mountains of Tibet*. Illustrated by the author. Harper & Row, 1987. ISBN 0-06-022149-6, $11.89. Ages 7-up.

When he looked up at the stars, the young boy in Tibet dreamed of someday visiting other worlds and other countries he knew existed beyond the mountains. As he grew to an old man, his dreams were never fulfilled: he never left his valley. When he died, he was given the choice to enter heaven or to live another life. Readers of all ages will be touched and delighted by his decision. Gerstein's tale, reflecting Chinese Buddhistic wisdom and inspired by the *Tibetan Book of the Dead*, is perfectly illuminated by his delicate watercolor and gouache drawings that capture the cultural setting.

Related Source

The Mountains of Tibet* is a perfect choice for storytelling. Beginners and experienced performers alike will recognize its strong story structure, depth of emotion, clarity of style, and rich imagery as essential ingredients for storytelling. Read the story several times, retaining the sequence of episodes, visualizing the character and various settings, and probing levels of personal meaning. Then tell it as frequently as possible to individuals and groups of any age available for the practice in recreating the whole of the story. Refinements, such as memorizing selected phrases (of which there are many beautiful ones), varying intonation and pacing, etc., can be made through continued practice-performance. Be sure always to acknowledge the author and source of the story to the audience.   H.M.

Storytelling
Primary
Intermediate
Middle School
Junior High School

40. Ginsburg, Mirra, reteller. *The Chinese Mirror*. Illustrated by Margot Zemach. Harcourt Brace Jovanovich, 1988. ISBN 0-15-200420-3, $14.95. Ages 4-8.

The Chinese Mirror is an unadorned adaptation of a Korean folk tale about a traveler who brought the first mirror to his village from China. Thinking that the mirror's magic would be lost if he showed it to everyone, he hid it away, taking it out in secret to look at it and laugh with pleasure. His wife sees this and, waiting until he goes out, takes the mirror out and looks into it. When she sees her own pretty face, she thinks that her husband has brought home a pretty young wife from China. Thus begins a chain of events caused when other family members look into the mirror and don't recognize themselves. This amusing tale is illustrated in watercolor paintings by Margot Zemach. Her characters are drawn with a brush, which gives an interesting thick and thin quality to the line. The clothing, settings, and colors also effectively evoke the Korean culture. Even the paper contributes to the oriental effect: its off white color reminds one of rice paper.

The structure of this story would make it easy to convert into a play. Each character would only have to remember what he/she thought he/she saw when looking into the mirror. The costumes would even be simple to make. The wife's skirt appears to be just material gathered at the waist. The mother-in-law wears a similar skirt and more material draped over her head and shoulders. Pants for the male characters could be long johns or pajama bottoms. A top could be made from a man's shirt with the collar tucked in and the front over lapped and pinned in a couple of places. Shoes could be slippers or beach thongs over socks. Some children could be set designers. They could put white paper on a bulletin board and paint a backdrop similar to the open-front house illustrated in the book. Invite other classes to attend a performance, providing the audience with playbills, complete with credits, "advertising," a story description, and an artfully designed cover, all produced by the students themselves.   M.A.C.

Drama, Language Arts
Primary
Intermediate

41. Goble, Paul. ***Buffalo Woman***. Illustrated by the author. Bradbury, 1984. ISBN 0-02-737720-2, $12.95. Ages 4-11.

ALA Notable Book

Paul Goble's books are a twofold delight. Like his five previous books of Native American legends, ***Buffalo Woman*** is a visual feast that tells a story of powerful significance to all. This transformation legend tells of the marriage of a hunter to a woman of the Buffalo Nation. When his wife and newborn son are driven from his village, the hunter pursues them to discover they have become part of a buffalo herd, her people. The buffalo people transform him into a buffalo so that he can remain with his wife and sons forever. The theme of the closeness of man and nature emerges clearly in this well told tale. Goble's impressive ink and watercolor drawings evoke strong images of the historical plains Indians and their art.

Art students may want to compare Goble's illustrations to copies of Sioux pictographic drawings from the 19th century. ***Buffalo Woman*** and ***The Girl Who Loved Horses*** (1978) are excellent for comparing to transformation tales from other cultures—e.g., "The Frog Prince" or the Celtic tradition of selkies. Students may wish to write Paul Goble to ask how he became interested in learning about Native American stories and art. They may write him c/o Bradbury Press, 866 Third Ave., New York, NY 10022.   H.M.

Related Source

Native American Studies,
Author Studies, Literature
Primary
Intermediate

42. Goble, Paul. ***Death of the Iron Horse***. Illustrated by the author. Bradbury, 1987. ISBN 0-02-737830-6, $12.95. Ages 5-8.

On August 7, 1867, a small group of Cheyenne braves derailed and raided a Union Pacific Railroad train, the only recorded occurrence of such an action in this nation's history. Loosely basing his story upon this incident, Goble effectively sets the stage with a Cheyenne prophet's ominous dream foretelling the coming of the white man and the killing, starvation, and the plundering of the earth that would follow. The book's message is clear: the Cheyenne acted to preserve their land and people against a fearful, unknown monster coming through their territory. Sometimes somber, sometimes amusing, this story comes to life with Goble's distinctive drawings, finely detailed and richly colored.

Students, especially those in upper elementary grades where American history is a social studies topic, should know the works of Paul Goble, winner of the 1979 Caldecott Medal for *The Girl Who Loved Wild Horses* (Bradbury, 1978). By setting up a display table with artifacts, traditional arts, and a historical map of the northern plains showing traditional Native American territories, children can be introduced to other titles as well, such as *The Gift of the Sacred Dog* (1984), *Star Boy* (1985), *Buffalo Woman* (1984), and *The Great Race of the Birds and Animals* (1985). All are carefully crafted, offering, through vivid words and colors, a beautiful and authentic glimpse into Native American life and legend.   A.S.

43.   Goble, Paul. *Her Seven Brothers*. Illustrated by the author. Bradbury, 1988. ISBN 0-02-737960-4, $13.95. All ages.

Admirers of Paul Goble will cheer this retelling of a Cheyenne legend explaining the origin of the Big Dipper. A Cheyenne maiden, who has the gift of understanding the spirits of all things and the ability to make beautiful clothing, makes seven sets of clothes for seven brothers she believes to be living in the north country. When she finally finds them, they welcome her as their sister and live peacefully together until the day the chief of the Buffalo Nation demands that she leave her brothers to live with him and his people. Their flight to safety takes them into the sky where they remain to this day. Goble's familiar watercolor and ink drawings are carefully researched to reflect authentic designs on the tipis and the clothing. Readers of all ages will come closer to understanding the spirits in all things in the closing lines: "Listen to the stars. We are never alone at night."

Transformation stories are prevalent in many cultures, especially among Native American cultures where the oneness of life is central to understanding the universe. Older children can compare many of the transformation tales of Goble's—e.g., *Star Boy* (1983) or *Buffalo Woman* (1984) both published by Bradbury—with tales from other Native American traditions; with the selkie legends from Scotland, Ireland, and Newfoundland; or with other tales from various cultures around the world as gathered in Jane Yolen's remarkable and appealing collection, *Shape Shifters* (Seabury, 1978).   A.S./H.M.

44.   Goble, Paul. *Iktomi and the Boulder: a Plains Indian Story*. Illustrated by the author. Orchard, 1988. ISBN 0-531-05760-7, $13.95. Ages 3-7.

Goble has created yet another remarkable rendering of a Native American story in this tale of Iktomi, the charming, but foolish mischief-maker. On this day, Iktomi feels very proud in his fine robes but soon swelters in the hot sun. He leaves his blanket on a convenient boulder, only to take it back when a rainstorm threatens. The boulder is not happy about this, and soon chases Iktomi and traps him. Iktomi is released only when he tricks some bats into knocking the boulder into pieces, which is why "bats have flattened faces today." Especially amusing are Iktomi's thoughts, which are printed in small type throughout the book. The story alternates with the narrator's comments in italicized text, which invite the audience's responses. Children should enjoy this humorous story, illustrated in Goble's distinctive and masterful style.

Goble's notes tell us that Iktomi is a hero in many stories. His most familiar name is Coyote. The trickster animal–god is found in many forms in stories throughout the world, including Raven, Hare, and Fox in Native American stories (e.g., in Dee Brown's *Teepee Tales of the American Indian* [Holt, Rinehart & Winston, 1979]); Anansi the Spider in Africa (see Courlander's *The Hat Shaking Dance and Other Tales from the Gold Coast* [Harcourt Brace Jovanovich, 1957] and McDermott's *Anansi the Spider: A Tale from the Ashanti* [Holt, Rinehart & Winston, 1977]); and Brer Rabbit in the United States (see Lester's *The Tales of Uncle Remus* [Dial, 1987]). Students are likely to find fun and satisfaction hearing about the mischief that these characters create and escape from. Discussing each story and charting the similarities of these folk tale characters is a useful first step in understanding comparative literature.   A.S.

Native American Studies, Literature Primary Intermediate

Related Sources

45. Goennel, Heidi. *Seasons*. Illustrated by the author. Little, Brown, 1986. ISBN 0-316-31836-1, $14.95. Ages 3-6.

One of the delights of the new picture books for 1986 was this simple and stunningly beautiful series of familiar children's seasonal activities. The text is brief and compact, consisting of short phrases describing favorite activities for each season. However, it is the beauty of the colorful and carefully designed paintings that creates the most lasting and pleasing effect. Broad areas of primary and complementary colors, few details, and careful placement of objects are fundamental to the deceptively simple illustrations. Adults and children alike should appreciate Goennel's ability to create mood as well as show setting and character. With a first book such as *Seasons*, one looks forward to many more contributions from this gifted artist.

Teachers of young children are quick to use seasonal changes and events as a focus for learning activities. Field trips, art activities, language experiences, and other lessons often center upon seasonal themes. Parents, grandparents, and other adults responsible for child care also look for suggestions and ideas for working with young children at home or during vacation periods. Teachers and librarians can offer parents many other suggestions for effective and enjoyable learning activities throughout the year through a regularly published list of books, magazines, films, videos, and other materials for use by adults with children. The list, along with suggested activities and adult roles and responsibilities, either can be mailed out monthly to the community or made available in the school or public library.   H.M.

Science, Art, Language Arts Primary

---

46. Goffstein, M.B. *School of Names*. Illustrated by the author. Harper & Row, 1986. ISBN 0-06-021985-8, $11.89. All ages.

Through simple pastel illustrations and sparse text, Goffstein ponders the idea that knowing the names of the objects of the natural world makes us one with them. "I want to go to the School of Names to know everybody with me on this globe...I would like to recognize and greet everyone by name. For all the years I may live, no place but the earth is my home." This idea, sometimes made complex by culture and ritual, is so simply presented by Goffstein that the beauty and awe of it can be grasped by even the youngest reader.

*Literature,
Language Arts
Intermediate
Middle School*

Related Source

Older children may want to explore other cultures in which it was believed that knowing an object's or person's true name gave one a oneness with, or even power over, that object or person. The idea shows up in other literature, notably in Ursula LeGuin's fantasy *A Wizard of Earthsea* (Parnassus, 1968) in which Ged seeks the true name of the shadow that stalks him, knowing that that is the only way he can conquer it. Students may want to write their own stories incorporating this ancient idea.   M.A.C.

47. Hadithi, Mwenye. *Crafty Chameleon*. Illustrated by Adrienne Kennaway. Little, Brown, 1987. ISBN 0-316-33723-4, $12.95. Ages 4-8.

In the tradition of a pourquois tale, *Crafty Chameleon* is the story of a chameleon who, fed up with the tricks played upon him by Leopard and Crocodile, decides to teach them both a lesson. By tying a vine around each of the animal's necks, Chameleon tricks Crocodile and Leopard into thinking that he is pulling them until they are exhausted and promise to never bother him again. But just in case the animals ever find out about the trick he played on them, Chameleon changes color to hide from them. Bold captivating illustrations by Kennaway not only complement, but also extend the text with the portrayal of interesting perspective and comical characterization. Children should enjoy finding the chameleon as he disguises himself among the colorful jungle foliage.

Related Sources

This story, because of its sparse text and appealing illustrations, would be a good example to use with smaller children first being exposed to the pourquois tales. After reading *Crafty Chameleon* aloud to the students, introduce them to other tales of this genre and discuss why these tales were told. Some examples are William Toye's *How Summer Came to Canada* (Walck, 1969), Paul Goble's *Star Boy* (Bradbury, 1983), Rudyard Kipling's *Just So Stories* (Doubleday, 1972), and Verna Aardema's *Why Mosquitoes Buzz in People's Ears* (Dial, 1975). As a creative writing exercise, develop a list of possible topics and write them on the board. Possible ideas could be: why thunder always follows lightning, why the leopard has spots, or why the elephant has a long trunk. Students could choose one of the topics on the board or one of their own and write their own pourquois tale. Students who are too young to write can dictate to an older student who can write the stories for them.   K.B.B.

*Literature,
Language Arts
Primary
Intermediate*

48. Haley, Gail E. *Birdsong*. Illustrated by the author. Crown, 1984. ISBN 0-517-55051-2, $10.95. Ages 4-8.

In this imaginative and romantic modern fairy tale, Jorinella the Birdcatcher takes in the orphan Birdsong in hopes that the girl's lovely pipe playing will attract more birds than ever to her snares, nets, limed strings, and bamboo traps. Then Jorinella can grow rich selling the birds at the marketplace. First she gives Birdsong a magic feather through which Birdsong is able to understand all of the birds' callings. Another feather, dropped from Jorinella's cloak, reveals her true self to Birdsong, who finally escapes in a glorious fashion. Haley's illustrations are medieval in tone and are richly colored in the jewel-like hues one sees in the feathers of birds. Gail Haley has carefully balanced picture and text, as well as researched her setting and creatures, in the tradition of her Caldecott-winning *A Story, A Story* (Atheneum, 1970).

A five-year-old, upon hearing about the first magic feather, remarked, "That feather is just like a bird dictionary!" Children might enjoy gathering materials, both real and imaginary, for their own special interest dictionaries. As they are gathered, they can be labelled and illustrated for complete identification.   M.A.C.

Related Source

*Language Arts
Primary*

49. Haley, Gail E. *Jack and The Bean Tree*. Illustrated by the author. Crown, 1986. ISBN 0-517-557177, $12.95. Ages 3-7.

"Poppyseed's a-telling stories" and this one is the Appalachian version of how "a mess of beans caused Jack to get into a real scrape." This Appalachian version of "Jack and the Beanstalk" is a delight to both the ear and the eye. Gail Haley, winner of both the Caldecott medal and the Kate Greenaway Award, sets inquisitive and headstrong Jack and his Maw in a mountain cabin. The bean tree sprouts from three magic beans and grows to the sky kingdom where it meets up with the giant Ephidophilus and his gentle wife, Matilda. In three trips to the giant's grand house "...with columns like the courthouse back home," Jack steals their magic tablecloth, a bantam hen that lays golden eggs, and a harp. The dialect is authentic, readable, and makes this version truly an American invention. The vertical portrait of the green giant, Ephidophilus, who stretches a mile and a half, and the three-quarter page close-up of giant Lady Matilda all in red are memorable. Haley presents inspired visual details of food, vines, animals painted on plywood with bits of moss, sticks, etc. This could become a children's favorite year after year.

The frontispiece is a circle of eight "Jacks" in different national costumes. The picture impels study of national folk heroes, their similarities and differences in character. Jack, as he is preserved by Appalachian folk tellers—notably Richard Chase—can be the focal point for study of regional and cultural history. Haley has included allusions to Jack in popular culture (e.g., The Jolly Green Giant). A search for Jack in Mother Goose or other folklore and popular culture is a natural activity based upon the background provided on the jacket and in the introduction to this book.   A.P.N./H.M.

*Literature
Primary
Intermediate*

---

50.   Haley, Gail E. *Jack and the Fire Dragon*. Illustrated by the author. Crown, 1988. ISBN 0-517-56814-4, $14.95. Ages 5-9.

Poppyseed, the storyteller, tells all who've come to her house on Story Mountain about the time when grown up Jack and his two brothers awakened the giant, Fire Dragaman, while clearing ground for their homesteads. Treasure-hungry Jack sought out the giant's hideaway in a deep cavern and discovered three sisters whom he rescued. Jenny, the one Jack fell in love with at first sight, gave him a wishing ring, a bottle of magic ointment, and a sword (Dragonteaser) before she was lifted to safety. Jack's greedy brothers left Jack in the cavern where he slew the giant and, with the wishing ring, returned to marry Jenny. Haley's richly colored and expressive linocut illustrations, like those in *Jack and the Bean Tree* (Crown, 1986) enhance her remarkable retelling of this American folk tale.

Children enjoy storytelling, both as listeners and as tellers. With the help of an interested teacher or librarian they can plan a school or community storytelling festival that features the humor and lore found in the Jack Tales. Begin with Haley's versions, Richard Chase's classic collection *The Jack Tales* (Houghton Mifflin, 1943), Still's *Jack and the Wonder Beans* (Putnam, 1977), and Cauley's *Jack and the Beanstalk* (Putnam, 1983). Be sure to included Briggs's parody *Jim and the Beanstalk* (Coward, 1970), and Ross's *Lazy Jack* (Dial, 1986) for their outrageous humor and modern flavor. Storyteller Donald Davis's retellings of several of the Jack Tales are the finest examples of these stories in oral form and his tapes should be made available for novice storytellers to study for technique. His tapes are available from the National Storytelling Resource Center, NAPPS, Box 309, Jonesborough, Tennessee 37659.   M.G.C./H.M.

Related Source

Storytelling, Social Studies Primary Intermediate

Related Sources

51.   Handford, Martin. *Find Waldo Now*. Illustrated by the author. Little, Brown, 1988. ISBN 0-316-34292-0, $10.95. All ages.

"Just find me in each picture and follow me through time." Easy for Waldo to say! This is a difficult challenge readers of all ages won't want to resist. Handford's cartoon-like, two-page murals chronicle the history of people, starting with "The Riddle of the Pyramids" and ending in "The Future." The minute detail and color combinations, unique to each ink drawing, delight the eye as readers search carefully, hoping to find Waldo among hundreds of miniscule people on each page. Just as readers are about to give up the search, Waldo is spotted in his stocking cap, arms piled high with history books. To give the eyes a rest, Handford provides a brief summary of each time period. For those unchallenged by the search for Waldo, "The Great Waldo Now Checklist" at the end of the book includes "Hundreds more things for time travelers to look for!" This is a happy addition to any library.

Waldo made his debut hiding among thousands of people populating modern day gathering spots like city streets and public beaches. After comparing earlier the ***Where's Waldo?*** (Little, Brown, 1987) with his latest expedition, Waldo fans will want to create their own drawing with someone or something hidden. The drawing should have some kind of theme—such as sports, marine life, or outer space—so that all parts of the drawing deal with the same topic. The artist should then decide what to hide within the drawing. For those who cannot draw with confidence, cutout collages would work as well. Finally, before handing it over to an expert eye, the creator should write a short summary of what the picture is about and what the viewer needs to find.　　J.T.

Related Source

*Art, Language Arts
Primary
Intermediate*

52.　Haugaard, Erik Christian. ***Prince Boghole***. Illustrated by Julie Downing.　Macmillan. 1987.　ISBN 0-02-743440-0, $13.95. Ages 5-8.

Prince Boghole is a literary fairy tale written in the rich language that characterizes fine storytelling. It is the story of Princess Orla of Munster, who was as good as she was beautiful, and the men who vie for her hand in marriage by going on a quest for the most wonderful of birds. There is subtle humor in the text too. The king, for example, tells Princess Orla that she made her bed and must lie in it, forgetting that it was he who set the task. The illustrations truly complement the text, reflecting both the beauty and the humor of the tale. The colors are jewel-like, the clothing is ornate in design, and the architecture and fluttering banners reflect the medieval Irish setting. Most striking is illustrator Julie Downing's composition: the figures sweep across the page.

　　Since there were no giants left and not even "a single dragon or two in Dingle," King Desmond had to come up with an appropriate quest for his time. Graham Oakley, in ***Henry's Quest*** (Atheneum, 1986), created a futuristic kingdom in which the characters set out on a quest for gasoline. After reading both of these books, students might enjoy playing with time and place settings to create their own kingdoms. In the stories the class creates, suitors could be sent on unusual quests through exotic or imagniary landscapes.　　M.A.C.

Related Source

*Literature,
Language Arts
Primary
Intermediate*

53.　Hearn, Michael Patrick. ***The Porcelain Cat***. Illustrated by Leo and Diane Dillon. Little, Brown, 1987. ISBN 0-316-35330-2, $12.95. Ages 6-8.

　　A simple task evolves into a complex quest as the old sorcerer sends his apprentice, Nickon, for a vial of basilisk blood so that he can work a charm on his porcelain cat, bringing it to life to chase the rats who gnaw his books. Nickon finds that to receive a favor he must do many, and he has an adventure that ends in first one surprise and then another. The illustrations, by Caldecott Medalists Leo and Diane Dillon, are beautifully designed, with curving page decorations reminiscent of illuminated manuscripts hand colored by monks. This medieval atmosphere is extended by the clothing, furniture, mystical characters, and dark forest settings. The pictures are also full of interesting facial expressions, hidden images, and sometimes cats to intrigue the viewer. At the same time, there is a subtle, but effective thread of humor throughout this beautifully-crafted book.

Students may want to look at Mercer Mayer's *The Pied Piper of Hamelin* (Macmillan, 1987) for another example of a way to get rid of rats. Teachers may want to introduce *The Giant Jam Sandwich* by John V. Lord and Janet Burroway (Houghton Mifflin, 1973) and *Cloudy With a Chance of Meatballs* by Judith Barrett (Atheneum, 1978) as examples of other town's visited by pests. Then students can invent new plagues and figure out ways, both magical and realistic, to obliterate them. Students can select story elements from the ideas discussed to develop another tale, which can be illustrated to reflect its time and place setting.   M.A.C.

54.   Hendershot, Judith. *In Coal Country*. Illustrated by Thomas B. Allen. Knopf, 1987. ISBN 0-394-98190-1, $13.99. Ages 5-10.

"Papa dug coal from deep in the earth to earn a living. He dressed for work when everyone else went to bed." So begins this warm and loving reminiscence of growing up as a coal miner's daughter. Hendershot's account is based upon memories—her own and those of her parents. From that first description, it is clear that this is a strong family, one in which everyone works hard, one in which affection is foremost. The overwhelming impression is of coal dust everywhere on Company Row: soot on the houses and the creek black with coal dust shot from the train that ran beside the Row. Equally as captivating as the text are Allen's full-page illustrations. Pastels and charcoal are the perfect media to capture the quality of life in a coal town. Each page seems sprinkled with siftings of gritty coal dust and the haze in the air is palpable. The most telling illustration that seems to embody the whole book is a close-up of Papa's face as he comes home, blackened with soot, but with blue eyes shining, and his daughter reflected in the lamp on his hat, running to meet him with outstretched arms. It is difficult to overpraise Hendershot's first book and Allen's artwork.

After sharing the book with students for the loving story and the fine art, make it available for them to quietly look through on their own. Then, depending upon their age and maturity, they might like to extend this experience with other childhood recollections such as Cynthia Rylant's *Waiting to Waltz* (1984), *When I was Young in the Mountains* (1983), or *A Blue-Eyed Daisy* (1985), all published by Bradbury, and Jean Fritz's *Homesick: My Own Story* (Putnam, 1982). Children could be encouraged to talk with their family about earlier childhoods and share these stories in class. They might also like to write about their life now (friends, games, special events, etc.), then give these descriptions to a family member to keep for some years, to be returned on a particular birthday.   B.B.

55.   Henkes, Kevin. *Chester's Way*. Illustrated by the author. Greenwillow, 1988. ISBN 0-688-07608-4, $11.88. Ages 4-up.

"Chester's way" is the only way to do things in this amusing and playful new book by Henkes. He always gets out of bed on the same side, always cuts his sandwiches diagonally, and never leaves the house without double-knotting his shoes. "You definitely have a mind of your own," says his mother. "That's one way to put it," says his father. But he is not alone. In fact, he and his best friend, Wilson, do everything alike. Then Lilly moves into the neighborhood: she does things her own way. "She definitely has a mind of her own," says Chester. "That's one way to put it," says Wilson. Eventually, they decide Lilly can be a good friend to have around. Henkes' frolicsome ink and watercolor illustrations mingle on the page with the text.

The story ends with "And then Victor moved into the neighborhood," leaving students with the structure of a story and an opportunity to create a new character and series of events. Working individually or in groups, they can write another episode about Victor. What is his way of doing things, and how does he go about making friends with his new neighbors? When this story is finished students can create the further adventures of an intriguing character like the slightly eccentric woman in Blake's *Mrs. Armitage on Wheels* (Knopf, 1988).   K.L.M.

ALA Notable Book

*Language Arts
Primary
Intermediate*

Related Source

56.   Hest, Amy. *The Purple Coat*. Illustrated by Amy Schwartz. Four Winds, 1986. ISBN 0-02-743640-3, $12.95. Ages 5-8.

Each fall Gabrielle, along with Mama, travels into New York City so Grampa, who is a tailor, can make her a navy blue coat. While Mama is off shopping in the city, Gabrielle asks Grampa to make her a purple coat, quoting him by saying, "It's good to try something new." Grampa recalls a time when Mama wanted a tangerine dress, and much to Gabrielle's delight, he devises a compromise sure to please all. This is a cheery story of a loving and thoughtful family. Warmth and compromise pour through in both the expressive text and the watercolored illustrations, making *The Purple Coat* worthy of the Christopher Award.

A sense of family and love runs deep within this book, providing an opportunity for youngsters to discuss experiences with and feelings about parents, grandparents, and other loved ones. Next children can dictate an ending to the statement "love is..." Print this at the bottom of a piece of paper for illustration. Encourage them to dedicate the picture to someone they love and present it to them, with love of course.   L.S.

*Art, Language Arts
Primary*

57.   Heyer, Marilee. *The Weaving of a Dream*. Illustrated by the author. Viking Kestrel, 1986. ISBN 0-670-80555-6, $12.95. All ages.

An old widow with three sons is known far and wide for her beautiful woven brocades. When she becomes entranced with a beautiful painting of a palace, she decides to weave it, spending three years on the task only to have it carried away by the wind when it is completed. One by one her sons search for it, but only the third son will endure the trials that bring him to the fairies of Sun Mountain, who have stolen the beautiful cloth. When he delivers the brocade at last to his dying mother, it comes to life and becomes their home, giving him also the lovely fairy who has woven herself into the cloth. This is a stunningly beautifuly book, its large illustrations so lifelike that one touches the pages almost expecting to feel a fuzzy caterpillar, a silken tassel, or old leathery skin. Both the pictures and story are enchanting—the words flow as smoothly as the pictures are gorgeous.

Literature,
Language Arts
Primary
Intermediate

This story has all the elements of a classic folk tale: the old parent, the pure-hearted third son successfully enduring horrible trials, the old person who helps him, the beautiful girl who becomes his bride, the two older brothers punished for their greed. Provide the children with a wide variety of folk tales from different lands through reading aloud, storytelling, records and tapes, and many illustrated versions of tales from around the world. They can compare and contrast their story elements, perhaps in chart form. They may also enjoy writing their own modern-day folk tales, following the classic format.   A.S.

58.   Hodges, Margaret, reteller. *Saint George and the Dragon*. Illustrated by Trina Schart Hyman. Little, Brown, 1984. ISBN 0-316-36789-3, $14.95. All ages.

Caldecott Award Winner
ALA Notable Book

Related Source

Illustrated by Trina Schart Hyman, *Saint George and the Dragon* was retold from Edmund Spenser's *Faerie Queen* by Margaret Hodges. Their collaboration has resulted in the 1985 Caldecott Medal winner. The text is vividly evocative of medieval England: the battle between Saint George and the dragon is described with such imagery that it is quite likely that the text could be used successfully without the pictures. Yet, Trina Schart Hyman's contribution to the whole is equal. She uses an interesting design device: on the text page she uses lines to create a frame that is filled with wild flowers, fairies, and action scenes from the story; and, on the illustration side these lines create the illusion of looking through a window as they visually tie text and picture together. Hyman's dragon is fearsome, her Saint George saintly, and her Una strong, solemn, and beautiful. Her scenery is picturesque and her compositions complex. Each figure is represented as an individual and there is enough detail in clothing, setting, and facial expression to satisfy even the most insatiable child. This is a stunning achievement in the art of the picture book.

Art, Language Arts
Primary
Intermediate
Middle School

By studying the design of Hyman's format, students could try their hand at a similar approach to illustrating a scene from a familiar folk tale (e.g., Little Red Riding Hood's first encounter with the wolf disguised as Grandmother). They could begin by drawing the frames, deciding what should be illustrated in each frame and what medium to use, then complete the drawing for display in the school entry area.   M.A.C.

59. Hoguet, Susan Ramsay. *Solomon Grundy*. Illustrated by the author. Dutton, 1986. ISBN 0-525-44239-1, $11.95. Ages 4-8.

In beautiful double-page wash illustrations, *Solomon Grundy* tells the story of two young married immigrants from Liverpool, England, who sail to America in 1830 to start a new life. The story follows the family's experiences through to 1910 when Solomon Grundy "died on Saturday, buried on Sunday. This is the end of Solomon Grundy." Through the appealing visual portrayal of the ups and downs of living in this young country in the 19th century, one comes to appreciate the changing American scene over the 80 years of Grundy's life. The well-known nursery rhyme, the text of which covers only eight pages, gives an added and familiar touch to the book, but this does not limit the story and is not what makes it a success. It is truly a "twice-told tale:" a story told in pictures as well as the text.

Hoguet's previously acclaimed book *I Unpacked My Grandmother's Trunk* (Dutton, 1983), Lawson's *They Were Strong and Good* (Viking, 1940), and Yarbrough's *Cornrows* (Putnam, 1979) would also be useful in helping young children see how they are all connected to an immigrant past and are a part of a still evolving nation. These and other books could be the basis for a larger instructional unit on immigration as the foundation of our multicultural society. E.A.H.

Related Sources

*Multicultural Studies
Primary
Intermediate*

60. Hurd, Thatcher. *Mama Don't Allow*. Illustrated by the author. Harper & Row, 1984. ISBN 0-06-022689-7, $11.89. Ages 4-8.

"Swamp bands play in the swamp," cries the whole town to Miles and his buddies! So they go to the swamp where they and their music are appreciated by the "sharp-toothed, long-tailed, yellow-eyed alligators." A quick switch from the jazzy "Mama don't allow no music playin' round here!" to "A Lullaby of Swampland" ("...lay your head awfully far down in the gooey, damp mud") saves the Swamp Band from the alligators' cauldron. Thatcher Hurd's illustrations are as delightfully comical as his text. His expressive colors are simple, but moving, and are a perfect complement the funky beat of the title song.

Thatcher Hurd provides his readers with the words and music to this traditional folk song. He also suggests that additional verses can be made up. Thus, a rollicking and creative singing session can follow a reading of his book. This type of holistic, integrated language arts experience is becoming more valued by educators for the rich background it provides for students. Other story poems that can easily be extended with extra verses are John Langstaff's exuberant *Oh, A-Hunting We Will Go* (McElderry, 1983) and N.M. Bodecker's "Let's Marry Said the Cherry" from his collection by the same title (Atheneum, 1974). M.A.C.

*Music, Language Arts
Primary
Intermediate*

Related Sources

---

61. Johnston, Tony. *Yonder*. Illustrated by Lloyd Bloom. Dial, 1988. ISBN 0-8037-0278-7, $12.89. Ages 4-8.

"Yonder is the farmer on a jet black horse./ Yonder are the hills that roll forever./ Yonder. Way over yonder." In such poetic prose, Tony Johnston tells of a young farmer's life as he builds his farm and raises his family. The story is derived from a tradition in Tony Johnston's family to plant a tree to commemorate the birth of each child. The cycles of life and of the seasons are richly depicted through image-laden text mirrored in Bloom's impressionistic, yet primitive, oil paintings in a spectrum of nature's finest colors. Pictures and text work as one as they showcase the warmth and pleasure of family in the simpler setting of days gone by. Watch for this one when the awards come out! Future collaborations by Johnston and Bloom would be welcome as well!

Social Studies
Primary
Intermediate

Yonder is a book that commemorates and celebrates family events and history. Trees were planted at the births and finally upon the farmer's death. How do other people mark the special occasions in their lives? This could be an interesting and worthwhile class project, especially for younger children. Students can search their memories and talk to family members about traditional celebrations. These could be listed and analyzed as to whether or not they reflect cultural tradition. Byrd

Related Source

Baylor's *I'm in Charge of Celebrations* (Scribner's, 1986) would be an excellent book to use to help children realize that they can start new traditions for celebration. A class project could be the planting of a tree to mark their eventual high school graduation. For current first graders, that means looking forward to the 21st century!   M.A.C.

62. Jonas, Ann. *The Quilt*. Illustrated by the author. Greenwillow, 1984. ISBN 0-688-03826-3, $9.55. Ages 3-6.

Ann Jonas always approaches her books with ingenuity, imagination, artistic integrity, and an obvious respect for her young audience. In *The Quilt* we share the excitement of a new quilt made up of cloth pieces from old and outgrown clothing and linens. We also are drawn into the young girl's dream in which the quilt, "like a little town," comes alive in rich and vibrant watercolors as the girl searches for her lost dog. We enter the world of imagination for a brief and satisfying episode in a young child's life. This is an excellent lap book for parents and children, as well as a visual feast for use with school groups.

Children's dreams are the subject of countless stories from "Wynken, Blynken, and Nod" to Mercer Mayer's popular *There's a Nightmare in My Closet* (Dial, 1968). Dreams can also be the basis

Related Sources

Art, Language Arts
Primary

for children's own writing or storytelling (see Kenneth Koch's *Wishes, Lies and Dreams* [Chelsea House, 1971]). An appropriate class project is the creation of class "Dream Quilt," with each piece or square being a representation of a child's experience or dream. The shared experiences in creating a group quilt will serve to remind all of our common fears, joys, and/or dreams.   H.M.

63. Jonas, Ann. *Reflections*. Illustrated by the author. Greenwillow, 1987. ISBN 0-688-06141-9, $12.88. Ages 5-8.

Like Jonas' previous *Round Trip* (Greenwillow, 1983), *Reflections* offers the reader a chance, this time in color, to read the book, turn it upside down, and read back to the first page. The simple story line follows a young boy through a day by the sea: seeing fishermen, the ferry boat, the beach, and other sights. It is the illustrations that star here—intriguing pictures that seem to transform magically when viewed from a different perspective—a boat yard into a campground, an orchard into a pond, a mill into a carnival. Each picture invites closer inspection as previously unnoticed details suddenly come alive. Here is an innovative idea, extended into color and executed well.

Children are usually fascinated by these pictures that change before their very eyes. They will clamor for more books that challenge their imaginations. Show them *The Trek*, also by Ann Jonas (Greenwillow, 1985), and Mitsumasa Anno's *Topsy Turvies: Pictures to Stretch the Imagination* (Weatherhill, 1970) and *Upside Downers: More Pictures to Stretch the Imagination* (Weatherhill, 1971). Your students will likely return to them again and again, delighting in their magical illustrations.   A.S.

Related Source

*Literature, Art
Primary
Intermediate*

Related Sources

64. Kellogg, Steven. *Pecos Bill*. Illustrated by the author. Morrow, 1986. ISBN 0-688-05872-8, $12.88. All ages.

A simple retelling of an old tall tale is enhanced by the abundance of comical and colorful illustrations by one of the country's most active and energetic artists. Tracing Pecos Bill's life from the time he was a baby until he marries and rejoins his lost family, Steven Kellogg provides an entertaining look at the situations that Bill encounters and handles along the way. Whether wrestling a rattlesnake or a monster, starting a rodeo, inventing steers with short legs on one side of their body, or just getting married, Pecos Bill makes a hero of himself without even trying. This version is so humorous and enjoyable it will probably be requested by young fans over and over again.

Share this book, and other picture books of tall tales, with older children. Discuss the characteristics of a tall tale—the challenges presented, the outrageous solutions, and the overall exaggeration—with the class. When the tall tale form is clear in everyone's mind, have students write and illustrate their own, self-created tall tales. Ask students to share their stories with the class either orally or by binding all students' stories together into one book.   L.S.

*Literature,
Language Arts
Primary
Intermediate*

65. Kuskin, Karla. *The Dallas Titans Get Ready for Bed*. Illustrated by Marc Simont. Harper & Row, 1986. ISBN 0-06-023563-2, $11.89. Ages 5-8.

Karla Kuskin, the author of *The Philharmonic Gets Dressed*, (Harper & Row, 1982), delights readers with a similarly structured

Related Source

glimpse at how a team of professional football players gets dressed after a game and, later that night, how they get into their sleeping clothes. Simont's cartoon-style drawings extend Kuskin's tongue-in cheek text. For example, Kuskin writes: "Jones cannot find his left loafer. Coach Scorch cannot find his lucky hat. Zelinka cannot find his little brother." The illustrations show Zelinka's little brother sitting behind a laundry bin clothed in both items. Readers will find themselves searching the illustrations often for the extra information they give. The overall effect is realistic and believable. It should be noted that the shower scene is strategically drawn: nothing more objectionable than a side view of a bare bottom shows.

Do the clothes "make the man?" *The Dallas Titans Get Ready for Bed* presents an ideal opportunity to discuss with children the "uniforms" our culture has sanctioned for various occupations. Why does the auto mechanic wear overalls while a businessman wears a three piece suit? What is "proper" dress for a wedding, a sleigh ride, a funeral, a baseball game, etc.? How many of our clothing decisions are based upon utility and how many upon culture? Can a person better himself or herself through dress? How much influence does peer pressure have upon dress? Encourage children to analyze the motivations behind their own clothing decisions. Students might then enjoy designing clothes for a paper doll (perhaps made from a magazine picture of a model mounted on cardboard and cut out) to suit a specific occupation or activity.   M.A.C.

Physical Education, Social Studies, Art Primary Intermediate

66.   Lattimore, Deborah Nourse. *The Flame of Peace: A Tale of the Aztecs*. Illustrated by the author. Harper & Row, 1987. ISBN 0-06-023704-0, $12.89. Ages 5-8.

"We know that the Aztecs feared nine evil lords of darkness and believed in a god of peace. Could a boy have outwitted those evil lords and struck a New Fire of Peace from the Morning Star? All we know is that during the time of Itzcoatl, a great Alliance of Cities marked the beginning of many peaceful decades." This compelling story of an Aztec boy's trek past those nine evil demons to find and return the symbol of peace to his people allows author/illustrator Lattimore to share with children her knowledge of Aztec mythology and pre-Columbian art. If one accepts the notion that bright, multicolored pictures attract like candy, then *The Flame of Peace* won't be left to gather dust on a classroom desk or library shelf. The variety of color, style, and amusing characters who dance across the double page spreads are strikingly attractive to the eye and lend authenticity to the depiction of the pre-Columbian story. In addition, the visual glossary on the end pages is helpful and the symbol system of page numbering is interesting. Some of the Aztec names are difficult but add to the sense of authenticity Lattimore wishes to convey to her readers.

What is peace? How can this concept be understood and expressed by younger children? Perhaps a beginning point is literature for children on the topic itself. How have authors and illustrators explored the topic? Here is an opportunity to share such books as Dr. Seuss's *The Butter*

Related Sources

Battle Book (Random House, 1984) or Lobel's ***Potatoes, Potatoes*** (Harper & Row, 1984). Next read Babbitt's ***The Search for Delicious*** (Farrar, Straus & Giroux, 1969) aloud. Then students can write about a search for peace modeled after the quest described in Babbitt's book.   J.A.F./M.A.C.

*Peace Studies
Primary
Intermediate*

67.   Leaf, Margaret. ***Eyes of the Dragon***. Illustrated by Ed Young. Lothrop, Lee & Shepard, 1987. ISBN 0-688-06156-7, $11.88. Ages 5-8.

   The villagers agree that the protective wall surrounding their modest town in China is plain. An artist agrees to paint a dragon on the wall provided his work is accepted without interference. When the magistrate breaks his word, the dragon comes to life and disappears into the sky leaving a crumbled wall as a reminder to always honor one's word. Ed Young's pastels sweep brightly and energetically across each page, carrying the eye and the imagination of the reader to the heart of this beautifully written literary tale inspired by an ancient Chinese essay.

   The ending of the story has an unfinished quality that requires thoughtful completion by the audience. Younger children may simply declare what happened to the village, or where the dragon and the artist went. Writing a "concluding" sentence or two, illustrated in pastels in the manner of Ed Young's drawings, is a satisfactory way to demonstrate the diversity of imagination and understanding that is found in any group. Jay Williams's ***Everyone Knows What a Dragon Looks Like*** (Four Winds, 1976), with paintings by Mercer Mayer, can be shared afterward. Older children who want to explore more deeply the significance and special honor that the dragon holds in Chinese mythology might begin Robert Wyndham's ***Tales the People Tell in China*** (Messner, 1971).   H.M.

*Art, Language Arts
Primary*

Related Sources

68.   Lee, Jeanne M. ***Ba-Nam***. Illustrated by the author. Henry Holt, 1987. ISBN 0-8050-0169-7, $12.95. Ages 5-8.

   There is a fairly limited body of literature for children about South Vietnam, particularly literature that doesn't involve destruction of life. This story by Jeanne Lee is especially welcomed. Author-illustrator Lee, raised in South Vietnam, shares a childhood experience with ancestor worship in this tale of meeting the grave keeper, Ba-Nam, while visiting the grave of her grandfather on Thanh-Minh, a day to honor ancestors by bringing offerings of incense, flowers, and cakes to place on the graves. Lee's family treated Thanh-Minh as a family outing day in which the children explore the land around the cemetery and climb trees to pick the popular mango and papaya fruits. As one reads this well written, authentically illustrated, and very personal story, one feels the joy of family life and tradition in South Vietnam, something long overdue for American readers.

   Lee's story might raise students' curiosities about how different cultures worship. Students might be challenged to investigate their national holiday that honors dead servicemen in all American wars (Memorial Day) or the American practice of publishing "in memoriam" messages in newspapers on special dates such as birthdays and anniversaries of relatives who have died. If those topics seem too somber, perhaps students would like to read other stories of Asia and

Southeast Asia by Jeanne Lee: *Legend of the Li River* (Holt, Rinehart & Winston, 1983), *Legend of the Milky Way* (Holt, Rinehart & Winston, 1982), and *Toad is the Uncle of Heaven* (Holt, Rinehart & Winston, 1985).   E.A.H.

69.   Lent, Blair. *Bayberry Bluff*. Illustrated by the author. Houghton Mifflin, 1987. ISBN 0-395-35384-X, $13.95. Ages 3-8.

Based upon the true story of Oak Bluffs on Martha's Vineyard, *Bayberry Bluff* is the simply told tale of the development of a tenting ground into a permanent vacation village. The style and media of the illustrations strongly evoke the essence of a bygone era. This is accomplished through an unusual method of combining printing and cardboard cuts, and through the design in the clothing and buildings. The decorations—shells, flowers, animal cutouts—with which the vacationers adored their tents and eventually their houses add to the charm of this captivating story.

Art students will surely enjoy trying the cardboard cut technique of Caldecott-winner Blair Lent which is described opposite the title page in

the book. In preparation they may want to look also at Margaret Hodges's *The Wave* (Houghton Mifflin, 1964), also illustrated by Blair Lent using the same technique. Older students might enjoy recreating in cardboard and fabric scraps a turn-of-the-century vacation village complete with decorations.   M.A.C.

70.   Levinson, Riki. *I Go with My Family to Grandma's*. Illustrated by Diane Goode. Dutton, 1986. ISBN 0-525-44261-8, $10.95. Ages 3-6.

Five cousins from different boroughs of New York City go to visit Grandma on the same day. The diversity of the city is shown by the various means each family uses to arrive at their destination. Set in the early 1900's, this book also provides the reader with a glimpse of New York and Grandma's house as they looked then. The typical realities of a large family gathering together—the scoldings, teasing, crankiness, exhaustion—are expressed clearly in the facial expressions of the round-faced children and parents. This exceptional picture book, showing a strong sense of family, offers a visual sense of the historical period that can be enjoyed by a wide range of readers.

This book is so packed with ideas that a multitude of extension activities quickly come to mind. One interesting aspect is the variety of

means of transportation used in the book. Mentioned and illustrated are a bicycle, a trolley, a horse-drawn wagon, trains, cars, and a ferry.

Students could discuss which of these are still used today, how they have changed, what is used now that was not used then, and so on. Consult other books on transportation to expand knowledge of the means the exist presently, were used in the past, or may be used in the future. Some suggested titles are *How Do We Travel?* by Caroline Arnold (Watts, 1983), *Things That Go* by Tadasu Izawa (Putnam, 1984), and *The Future World of Transportation* by Valerie Moolman (Watts, 1984).   L.S.

Related Sources

71.   Levinson, Riki. *Watch The Stars Come Out.* Illustrated by Diane Goode. Dutton, 1985. ISBN 0-525-44205-7, $12.95. Ages 4-8.

ALA Notable Book

Two small children journey alone aboard ship from the "Old World" to a new life in American at the turn of the century. Their experiences aboard ship and the excitement of their arrival in New York City becomes a story passed down from generation to generation in this charming picture book. Through captivating illustrations and simple text, a young reader can follow the round-faced, sturdy young immigrants as they view the Statue of Liberty and pass through immigration on Ellis Island. Their joyous reunion with their parents and their arrival at their new home on Hester Street, which is teaming with activity, are perfectly captured in Diane Goode's simple, detailed pictures. This is a very special book which introduces young readers to that exciting period when immigration to the United States was at its peak and extols the universal experience of a warm, loving family life.

With the recent interest in the restoration and anniversary of the Statue of Liberty, teachers will certainly wish to use *Watch The Stars Come Out* in conjunction with one of the many fine informational books, such as Mary J. Shapiro's *How They Built The Statue of Liberty* (Random House, 1985) or the S.V.E. filmstrip *The Statue of Liberty*. While the latter provides the historical background, *Watch The Stars Come Out* shows the emotional impact that viewing Miss Liberty for the first time had on generations of immigrants. Librarians in ethnic neighborhoods will surely wish to include this picture book in their collections to help acquaint children with their heritage. A special speaker or display of materials from the library collection could create broad interest in the topic among all family members.   S.L.W.

Related Sources

Multicultural Studies
Primary
Intermediate

72.   Lionni, Leo. *Frederick's Fables.* Illustrated by the author. Pantheon, 1985. ISBN 0-394-97710-6, $14.99. Ages 3-8.

For longer than some of us may recall, Leo Lionni has brought delight, humor and morality to generations of readers. It is, therefore, a proper tribute to his genius to have this most welcome collection of his thirteen best-known stories in one handsome volume. Here are Frederick the word-gathering mouse and Willy the wind-up mouse, plus Cornelius, Swimmy, and Lionni's other animal characters so immediately identifiable by children. The introduction by Bruno Bettelheim speaks clearly to the vital role illustrations play in picture story books and to the underlying themes in Lionni's slightly rewritten fables. This is a book not to "buy," but to invest in for the years of pleasure it will provide to future generations of readers young and old.

Like Frederick, children can become word-gathers and take pride and pleasure in what they collect. Language arts classes can be enriched by such activities where children explore in groups or individually descriptive words and action words that are related to a chosen topic or theme. Read and discuss "Frederick," one of Lionni's stories included, and the importance of words in enriching our lives. Lists displayed prominently around the room will serve as daily reminders.   H.M.

73.   Lobel, Arnold. *The Turnaround Wind*. Illustrated by the author. Harper & Row, 1988. ISBN 0-06-023988-3, $12.89. Ages 4-8.

It was a beautiful day and the countryside was full of people taking the air. Suddenly a wild wind descends and turns everyone topsy-turvy. Lobel first presents small cameos of these characters as they stroll about. Then he shows close-ups of them after the wind has played its tricks. These pages are to be turned upside down, where one of the other characters is revealed imbedded in the first. The sketchy cartoon-style drawings, colored with watercolors, are intriguing, enticing the eye to search for the characters. Text at the bottom of each picture, and thus at the top and bottom of each page, describes what has happened to each character. This is an ingenious book, a fine final contribution by a talent who will be missed in the world of children's literature.

Other illustrators have experimented with upside down designs in various ways, resulting in some very clever books. Gather the following: *Upside-Downers* by Mitsumasa Anno (Weatherhill, 1971), *Round Trip* (Greenwillow, 1983) and *Reflections* (Greenwillow, 1987) by Ann Jonas, and *The Look Again and Again and Again... Book* by Beau Gardner (Lothrop, Lee & Shepard, 1984). After studying the designs and the techniques these authors used to create them, allow children to try an upside down design themselves. The easiest form to model would be Gardner's simple graphics. Even so, this is a demanding task and one design per child is sufficient. The class could come up with a vehicle for uniting the individual drawings into a unified story, as Arnold Lobel did with his big wind. This could result in a class book for all to enjoy.   M.A.C.

74.   Locker, Thomas. *Family Farm*. Illustrated by the author. Dial, 1988. ISBN 0-8037-0489-5, $14.89. All ages.

As we know from daily headlines, the future of the family farm is bleak. For younger readers, *Family Farm* explains the familiar, realistic situation in which the father must take a job in the city and all the family must assume more responsibilities in order to save the farm. In this story, there is a happy ending: a new cash crop saves the farm—

Language Arts Primary

Related Sources

Art, Language Arts Primary Intermediate

at least for another year. Locker's text is well written and equal to his usual detailed and realistic oil paintings, in which shadows, light, and shading effectively convey the moods of the story and the characters.

A unit on "The Farm" remains a mainstay of primary social studies programs. *Family Farm* can be used by a primary teacher who believes studying the farm should not be a superficial survey of 19th century rural life. Too many urban children know the fragility of our industrial economy; it is appropriate that they learn that life in rural America can be as precarious as life in the city. Although the book ends "sort of" happily, the story is an excellent stimulus for such critical questions as: What do you think will happen next year? Is this like anything that has happened to someone you know? Are endings always this happy?　　J.F.A.

Language Arts, Social Studies Primary Intermediate

75.　Locker, Thomas. *Where the River Begins*. Illustrated by the author. Dial, 1984. ISBN 0-8037-0089-X, $15.00. Ages 4-8.

This is the simply-told story of two boys and their grandfather who hike to the source of the river that flows near their home. They pass fields and climb into the foothills to an upland meadow where the river begins. It is a gentle story that lets artist-teacher Thomas Locker display his considerable skills as a landscape painter in the tradition of Constable, Turner, Lorrain, and the Hudson River School artists. The characters are clearly secondary to the low hills, the trees and fields, the sky, and the ever-present river that flows through the heart of the book. The reader, in fact, is held at a peaceful distance from the story and is compelled to admire the illustrations like a painting on a museum wall.

Picture story books are often a child's first introduction to art. Repeated experiences with book illustration can greatly influence a child's growing sense of aesthetic judgment and taste. Locker is a fine painter whose style is comparable to American and European landscape painters of the 18th and 19th centuries. Sharing *Where the River Begins* is an opportunity for teachers to show the connections between painters and styles of the past with contemporary artists who illustrate books for young people.　　H.M.

Art Primary Intermediate

76.　Lussert, Anneliese. *The Farmer and the Moon*. Illustrated by Jozef Wilkon. North-South, 1987. ISBN 0-8050-0281-2, $12.95. Ages 5-8.

Money from the moon? This is the unexpected solution to the problems of Mark, the poor but honest farmer, when he tangles with his rich but miserly neighbor, Luke. Lussert has created a charming, tightly-told tale with a European flavor in the ancient tradition of innocence triumphing over calculated greed. Appealing characters and intriguing plot twists will keep the pages turning as the reader roots for Mark all the way. Equally appealing are the stunning full-page illustrations, one for each page of text, in glowing pastels that range from a transparent, chalk-like quality to a solid, waxy appearance.

This is a perfect tale for creative drama. The three main characters (Mark, Luke, and the moon) may be supplemented by imaginatively conceived farm animals reacting to the action, as suggested by tongue-in-cheek details in the illustrations. The tight structure lends itself to an investigation of story structure. Children may wish to write the story from Luke's point of view, or write a sequel, speculating upon what happened to Luke and including their own pastel illustrations.   B.B.

77.   Lyon, George Ella. *A Regular Rolling Noah*. Illustrated by Stephen Gammell. Bradbury, 1986. ISBN 0-02-761330-5, $13.95. Ages 4-7.

What with chickens and guineas to tend on the railroad journey, not to mention Rosie and her calf and Bad Patch, the mare, it is no wonder young Gabbard came to be called a "regular Rolling Noah." George Ella Lyon relives the journey of her grandfather as he traveled through Canada in a box car. His job was to deliver some former neighbors' livestock to their new homestead in the northern plains. Told in the sparse, whittled down style of a country boy from the hollows, Lyon realistically portrays this unique true-to-life adventure. Gammell's airy hues combine with beautiful detailing to create watercolor illustrations inviting enough for any would-be box car gadabout. Although his trip is exciting and Gabbard is much more worldly after his adventure, he concludes there truly is no place like home and the hills of Kentucky.

Although American children recently enjoyed the refurbishing of the Statue of Liberty and took pride in their ancestors' voyages to Ellis Island, the trip for some did not end in America. Two films that may be available from a public library, *We Came to America* (color, 15 minutes, 1964) and *Valley of a Thousand Peaks* (color, 25 min., 1978), dramatize the beauty of Canada as well as the pioneering spirit which led families to search for a better life. Students might be interested in serving as "diplomats" for Canada (or another country) can speak on the advantages of moving to a new homeland. Travel posters from other countries could entice would-be "expatriates" to new lands.   G.G.

78.   Mahy, Margaret. *17 Kings and 42 Elephants*. Illustrated by Patricia MacCarthy. Dial, 1987. ISBN 0-8037-0458-5, $10.95. Ages 4-8.

In a near-perfect marriage of text and illustration, Mahy and MacCarthy have created a sensory delight for readers of all ages. Reading the rhyming text, one cannot help but feel the rhythmical quality that begs to be read aloud. The reader meets all sorts of animals as the seventeen kings travel through the jungle infecting every creature within earshot with their contagious pulsating beat. Creatures such as "Tinkling tunesters, twangling trillicans,/ Butterflied and fluttered by the great green trees./ Big baboonsters, black gorillicans/ Swinging from the branches by their hairy knees" joined in and "…Bibble-bubble-babbled to the bing-bang-bong!" MacCarthy's batik paintings on silk are vividly intense and richly exotic in their color quality. Her illustrations perfectly capture the gaiety of the jungle romp through her characterization of the animals and luminous paintings of the lush jungle habitat.

Teachers and librarians should not be the only ones to read this book aloud: children will also want to join in as it has the makings of a terrific responsive or choral reading. With the help of some percussion instruments, perhaps homemade, "write" a script blending the reading of the text with some rhythmic patterns adapted to the age of the children. Music teachers could also use this book to encourage young children to clap out and march to rhythms.   K.B.B.

Music, Language Arts
Primary

79.   Marshall, James. *The Cut-Ups*. Illustrated by the author. Viking, 1984. ISBN 0-670-25195-X, $10.95. Ages 3-8.

First in Marshall's
Cut-Ups series

Quite simply, this is probably the funniest book of 1984! Spud Jenkins and Joe Turner are neighborhood terrors who "made their mothers old before their time." They get their comeuppance at the hands of wily Mary Frances Hooley and Lamar J. Spurgle ("He just loves kids. He used to be an assistant principal."). Though the boys escape Mr. Spurgle's wrath, when they return to school at the end of the summer, a surprise awaits them—and the reader as well. Children and adults alike should find a laugh on every page. The farcical humor can be found in the story and in Marshall's cartoon illustrations, bringing children back to this book again and again.

James Marshall has been successfully illustrating books for young people for many years. He would be an appealing object for an author–artist study project for younger children. With the help of a good reference librarian, find biographical sources that young readers can use to learn about him. Arrange with his publisher for any promotional materials and photographs they may have of him and, if possible, plan a time for a conference call for the class with him. Prepare the class by studying all available books by him and the biographical information. Then plan what questions to ask during the phone interview.   H.M.

Author Studies
Primary
Intermediate

80.   Marshall, James. *Goldilocks and the Three Bears*. Illustrated by the author. Dial, 1988. ISBN 0-8037-0542-5, $10.95. Ages 4-8.

Caldecott Honor Book
ALA Notable Book

James Marshall, the clown prince of children's picture books, brings his outrageous brand of humor to retelling one of children's favorite and most familiar tales. The rosy-cheeked innocence of Goldilocks hardly hides the brat within ("she was one of those naughty little girls who do exactly as they please"). While the bear family is out riding on their rusty tandem bicycle waiting for the porridge to cool, Goldilocks walks in, eats baby's porridge, breaks his chair and is caught sleeping in his bed when the bears return. However, this is hardly the same beloved, often "cute," traditional story. Marshall's Caldecott Honor Book-winning illustrations create an off-beat retelling that pumps new life into the old yarn and should leave today's audiences in stitches.

Marshall's retelling is the latest in a long history of illustrated versions of an old English folk tale that began with Eleanor Mure's *The Story of the Three Bears*, printed in 1831 and considered the first illustrated version (a facsimile copy may be available from the Osborne Collection of the Toronto Public Library, where the original may be seen, or from Oxford University Press in Toronto). Younger readers will gain much from the opportunity to examine as many different versions as local libraries can supply; the librarian can also help find non-illustrated versions in folk tale anthologies. The books gathered could be made into an especially attractive display in the class or library. Students can compare how the bears and the girl/woman are portrayed by the artists, how the settings in each version differ, and how each episode in the story is alike or different. Discussing and charting their observations can be an enjoyable and challenging first step toward an awareness of criteria for evaluating books, especially those with illustrations.   H.M.

Related Source

*Literature
Primary
Intermediate*

81.   Martin, Jr., Bill and John Archambault. *The Ghost-Eye Tree*. Illustrated by Ted Rand. Holt, Rinehart and Winston, 1985. ISBN 0-03-005632-2, $11.95. Ages 6-8.

Originally developed by the authors as a reader's theater selection, this chilling story is meant to be read aloud. Though told in language that plays with sounds and rhyming, the story is not light. Rather, it deals with very real fears of two children who must walk by "the ghost-eye tree" after dark as they go for milk for their mother. The children sometimes feel they've conquered the tree and other times feel the tree has "gotten" them! The suspense is enhanced by Ted Rand's dark, eerily-moonlit watercolor pictures. His gnarled ghost-eye tree invites close scrutiny as the reader attempts to figure out just what the children saw moving in the tree and why they came to call it the ghost-eye tree.

The Ghost-Eye Tree provides an opportune moment for discussion of children's fears, both real and imagined. Because either type is just as scary to the child, this discussion should be conducted in an atmosphere of acceptance. Even so, some helpful differentiation between what is a legitimate fear and what is probably a figment of the imagination, and thereby more easily conquered, can result. This could begin with an analysis of what the children feared in *The Ghost-Eye Tree* and how they handled it. A classroom book entitled "Fears and How to Conquer Them" could be a culminating project.   M.A.C.

*Social Studies,
Language Arts
Primary*

82.   Mayer, Mercer, reteller. *The Pied Piper of Hamelin*. Illustrated by the author. Macmillan, 1987. ISBN 0-02-765361-7, $16.95. Ages 5-8.

Mayer has done a fine job both retelling and illustrating the eerie tale of *The Pied Piper of Hamelin*. His rats are red-eyed and disgusting, his adults self-centered, and his children touchingly innocent. The piper himself is depicted as mysterious, yet kind to the children he led away from an ungrateful town. The final song explains the expression, "the piper must be paid." Mayer's text is very readable. He avoids telling the entire story in poetry. Rather, he tells the story simply, with interesting language and plenty of imagery, as is appropriate for his intended audience. This is a memorable version of a favorite old tale.

The ending of *The Pied Piper of Hamelin* may leave children dangling. What was behind the door in the mountain? What happened to the children? Did the townspeople try to get them back? Did they ever pay the piper? What happened to the piper himself? After discussing these questions, students may be motivated to write or tell sequels to Mercer Mayer's version of this traditional folk tale.   M.A.C.

*Literature,
Language Arts
Primary
Intermediate*

83. Mayer, Mercer. *The Sleeping Beauty*. Illustrated by the author. Macmillan, 1984. ISBN 0-02-765340-4, $14.95. All ages.

Mercer Mayer has retold the classic fairy tale of "Sleeping Beauty" in a richly detailed, Gothic style that would put even Walt Disney to shame. The reader's sympathies are immediately in the king's camp. Unlike earlier versions of the story in which the king insults the faerie by being too cheap to buy another gold plate, Mayer tells us that the insult was the steward's fault: he had replaced one of the golden goblets with a gold painted lead one so he could use the real one to pay off his debts. The plot is complicated by the king's jealousy over the silver owl who portends his daughter's birth. The silver owl is the brother of the Blue Faerie (the insulted faerie) so her curses rain down upon the king again. It is eventually the Blue Faerie's own son who kisses and awakens Sleeping Beauty. Mayer's illustrations are as complex and finely wrought as his text. Lovers of art nouveau will especially enjoy Mayer's undulating design and heads of swirling hair. Mercer Mayer has worked hard to achieve that artful blend of picture and text.

Folk tales, even those thought of as "by " individual writers—e.g., the Grimm Brothers and Perrault—have always been fair game for storytellers and other revisionists. Different versions reflect the interests of the tellers and the culture and times of the retelling. Several illustrated versions of "Sleeping Beauty" could be shared with younger children and examined for their similarities and differences: Hyman's *The Sleeping Beauty* (Little, Brown, 1974), Le Cain's *Thorn Rose or Sleeping Beauty* (Bradbury, 1975), and Hoffman's *The Sleeping Beauty* (Oxford, 1959).   M.A.C./H.M.

*Literature
Primary
Intermediate*

Related Sources

84. McKissack, Patricia C. *Mirandy and Brother Wind*. Illustrated by Jerry Pinkney. Knopf, 1988. ISBN 0-394-98765-9, $13.95. Ages 4-8.

Mirandy knows that if she could capture the wind for a dancing partner, she would win a prize in the upcoming junior cakewalk contest. She asks everyone for advice and suggestions about how to capture the

*Caldecott Honor Book
ALA Notable Book*

wind, but none work. In the end she traps Brother Wind in the barn, gets his help and, with her clumsy friend Ezel as her partner, wins the contest to the surprise and entertainment of all. McKissack speaks to the reader in language musical in its rhythms and cadences, language that should be heard and savored. Pinkney's watercolors combine elements of fantasy with the colorful exuberance of Mirandy and her friends.

Spring is usually a good time of the year to plan a "Windy Week" at school or at the library when everyone focuses their attention upon stories, songs, poems, plays, games, and other activities that pay homage to the wind. Bauer's *Windy Day: Stories and Poems* (Lippincott, 1988) is an excellent starting place for gathering ideas. *A To Zoo: Subject Access to Children's Picture Book*s (Bowker, 1985) is an excellent guide to 4,400 other books for younger children. Dorson's *Buying the Wind: Regional Folklore in the United States* (University of Chicago, 1964) is a useful resource for teachers who wish to locate myths, folk tales, and other traditional materials. Culminate "Windy Week" with a school-wide kite flying festival where the presence of "Brother Wind" takes on immediate importance.   H.M.

Literature, Music, Language Arts
Primary
Intermediate

Related Sources

85. McPhail, David. *First Flight*. Illustrated by the author. Joy Street, 1987. ISBN 0-316-56323-4, $13.95. Ages 4-8.

A young boy's stuffed bear provides a measure of security for his first airplane flight. While the boy takes each phase of the trip in stride, his bear—now a life size passenger—suffers many of the discomforts normally experienced by travellers: take-off anxiety, upset stomach, fatigue, and occupied lavatories. Anyone who has travelled by air, or who is about to take a plane trip for the first time, will appreciate the bear's predicaments and facial reactions. This is just the ticket for sharing with a large group or by a parent with a young traveler.

As he did so successfully and appealingly in *The Bear's Toothache* (Little, Brown, 1978) and *The Bear's Bicycle* (Little, Brown, 1975, with Emilie McLeod), McPhail contrasts so clearly the humorously stressed-out bear (as a child) with the calm handling of the situation by the child (as the adult) that even younger children will be able to understand both points of view. With the guidance of a sensitive adult, children can discuss other situations in which they have felt, as the bear did, uncertainty or lack of control (e.g., a first music lesson, a first day at a new school, a first visit to a relative's home). Then they can contrast those feelings with how they would have responded as the "grown up," just as the boy does in McPhail's stories.   H.M.

Related Sources

Social Studies
Primary

86. Meyers, Odette. *The Enchanted Umbrella*. Illustrated by Margot Zemach. Harcourt Brace Jovanovich, 1988. ISBN 0-15-200448-3, $13.95. Ages 4-8.

Patou is helper to an umbrella maker, for whom he cares deeply. When the old man dies, his selfish nephew cheats Patou out of his half of the inheritance, giving him only a ragged umbrella. The umbrella, however, is enchanted and saves Patou from more than one disaster, finally flying him to an island where umbrellas are unknown. The people there make him king, and he sets up shop, supplying umbrellas to everyone. Zemach's watercolor paintings, with their impressionistic backgrounds and lively action, capture the flavor of the text, an adaptation of a French folk tale. The book is reminiscent of Mitchell's *The Baron Rides Out* (Philomel, 1985): the wild adventures of Patou have a tall tale quality like those of the Baron Munchausen.

Related Source

Umbrellas used to be a sign of power. The illustrations of umbrellas from all over the world are lavish in their design. After hearing *The Enchanted Umbrella* read aloud, children might enjoy designing their own umbrella fit for a king. These would make a bright display in a classroom, hallway, or library. The children might even take this one step further and decorate their own real umbrellas (which can be purchased for as little as $3.00) using magic markers, fabric scraps, feathers, or other materials.   M.A.C.

Art
Primary

87.   Mikolaycak, Charles. *Babushka*. Illustrated by the author. Holiday House, 1984. ISBN 0-8234-0520-6, $14.95. Ages 3-8.

This is a retelling of the classic Russian folk tale of the peasant woman who was too busy polishing and cleaning her cottage to join the Three Wise Men of their journey to Bethlehem. When she does try to follow them, they are lost to her forever. She still wanders the earth, looking for the baby King, leaving toys, candy, and the warm smell of cinnamon behind her. The religious significance is less apparent than Babushka herself, endlessly seeking. *Babuskha* is a handsome book with glowing watercolor and colored pencil illustrations artfully combined with text. The artist suggests the passage of time from ancient to modern times with rich details.

Students may compare Mikolaycak's vision of this old tale with those by other artists, particularly the Caldecott-winning *Baboushka and the Three Kings* by Ruth Robbins and illustrated by Nicolas Sidjakov (Parnassus, 1960). Young children can begin to compare such features as the medium, size, format, and color, as well as the content of the illustrations in finding points of contrast. In addition, they can compare this "seeker" with versions from other cultures, e.g., La Befana from Italy. Helping young children to respond consciously to elements of literature and art are critical first steps in developing appreciation and judgment in the arts.   B.B./H.M.

Related Source

Literature
Primary
Intermediate

88.   Mitchell, Adrian. *The Baron on the Island of Cheese*. Illustrated by Patrick Benson. Philomel, 1986. ISBN 0-399-21309-1, $12.95. Ages 8-up.

The Baron on the Island of Cheese is one of many little-known tales dating from the late 1700's that are told about a real man, Baron Hieronymus Karl Friedrich Munchausen, a gifted prevaricator who took himself quite seriously. In this story, the Baron falls through the volcano Etna on a bet, having arrived there via a cannon shot. From there his adventures continue through the center of the earth, onto an iceberg and the island of Cheese—which is inhabited by tall and tiny purple people with three legs and one arm—and into the belly of a whale. Adrian Mitchell tells his tale in rich language full of imagery, wry humor and the exaggeration for which the Baron tales are so well loved in Germany. Patrick Benson's illustrations, in ink and watercolor, are precisely and comically executed. Most notable are his perspectives: we see the Baron from the back of an eagle, perched in a giant bird's nest high in a tree, and shooting skyward from a cannon. This is an exciting introduction to one of literature's most colorful characters.

The Baron Munchausen tales are similar to American tall tales, with their outrageous exaggeration, yet they were first recorded many years before the tall tales. Children can be introduced to the Baron tales through *The Baron Rides Out* (Putnam, 1985), an earlier collaboration of Mitchell and Benson, and *The Real Munchausen* (Devin-Adair, 1960), written by Angelita von Muchausen, the five times great grand-niece of the true Baron. Then children can compare the tales to American tall tales about Pecos Bill, Davy Crockett, Paul Bunyan, etc. Students might enjoy making up some outrageous plot and deciding which character would be likely to have such an adventure.　　M.A.C.

Related Sources

Literature,
Language Arts
Primary
Intermediate

89.　　Mori, Tuyosi. *Socrates and the Three Little Pigs.* Illustrated by Mitsumasa Anno. Philomel, 1986. ISBN 0-399-21310-4, $11.95. Ages 7-up.

Mitsumasa Anno, winner of the 1984 Hans Christian Andersen Prize, has joined forces with mathematician Tuyosi Mori to produce a fascinating book illustrating the principles of combinatorial analysis, permutations, and combinations. Socrates, a wolf, must decide how he can most likely find one or more of three little pigs in five houses. With the help of his mathematical frog friend, Pythagoras, and the nagging of his hungry wife, Xanthippe, Socrates considers all the possible combinations and permutations. All of the choices are elaborately drawn out and explained as the reader is gradually led to explore various questions: How many choices are there if only one pig can be in a house? More than one pig? If the pigs are differentiated (red, yellow, and blue clothes) or treated as identical? This book requires slow, careful reading but explains the choices clearly, leading the reader from complex to simple to complex. Anno's cheerful little pigs and philosophical wolf and frog lend a congenial air to the story. An extensive note to parents and teachers is added to explain the principles involved.

Math, Science
Primary
Intermediate
Middle School

Children will understand these principles best when they have a chance to work out similar problems on their own. How many ways can you arrange two pigs in four houses? Two pigs in five houses? The importance here is not to solve a particular problem but rather to learn to work in a systematic fashion. Children should see the pattern develop and may gradually be able to predict solutions without drawing each choice.　　A.S.

90. Noble, Trinka Hakes. *Apple Tree Christmas*. Illustrated by the author. Dial, 1984. ISBN 0-8037-0102-0, $10.95. Ages 4-8.

Apple Tree Christmas is a touchingly nostalgic look at a rural family's life in the early 1880's. Much of the story line and detail was taken from the author's family's experiences in rural Michigan. This is the story of how much an old apple tree means to the Ansterburg family, particularly to young Katrina. The apples are used for cider, for feeding the family and livestock, and decorating the Christmas tree and table. The younger child, Josie, swings from a wild grape-vine that hangs from the tree, and the older girl, Katrina, uses a large branch as her studio and drawing board. When a terrible blizzard destroys the apple tree, Katrina is crushed. Her father, however, saves what he can: the vine for Josie and the studio for Katrina. This is a touching family story, reminiscent of Laura Ingalls Wilder's writings.

This could be an excellent book to use with older children in conjunction with the Wilder books. Children could discuss those simpler times and try to rate the pros and cons of living then and living now. This might spark further research on living conditions, medical facilities, entertainment opportunities, etc., so that their decisions could be justified. A visit to a house or farm museum would allow children to see artifacts from those times firsthand.   M.A.C.

Social Studies
Primary
Intermediate

91. Noble, Trinka Hakes. *Meanwhile Back at the Ranch*. Illustrated by Tony Ross. Dial, 1987. ISBN 0-8037-0354-6, $10.89. Ages 4-8.

Nothing much ever happens on Rancher Hick's farm out West, so one day he drives eighty-four miles to Sleepy Gulch to see what's new there. His wife, Elna, stays home to dig potatoes. What follows is the humorous juxtaposition of Rancher Hick's visit in Sleepy Gulch—including a long, slow amble through (yawn) a checker game that has lasted for weeks and watching a turtle crossing the road—with Elna's "boring" day as she wins a refrigerator, receives a surprise inheritance, strikes oil, is discovered by a movie producer, and is visited by the President. Children will be chuckling at each new revelation of this funny tall tale and chanting "Meanwhile...back at the ranch" right along with you. Tony Ross's droll illustrations are the perfect companion to this wacky tale.

This book shows clearly the contrast between two very different days: boring and exciting. Children can follow this pattern to create a story showing the contrast between days that are lucky and unlucky, hot and cold, happy and sad, or busy and relaxed. The titles can reflect different settings, e.g., "Meanwhile back at the school..." or "Meanwhile back at the ball park..." Children should enjoy reading their final stories to each other and to younger students. With a little planning, it might be possible to string the stories together into a single coherent narrative.   A.S.

Language Arts
Primary
Intermediate

---

92.   Novak, Matt. *Claude and Sun*. Illustrated by the author. Bradbury, 1987. ISBN 0-02-768151-3, $12.95. Ages 4-7.

This simple fantasy for younger children illustrates the close relationship between the sun and Claude, an affable farmer and Santa Claus look-alike. Novak's subtle and soft illustrations remind one strongly of the pointillist works of Seurat. He has used points of color to depict subtle changes in light as the day dawns, as the sun gets hot in the sky, as it rains, and then as night comes. Though the story is not complex, when Claude and sun go through "a secret passage to the rain spot" the reader is left wondering about who Claude really is and what the secret passage is all about. Thus the simple format is deceiving: there is sufficient substance to provoke thought and stimulate the child's imagination.

Art
Primary
Intermediate

Few children's books have been illustrated in the pointillist style. Students might enjoy studying this technique in this book, through general books on art and artists, and by a visit to an art museum that displays the works of Seurat and other pointillists. Students may want to try doing a series of impressionist drawings that reflect changes in light due to the time of day or weather conditions.   M.A.C.

93.   Oakley, Graham. *Henry's Quest*. Illustrated by the author. Atheneum, 1986. ISBN 0-689-31172-9, $12.95. All ages.

In both picture and text, Oakley takes the reader on a trip into the future. Henry is a shepherd in a small kingdom ruled by King George XXXXVII. Only two books had survived the book burning ordered by the king's great-great-great grandfather: *King Arthur and the Knights of the Roundtable* and *Aunty Mabel's Fairy Tale Book*. Thus, we find the king has renamed himself Arthur II and has encouraged chivalry and knight errantry among his subjects. When it comes time for the eldest princess, Isolde, to marry, Arthur II issues a proclamation that whatever knight successfully undertakes a quest for gasoline—a magical substance necessary to make the royal family's shiny heirlooms move—will win the princess's hand in marriage. Henry, who read and believed *Aunty Mabel's Fairy Tale Book*, decides this is his chance to have some similar adventures. Through his journey the reader is treated to a provocative view of what the future might bring. Oakley's complex illustrations, some of which look like impressionistic paintings, are full of detail and extensions of the ideas in the text.

Social Studies,
Language Arts
Primary
Intermediate

Related Resource

As we near the turn of the century, we will undoubtedly indulge in more and more speculations about what the future will be like. Students, after reading and studying *Henry's Quest*, can discuss how much of Oakley's story could come true. They may also want to present their own future view. A different perspective on futurism can be found in Isaac Asimov's more sophisticated *Futuredays* (Henry Holt, 1986), which is a presentation for older readers of a series of cards designed in 1899 to depict what might be possible in the year 2000. These are accompanied by Asimov's comments about the sources and accuracy of that artist's vision.   M.A.C.

94. Phillips, Mildred. *The Sign In Mendel's Window*. Illustrated by Margot Zemach. Macmillan, 1985. ISBN 0-02-774600-3, $12.95. Ages 5-8.

The story line and Zemach's illustrations are clearly reminiscent of the tales of European origins where the clever woman solves the predicament and saves the skin of the fumbling, bumbling man. Molly and Mendal rent part of their home to a stranger named Tinker. One day, Tinker hears Mendel count his money and decides to accuse Mendel of stealing the money from him since he knows the exact amount of money that is in the drawer. The soldiers are ready to arrest Mendel when Molly saves her husband with a clever scheme for uncovering Tinker as the culprit. This is a humorous story told with the wit and panache of a seasoned storyteller. Margot Zemach's watercolors capture the Old World setting and the vigor of this charming tale.

The Sign In Mendel's Window is a good read-aloud book for third and fourth graders who might be challenged to speculate about the way in which Molly will save her husband from going to jail. This story would be especially good for a study of folk tale heroes and motifs from other countries, examining the trickster, simpleton, and the problem solver. Since this tale is not associated with a particular country, where do the children think it might have originated, given the characteristics of the story and the content of the pictures?   B.C.

ALA Notable Book

Literature
Primary
Intermediate

95. Prusski, Jeffrey. *Bring Back the Deer*. Illustrated by Neil Waldman. Harcourt Brace Jovanovich, 1988. ISBN 0-15-200418-1, $13.95. Ages 4-8.

This first picture story book by both author Prusski and illustrator Waldman leaves one hoping that it will be the first of many collaborations. The book is beautiful in page design and layout, as well as in text and illustration. The story is of a Native American boy undergoing rites of passage. His father has gone hunting and has not returned, leaving the family with very little food. The boy offers to go into the forest and "bring back the deer." He is instructed to "become the deer" by his grandfather, for then the deer will "give himself to you. It is a sacred thing." After various misadventures, the boy does become a deer while chasing a buck and a wolf. These, it turns out, are his father and grandfather. This is a mystical story and reflects aspects of various Native American cultures without being taken from their folk lore. The air of mystery is just as evident in the black and pastel-colored pictures. Animals are incorporated into the natural backgrounds in the manner of Peter Parnall, and Native American symbols appear throughout as well.

It might be an interesting project for older children to research the aspects of the story representing Native American culture to determine their origins. Features to investigate include the clothing of the boy and his family, the skin lodge, the face paint of the boy when he goes out to hunt, the idea of "becoming" the deer or unity with nature, the customs of the wolf and their relationship to those of the boy's people, and the symbols found throughout the illustrations. This could be done in small

Native American Studies
Primary
Intermediate
Middle School

groups with each group focusing upon one aspect of the story and reporting back to the class.   M.A.C.

96.   Pryor, Bonnie. *The House on Maple Street*. Illustrated by Beth Peck. Morrow, 1987. ISBN 0-688-06381-0, $12.88. Ages 5-8.

The House of Maple Street is a richly-painted picture book that treats readers to a trip into the past. In a simple story line that flows with the illustrations, Bonnie Pryor tells the history of a particular area of land, now known as Maple Street, for the past three hundred years. From forests and roaming animals to the Native Americans who followed the buffalo and the immigrants who came westward, from young farmland to current city neighborhood, Beth Peck has beautifully portrayed the past with soft paintings which help readers visualize the progression of the land use. Within the history is the story of an arrowhead lost by a young boy and found years later by a young girl, who then loses the arrowhead and a china cup. These are found at the end of the story by the current residents of the house on Maple Street, who wonder about the people who lost the items. An intriguing and plausible story, *The House on Maple Street* is an appealing and archaeologically sound glimpse into the past.

Local History,
Language Arts
Primary
Intermediate

This book offers an wealth of ideas that could be exciting for building into the curriculum in an intermediate or middle students. Divide students into groups and ask each group to research one facet of the history of the area where their school is located—e.g., animal life, architecture, original inhabitants. Library materials are only one resource. Other materials could be from a state or local historical society, a local university's archeology and sociology departments, architectural firm, and interviews with people who have lived in the neighborhood for many years. After students have compiled their data, they could report their information in the form of a school newsletter for other classes, as well as for parents and the community.   L.S.

97.   Reading is Fundamental. *Once Upon A Time...* Illustrated by various artists. Putnam, 1986. ISBN 0-399-21369-4, $14.95. All ages.

This carefully edited and appealing volume seems more a keepsake than the treasured resource it really is. Twenty-eight of the ablest writers and illustrators of young people's books have contributed their talents to this resounding affirmation of the joys of children's literature. Short stories, remembrances, and excerpts from books by Virginia Hamilton, Jean Fritz, Natalie Babbitt, Katherine Paterson, and other writers; illustrations by Dr. Seuss, Maurice Sendak, Leo and Diane Dillon, Tasha Tudor, and others; and poems by Shel Silverstein, Myra Cohn Livingston, Jack Prelutsky, and others—these and more comprise this collection that honors the creators of children's books. At the same time, it serves children through supporting RIF, the nation's largest reading motivation program outside of the classroom.

Reading from *Once Upon a Time...* should whet the appetite of children to find the complete story or other selections from the entire anthology of poems. For example, hearing the selection from *Eyes of Darkness* by Jamake Highwater (Lothrop, Lee & Shepard, 1985) read aloud is an excellent introduction to his remarkable book for older readers. Learning about the childhoods of Natalie Babbitt, Ashley Bryan, or Jean Fritz can be an incentive to read their books and make that important connection between the writer and the work. Studying closely the fine artwork of Steven Kellogg, James Marshall, and the Dillons could lead children to other illustrations by these remarkable artists. Let *Once Upon a Time...* serve to guide children to further pleasures by these gifted creators of books for children.   H.M.

Related Source

Author/Illustrator Studies
Primary
Intermediate

98.   Rogasky, Barbara. *The Water of Life: A Tale from the Brothers Grimm*. Illustrated by Trina Schart Hyman. Holiday House, 1986. ISBN 0-8234-0552-4, $14.95. Ages 5-8.

When an old king becomes very ill, one by one his three sons search for the "Water of Life" which will cure him. Only the third son speaks kindly to the little man who helps him find the precious water and with it, a beautiful princess. But the prince must overcome the treachery of his older brothers before he can save his father and claim his bride. Rogasky and Hyman, former collaborators on *Rapunzel* (Holiday House, 1982) have created a magical world that brings this fairy tale to life. Here we see cool forests, rich tapestries, and sparkling stained glass, all in luxurious full-color detail. What a beautiful version with which to introduce children to this lovely story!

Fairy tales need to be a part of every child's life. Have a Grimm's fairy tale festival in your class or media center. Collect as many versions of the tales as you can, both collections and individual titles. Besides Hyman, notable illustrators to look for are Michael Hague (*Beauty and the Beast* [Holt, 1983]), Paul Galdone (*Rumplestiltskin* [Clarion, 1985]), and Susan Jeffers (*Hansel and Gretel* [Dial, 1980]). Introduce the Brother Grimm with *Once Upon A Time: A Story of the Brothers Grimm* by Robert Quackenbush (Prentice-Hall, 1985). Have children compare and contrast different versions of the same story, read fairy tales to younger children, and learn the pleasures of storytelling. Even the oldest and most familiar stories will be fascinating and enriching to your children.   A.S.

Related Source

Literature,
Storytelling
Primary
Intermediate
Middle School

Related Sources

99.   Romanova, Natalia. *Once There Was A Tree*. Illustrated by Gennady Spirin. Dial, 1985 (1st Am. ed.). ISBN 0-8037-0235-3, $10.95. Ages 5-up.

Even a quick glance at *Once There Was A Tree* makes it immediately clear that a great deal of care and love of fine books went into writing, illustrating, and designing Natalia Romanova's evocative story. Originally published in Russia, it tells of a woodsman who cuts down a broken tree leaving a stump for a beetle to lay its eggs, for a colony of ants to bore into, for a frog to find shelter within, for an earwig to make its home, and, finally, for a hiker to rest his feet. Gennady Spirin's dark detailed drawings invite the reader to look deep into each picture for the beauty within. The story effectively assures young children that nature belongs to all living beings, and that each of us is responsible for living cooperatively with our natural world. This book is a small treasure that delights the eye, offers inspiration, and reminds us that bookmaking can be an art.

*Science
Primary
Intermediate*

Old stumps or rotting logs found in words or vacant lots represent a microclimate to the plants and animals that are sustained by the protective decaying material. With guidance young children can systematically explore the self-enclosed "world" of living things that are found inside of, beneath, on top of, and close around stumps, fallen logs, piles of rocks, etc. Careful observation, census taking and record keeping, inferential and relational thinking are all basic science-thinking skills that can be taught in this activity.   H.M.

100.   Rylant, Cynthia. *Birthday Presents*. Illustrated by Sucie Stevenson. Orchard Books, 1987. ISBN 0-531-05705-4, $12.95. Ages 4-6.

This happy book depicts the birthdays of a young child, from her real birthday to age six. Her parents bring back memories of each year's celebration and her age-appropriate responses—sucking icing off her fingers, wanting only presents, etc.—and always say "we told you we loved you." Before age six the girl returns the thoughtfulness, helping to bake her parents' cakes and telling them she loves them. The tenderness, security, and love of this family spill over onto each colorful page, making this book a joyous experience of family sharing.

*Social Studies,
Language Arts
Primary*

This book could prompt children to remember their own birthday celebrations and traditions. It could also start them thinking about themselves at each stage of growing older. Have children ask their parents to share memories and photographs of them at each age—When I was one year old..., When I was two years old... etc. Each child can create an individual illustrated booklet of memories to be presented to his or her parent(s). It should become a treasured family favorite.   A.S.

101.   Rylant, Cynthia. *Night in the Country*. Illustrated by Mary Szilagyi. Bradbury, 1986. ISBN 0-02-777210-1, $12.95. Ages 3-6.

Cynthia Rylant and Mary Szilagyi have created a nighttime for younger children that describes in words and images the sights and sounds that are alive during a night in the country. Children are asked to "listen" to familiar sounds (the "reek reek reek" of the frogs and the plop of an apple dropping to the ground) and to "see" what animals are doing while children sleep (rabbits eating the apples that fell and a cow nuzzling her calf). When day comes, the animals will "spend a day in the country listening to you." This gentle book appeals to all the senses through the appropriately simple text and the vibrant drawings that evoke both the rural setting and the night environment.

Nighttime sounds can be frightening to young children, but this book invites readers to enjoy and be reassured by the country atmosphere. Teachers and children can talk about things that make people scared and the ways in which they can be explained. Mercer Mayer's *There's a Nightmare My Closet* (Dial, 1968) and *You're a Scaredy-Cat* (Scholastic, 1980) are appropriate companion books. Children might want to tape record sounds in their yard or home for a short period and then write words that imitate each sound.   B.C.

*Language Arts
Primary*

Related Sources

102.   Rylant, Cynthia. *The Relatives Came*. Illustrated by Stephen Gammell. Bradbury, 1985. ISBN 0-02-777220-9, $12.95. Ages 5-9.

The most joyous book of 1985 certainly must be *The Relatives Came*, an exuberant blend of Cynthia Rylant's loving homespun recollections and Stephen Gammell's illustrations that dance and leap and career across each page. They came in a station wagon ("that smelled like a real car") filled with an ice chest of soda pop and bologna sandwiches to spend time eating, playing, working, singing, and sleeping as one huge and very happy family. Rylant's narrative has never been cleaner and more lyrical; she distills the essence of this extended family. Gammell's colored pencil drawings capture all the feelings of the people and the places in a book certain to be treasured by all who make this part of their extended family.

*Caldecott Honor Book
ALA Notable Book*

Visits by relatives or old family friends are celebrated differently by every family. Younger children usually find such occasions special and eventful, remembered fondly as strong images that can be drawn, dramatized, written about, or shared as a source of storytelling. *The Relatives Came* is likely to be a stimulus for recalling those special days or weekends. Let the power of the words and the illustrations work their magic on your class by reading it aloud and letting the children linger over the illustrations. They may be motivated to write their account of a similar visit by their favorite relatives.   H.M.

*Art, Language Arts
Primary
Intermediate*

103.   Snyder, Dianne. *The Boy of the Three-Year Nap*. Illustrated by Allen Say. Houghton Mifflin, 1988. ISBN 0-395-44090-4, $14.95. Ages 5-8.

Snyder heard many tales like *The Boy of the Three-Year Nap* during her childhood in Japan. Her collaboration with Japanese native Say has resulted in this 1989 Caldecott Honor Medal winner. It is a trickster tale about Taro, a boy who loved to sleep so much that the villagers called him "The Boy of the Three-Year Nap." Taro is not mentally lazy, however, for he comes up with a plan to marry a rich merchant's daughter. What he doesn't count on is the fact that his mother is a little cleverer, turning the plan on him so that he not only

*Caldecott Honor Book
ALA Notable Book*

gets a wife, but also a job! The illustrations are done in brush line and watercolor. Say draws simple, expressive characters housed in traditional Japanese dwellings and clothed in authentic dress. The straight, pure lines in this architecture contrast with the soft washes of his natural backgrounds. Subtle humor is a unifying thread in both text and illustration, as shown by the comparison of the mother to a cormorant and the emotive facial expressions.

Related Sources

Say's background as apprentice to a Japanese cartoonist is intriguing. Children in America may tend to think of the cartoon as an American invention limited to Sunday newspapers or Marvel Comics. Bailey's *Great Cartoons of the World* (Crown, 1971) would be a good resource to show children that cartooning cuts across all cultures. For those children interested in trying the art themselves, Tallarico's *Guide to Drawing Cartoons: A Step by Step Fun Guide* (Putnam, 1975) and Zaidenberg's *How to Draw Cartoons: A Book for Beginners* (Vanguard, n/a) are but two of many "how-to" books listed under "Caricatures and Cartoons" in *Books in Print*. This listing is worth a look for those children with special interests, for there are cartoon books on subjects ranging from dancing cats to theatrical caricatures, including such all-time favorites as "Snoopy" and "Garfield." A cartoonist from a local newspaper could be invited to speak to the class about his/her profession as well.   M.A.C.

Art, Language Arts Primary Intermediate Middle School

104.   Steig, William. *Spinky Sulks*. Illustrated by the author. Farrar, Straus & Giroux, 1988. ISBN 0-374-38321-9, $13.95. Ages 3-up.

ALA Notable Book

Poor Spinky! When insensitive family members hurt his feelings he is forced to throw himself into a deep and lasting sulk. Though they try to make amends, Spinky has no use for kisses and apologies that come too late. His brother, Hitch, even gets "down on his ugly knees" and begs forgiveness for "anything he had ever done that Spinky took exception to." Their injustices are merely hinted at, but Spinky's suffering is obvious as he lies "like a pile of laundry" in the backyard hammock. With his tongue squarely in his cheek, Steig shows the driving force of pride that keeps a good sulk going. His hilarious text is bettered only by Spinky's expressions in distinctive cartoon illustrations. A classic in the making, *Spinky Sulks* is not only a rollicking but also a poignant slice of family life.

Spinky's dilemma is a familiar one in many families: how can he forgive his family and keep his integrity at the same time? His solution is to throw a grand breakfast party, disguising himself as a clown. In classrooms, as well as families, feelings are often hurt and resentment can linger for some time. In the spirit of Spinky's genius, the class could throw itself a party for everyone to make amends for past indiscretions and start anew. Dressing up as a clown and throwing a brunch bash is great fun. It is also a gentle reminder to everyone that emotions bruise easily, and the feelings of others are important and need to be treated with great care.   K.L.M.

Social Studies Primary

105. Steptoe, John. *Mufaro's Beautiful Daughters*. Illustrated by the author. Lothrop, Lee & Shepard, 1987. ISBN 0-688-04046-2, $12.88. Ages 5-8.

Steptoe demonstrates that he is as gifted a storyteller as he is an artist in this literary tale based upon a Zimbabwean folk tale. Manyara and Nyasha are beautiful sisters with very different personalities. When the king sends for beautiful young women to appear before him so that he can select a bride, Manyara schemes to get there before her kind sister. In doing so she demonstrates her selfishness and thus ends up as a servant to her sister, who is selected as the new queen. The language evokes the culture and the strong emotions of the folk characters. Just as important are the exquisite illustrations which are rooted in the details of the place and time where the story is set. This is a straightforward tale employing several motifs found in Cinderella tales in other cultures for both younger and older audiences everywhere to be enchanted by and to enjoy.

The illustrations are so stimulating that children should not be blamed for wanting to create their own tropical jungle filled with exotic birds, plants, and distant cities. Children—individually or in pairs—can select from a variety of media (e.g., tissue paper, yarns, markers, feathers, spray paints, melted crayons, etc.) with which to work. Tree branches can be tied together to make mobiles from which the flowers and birds can be attached for display in the hallway, cafeteria, or in the school entry area.   H.M.

Caldecott Honor Book
ALA Notable Book

Related Sources

Art, Language Arts
Primary
Intermediate

106. Stevenson, James. *There's Nothing To Do*. Illustrated by the author. Greenwillow, 1986. ISBN 0-688-04699-1, $11.88. Ages 5-8.

When Louis and Mary Ann complain of boredom to their grandfather, they are treated to one of his wild stories about his own experience being bored as a child. For those readers who have chuckled over Grandpa's stories in *That Terrible Halloween Night* (1980), *We Can't Sleep* (1982), or *What's Under My Bed?* (1983), all published by Greenwillow, this new yarn will be as welcome as an old friend. For those who are not familiar with Grandpa, this is a good introduction. Stevenson's drawings are animated and comic, and they are a perfect complement to Grandpa's zany stories. Readers of *There's Nothing To Do* are likely to get a giggle over baby Wainey, who is completely bald except for one curly hair and the expected moustache *à la* Grandpa-as-a-boy and the birds who "were so bored they keep dozing off and falling out of the trees."

After sharing this and Stevenson's other Grandpa books, students may want to create their own Grandpa story. This can be done as a group effort or individually. First, the students will want to think of a situation for Louis and Mary Ann to complain about to Grandpa (Stevenson's occasion for setting Grandpa off on yarn spinning). Next, students will want to brainstorm all the crazy things that could have happened to young Grandpa in that situation. Finally, a polished story

Related Sources

Language Arts
Primary
Intermediate

could be produced through careful selection and editing of events. This could be sent to James Stevenson, c/o Greenwillow Books, 105 Madison Avenue, New York, NY 10016.   M.A.C.

107.   Stolz, Mary. *Zekmet, the Stone Carver*. Illustrated by Deborah Nourse Lattimore. Harcourt Brace Jovanovich, 1988. ISBN 0-15-299961-2, $13.95. Ages 7-10.

Stolz and Lattimore have combined their talents to create one of the best fictitious stories surrounding the creating of the sphinx. Stolz tells the story of Zekmet, who was a peasant, yet a great sculptor who designed the mighty sphinx. The strength of the story lies in Stolz's superb portrayal of the people and their customs. She has given her characters distinct personalities: the Pharaoh is arrogant and pompous; his vizier, Ho-tep, is respectful in the Pharaoh's presence, yet speaks unfavorably of him every time he can get away with it; and Zekmet, who takes full advantage of his situation with Ho-tep to request a handsome payment for his design. Lattimore's background as an art historian is evident in this well-researched picture book. Lattimore has chosen to illustrate her characters as they were represented in ancient drawings, using white, grey, and black colored pencil. The colors and media reflect the barren desert climate and the stone and marble representative of the Pharaoh's palace.

Language Arts
Primary
Intermediate

Related Sources

Lattimore cleverly uses the borders in the book to retell the story in hieroglyphs, while her end pages serve as a dictionary of terms. "Reading" the story in the borders using the end pages as reference is challenging, even for older children. Younger children may enjoy hearing and seeing a facsimile copy of *Mother Goose in Hieroglyphics* published in 1855 (reprinted in Haviland and Coughlan's *Yankee Doodle's Literary Sampler* [Crowell, 1974]).   K.B.B.

108.   Szilagyi, Mary. *Thunderstorm*. Illustrated by the author. Bradbury, 1985. ISBN 0-02-788580-1, $11.95. Ages 4-7.

In language that is appropriately and effectively spare and accompanied by illustrations that shimmer and shift to match the moods of the story, Mary Szilagyi captures the sights and mood of a sudden summer thunderstorm. A young child's fears are comforted by a caring mother until the rain stops and the storm passes. Between the clear skies at the beginning and end of the story, readers see darkening clouds, the flash and crackle of lightning, and torrents of rain. The full-color drawings evoke authentic images that are strong and lasting. Young children should easily recognize feelings they have experienced and warm to the calm reassurance given by the girl's mother.

Science
Primary

Related Sources

If fear often results from ignorance, then young children should benefit from learning what causes lightning and thunder. Franklyn Branley's *Flash, Crash, Rumble and Roll* (Crowell, 1985) is excellent for this age group. In addition to using *Children's Catalog* to identify other appropriate informational books for this younger audience, teachers and parents can extend children's understanding of this natural occurrence through fiction, poetry, and folk tales.   H.M.

109.   Tejima. *Owl Lake*. Illustrated by the author. Philomel, 1987. ISBN 0-399-21426-7, $13.95. Ages 2-6.

Owl Lake begins a series of large-format books about woodland animals with woodcuts by the talented and prize-winning Japanese artist, Tejima. In this dramatic and haunting story, the grace and majesty of an eagle owl in its natural habitat is exquisitely portrayed in both appropriately simple prose and Tejima's striking illustrations. Evening comes and signals the owl family that it is time to start their search for food. The luminous images give the feeling of moonlit darkness while father owl soars over the dark water searching for food. As dawn's sun rises, the owl family settles down for sleep. *Owl Lake* won the Japan Prize for Outstanding Picture Books in 1983.

    This is an opportunity to introduce young people to the habits and behaviors of nocturnal animals. Other books that could be used as well are Margarete Goug-Sigman's *Animals of the Night* (Silver Burdett, 1983), Carol Lesser's *The Goodnight Circle* (Harcourt Brace Jovanovich, 1984), and Jane Yolen's *Owl Moon* (Philomel, 1987). A visit to a zoo would also be useful to see different animals that are active at night or an evening walk with a flashlight to observe local nocturnal animals. Both of these activities could be the basis for writing about what each student experienced.   C.A.Y.

ALA Notable Book

Related Sources

*Science
Primary
Intermediate*

110.   Thomas, Marlo, et al. *Free To Be...A Family*. Illustrated by various artists. Bantam, 1987. ISBN 0-553-05235-7, $19.95. All ages.

This was an ambitious and risky project. Like its successful and widely read predecessor, *Free to Be...You and Me* (McGraw-Hill, 1974), this diverse collection of stories, songs, poems, skits, and essays brings together the efforts of over 70 creative artists to illuminate the many faces of the contemporary American family. Each selection successfully and uniquely sheds light on some aspect of family relationships, economic and social uncertainties, and individual feelings—always from a young person's perspective, which is the key to the success of the book. The images range from comic ("Boy Meets Girl Plus One") and hip (a rap song, "Yourself Belongs to You") to selections that are thoughtful (Lucille Clifton's "We and They") and poignant (Whoopi Goldberg's "Doris Knows Everything"). For hours of individual reflection or for family sharing, this collection prompts consideration of the values and aspirations we all have as members of a family. *Free To Be...A Family* is one of the most evocative and joyous books of 1987.

    This is a rich source of material for reading aloud to groups of young people. The selections are brief and appealing, and each deals with situations or emotions that are universal. Readers of all ages can find at least one selection from this collection that prompts a very strong

Related Source

and highly personal response. The lively and enlightening follow-up group discussions could lead to a writing activity, such as a letter to another family member or a letter to the author of the particular selection. Keeping a one-week diary of responses to family experiences often produces individual insights possible in no other way. Creating that personal response in the same form as the selection (poem, song, skit, etc.) is a challenging alternative for older students.   H.M.

111.   Turner, Ann. *Nettie's Trip South*. Illustrated by Ronald Himler. Macmillan, 1987. ISBN 0-02-789240-9, $11.95. Ages 6-10.

Detailed, penciled illustrations and blank verse are effectively used to document the impact of a ten-year-old's visit to the antebellum South. Few words are used to powerfully remind the reader that the Constitution classified Black Americans as three-fifths of a person, that slaves were not allowed last names, that personal humiliation was characteristic of slave auctions, that children were separated from their families, and that reading was forbidden to those enslaved. Based upon the actual diary of the author's great-grandmother, its message will be felt strongly as children read this emotion-filled book.

What would your feelings be if you observed the practices of slavery? Would you be frightened or have bad dreams like Nettie? Children should be encouraged to think about significant historical periods and to articulate not only their emotional responses, but also their evaluation of American's times of shame as well as of pride. *Nettie's Trip South* work helps students to do this because it highlights the evil that corrupted this nation's ideals during slavery times.   J.F.A.

112.   Tusa, Tricia. *Maebelle's Suitcase*. Illustrated by the author. Macmillan, 1987. ISBN 0-02-789250-6, $12.95. Ages 5-8.

Bumpy-lumpy, soft-as-a-cushion Maebelle is clearly the focus of this delightfully illustrated tale of friendship. Maebelle, 108 years old, is a hatmaker who lives in a fascinating treehouse to be near her friends the birds. Warm-hearted, imaginative, and independent, she is the best model of a (so-called) senior citizen. When her friend, Binkle, a whimsical, one-of-a-kind bird has a problem flying south, Maebelle creates a one-of-a-kind hat. Though it fails to win the annual hat contest, it does solve Binkle's problem and brings Maebelle an unexpected reward for her unselfishness. Glowing pencil and watercolor illustrations are a joy for silly details (e.g., the egg from which Binkle was hatched; captivating perspectives of Maebelle from above, below, sideways, leaning out of windows, or flopped in an over-stuffed, homemade hammock). Unlike many picture book characters, Maebelle's constantly changing expressions portray her as a very real person—someone you wish lived next door.

Maebelle's Suitcase is a richly imaginative book to have fun with, so let go! Start with a classroom hat contest or, less competitively, a hat parade. Maebelle's own creations will provide inspiration for the silliest hats possible. From this event may come a display of student's snapshots, written descriptions, or a videotape. Children may also design the most unimaginable bird ever seen—as a class project or individually, in papier-mache or as drawings. Maebelle's inventive dwelling begs for more house designs as well. For this activity, see *Need a House? Call Ms. Mouse* by George Mendoza (Grosset & Dunlop, 1981).　B.B.

113. Van Allsburg, Chris. *The Polar Express*. Illustrated by the author. Houghton Mifflin, 1985. ISBN 0-395-38949-6, $15.95. All ages.

No book has so captured the hearts of so many children, parents, and critics with equal force than the 1986 Caldecott Award winner, in which a young boy boards the "Polar Express" bound for Santa's village at the North Pole. There he meets Santa Claus and is granted a gift wish: a bell from a reindeer's harness. When he returns, he wakes Christmas morning to find a silver bell under the tree. While the story is appropriately childlike and evocative of the mystery surrounding Christmas, the masterful color illustrations draw the reader directly to the heart of the story to travel over land, through forests, and high above the crowd gathered in the streets at the North Pole. Van Allsburg moves the eye and the imagination of older and younger readers alike. This is a book for a family to treasure from one generation to another.　H.M.

114. Van Allsburg, Chris. *The Stranger*. Illustrated by the author. Houghton Mifflin, 1986. ISBN 0-395-42331-7, $15.95. All ages.

A thump on the fender; a foot jams the brakes. "Oh no!" senses Farmer Bailey, "I've hit a deer." Fawn-colored end plates entice the reader to journey on a mystical pilgrimage into autumn with a silent stranger who seems ill-equipped for even ordinary society. Through the magic of Chris Van Allsburg's stunning autumn-hued oil pastels, the reader is swept along country roads as summer slips between fall's waiting fingers. But here is where the magic begins. Who is this quiet man who seems so much a part of nature that the seasons hesitate and wait to take their cue from him? This untraditional account of the change in seasons grows more lovely and reflective with each delightful reading. Van Allsburg's alluring illustrations burn with a depth and mystery all their own, and must be seen to be appreciated.

Van Allsburg's metaphor of the stranger as fall has familiar parallels in other volumes of children's literature. A most sensitive example is Chapter 8 in Felix Salten's *Bambi* (Simon & Schuster, 1970), a timeless conversation between two leaves who contemplate death as winter grasps at their failing hold on life. A more visual example is *Grandfather Twilight* by Barbara Berger (Philomel, 1984), in which the moon is depicted as a pearl which grows as

Grandfather walks twilight into the world. After discussing examples of metaphors in literature, spring and summer could be characterized and accompanying stories written by children. Illustrations reflecting the same mood as the season could complement these stories, remembering Van Allsburg's stunning use of color to portray the season and medium to create a sense of texture, shape, and design. Through this exercise a total image could be created by young artist–illustrators.   G.G.

115. Wiesner, David. *Free Fall*. Illustrated by the author. Lothrop, Lee & Shepard, 1988. ISBN 0-688-05583-4, $13.95. Ages 6-10.

Caldecott Honor Book
ALA Notable Book

This 1989 Caldecott Honor Medal book was certainly worthy of the award. It is a wordless picture book and a visual feast that takes its viewer on a fantastic trip into the land of dreams and the subconscious. Using watercolors in slightly softer than lifelike tones, Wiesner creates a complex series of paintings both beginning and ending with the young boy in bed. Each page flows visually into the next, showing how the dream segments are all interrelated. Additional details illustrate how things from our reality intricately enter into our subconscious. For example, the boy falls asleep with his atlas and his box of chess pieces open. The first dream segment results when a page from the atlas drifts into a checkered landscape, which turns into a chessboard peopled with real medieval characters found in the game of chess. Three of these have strange plain faces and accompany the boy on the rest of his journey. It turns out in later pages that they were two pawns and a shaker of salt, an interesting image, as the "salt" is a steadfast friend throughout the adventure. There is such depth of detail in Wiesner's friendly twisting of reality that children are likely to always find something new.

Language Arts
Primary
Intermediate
Middle School

It might be interesting to put *Free Fall* in a center for intermediate children with instructions to write a narrative to accompany the illustrations. The children could be told that their story doesn't necessarily have to follow the boy, but could trace one of the other characters or follow objects that show up throughout the book, such as the maps from the atlas. The children could be instructed to keep their story a secret while they are writing it. When everyone has had a chance to finish, the stories could be shared aloud. It is quite likely that a surprising variety will result and that there will be cries of "Where was that? I didn't see that when I read the book!" The book together with the students' stories could be displayed in the library for others to explore.   M.A.C.

116. Williams, Vera B. *Music, Music for Everyone*. Illustrated by the author. Greenwillow, 1984. ISBN 0-688-02604-4, $11.88. Ages 4-8.

ALA Notable Book

Sequel to
A Chair for My Mother

Vera Williams continues the story of Rosa that she began in Caldecott Honor Book *A Chair for My Mother* (Greenwillow, 1982) and *Something Special for Me* (Greenwillow, 1983). This time Rosa's grandmother is ill and must stay upstairs in bed, so the beautiful, rose-covered chair sits empty and the money jar in which the family saved for the chair and the accordion of *Something Special for Me* is also forlornly unfilled. Rosa and her friends make music to cheer Grandma and hit upon the idea of forming a band. Rosa especially likes this idea for it will give her the means to start filling the jar once more. The pictures in this book are very consistent with the other two—the three books make a nice trilogy.

Vera Williams's illustrations demonstrate her award-winning use of watercolor. Careful examination of the paintings reveals bleeds and runs that are integral to the design. This is not easy to do, but children should certainly enjoy trying it with the guidance of an expert art teacher. Children might also enjoy writing about what they would do with a jar of money they had saved through months of sacrifice. A discussion of times we need to sacrifice and people we sacrifice for might also be thought provoking.   M.A.C.

Art, Language Arts
Primary
Intermediate

117.   Williams, Vera B. *Stringbean's Trip to the Shining Sea*. Illustrated by the author and Jennifer Williams. Greenwillow, 1988. ISBN 0-688-07162-7, $11.88. All ages.

ALA Notable Book

This inventive and fascinating book is made entirely of postcards and "photos" created by Vera Williams and Jennifer Williams to illustrate Stringbean's trip from Jeloway, Kansas, to the Pacific Ocean. The letters on the backs of the postcards, written by Stringbean and his brother, chronicle their trip and tell two side stories: of finding and returning a clown's big shoe, and of the arrival of Stringbean's dog, Potato, who had followed them on their trip. The postcards show the sights and give some history. The letters do the same and focus upon events of typical interest to a boy Stringbean's age (though they do not reflect the invented spellings typical of a child that age). Vera and Jennifer Williams even illustrated the funny truck with the homemade house on the back, which was Stringbean's and Fred's camper, and the postage stamps on the postcards.

The best thing about *Stringbean's Trip to the Shining Sea* is its potential for use as a model for similar projects. The old "How I Spent My Summer Vacation" theme takes on a new twist here. Students can create a series of postcards to tell about a trip they took or about what they did all summer. Even swimming, reading, biking, and being lazy can be illustrated on a postcard. Making these in postcard style and creating stamps to "mail" them with makes the project that much more interesting. Another activity would be to create postcards to chronicle an imagined trip to a place they have always wanted to visit.   M.A.C.

Art, Language Arts
Primary
Intermediate
Middle School

118.   Winter, Jeannette. *Follow the Drinking Gourd*. Illustrated by the author. Knopf, 1988. ISBN 0-394-99694-1, $13.99. Ages 5-9.

In richly evocative images, Jeannette Winter tells a tale that might be true about Molly and her man James, slaves whose family was going to be separated by the auction of James. They heard the quail call, though, and remembered the song old Peg Leg Joe had taught them: "When the sun comes back, and the first quail calls,/ Follow the drinking gourd./ For the old man is a-waiting to carry you to freedom/ If you follow the drinking gourd." Thus begins the harrowing trip north for Molly, James, little Isaiah, old Hattie, and her grandson George as they follow the map of the Underground Railroad hidden in the lyrics of the song. Winter is successful with pictures and text: both are poetically simple. Short sentences mirror the style of the song and primitive paintings perfectly represent the harsh reality of the fugitives. Like the song, this is a book that has lasting value.

Black Studies, Music
Primary
Intermediate

Related Sources

Be sure to let the children hear the song, especially a version by The Weavers or Leadbelly. Then, they will surely want to learn to sing "Follow the Drinking Gourd" themselves. They are likely also to want to know more about the Underground Railroad after hearing this story. Levine's *If You Traveled on the Underground Railroad* (Scholastic, 1988) and McGovern's *Runaway Slave: The Story of Harriet Tubman* (Four Winds, 1968) can answer their questions. Another outstanding book for this age group is Turner's *Nettie's Trip South* (Macmillan, 1987), which chronicles the reactions of a northern girl when she encounters slavery for the first time.   M.A.C.

119.   Wood, Audrey. *Elbert's Bad Word*. Illustrated by Audrey and Don Wood. Harcourt Brace Jovanovich, 1988. ISBN 0-15-225320-3, $13.95. Ages 4-8.

In the Woods' newest adventure, young Elbert is attending an elegant garden party when he catches a bad word in the form of an ugly, bristly-haired creature. When a series of calamities results in Sir Hilary's croquet mallet landing on Elbert's great toe, the bad word springs from his mouth, more huge and ugly than ever. The word's effect is shocking, and Elbert realizes that he is in need of a cure. The wizard gardener comes to his rescue by baking a cake filled with powerful words. They turn out to be so effective that the bad word shrinks to the size of a spider and scurries down a black hole in the ground. Many children have the unfortunate experience of discovering the effect a bad word can have. Never has such sound advice been more delightfully packaged! Collaborating on the zany illustrations, the Woods' have given the book a unique flavor that sets it apart from their earlier works. Also, the power of the bad word is emphasized as it grows to an enormous size on the book's pages.

Language Arts
Primary
Intermediate

Everyone needs a list of powerful words to express frustrated emotions. Stack up dictionaries and thesauruses and help the whole class bake a word cake. Students can spell words they have chosen with raisins or nuts, write them in flour before it is added to the batter, or simply write them on slips of paper and sift their magic into the mixture! Once the bakers have had generous helpings of word cake, encourage them to test their new vocabularies during exasperating moments or write a story illustrating the use of their new words during such a moment.   K.L.M.

120. Wood, Audrey. *Heckedy Peg*. Illustrated by Don Wood. Harcourt Brace Jovanovich, 1987. ISBN 0-15-233678-8, $14.95. Ages 4-8.

A mother promises to return from the market with a special present for each of her seven children. While she is gone, a witch snatches the children from their home, transforms them into different foods, and takes them to her hut for her dinner. The clever and determined mother ultimately outwits the hag and saves her children in the nick of time. Don Wood's oils set the tone for the story and are a perfect balance to the tale, depicting not only the movement of the story, but also the detail of the setting and the emotions of the characters. Together, the Woods have created a darkly rollicking story of enchantment, strong emotions, and human triumph to share for generations.

This story is similar to an old childhood game: a group of children choose the mother, the witch, and the children. The "witch" hides and "Mother" leaves the "children" to go to town, first warning them not to let the mean witch in and promising to spank them if they do. The witch, pretending to be a nice neighbor, comes to borrow sugar and, while the children are getting it, she "steals" them one at a time, taking each back to her hiding place. Mother returns and must find the witch's house by following the cries of her children. The witch and Mother then make a deal: if Mother can guess the type of food the children have been turned into, and then the flavors, the children may go. Mother guesses food types—pies, pudding, cakes—and when she's found the correct one, such as puddings, yells out flavors—banana, custard, tapioca, etc. When the child's flavor is called, he/she runs home as fast as possible. If Mother catches the child, she may "spank" him/her. If the child beats the mother, he/she is home "free." Play continues until all children have raced Mother home.   H.M./L.S.

*Language Arts,
Social Studies
Primary*

121. Wood, Audrey. *King Bidgood's in the Bathtub*. Illustrated by Don Wood. Harcourt Brace Jovanovich, 1985. ISBN 0-15-242730-9, $12.95. Ages 4-8.

What do you do with a king who is enjoying his bath so much that he won't get out? First, you send in the knight to try to lure him into battle. When duty doesn't move him, you appeal to his baser desires— his love of food, fishing, and dancing. Lively King Bidgood still enjoys all of those pleasures, but in the tub rather than out of it. King Bidgood is a Renaissance king, as suggested by the details Don Wood put into the clothing and food. Subtle color changes reflect the sun's passage through a day; yet the overriding tone is quite dark, as if viewed from the inside of a castle. To the child, though, the appeal lies in King Bidgood's bath time shenanigans: thankfully, such extravagances are likely to be found only in children's imaginations.

Though the picture book format may not immediately attract upper elementary readers, older students studying the Renaissance can benefit from looking through *King Bidgood's in the Bathtub*. What life was really like in the Renaissance could be explored in Wood's

ALA Notable Book

*Emerging Readers,
Social Studies
Intermediate
Middle School*

illustrations. How did people dress and behave during the Renaissance? What did they eat? What were the roles of men, women, and children? What kinds of work did people do? What inventions that we enjoy today were unheard of then? Sharing Joe Lasker's *Merry Ever After* (Viking, 1976) is an excellent follow-up to look through for another view at that historical period.   M.A.C.

122.   Wood, Audrey. *The Napping House*. Illustrated by Don Wood. Harcourt Brace Jovanovich, 1984. ISBN 0-15-256708-9, $11.95. Ages 4-8.

It is a rainy afternoon in the "napping house where everyone is sleeping." With each page turn, the pile on the cozy bed grows higher as a snoring granny is joined by a dreaming child, a dozing dog, a snoozing cat, a slumbering mouse, and, finally, a wakeful flea who starts a chain reaction of everyone waking up. Don Woods raises the perspective with each addition to the pile on the bed and subtly and gradually changes this palette from rainy grays and blues to sunny greens and yellows. By the time the cast of characters is ebulliently awake, of course, there is no need to nap for the day has become beautiful. The back cover, picturing the Woods in front of their own home, reveals that the napping house is theirs. This perfect union of text and illustration showcases two talented contributors to the field of children's literature.

Predictable tales such as this story with accumulative structure and its repeated phrases will first amuse younger children and then will encourage them to "read it by myself." Success is almost guaranteed because of the predictable language patterns and the lively illustrations. This book would be an excellent source for emergent readers and beginning reading programs. It can also be used as a pattern for making similar big books for shared reading experiences.   M.A.C..

123.   Wright, Jill. *The Old Woman and the Willy Nilly Man*. Illustrated by Glen Rounds. Putnam, 1987. ISBN 0-399-21355-4, $12.95. Ages 5-8.

Well, the Willy Nilly Man is magic, and iffn you hev a problem, mebbe you should walk through the woods to his rickety-rackety shack. Iffn you ain't afeard. The old woman whose shoes wouldn't stop a-dancin' and a-singin' all night did, and she was scaired. Iffn you want to know what the Willy Nilly Man did to help her, and why the old woman mixed up a mess of mighty peculiar blackbury jam, you'll jes have to read the story yourself. It's a mighty amusin' backwoods tale, and the pictures is purty too—looks jes like them two folks.

This is a fine story for readin' aloud, or iffn you've a mind to, for storytellin'. It's also mighty good for play-actin'. Besides the old woman and the Willy Nilly Man, them dancin' shoes need showin' off, as well as them magical movin' objects around the Willy Nilly Man's shack. All these tricks would go well with a dash of Brer Rabbit and Jack Tales, too.   B.B.

Related Source

ALA Notable Book

Emerging Readers, Language Arts Primary

Drama, Storytelling Primary Intermediate

Related Sources

124.   Yolen, Jane. *Owl Moon*. Illustrated by John Schoenherr. Philomel, 1987. ISBN 0-399-21457-7, $13.95. Ages 2-6.

The 1988 Caldecott Medal winner tells of the quiet magic of a winter's night as a young girl and her father search for the mysterious owl. The words and illustrations of *Owl Moon* blend in such an intimate way that the reader is not surprised to find that both artists have personal experiences owling. Yolen shares her quiet sensory impressions with eloquent, poetic prose. Schoenherr indulges in visual remembrances of crisp winter nights using muted watercolors and angular shapes that cradle and enhance the text. His use of white space suggests the vastness of snow covered fields or the comfort of a clearing in the woods. Yolen's words etched on the snowbanks are as natural as a set of animal tracks on the winter's landscape.

Caldecott Award Winner
ALA Notable Book

Expand the age range of this Caldecott winner by using it with intermediate age children to examine and experiment with descriptive language and sensory impressions. First, read the book aloud to the class directing the students to listen for language that describes sensory impressions. Talk about the sensory appeal of phrases such as, "I could feel the cold as if someone's icy hand was palm-down on my back" and "my mouth felt furry, for the scarf over it was wet and warm." Finally, have students consider personal sensory impressions of the night or another similar topic of their choice and encourage them to write them in a short story or descriptive paragraph.   L.B.

Language Arts
Primary
Intermediate
Middle School

125.   Yorinks, Arthur. *Bravo, Minski*. Illustrated by Richard Egielski. Farrar, Straus & Giroux, 1988. ISBN 0-374-30951-5, $13.95. Ages 3-up.

Count on the Caldecott Award-winning team of Yorinks and Egielski to create a vision of the world that is fresh, witty, and slightly off center. *Bravo, Minski* is all of that and more. Minski grows up in an implausible European setting where he has become famous for his inventions: aspirin, eyeglasses, the automobile, rockets, and more. As Leonardo da Vinci said of young Minski, "Has this boy got brains? What a noodle!" But Minski longs for a singing career and turns his genius toward that goal. Yorinks's writing is exuberant and animated in establishing the story's pace and emotional atmosphere. Egielski's richly expressive watercolors seem to have a life of their own as we watch the 18th century costumed characters cavort across the pages in the most playfully original story of the year. Bravo Arthur! Bravo, Richard!

If Minski didn't really invent the aspirin, who did? Or the automobile? Or the telephone? Or the other inventions attributed to Minski? And where? And when? Who were da Vinci and Caruso and Einstein? And where and when did they live? Finding out the historical facts that are oddly mixed together in Minski's story will be a practical adventure in elementary library research that will in no way detract from the pleasure of hearing the story again and again.   H.M.

Social Studies
Primary
Intermediate

126. Yorinks, Arthur. *Hey, Al.* Illustrated by Richard Egielski. Farrar, Straus & Giroux, 1986. ISBN 0-374-33060-3, $13.95. Ages 3-up.

Caldecott Award Winner
ALA Notable Book

"There's no place like home" is the philosophy in the 1987 Caldecott Award-winning *Hey, Al.* Like many others, Al and his faithful dog, Eddie, are not satisfied with their home life. A large colorful bird gives them the opportunity to taste the pleasures of a life of luxury in an island in the sky. Unfortunately, they also begin to turn into birds. How happy they are to return unscathed: the last sentence in the book is "Paradise lost is sometimes Heaven found." The illustrations are worthy of the award for both color and design. Al's dreary life is reflected in the drab browns of his apartment. This is contrasted with the bright plumage of the birds in the middle pages and the changes Al makes to his apartment in the end. The closeness of Al's environment is emphasized by the design, which shows each room as a shadowbox with extensions out the door.

Science, Art
Primary
Intermediate

The birds are particularly intriguing: a mixture of genuine as well as imaginary. Among the more unusual birds depicted is the extinct dodo bird. How many birds in the full two-page spreads in *Hey, Al* can students identify? Use handbooks on birds from the library. Students may create equally fantastic birds of their own with crayons or paint or colored paper. Brian Wildsmith's *Birds* (Watts, 1967), Leo

Related Sources

Lionni's *Inch by Inch* (Astor-Honor, 1960) or his *Tico and the Golden Wings* (Pantheon, 1964), or the innovative *Birds of a Feather* by Willi Baum (Addison-Wesley, 1969) can extend the study of birds or be compared to *Hey, Al.*.   F.M.H.

127. Zelinsky, Paul O. *Rumpelstiltskin.* Illustrated by the author. Dutton, 1986. ISBN 0-525-44265-0, $12.95. Ages 7-up.

Caldecott Honor Book

Zelinsky has included text notes in this rendition of "Rumpelstiltskin," a Caldecott Honor Book for 1987, to explain five variants of this tale since 1806. His version is based primarily on the 1819 text with some changes that he felt were necessary to accompany his drawings. The illustrations are large and bold; minimal text on each page let Zelinsky's illustrations dominate this rendition as they should. His respect for historical authenticity and his ability to reproduce social and cultural details in his art work make this version of *Rumpelstiltskin* a useful guide to dress, architecture, and art of the Middle Ages in Europe.

Literature
Intermediate
Middle School

For older children studying folk tales, use Zelinsky's version and earlier presentations of this story to compare for similarities and differences among them, both in their storyline and in the style of illustrations. Among those which would be useful are Donna Diamond's eerily photographic *Rumpelstiltskin* (Holiday House, 1983), Evaline Ness's English *Tom Tit Tot* (Scribner's, 1965), and Margot Zemach's wonderfully comic Cornish version, *Duffy and the Devil* (Farrar, Straus & Giroux, 1973).   H.M.

Related Sources

128. Zhang Xiu Shi. *Monkey and the White Bone Demon*. Illustrated by Lin Zheng, et al. Viking, 1984. ISBN 0-670-48574-8, $10.95. Ages 6-9.

On his journey to the Western Heaven, the pious monk, Hsuan Tsang, is deceived by the White Bone Demon, who takes him and his felllow travelers prisoner with the intent to feast upon them. They are saved by Monkey who tricks the Demon into revealing her evil deception; Hsuan Tsang thus learns the importance of "distinguishing between right and wrong, between friend and foe." This ancient story is remarkably illustrated in vivid colors, stylistic designs, and characters that are clearly modern but which evoke China. The total effect of both story and art is a distinctive literary encounter for young and old alike.

Children around the world enjoy stories with adventure, with characters that are believable and triumphant, and with beautiful illustrations that complement and extend the story. There are many opportunities for American children to share the delights of children in other countries and cultures through the many books translated into English. Any multicultural program or social studies curriculum could draw heavily upon these materials; for those groups studying China, *Monkey and the White Bone Demon* should be required.   H.M.

Multicultural Studies
Language Arts
Primary
Intermediate

FICTION FOR YOUNGER READERS

FICTION FOR YOUNGER READERS

129.   Aiken, Joan. *Past Eight O'Clock*. Illustrated by Jan Pienkowski. Viking Kestrel, 1987 (1st Am. ed.). ISBN 0-670-81636-1, $14.95. Ages 7-11.

This collection of eight short stories is based upon popular bedtime nursery rhymes, but these are not syrupy, watered-down versions. They have the same drama, sadness, and candor that some traditional fairy tales and rhymes had before fashion dictated that they be rewritten. For example, in "Your Cradle is Green" the babies are left in the care of kind Gerda because their parents were too poor to care for them. In "Past Eight O'Clock," the little girl's mother died. Each story has a happy or amusing ending that will leave the audience relaxed and satisfied. Pienkowski's illustrations are pitch black against white with occasional bursts of primary colors. Though done mostly in black and colored silhouette, the cutouts still show such fine detail as the stiff hair of a horse's tail or a smile in profile. Aiken's skills as a storyteller, however, remain this book's strongest feature.

Here is an opportunity to re-interest children in nursery rhymes. Select some popular nursery rhyme titles and encourage students write down—or tell the teacher to write down—what they think the story behind the rhyme might be about based solely on the title. This could be a good language experience and help them to predict or anticipate during reading. Children could also draw their ideas or make their own paper silhouettes. For older children, a trip to a library would reveal different versions of the same fairy tale or nursery rhyme. Children could discuss why the stories change over the years and decide which versions are more appealing and why.   L.A.B.

*Language Arts, Art,
Literature
Primary
Intermediate*

130.   Aiken, Joan. *The Moon's Revenge*. Illustrated by Alan Lee. Knopf, 1987. ISBN 0-394-99380-2, $12.95. Ages 8-12.

In the flavor of a tale of long ago, when "women wore shawls and men wore hoods and long pointed shoes, and the cure for an earache was to put a hot roasted onion in your ear," Aiken tells the story of Seppy, the seventh son of a seventh son, who wishes to become the best fiddler in the world. He learns that if he throws his shoe at the moon each night for seven nights, the moon must give him his wish. Seppy does become a great fiddler, yet also learns, as in all good fantasy stories, that magic has consequences, some of it not very pleasant. Accompanying Aiken's story are Lee's exceptional realistic paintings which help transport the reader back into time to feel the cold icy glow of the moon, view the vastness of the countryside, and hear the deafening roar of the ocean. Together, they create a delicious faerie quality and atmosphere.

*Literature
Intermediate
Middle School*

Here is an opportunity to discuss the concept of magic having consequences. Elicit responses from the students about other stories they have heard or read in which getting something through magic has consequences. Highly entertaining books that also illustrate this theme are Bill Brittain's *The Wish Giver* (1983) and *Dr. Dredd's Wagon of Wonders* (1987) both published by Harper & Row. Write their responses on the chalkboard. Next, introduce the class to the problem-centered story structure, i.e., setting, character, problem, attempt at solution, and result. Chart *The Moon's Revenge* according to the story structure either on the chalkboard or on large paper. Finally, have small groups analyze in the same manner either *The Wish Giver, Dr. Dredd's Wagon of Wonders*, or one of the magic-centered stories the students identified.   K.B.B.

Related Sources

131.   Alexander, Lloyd. *The El Dorado Adventure*. Dutton, 1987. ISBN 0-525-44313-4, $12.95. Ages 10-14.

Second of a series of adventures featuring Vesper Holly

Vesper Holly burst into life in 1986 in Alexander's *The Illyrian Adventure,* published by Dutton. She proved so indomitable and spirited that this new adventure was inevitable. Set in the mythical Central American republic in El Dorado in the 1870s, Holly must act swiftly and courageously to save the few remaining Chirica Indians from destruction by the evil Dr. Helvitius, who plans to build a canal across their traditional homelands. The tale of how she succeeds will be welcomed by those seeking first rate adventure, clear villainy and heroism, and writing that is witty and clean. Alexander is a master storyteller who demonstrates here the same skill that won him the Newbery Medal and the National Book Award, as well as the acclaim of middle grade lovers of fantasy-adventure stories.

Related Sources

When the Suez Canal (1869) and the Panama Canal (1914) were finally completed, these remarkable achievements changed forever patterns of world travel. There has been a great deal written about how each of these projects was planned and engineered; for example, Markun's *The Panama Canal* (Watts, 1979), Stein's *The Story of the Panama Canal* (Children's Press, 1982) and Garrett's *The Suez Canal* (Greenhaven, 1980). However, less is discussed about the ecological upheaval caused by these intrusions on their environments, nor is much written about the immediate and long range impact on the communities who were removed by these projects. Using the situation of the Chirica Indians as described in *The El Dorado Adventure*, students can analyze the merits and dangers of constructing the canal as hypothesized. For older students, the issue can serve as a debate topic for two opposing teams of debaters.   H.M.

*Social Studies,
Science
Intermediate
Middle School
Junior High School*

132.　Bauer, Caroline Feller. *Windy Day: Stories and Poems*. Illustrated by Dirk Zimmer. Lippincott, 1988. ISBN 0-397-32208-9, $11.89.　　Ages 7-10.

This anthology is a rich literary collage of words and rhythms that evoke a variety of images about wind. Young and intermediate readers should enjoy the humor of "Little Pieces of the West Wind" and "When the Wind Changed," as well as the sensitive Chinese folk tale "The Girl Who Could Think." Interspersed are poems by Merriam, Prelutsky, Milne, Kuskin, and many other writers who explore the diversity of ways to know and to feel about the wind. This is an excellent addition to a collection of books for reading aloud.

Science, Literature, Language Arts Primary Intermediate

Related Sources

Science units on weather can be enlarged to look into how non-scientists have tried to "know" aspects of weather. Using this collection of narrative materials, as well as Bauer's other anthologies on rain and snow (*Rainy Day* [Lippincott, 1986] and *Snowy Day* [Lippincott, 1986]), have children scour other sources of stories, folk tales, and poetry in the library to create a classroom anthology of weather-related narrative materials. Bauer has included a bibliography of nearly two dozen books to begin this search. Put the materials in an oversized format and be sure to illustrate your class book. Each selection should be discussed, evaluated, and selected by consensus of the group as appropriate for the collection.　　H.M.

133.　Bauer, Marion Dane. *On My Honor*. Clarion, 1986. ISBN 0-89919-439-7, $11.95. Ages 9-12.

ALA Notable Book

"On my honor," Joel promised his father, "we won't go anywhere but the park." But when his friend, Tony, challenges him to swim in the treacherous Vermillion River, Joel doesn't want him to think he is scared. Joel dares Tony to swim out to a sandbar, but it's only when Tony disappears that Joel realizes that he can't swim. Back at home, Joel cannot rid himself of the stench of the river. Guilt-ridden and afraid, Joel must find the courage to tell the horrible truth: Tony is dead! With power and sensitivity Bauer tells a gripping, action-filled story. The moral issues are presented realistically through strong and down-to-earth characterizations.

Children are never prepared for the death of a peer. Death often seems removed from their daily lives as they know it, restricted to pets, unknown people in news stories, or older people of different generations. When a peer dies, it can be someone who sat right next to them, someone they played with, and there is a void. *On My Honor* deals realistically and honestly with the beginning stages of the grieving process. Other helpful books are Katherine Paterson's *Bridge to Terabithia* (Crowell, 1977), Candy Dawson Boyd's *Breadsticks and Blessing Places* (Macmillan, 1985), Doris Buchanan Smith's *A Taste of Blackberries* (Crowell, 1973), and Anna W.M. Wolf's *Helping Your Child to Understand Death* (Child Study, 1973). These may deepen children's understanding of death.　　J.P.

Social Studies Intermediate Middle School Junior High School

Related Sources

---

134.   Baylor, Byrd. *I'm in Charge of Celebrations*. Illustrated by Peter Parnall. Scribner's 1986. ISBN 0-684-18579-2, $13.95. Ages 6-9.

Related Sources

As they did in *The Desert is Theirs* (1975), *Desert Voices* (1981), and *Everybody Needs a Rock* (1974) all published by Scribner's, Byrd Baylor and Peter Parnall have successfully collaborated on a book about the desert. In this one, a desert dweller, accused of being lonely, describes how her fascination with the desert and its creatures keeps her occupied. Living as close to nature as she does, she notices things—falling stars, a strange, parrot-shaped green cloud, dust devils, a spring beginning—and she celebrates their happening. For example, August ninth is Rainbow Celebration Day, the day she and a jackrabbit stood on a misty hill watching a triple rainbow. Baylor's text is serene and yet personal: it celebrates and invites the reader to join in. Peter Parnall joins the celebration with his colorful stylized illustrations that capture the setting and the people who live there.

Social Studies
Primary
Intermediate

After sharing this book with a class, the group may decide it is time to respond to Byrd Baylor's invitation to celebrate special, personal days. Children will surely enjoy thinking about something that touched them so deeply that they never want to forget it. This can be anything. The class could even go on a very quiet walk, keeping eyes wide open, to see if anything noticeable is happening that is worth celebrating—as Byrd Baylor says, you have to be choosy. Each child can pick a date, name his or her special day, and decide how it will be celebrated. The special days can then be compiled on a calendar, which could be displayed on a bulletin board surrounded by the children's descriptions of how to celebrate each day. This would be an acceptable alternative to celebrating traditional American holidays in schools, so that children whose culture or religion makes the celebration of those holidays uncomfortable can be included.   M.A.C.

135.   Beatty, Patricia. *Be Ever Hopeful, Hannalee*. Morrow, 1988. ISBN 0-688-07502-9, $11.95. Ages 10-14.

Sequel to
Turn Homeward,
Hannalee

Be Ever Hopeful, Hannalee is a sequel to *Turn Homeward, Hannalee* (Morrow, 1984). Set during the Civil War and its aftermath, both books are based upon the author's family history and her careful research of the times, places, and related events. Hannalee's father died of malaria during the war, her brother lost his arm, and her family is left in upheaval and in even greater poverty than they had known before the war. Though her family had not supported slavery, they had supported the South. They move to Atlanta where they hope to begin a new life and acquire some riches. When her brother is accused of a crime he did not commit, Hannalee must trust a Yankee girl and a Black girl to help her prove his innocence. Not only does she tell an appealing story, but Beatty's fiction realistically and authentically portrays the Regulators, the Ku Klux Klan, the refugee camps, and both whites and Blacks during this period.

The listing of good children's fiction, poetry, nonfiction, and biography dealing with the Civil War is so extensive that teachers could plan an entire unit of instruction using just trade books. Begin by identifying two or three broad objectives, e.g., significant events leading up to the war, the impact of war on families both in cities and on farms, etc. The class can be organized into interest groups based upon topics related to the objectives, e.g., one group can look at farm and city families in the South, another at their counterparts in the north. With the help of a school or public librarian, and sources like *Children's Catalog*, gather together a wide variety of books for the range of reading abilities in the class. Keep several social studies textbooks available for reference as well as an historical atlas. Finally, provide discussion questions for each topic/group that could be the basis for a written project or presentation.   V.H.S.

Black Studies,
U.S. History
Intermediate
Middle School
Junior High School

Related Source

136.   Bellairs, John. *The Spell of the Sorcerer's Skull*. Dial, 1984. ISBN 0-8037-0120-9, $11.95. Ages 10-up.

The Spell of the Sorcerer's Skull is an exciting mystery, suggestive of Halloween, but set in the spring. Johnny Dixon, from previous Bellairs mysteries, is back with his friends Fergie, Father Higgins and Professor Childermass, this time in a wild chase to the islands of Maine. When the Professor disappears, the clues are few: a haunted dollhouse and a menacing jack-o'-lantern (in March?). Demonic forces lead Johnny and his friends on to the final, terrifying rescue. The familiar characters and patterns of Bellairs's mysteries are particularly well-handled here with just the right amount of terror, suspense and red herrings to keep mystery fans turning pages until the very end.

Prediction is always an appropriate thinking/reading skill to emphasize. The episodic structures and cliff-hanger chapter endings to Bellairs' mysteries make them perfect for reading strategy lessons. Teachers might read this story aloud, chapter by chapter, asking the class to predict what will happen next and why. Allowing children to share and discuss the reasons for their predictions should provide opportunities to help children identify and attend to significant information in a story and use that information to build meaning.   B.B.

Language Arts
Intermediate
Middle School

137.   Blume, Judy. *Just as Long as We're Together*. Orchard, 1987. ISBN 0-531-05729-1, $12.95. Ages 10-13.

Just as Long as We're Together is the story of the seventh grade year of Stephanie and her two friends, Rachel and Alison. It is reminiscent of many of Blume's previous books in that it deals with typical adolescent problems and feelings. In this case, adjusting to the separation of her parents is the preoccupation of Stephanie, along with dealing with a three-way friendship and an emerging awareness of the opposite sex. Blume's dialogue is true and her characterizations are clear. The resolution is hopeful—Stephanie's reconciliation with Rachel coincides with moves her parents make toward resolving their difficulties. If anything is lacking here, it is a generous dose of the appealing humor that make Blume's *Fudge* books so captivating to middle grade readers.

Stephanie's response to the news of her parents' separation was to overeat. Throughout the book she has difficulty opening up to anyone— friends, family, guidance counselor—and discussing her problems. *Just as Long as We're Together* could be used effectively as a vehicle for discussing self-destructive responses to problems and possible avenues for help when one is experiencing difficulties. Would the story have been different if Stephanie had not kept everything bottled inside? Did her one heart-to-heart communication with her father influence his decision to move back closer to his family? After discussing such questions, students might enjoy selecting a particular scene from the book and rewriting it to illustrate a different course of events that might have occurred if Stephanie's response to her problems had been more open.   M.A.C.

138.   Boyd, Candy Dawson. *Breadsticks and Blessing Places*. Macmillan, 1985. ISBN 0-02-709290-9, $11.95. Ages 10- 14.

This compassionate story is told with sensitivity as twelve-year-old Toni Douglas struggles with the untimely death of one of her best friends. As those around her resume their normal lives, Toni cannot cope with the reality of Susan's death. When Toni's other best friend, Mattie, confesses to Toni how she finally reconciled herself to her father's death, Toni is able finally to say good-bye to Susan in her own special way. *Breadsticks and Blessing Places* portrays a gripping, realistic picture of how death can affect young people. It is heart- wrenching and down-to-earth, depicting life and death with truthful- ness, tenderness, and sincerity.

This book would be an excellent choice for children who are dealing with the death of a friend or relative. The characters truthfully discuss what must be on every young person's mind when experiencing death and the realization that life goes on. A book for parents or teachers which would be helpful in explaining death and the grieving process are *Telling a Child About Death* by Edgar N. Jackson (Dutton, 1965). Choices for children to read could be *Death Is A Noun* by John Langone (Little, Brown, 1972) and, for older readers, *Death Be Not Proud* by John Gunther (Harper & Row, 1971).   J.P.

139.   Boyd, Candy Dawson. *Charlie Pippin*. Macmillan, 1987. ISBN 0-02-726350-9, $12.95. Ages 8-12.

Charlie is a determined eleven-year-old entrepreneur who, with her classmates Chris and Katie Rose, is placed on the War and Peace Committee as a class project. Their topic, the Vietnam War, stirs many emotions in Charlie because her father and Uncle Ben survived it, yet will not discuss it. Charles wants to understand her father's anxiety about the war, so she continues the report against his wishes. In Washington, D.C. with Uncle Ben, she goes to the Vietnam Memorial and finds the names of two of her father's former friends. Although she went without parental permission, Charlie felt that through this experience she would better understand the memories harbored within her father, whose unspoken bitterness about the war has affected his entire outlook on life, love, and his family. Anguish and the subtle fear of war are tastefully manifested through Boyd's characterization and language. Her style incorporates the steadfast yet timid thirst for explanations Charlie demonstrates throughout her search.

Peace Studies Intermediate Middle School Junior High School

Students can study the impact of the Vietnam War on others in much the same manner that Charlie did. They can interview three people and compare their answers to the others' and to those from the rest of the class. Students can compare their feelings with those of Charlie. Finally, students might want to find out what they can do to promote peace throughout the world. They can begin by writing to their national legislators. To do this, send letters to the following: The Honorable (your senator's name), United States Senate, Washington, D.C., 20510; or The Honorable (your representative's name), United States House of Representatives, Washington, D.C. 20515. Teachers and librarians may also wish to use the services and materials at the Lion and the Lamb Peace Arts Center, Bluffton College, Bluffton, Ohio 45817. Katherine Paterson's *Park's Quest* (Lodestar, 1988) is an excellent companion book that deals with many of the same issues related to the aftermath of the Vietnam War.   M.M.S.

Related Sources

140. Brittain, Bill. *Dr. Dredd's Wagon of Wonders*. Illustrated by Andrew Glass. Harper & Row, 1987. ISBN 0-06-020714-0, $11.89. Ages 8-12.

Sequel to The Wish Giver

Trouble comes again to the good folks of Coven Tree. This time drought has so cursed the farmers and the livestock that townspeople are desperate for relief. When a stranger promises to make rain in return for "some small recompense" to be named later, the town officials eagerly agree. But when they learn of Dr. Dredd's incredible powers of evil, they regret their bargain. As in other tales of good versus evil, the diabolical Dr. Dredd is vanquished by the caring and cunning of spunky Ellen McCabe and young Calvin Huckabee. Brittain's folksy style is music to the ear, as though the storyteller were present. Rich in imagery, filled with characters that will enchant and delight, and tightly plotted for broad appeal, this witty sequel to *The Wish Giver* (Harper & Row, 1983) should work its magic on all who enter.

Related Source

Rainmaking has been the object of wonder, magic, religion, and science since the dawn of time. Here is an opportunity for students to learn about this aspect of cultural history throughout the world by studying myths and legends, rituals and customs, and scientific and pseudo-scientific experiments that have been used to predict or control the weather (and other natural phenomena). Which customs and inventions persist to this day should make an interesting topic for intermediate grade student research and discovery.   H.M.

Science, Social Studies Intermediate Middle School Junior High School

141.   Bulla, Clyde Robert. *The Cardboard Crown*. Illustrated by
Michele Chessare. Crowell, 1984. ISBN 0-690-04360-0,
$10.95. Ages 7-10.

Lonely eleven-year-old Adam finds a strange girl at his door. She
is dressed in a long white dress and has a golden crown on her head.
She says she is a princess. Intrigued, Adam befriends her and sells a
prized possession to help her get home to her father. After her father's
cruel betrayal, it is again Adam who helps her put her life back together.
Bulla tells a simple, compassionate tale for younger readers. Still, there
is ample suspense, and the reader is skillfully drawn from one chapter to
the next in this appealing mystery.

Everyone has experienced disappointments, though some are more
memorable than others. *The Cardboard Crown* could be a good
vehicle for discussion of how sometimes things are not what they
appear to be—the crown was cardboard, the princess imagined, and the
father not as devoted as he pretended to be. Children might be willing to
share a disappointment they have encountered—from a broken promise
to a toy that was not what it was advertised to be—either in discussion
or, more privately, in writing. Especially important is how we learn to
handle disappointments. Vera Cleaver's *Sweetly Sings the Donkey*
(Lippincott, 1985) effectively deals with the same theme of young
people coping successfully with hardships and disappointments. The
discussion or writing activity should include how a person might best
repond to specific setbacks.   M.A.C.

*Social Studies,
Language Arts
Primary
Intermediate*

Related Source

142.   Bunting, Eve. *Sixth-Grade Sleepover*. Harcourt Brace Jovanovich, 1986. ISBN 0-15-275350-8, $13.95. Ages 8-12.

Janey belongs to a special co-ed reading club that has been invited
to attend a sleepover in the school cafeteria, chaperoned by three
teachers. Janey and her friends are all excited about attending the event,
but Janey has a problem—she is afraid of the dark. We learn of her
terrible experience when she was placed in a closet by her baby sitter
and how she still carries this fear. Other areas of concern are "typical" of
sixth graders (boyfriends, pajamas, slippers, etc.). While the author
mentions "the problem" early in the book, it is not explained and
children will probably make interesting predictions. However, the
charm of the story is the love for reading that Bunting models through
her characters. Janey says, "I don't think there's anything as cozy in the
world as lying on a sleeping bag with your friends all around you,
munching celery with peanut butter and reading a good book. Magic is
right!" Bunting demonstrated she has the ability to capture the varieties
of sixth graders in their language, their thinking, and their outlook on
life.

Why not consider a similar sleepover in your own school? There
are many specific titles of books mentioned that could be a starting point
for reading and sharing in that unique setting. Students could then guess
why Eve Bunting mentioned these particular titles and write to her either

*Language Arts
Primary
Intermediate*

agreeing with her choices or suggesting better titles. Another way to organize the sleepover would be to have students come dressed as a favorite character in a book they plan on sharing. Then they could trade books for a timed session of sustained silent reading (SSR).   B.C.

143.   Byars, Betsy. *Cracker Jackson*. Viking Kestrel, 1985. ISBN 0-670-80546-7, $11.95. Ages 9-12.

ALA Notable Book

Award-winning author Betsy Byars has written a timely novel on a subject very much in the news: wife and child abuse. When thirteen-year-old Cracker Jackson discovers his ex-babysitter and her child are being physically abused, he takes on the responsibility for helping his friends out of their perilous situation. Cracker is all seriousness, while his friend and constant companion, Goat, is forever getting involved in ludicrous escapades, but both are believable characters. The story evokes laughter but never down plays the evils of physical abuse. The subject matter in this novel is treated honestly and at a level appropriate for middle grade readers. The author does a careful job of balancing humor and despair.

Local Family and Child Abuse Prevention Centers often have excellent programs on physical and sexual abuse. If there is a need in your area for a child abuse center, contact the National Exchange Club in your area. They have a foundation that sets up and supports child abuse centers across the country. A child abuse prevention kit is available at no cost from NCPCA Information Services, P.O. Box 2866, Chicago, IL 60690. Finally, local YWCA's have many programs for women and children concerning abuse.   M.E.H.

Family Life,
Social Studies
Intermediate
Middle School
Junior High School

144.   Carrick, Carol. *Stay Away From Simon*. Illustrated by Donald Carrick. Clarion, 1985. ISBN 0-89919-343-9, $10.95. Ages 7-10.

This sensitively-written story takes place on Martha's Vineyard in the 1830s. Simon is the retarded son of a miller. They say that his mind is too slow for learning, so he is given no schooling. The children his own age do not play with him, calling him "Simple Simon." In his loneliness he seeks out the companionship of younger children. Many of the parents think that this is not natural and they warn their children, "Stay away from Simon." One day Simon follows Lucy and her little brother home from school. Lucy is frightened, but with the help of her understanding parents, Lucy discovers something quite remarkable about Simon. Donald Carrick's strong illustrations enhance this provocative story.

Schooling during the 1830s is aptly described: in the one-room schoolhouse children next to the stove were too hot, and the ones next to the door were too cold, older boys had to stay on the farm to help with the work and were only released to attend school in the dead of winter, and notebooks were made at home out of smoothed-out wrapping paper sewn together; a one-legged stool was used for

Social Studies
Primary
Intermediate

punishment. This can be brought vividly to life for children by visiting, where possible, a local museum complex that includes a one-room school interpreted by skilled guides. Back at school, the classroom can be set up for a day or a week as a one-room school so that students might experience the past firsthand. The educational ways of the past century can then be compared with those of the present.   M.E.M.

145.   Cassedy, Sylvia. *M.E. and Morton*. Crowell, 1987. ISBN 0-690-04562-X, $12.89. Ages 8-12.

ALA Notable Book

People in all walks of life must learn to cope with the problems of the human condition—birth, pain, isolation, poverty, illness or death. Sylvia Cassedy introduces us to eleven-year-old Mary Ella (M.E.), a gifted child who must bear the "burden and shame" of Morton, her older brother, who is a slow learner. Living with the loneliness and isolation of her giftedness, M.E. also longs for a friend of her own. During one special summer, M.E. meets Polly and is astonished when this flamboyant new girl on the block also picks Morton for a friend. The three children learn about each other's need for a special kind of love in a kaleidoscope of activities that they share in a summer together. Through her characters Cassedy shows that children are not immune to the problems inherent to being human. Her story gives readers a window for looking at life from different perspectives.

Social Studies
Intermediate
Middle School
Junior High School

Good stories of coping with the problems of the human condition, especially disabilities, serve several purposes. For disabled youngsters, they provide positive images of a negative situation, and they help those who are not impaired develop a more healthy and intelligent under-standing of some of the problems that a disabled person may face. *M.E. and Morton* should be added to the list of well-written books on this topic. Several good complementary fiction books are *Kelly's Creek* by Smith (Crowell, 1975), Byers's *Summer of the Swans* (Viking, 1970), and Wrightson's A *Racecourse for Andy* (Harcourt, 1968). An excellent resource for an analysis and annotation of books about the disabled is Barbara Baskin and Karen Harris's *More Notes from a Different Drummer: A Guide to Juvenile Fiction Portraying the Disabled* (Bowker, 1984).   L.P.B.

Related Sources

146.   Chaiken, Miriam. *Yossi Asks the Angels for Help*. Illus-trated by Petra Mathers. Harper & Row, 1985. ISBN 0-06-021196-2, $8.89. Ages 8-10.

Yossi can't keep his mind on his studies. He had planned to buy his Hanukkah gifts after school, but his eight quarters have disappeared, probably through the hole in his pants pocket. He looks for angels to provide a miracle when the Sabbath candles are lit. He prays to God to intercede. His Rebbe's advice to "act as if God doesn't exist," i.e., to think and act for himself, teaches him a valuable lesson and results in a satisfying conclusion to this brief (52 pages) story. Chaiken's believable characters reflect the joys and problems growing up in a Chassidic family; yet she writes with a sure sense of the universal feelings of all children in this touchingly warm and insightful story.

For many children the Chassidim seem as though they belong to another time and place. Children may be surprised to learn that Chassidic Jews maintain their orthodox beliefs and customs in many communities throughout this country. Other stories about Jewish life for this age group include Chaiken's *How Yossi Beat the Evil Urge* (1983) and *I Should Worry, I Should Care* (1979), both published by Harper & Row; M.B. Goffstein's *Family Scrapbook* (Farrar, Straus & Giroux, 1978); and the popular Ike and Mama books by Carol Snyder (published by Lothrop, Lee & Shepard). Adult and young adult readers will enjoy reading the insightful and best-selling novels by Chaim Potok: *My Name is Asher Lev* (Knopf, 1972), *The Promise* (Knopf, 1969), *The Chosen* (Fawcett, 1986), or *In the Beginning* (Knopf, 1975). All offer an honest and understanding picture of Jewish-American life while portraying universal human characteristics that can be recognized by all.   H.M.

Jewish-American Studies
Intermediate
Middle School

Related Sources

147.   Cleaver, Vera. *How Sweetly Sings the Donkey*. Lippincott, 1985. ISBN 0-397-32157-0, $11.89. Ages 10-14.

"If life hands you lemons, make lemonade" best sums up fourteen-year-old Lily Snow's approach to life. Lily's father is in poor health in addition to being a day dreamer and a wanderer who has uprooted his family several times to follow his dreams. Lily's mother is weak and unable to cope with her husband's disposition any longer, so she takes off with a man who will care for her. Lily assesses the reality of her family's situation and becomes determined to improve their lives. The author's strong characterizations, especially of Lily, and the well-developed plot provide for pleasurable reading. Readers who remember the determined and resourceful Mary Call in *Where The Lilies Bloom* (Lippincott, 1969) will want to read this equally fine novel.

Related Source

If students admire Lily Snow and her determination, they may enjoy reading biographies of women who channeled their determination to reap productive results. The following books include biographical sketches of women whom students may find inspiring: *Women Pioneers in Science* (Harcourt Brace Jovanovich, 1979) by Louis Haber; *Young and Female*, compiled by Pat Ross (Random House, 1972); *Twentieth Century Women of Achievement* by Samuel Kastman (Richard Rosen Press, 1976); and *Wise Women* by William P. Rayner (St. Martins Press, 1983). By reading Lily's story and biographies of women who exemplified the value of determination in their lives, students may find inspiration for their own lives.   M.E.H.

Women's Studies
Intermediate
Middle School
Junior High School

Related Sources

148.   Cole, Brock. *The Goats*. Farrar, Straus & Giroux, 1987. ISBN 0-374-32678-9, $11.95. Ages 8-12.

Stripped of their clothes and left with no provisions, a boy and girl—designated as the summer camp "goats"—are left to spend the

ALA Best Book
ALA Notable Book

night on a deserted island. The pair decide to leave the island instead of spending the rest of the summer as the camp jokes. Their rather haphazard journey through the area, "borrowing" food, shelter, and clothing to survive, helps them strengthen their perceptions of themselves and self-confidence. They manage some harrowing escapes due to their cunning and determination to stay together and outwit authority. Brock handles the friendship which develops between them in a convincing and realistic manner. Readers can empathize with these two characters as they feel their pain and humiliation grow into self-determination and triumph in this touching human drama.

Literature ,
Social Studies
Intermediate
Middle School

Related Sources

The theme of friendship between the sexes is an important topic for young people on the verge of adolescence. One of the major issues in this story is the relationship which evolved between Howie and Laura, and the strength they drew from it. Among the many other books which deal in a positive way with a strong and growing friendship between a boy and a girl who face adversities are *Bridge to Terabithia* by Katherine Paterson (Avon, 1979) and *Sometimes I Think I Hear My Name* by Avi Wortis (Pantheon, 1982).   K.B.B.

149.   Conly, Jane Leslie. *Rasco and the Rats of NIMH*. Harper & Row, 1986. ISBN 0-06-021361-2, $11.89. Ages 9-12.

Sequel to
Mrs. Frisby and the
Rats of NIMH

Related Source

A colony of rats that can read, write, and program computers? Impossible? Rasco, a city-wise rat, hooks up with a group of academically sophisticated country rats to destroy a hydro-electric dam. Struggling to preserve the natural resources and peace of their home, Thorn Valley, the rats frantically work to outwit the engineers and construction workers. Conly has written an ingenious and successful sequel to her father's Newbery Award-winning book *Mrs. Frisby and the Rats of NIMH* (Atheneum, 1971). She creates a boastful, brazen Rasco who is capable of turning the quiet colony into chaos with his spontaneous ideas and schemes. Gradually Rasco learns what it is really like to be a leader and a hero.

Language Arts
Intermediate
Middle School

Every student knows a Rasco-type personality and can relate to the problems and frustrations he or she can create. Energetic, enthusiastic, and desperately in need of being liked, Rasco constantly gets himself into trouble. This story provides the class with the opportunity to look at life through his eyes. This can begin by discussing Rasco's feelings as well as others' reactions to him. With the rats' conquest and discovery at the end of the story, students can write their own sequel in which they may or may not agree about how Rasco has changed and what he is most likely to do next.   M.B.C.

150.   Corcoran, Barbara. *The Sky is Falling*. Atheneum, 1988. ISBN 0-689-31388-8, $13.98. Ages 8-12.

When Annah's father loses his job at the start of The Depression in 1929, her affluent private-school lifestyle goes through unwelcome changes. The family house in a Boston suburb is put up for sale, the family is scattered, and Annah finds herself living with a widowed aunt in a rural lakeside cottage in New Hampshire. Through her friendship with a poor and abused, but independent girl, Dodie, and the support of her understanding aunt, Annah gradually matures and learns to look beyond herself. Corcoran has written a thoughtful book about how one can grow in positive ways through the acceptance of change. The characters are convincing and provide valuable insights into human behavior for today's readers.

Annah's Boston life is predictable and her future is planned. The changes forced by her father's job loss impact in many ways on each family member. Students can discuss how these changes actually worked positively in the lives of the characters. Many students may recall unwelcome changes in their lives and how they resulted in positive or negative outcomes. They can learn that change is inevitable in life and that learning to grow with change is one sign of maturity. Those who have not read Irene Hunt's moving *No Promises in the Wind* (Follett, 1970) may enjoy another view of the same time and similar family problems.   A.S.

Family Life, Language Arts Intermediate Middle School

Related Source

151.   Dahl, Roald. *Matilda*. Illustrated by Quentin Blake. Viking Kestrel, 1988. ISBN 0-670-82439-9, $13.95. Ages 8-12.

By the time Matilda enters school she has not only read through the entire children's section of the local library, but she has also knocked off an impressive list of adult classics. Her parents, in their abysmal ignorance, treat their genius daughter as a blockhead. Matilda's mother is TV and bingo crazed, while her father is busy turning back the odometers on the used cars he sells. Readers will cheer Matilda's ingenious tricks to square herself with such insensitive parents. Her fertile mind meets the ultimate test in "The Trunchbull," a former Olympic hammer thrower and the most wicked and unfeeling school headmistress in all literature. Matilda brings order to the chaos of her life in a happy and satisfying ending. Children will cheer her every triumph. Dahl's characters are sharply drawn and the suspense is delicious. The story moves quickly through an abundance of dialogue, wickedly funny scenes, and exaggerated classroom humor. *Matilda* should be a good choice to share aloud with upper elementary classes.

Matilda was an avid reader. Thus, this is a good opportunity to discuss the notion of "good" books. Each individual can compile a list of "Ten Books Everyone In This Class Should Read." Then the lists can be shared with the class and the selections defended. Ultimately, the class could develop a single list of ten books at the beginning of the school year. The class could set a goal for everyone to have read of the books on the list by the end of the year.   B.B.

Literature Intermediate Middle School

152.   Danzinger, Paula. *Remember Me To Harold Square*. Delacorte, 1987. ISBN 0-385-29610-X, $13.95. Ages 10-14.

"We, the loving parents, in order to form a more perfect union, do hereby devise an absolutely, wonderful, marvelous educational experience in which our children search for objects, facts, people, and places." Thus begins the Serendipity Scavenger Hunt that takes fourteen-year-old Kendra Kaye, her precocious little brother Oscar (nicknamed, O.K.), and a visiting family friend on a 35-day field trip around New York City, with a trip to England as a prize for the completion of all the requirements. The three find themselves doing things, going places, and eating foods they never would have thought possible. Most important, they find they are really enjoying themselves while learning about New York. In her fast-paced, humorous style, Danzinger has taken what might have been an ordinary sightseeing trip and turned it into a fun-filled, challenging experience where the characters also learn a great deal about each other.

Related Source

After reading this book, students could be challenged to make up a scavenger hunt of their own community. They may want to start by following the book's format of rules and regulations, or make up their own. A useful resource book for children and adults is *City Safaris* by Carolyn Shaffer and Erica Fiedler (Sierra Club, 1987). A facts hunt can be put together by conducting research at local libraries or historical societies. If your community does not offer enough variety, extend the hunt to neighboring communities. Places of interest, museums, and different neighborhoods could be on the list of places to visit. A list of foods to try can be compiled after checking area restaurants in the phone book to see what international or ethnic foods are available in the area. After putting together a scavenger hunt of their community, students might challenge their families to go on the hunt together.   K.B.B.

Local History,
Language Arts
Intermediate
Middle School
Junior High School

153.   Edwards, Sally. *George Midgett's War*. Scribner's, 1985. ISBN 0-684-18315-3, $12.95. Ages 10-13.

The Revolutionary War seemed distant and remote to the people of Okracoke, an island off the coast of North Carolina, until British raiders murdered Hannah, a deaf-mute who was well–liked by her neighbors. Suddenly, the war was viewed from a different perspective and the hearty islanders choose to become involved by furnishing badly needed supplies to the tattered Revolutionary Army at Valley Forge. Fourteen-year-old George Midgett and his father take on the task of delivering the valuable supplies. This impressive work of historical fiction provides readers with an understanding of the people and territory in this part of America in 1777-1778. The story line is enhanced by the realistic dimension of a boy growing in understanding of himself and his father. The author does an excellent job of blending an history and fiction.

U.S. History
Intermediate
Middle School
Junior High School

Related Sources

Okracoke Island lies at the southern tip of North Carolina's Outer Banks. Students may enjoy learning more about this island and two pirates long associated with its history: Edward Teach, better known as Blackbeard, and Stede Bonnet. The following books are among those that provide information on one or both of these men and the events involving the men and the island: *Pirates and Buccaneers* by Robert D. Larranaga (Lerner, 1979) and *Buccaneers and Pirates of Our Coast* by Frank R. Stockton (Macmillan, 1967).   M.E.H.

154.   Fleischman, Sid. *The Whipping Boy*. Illustrated by Peter
Sis. Greenwillow, 1986. ISBN 0-688-067216-4, $11.75.
Ages 7-11.

Newbery Award Winner

"Fetch the whipping boy!" Since it is forbidden to spank the heir to
the throne, Jemmy, the orphaned son of a rat catcher, has been pulled
from the streets to take Prince Brat's punishments. The prince lives up
to his name—tying the wigs of the lords and ladies to the backs of their
chairs, refusing to learn to read and write and the like. Jemmy takes the
whipping silently, which angers the young prince. But when Prince
Brat decides to run away, it is Jemmy he takes with him. On his flight,
the prince learns about life outside the castle, real people, and himself.
This tale of high adventure is fast-paced and suspenseful. The characters
are lively and colorful. *The Whipping Boy*, winner of the 1987
Newbery Award, demonstrates both Fleischman's familiar humor and a
strong sense of compassion for both boys as Jemmy's and Prince Brat's
lives ultimately merge together in friendship.

There are many exciting scenarios in *The Whipping Boy* which
could be easily adapted for reader's theater or as a skit by pairs or small
groups of students. There is an abundance of lively dialogue and
descriptive details of the various settings where the action takes place.
Students could make their own simple sets and create their own
costumes. Among the several episodes from which to develop a script
or a skit, especially good choices are those chapters which involve the
notorious highwayman, Hold Your Nose Billy, so named because of
his love of garlic.   J.P.

*Drama, Language Arts
Social Studies
Intermediate
Middle School
Junior High School*

155.   Forrester, Victoria. *The Candlemaker and Other Tales*.
Illustrated by Susan Seddon Boulet. Atheneum, 1984. ISBN
0-689-31013-7, $10.95. Ages 8-12.

Victoria Forrester is an accomplished storyteller. These four
literary tales are, in style and mood, in the tradition of fairy and folk
tales found in all cultures. They contain magic, three wishes granted and
used foolishly, task and trials, and pourquois stories. Forrester's
language is playful, elegant, yet reminiscent of the oral storyteller.
Susan Seddon Boulet's finely exquisite illustrations sustain the fairy
quality of the collection. She is an artist whose work is deserving of a
wider audience.

Though upper elementary readers will enjoy these stories by
themselves, they are excellent for sharing aloud with the whole class,
for there is a richness of language to delight the audience along with
substance to provoke thought and discussion. Reading aloud, therefore,
is an opportunity to demonstrate the power and beauty of the sound of
literature and of language. By scheduling a regular time for oral
literature, expectations will develop for stories heard, thereby making
oral literature a significant part of young people's language education.
Forrester's stories are an excellent place to begin.   H.M.

*Literature,
Language Arts
Intermediate
Middle School*

156.   Fox, Paula. *One-Eyed Cat*. Bradbury, 1984. ISBN 0-02-735540-3, $11.95. Ages 11-14.

Newbery Honor Book
ALA Best Book
ALA Notable Book

One-Eyed Cat is a charming and sensitive story full of fully-drawn characters in a setting both tranquil and haunting. Ned's childhood during the Great Depression has been a mixture of loving family life and the loneliness of a small boy learning to move silently through life in an effort not to disturb his mother, who has become an invalid. When Ned's Uncle Hilary gives him an air rifle for his eleventh birthday, his life is radically changed. The gift brings disaster as Ned shoots into the dark, and later discovers what had been his target. Feelings of guilt infect Ned's life when he meets the one-eyed cat and struggles to make amends for what he has done.

Paula Fox has written a novel for children that has gained her further praise from critics and a 1985 Newbery Honor Award. She has previously received the Newbery Medal (*Slave Dancer* [Bradbury, 1973]), the American Book Award (*A Place Apart* [Signet, 1983]), and the Hans Christian Andersen Medal. These are just a few of the scores of awards given to writers and illustrators of books for young readers. Students may wish to learn which authors and artists have won which awards by reading *Children's Books: Awards and Prizes* published by the Children's Book Council, 67 Irving Place, New York, NY 10003.   R.M.G.

*Author Studies
Intermediate
Middle School
Junior High School*

157.   Garrigue, Sheila. *The Eternal Spring of Mr. Ito*. Bradbury, 1985. ISBN 0-02-737300-2, $11.95. Ages 10-12.

*Sequel to
All the Children
Were Sent Away*

All the Children Were Sent Away (Bradbury, 1976) introduced Sarah Warren, an English child sent to live with relatives in Canada to avoid the dangers of England during World War II. In this sequel, Sarah, still living with her aunt and uncle in Canada, befriends her uncle's Japanese gardner, the kind and gentle Mr. Ito. Everyone in the community was very accepting of Japanese-Canadians until the bombing of Pearl Harbor. A bewildered Sarah watches as Japanese-Canadians are herded off to isolated internment camps. Only by accidentally finding Mr. Ito, who hid himself in a remote cave, is Sarah consoled about a world grown ugly by war. The author's perceptive explanation about the causes of war and her basic understanding of human nature make this touching story well worth reading.

In *The Eternal Spring of Mr. Ito* readers learn that citizens of Japanese descent were imprisoned in Canada, just as they were in this country during World War II. Those who wish to learn more about this dark period in the history of our country have several excellent sources to which to turn, including Yoshiko Uchida's *Journey to Topaz* (Scribner's, 1971) and *Journey Home* (Atheneum, 1978) for which she draws from her and her family's experiences of being sent to a camp at Topaz, Utah. For a true story of life in a Japanese-Canadian internment camp, students can turn to Shizuye Takashima's *A Child in Prison Camp* (Tundra Books, 1971).   M.E.M.

*Asian-American Studies
Intermediate
Middle School*

Related Sources

158.   Gilson, Jamie. *Hello, My Name is Scrambled Eggs.* Illustrated by John Wallner. Lothrop, Lee & Shepard, 1985. ISBN 0-688-04095-0, $10.25. Ages 9-12.

Hello, My Name is Scrambled Eggs is a fast-moving story of seventh grader Harvey Trumble's attempt to Americanize a Vietnamese boy whose family has been brought to America by Harvey's church. Harvey takes Tuan under his wing and, as their friendship grows, leads him through both touching and funny experiences, teaching him the English language and the "American way" of life. Through Tuan, Harvey learns some valuable lessons about people and the importance of one's heritage and culture. This warm-hearted book portrays characters as realistic as the kids next door.

This would be an worthwhile book to use in a multicultural lesson incorporating social studies and language arts. In groups have children read this and other books on Asian immigrants, such as *In the Year of the Boar and Jackie Robinson*, by Bette Bao Lord (Harper & Row, 1984), *Angel Child, Dragon Child* by Michele Maria Surat (Raintree, 1983), or *Dragonwings* by Lawrence Yep (Harper & Row, 1975). Current sources of information can be obtained from newspapers or programs from the local PBS station. After information has been gathered and shared, have students write about their experiences with someone from another country or an experience that someone they know has had with a person from another country.   J.P.

Related Sources

Asian-American Studies
Intermediate
Middle School

159.   Greer, Gery and Bob Ruddick. *Max and Me and The Wild West.* Harcourt Brace Jovanovich, 1988. ISBN 0-15-253136-X, $12.95. Ages 9-12.

In this fast-moving fantasy–mystery, Steve Brandon and Max Zilinski use Professor Flybender's Fully Guaranteed One-Of-A-Kind Time Machine as a gateway to the Wild West. When they "arrive" in Silver Gulch, Steve finds he has been transformed into Desmond Langsfield, a renowned actor and undercover agent for the Pinkerton Detective Agency, while Max has become Ed Huff, a popular journalist. Steve discovers that as Desmond Langsfield he is scheduled to entertain the town at Nellie Bradshaw's Last Chance Theater. In a secret meeting with the sheriff, however, he learns that his real job is to find and capture Gentleman John Hooten, the Rhyming Robber of the Rockies. The plot moves quickly and the tone is light and humorous. To the delight of young readers, Steve and Max go from one entertaining situation to another in a light-hearted, playful way. Students who have not read previously published *Max and Me and the Time Machine* (Harcourt Brace Jovanovich, 1983) may enjoy both stories.

Investigating the "Wild West" can be fun and informative. Students might research any of the real-life outlaws mentioned in the story. This can lead to details about life in the west around 1882, when Max and Steve's visit takes place. This information might be used to produce a fact sheet about the life and times of the outlaws. Students can also design wanted posters, either by hand or using a computer program

Related Source

U.S. History,
Computers,
Language Arts
Intermediate
Middle School

such as *Print Shop*, for the outlaws they researched. Building on the use of theater in the story, students might write and present, at their own Last Chance Theater, short plays about the outlaws and their times. This idea can be extended to include student productions of the three short plays which Desmond Langsfield was supposed to present in Silver Gulch. A brief four-line synopsis of each play is given in the book. Students can rewrite and produce one of the plays.   G.B.

160.   Grove, Vicki. *Good-bye My Wishing Star*. Putnam, 1988. ISBN 0-399-21532-8, $13.95. Ages 8-12.

Just as the title suggests, *Goodbye My Wishing Star* is a story about leaving a cherished place of precious memories and friends. Jens Tucker has spent all of her twelve years on the family farm. When hard times suddenly force her parents to sell it, Jens is bewildered, resentful, and worried. In order to sort out her emotions, she records her thoughts in a special diary, which she plans to leave under a bale of hay in the barn for the new owners. Grove so convincingly presents Jens's feelings that the reader empathizes with her as she wishes on her special star for a stroke of luck to keep her family from leaving and cheers for her as she discovers, through the help of her best friend, the excitement of moving on. The rural setting and language make Grove's story authentic and believable. The characters blend everyday practicality with optimism.

Language Arts Intermediate Middle School

To most, home is a special place and Grove treats it warmly and lovingly. The story's message is that although we may physically leave a place, it remains with us deep in our hearts to be remembered fondly and often. Jens left her diary so that the new owners could "appreciate every minute and every second of what they've got." After reading the story aloud, teachers could ask intermediate students to imagine themselves in Jens's position and have them write letters to future owners of their homes. In the letters, students can include their favorite memories and funny stories that have made their home a special place. Because the letters will be personal, students should be asked to share them only on a volunteer basis.   J.B.R.

161.   Hadley, Irwin. *I Be Somebody*. Atheneum, 1984. ISBN 0-689-50308-3, $11.95. Ages 9-12.

This novel is based upon a little-known incident in Black American history. At the turn of the 20th century the vast majority of citizens in a Black Oklahoma town decided to migrate to Athabasca in Canada to homestead and escape white supremacy and prejudice. Ten-year-old Rap is the main character who, along with his Aunt Spicy, decided to chance the unknown. *I Be Somebody* has all the elements that make reading enjoyable: an interesting plot and premise, a range of emotions, and a cast of well-drawn and unforgettable characters. It combines good writing, worthwhile characters, and a factually-based story of human courage and determination.

There are many little-known events in the history of Blacks (and other minority groups) in this country. There are, however, other titles that might easily be companion books in an organized reading experience for upper grades and middle school readers on aspects of Black history. *The Black Experience in Children's Books*, now in its 3rd edition, is an outstanding list of fine books edited by Augusta Baker and published by The New York Public Library. It is a worthwhile reference for every school and public library. Teachers can also consult a librarian for a list of resources available locally. If there isn't one, create one with the help of your students. This can be donated to the public or school library for reference by other interested teachers and students.   H.M./M.A.C.

Related Source

Black Studies, Literature Intermediate Middle School Junior High School

162.   Hamilton, Virginia, reteller. *In The Beginning*. Illustrated by Barry Moser. Harcourt Brace Jovanovich, 1988. ISBN 0-15-238740-4, $18.95. All ages.

In this 1989 Newbery Honor book, Hamilton retells twenty-five creation myths from around the world. The familiar Biblical creation story, as well as several Greek myths, are joined in this brilliant collection of fascinating and lesser-known stories from other traditions, including Eskimo, Native American, African, and Tahitian. *In The Beginning* transports the reader beyond the recognizable past into the time before anything existed. Out of the void, gods emerge from eggs, water, huge stones, and darkness in the shape of ravens, giants, and man. These intriguing images are clarified through Moser's hauntingly beautiful watercolors.

Newbery Honor Book ALA Best Book ALA Notable Book

After each story the author comments about the type of myth and its cultural origins. In addition, a section relates the myths by motif. Teachers can make use of this information by encouraging students to listen for common motifs. The length of the stories, as well as the language, make them ideal to read aloud. After reading to your students, lead them in a discussion to chart such story elements as type of creation, appearance (or absence) of death or evil in the creation act, and the number and type of gods represented. After several stories, students will be able to infer the common themes, motifs, and charcters among some of the stories regardless of country of origin. This could be an effective activity to combine with the study of world history.   L.B.

Multicultural Studies, Literature Middle School Junior High School

163.   Hamilton, Virginia. *The Mystery of Drear House*. Greenwillow, 1987. ISBN 0-688-04026-8, $11.75. Ages 10-up.

In this compelling sequel to *The House of Dies Drear* (Macmillan, 1968) the pervasive secrets of the Drear House, as well as those of the neighboring Darrow House, continue to unfold. Startling new discoveries, expertly wrapped in fascinating history about the underground railroad, are presented at a quick, even pace—a ghostly Indian maiden, slave orphans, a tunnel between the Drear and Darrow Houses, and yet another treasure hoarded by abolitionist Dies Drear.

Sequel to The House of Dies Drear

Mrs. Darrow, a mentally unbalanced invalid caught between the past and present, plays a pivotal role in the final airing of all the secrets and in initiating peace and trust between the two families. As she has in so many prior books for young people, Hamilton provides readers with a captivating story that entertains as well as challenges its readers.

Black Studies,
Literature
Intermediate
Middle School
Junior High School

Related Sources

This book, along with *The House of Dies Drear*, could be used to investigate the underground railroad and the bravery of the conductors who defied federal fugitive slave laws to operate stations and aid escaping slaves. Share the chapter called "On the Underground Railroad" from Milton Meltzer's *A History in Their Own Words: The Black Americans* (Harper & Row, 1984, paperback) with your students. They would also learn a great deal from such sources as Marcy Heidish's *A Woman Called Moses* (Houghton Mifflin, 1976) and Barbara Smucker's *Runaway to Freedom* (Harper & Row, 1977). Someone might contact a local historical society to locate underground railroad stations in your area as well as guest speakers for your class who could recount local events or people that figured prominently in the underground railway, the abolitionist movement, or similar human rights effort.   L.B.

164.   Hamilton, Virginia. *The People Could Fly*. Illustrated by Leo and Diane Dillon. Knopf, 1985. ISBN 0-394-96925-1, $13.99. All ages.

The People Could Fly is a remarkable group of Black American folk tales that should become a treasured part of folklore collections. Award-winning writer Hamilton has researched her tales thoroughly, providing notes at the end of each explaining its origins or dialect, along with an extensive bibliography of resource materials. She has maintained a delicate balance between dialect and readability, including the definitions for some of the more unfamiliar words in the story notes. Thus, the flavor of the stories is not sacrificed to her audience's understanding. It is, however, the selection of the stories that sets this collection apart from others like it. The reader not only gets a taste of the various cycles of folktales that originated in Black America, but also is presented with a poignant and realistic view of slaves and slavery. The stories represent the collective imagination of a people who were subdued, yet were unconquerable—people who were victims of intolerable cruelty, yet were still capable of laughter and dreams.

Related Sources

Black Studies,
Literature, Storytelling
Intermediate
Middle School
Junior High School

After reading *The People Could Fly*, older students might enjoy reading an earlier Virginia Hamilton work, *The Magical Adventures of Pretty Pearl* (Harper & Row, 1983). In that book, Hamilton interweaves Black American folklore with Black history and the story of how her own family came to Ohio from the South. *The People Could Fly* contains stories about many of the folk characters that appear in *The Magical Adventures of Pretty Pearl* and the story notes help explain their origins. Both books powerfully portray the Black experience and serve to put slavery into a larger perspective that is worth exploring.   M.A.C.

165. Heide, Florence Parry. *Tales for the Perfect Child*. Illustrated by Victoria Chess. Lothrop, Lee & Shepard, 1985. ISBN 0-688-03892-1, $13.00. Ages 8-12.

What do all parents want? Perfect children. What happens when parents get their wish? Disaster! Only funny disasters are allowed in this light-hearted album of animal children who drive their elders crazy merely by following the letter of parental law. Children should not only laugh at the whacky illustrations by Victoria Chess, but giggle at the aggravatingly true-to-life parent-child situations and their outcomes. This collection of outrageous tales is for sharing for the delight of adults and youngsters alike; it is an opportunity for both to be in on the humor of these comic situations.

Jack Prelutsky's *New Kid on the Block* (Greenwillow, 1984) is as full of remarkable children as Heide's *Tales for the Perfect Child*. Strange conduct can be very good (as seen in Prelutsky's "Dainty Dottie Dee") or shockingly naughty (as seen in the poems "My Mother Says I'm Sickening" and "Sidney Snickle"), depending upon the person's motives. Another author who had some fun with the perfect child was Myra Cohn Livingston in *Higgledy Piggledy: Verses and Pictures* (McElderry, 1986). Children could write and illustrate their own books about when things went wrong and they wanted them to be right; about a situation in which they were trying to be a "perfect child" (and enjoyed the problems this caused); or about a time when something good came out of bad behavior.   G.G.

Related Sources

Language Arts
Primary
Intermediate

166. Heide, Florence Parry. *Treehorn's Wish*. Illustrated by Edward Gorey. Holiday House, 1984. ISBN 0-8234-0493-5, $9.95. Ages 6-12.

Heide's whimsical story, which is perfectly complemented by Gorey's pen and ink drawings, is definitely for the reader who wants something out of the ordinary. Treehorn prepares to celebrate his birthday by clearing out his bureau drawers and closet to make room for the many presents his parents will give him. Ever hopeful, Treehorn expects many presents in spite of the fact that his parents have not given him much for his past few birthdays. Treehorn's self-involved parents, his discovery of a jug containing a genie who will grant him three wishes, and Heide's subtle humor become engagingly entangled to produce a very amusing object lesson. The pathos of the situation is lightened by Heide's first rate sense of the absurd.

A list of books children find truly funny—ones that make them laugh out loud—is a valuable resource for any teacher or librarian. A group project might be to develop such a list through a questionnaire involving young people from schools throughout the district for use at home, as well as in school. Questionnaires can be sent and returned through regular inter-school mails at no charge. Tabulating the results could be a challenging math lesson in statistics.   S.L.W.

Literature, Math
Primary
Intermediate

167.   Henry, Maeve. *The Witch King*. Orchard, 1988 (1st Am. ed.). ISBN 0-531-05738-0, $12.95. Ages 9-12.

Robert Harding, son of a poor fisherman, believes the stories of old Granny Fishbone, even if no one else in his poor seaside village does. His imagination is fired by her images of a great city born out of the seed of one tree and of the Witch King who will someday destroy the City to save it. Finally Robert decides to seek the City himself, even though others who had undertaken such a quest had never returned. He does indeed find the City and sees the fulfillment of the prophecies in a way undreamed of in his wildest imaginings. Maeve Henry has written a powerful first novel: in just 126 pages, she has created a captivating world full of magic; peopled it with characters her reader can love, hate, and wonder about; and spun a mythology that is both believable and fantastic. A sequel would be welcomed.

Literature
Intermediate
Middle School
Junior High School

This could be a good book to use to introduce third or fourth graders to author-created worlds of fantasy. Because the book is short, it can easily be read aloud in a few sessions; because the plot is complex, it would probably help students in their understanding if the major events of the story were charted, along with the prophecy. Students could then visualize how the prophecy came true. They might want to discuss whether they had guessed how this would happen. Students could also list elements that illustrate the world Maeve Henry created. These could be designated with a check if they can be found in our world and with a star if they are purely Henry's fantasy. Students might want to do the same with some other works of fantasy, perhaps read in small groups. Allan Eckert's *The Dark Green Tunnel*

Related Sources

(Little, Brown, 1984) and its sequel, *The Wand* (Little, Brown, 1985), would be appropriate for the younger age level. Laurence Yep's *Dragons of the Lost Sea* (Harper & Row, 1982) and *Dragon Steel* (Harper & Row, 1985) would be effective sources to use with older students.   M.A.C.

168.   Hilts, Len. *Timmy O'Dowd and the Big Ditch: A Story of the Glory Days on the Old Erie Canal*. Gulliver, 1988. ISBN 0-15-200606-0, $13.95. Ages 8-12.

Related Source

Len Hilts, the author of *Quanah Parker* (Gulliver, 1987), once again has demonstrated that history told through story can be interesting indeed. This well-written adventure is set along the Erie Canal in 1845, a time when westward expansion was into today's Midwest. Fascinating facts about the canal system in New York are interwoven into the story of twelve-year-old Timmy O'Dowd, whose father is superintendent of a section of the canal. In those days the canal was nothing more than a big ditch protected on either side by berms made of the earth from the original digging. There was no such thing as a canal engineer when the canal was built, so digging and maintaining it required "Yankee ingenuity." When heavy rains and the tunnels of muskrats cause a breach in the berm, Timmy's cousin Dennis, visiting from New York City, comes up with a novel way to channel the water away from the breach until it can be filled. Timmy thus learns to be a more realistic judge of people, including his cousin and the canal boat captain he has idolized.

Canals made farming in the Midwest profitable as it allowed farm goods to be taken to market cheaply. Still, they were a costly and not always popular project. Some students might enjoy researching other such foresighted projects, such as the Panama and the Suez Canals. Still others might like to research proposed projects that never got off the ground because of lack of support or lack of funding. Some students could share folklore and/or songs that grew out of the canal system. Peter Spier's *The Erie Canal* (Doubleday, 1970) is an illustrated version of the song that is packed with pictorial detail that is lacking in Hilts's book. Lloyd Alexander's *The El Dorado Adventure* (Dutton, 1987) is another work of fiction which explores the social and political issues related to canal building. A class could work on individual or small group canal-related projects—perhaps someone might even like to build a working model of a lock—and then learn from each other as they report back to the whole group.   M.A.C.

U.S. History, Science, Music, Literature Intermediate Middle School

Related Sources

169. Howard, Ellen. *Her Own Song*. Atheneum, 1988. ISBN 0-689-31444-2, $12.95. Ages 8-12.

In 1905, most of the white people in Seattle wouldn't have dreamed of associating with the large Chinese population. But why did Millie, adopted but now motherless and living with her depressed father and his sister, feel so comfortable with the Chinese laundryman? And why would he risk his life to help her? Millie's oppressive dreams hold the surprising secret. Award-winning author, Ellen Howard, is at her best when she entices her readers with the exotic and mysterious flavor of the Chinese culture. Her characters are as irresistible as the intriguing plot, which is based on a true incident in the author's life. As usual, her writing is rich with description without slowing the momentum of the story.

Students can trace the first wave of immigration from China in the middle 19th century and the reasons for leaving China and choosing the United States in which to settle. Lawrence Yep is an outstanding writer who has explored these themes in *Dragonwings* (Harper & Row, 1975) and others of his books for older readers. Students can read about present day China to see how many of the customs described in *Her Own Song* are still followed today. Carter's *Modern China* (Franklin Watts, 1986) and Wolf's *In the Year of the Tiger* (Macmillan, 1988) are good sources for this age group.   L.A.B.

Asian-American Studies Intermediate Middle School Junior High School

Related Sources

170. Howe, James. *Nighty-Nightmare*. Illustrated by Leslie Morrill. Atheneum, 1987. ISBN 0-689-31207-5, $11.95. Ages 8-12.

Chester, the Monroes' well-read and overly imaginative cat, is more than a little nervous when the family decides to camp out on St.

George's Day, the day the "devil has sway." The appearance of two strangers at the campsite, accompanied by a drooling scarred bulldog, Dawg, convinces Chester and the two Monroe dogs that evil does indeed lurk in the woods. As usual Howe's wise-cracking characters cleverly play with their words. Fans of Howe's earlier mysteries will be amused when Dawg deliberately gets the pets lost in the forest and Chester tries to lure him to sleep with a tale about Bunnicula, "...a hare with dark roots." This fourth in a series of lighthearted, humorous mysteries narrated by Harold, the dog, is almost guaranteed to delight youngsters.

Literature,
Language Arts
Primary
Intermediate

Related Source

Howe's appeal to readers is, at least in part, due to his joyful and playful use of language. Have students examine the books in this series specifically to find puns. Then discuss with them how puns are structured and why they make us laugh. For example, why is Harold's explanation of tracking (which makes good "scents") amusing? Develop and display a class list of homophones and puns. Then read *A Very Mice Joke Book* by Karen Jo Gounaud (Houghton Mifflin, 1981) to your class to further explore the concept of puns. Finally, have students create their own playful puns, illustrate them if appropriate, and then compile them into a book or use them to make a bulletin board.   H.M.

171.   Hunt, Irene. *The Everlasting Hills*. Scribner's, 1985. ISBN 0-684-18340-4, $12.95. Ages 10-14.

Memorable characters and sincere human emotion are hallmarks of novels by Newbery honoree Irene Hunt. Set in Colorado's Rocky Mountains in the 1930's, *The Everlasting Hills* is the story of twelve-year-old Jeremy Breck, mildly retarded and the object of his father's harsh contempt and bitter disappointment. Only in his older sister Bethany can Jeremy find protection from his father's rages and experience the love and support he so desperately seeks. When Bethany's attentions are captured by a suitor, even this security is threatened. However, by chance, Jeremy is befriended by a recluse named "Ishmael," and his thirteenth year marks his passage into adulthood. He gains a new sense of confidence and begrudging respect from his father. Hunt continues to offer her readers honest feelings and characterizations that are uplifting and probe the depths of the well of humanity she knows is in each of us.

Social Studies
Intermediate
Middle School
Junior High School

Related Sources

With more schools mainstreaming handicapped children, teachers may be seeking ways to help *all* students better understand and be sensitive to the needs and feelings of each other. After reading *The Everlasting Hills*, the reader could compare the attitudes and methods of dealing with "retardation" in this book to those in other books such as Betsy Byar's *The Summer of the Swans* (Viking, 1970) or Jean Little's *Take Wing* (Little, Brown, 1968). Discussions of the attitudes in these and other similar books, as well as the reader's feelings and attitudes about being handicapped, could help both handicapped and non-handicapped young people understand each other better, especially where mainstreaming has not occured.   L.M.H.

172.   Jacques, Brian. *Redwall*. Illustrated by Gary Chalk. Philomel, 1987 (1st Am. ed.). ISBN 0-399-21424-0, $15.95. All
ages.

In the Summer of the Late Rose, as the gentle mice of Mossflower
Abbey and their neighboring animal friends are getting ready to celebrate
the year of abundance and blessing, word comes that Cluny the
Scourge, the dreaded one-eyed rat, and his army of vile and despicable
warriors are coming to conquer Redwall Abbey. Matthias, a young apprentice mouse, wishes that Martin the Warrior was still alive to protect
them with his legendary sword. By solving the riddle of the location of
Martin's sword, Matthias becomes the leader of this important battle.
This book is one which sweeps the reader to the exact time and place of
the story, guided by Jacques' masterful ability to establish the languages of the cast of characters. Readers are easily able to believe in the
well-developed animal characters. This appealing and unforgettable
drama is filled with mystery, high adventure, and humor.

Jacques's ability to give each animal its own personality and
language is part of this book's success. Older students may want to
discuss the personality traits of each of the characters—the one-eyed
rate, Cluny the Scourge; the sly fox Chicken-hound; the evil snake
Asmodeus; or the heroic Basil Stag Hare—and why the author portrayed them as he did. As a follow-up writing activity, students could
choose an animal, give it certain characteristics and a suitable name, and
write a short story about their new character. Students may opt to do
this in small groups and have their animal interact with others which
were created by the members in their groups.   K.B.B.

Language Arts
Intermediate
Middle School
Junior High School

173.   Kaufman, Stephen. *Does Anyone Know the Way to
Thirteen?* Houghton Mifflin, 1985. ISBN 0-395-35974-0,
$11.95. Ages 9-12.

This fast-moving book gives substantial insight into the life of a
Jewish boy in the 1950s. Approaching thirteen, Myron Saltz has two
wishes: to skip his dreaded Bar Mitzvah and to be a Little League
baseball star. Myron's troubles are compounded when he learns that his
study partner is the public school bully and his Hebrew teacher the
terrible-tempered Mr. Leibensohn. During his months of study,
however, Myron comes to realize the importance of being Jewish and
gains respect and pride for his heritage and upbringing. Myron shows
personal courage when he goes through with his Bar Mitzvah despite a
serious injury. Kaufman gives good information on Jewish heritage and
through strong characterizations brings the story alive with humor and
understanding.

Students can become aware of the cultural, racial, and individual
differences of America's pluralistic scoiety through the use of a bulletin
board entitled "Who Are These Americans?" Students can contribute by
cutting out magazine pictures identifying Americans of different ethnic
groups. The teacher might also provide a book table with samplings
from groups. Some recommended books to start with are *...And Now*

Multicultural Studies
Intermediate
Middle School
Junior High School

Related Sources

Miguel by Joseph Krumgold (Crowell, 1953), *Fast Sam, Cool Clyde, and Stuff* by Walter Dean Myers (Viking, 1975), *When Thunders Spoke* by Virginia Driving Hawk Sneve (Holiday House, 1974), and *In the Year of the Boar and Jackie Robinson* by Bette Bao Lord. Other books focus on regional and religious groups and other ethnic minorities. Books for teachers to refer to are *Children's Literature: An Issues Approach* by Masha Kabakow Rudman (Heath, 1984) and *Shadow and Substance* by Rudine Sims (NCTE, 1982).   J.P.

174.   Kaye, Marilyn. *Phoebe*. Illustrated by Roberta Ludlow. Harcourt Brace Jovanovich, 1987. ISBN 0-15-200430-0, $13.95. Ages 10-up.

Phoebe, the youngest of the four Gray girls, comes back from summer camp and realizes that her family and friends have all changed. Assuming everyone would be anxiously awaiting her arrival, she finds her friends aren't acting the same: they are interested in makeup, earrings, clothes, and boys. Since she is not interested in any of those things, "Fee" isolates herself from the others and finds consolation in working as a volunteer in the library, where her growing up begins. She organizes a group to help defend the librarian in a book banning attack. Her convictions and courage help her realize she is growing up—in her own way. Kye realistically captures the language and feelings of adolescents in a way that is believable and appealing. This is fast-paced novel has been skillfully written for younger teens on the verge of adult decisions.

Reading *Phoebe* may prompt an exploration of censorship. What is censorship? Who are the censors? What does the First Amendment to the U.S. Constitution guarantee? Students can research these and other questions and report back to the entire group. Part of the resulting discussion is likely to include whether individuals, groups, or parents have the right to tell students—or anyone—what they can or cannot read. They may complete their study by finding out whether their own school district has a censorship policy and if any specific books have been the object of censorship attacks. If there is no policy in place, they may want to offer their own and present it at the next meeting of their school board. For more information, students or teachers may contact: National Coalition Against Censorship, 22 E. 40th St., New York, NY 10016, or People For the American Way, 1015 18th St. NW., Suite 300, Washington, D.C. 20036.   J.F./M.A.C.

Government, Social Studies Intermediate Middle School Junior High School

Related Sources

175.   Kennedy, Richard. *Amy's Eyes*. Illustrated by Richard Egielski. Harper & Row, 1985. ISBN 0-06-023220-X, $13.89. All ages.

ALA Notable Book

"I saw a ship a-sailing, a-sailing on the sea/And oh, but it was laden with pretty things for thee." *Amy's Eyes* is laden with both treasure and mystery, including Amy, an orphan who turns into a doll;

her beloved sailor doll, who turns into a real live sea captain; and a crew of Mother Goose animals brought to life to man the frigate *Ariel*. Together with first mate Mr. Cloud, the inscrutable Bad Sister, and the deeply-troubled Skivvy, they set off the find the X on a treasure map. Beset by pirates, and drawn by the strange Mama Dah-Dah and her giant albatross, the *Ariel* sails to meet the destiny of all aboard. Part allegory, part myth, part nursery tale, this is above all a rousing sea adventure in the tradition of ***Treasure Island***, sweeping along in cliff-hanging suspense. The language is salty and evocative: "Hook their guts!" or "...small boats tied closely at the fringe of ocean, as if held by strings to the apron of the village." *Amy's Eyes* is an experience at many levels, rich in metaphor, language, humor, and excitement, all wrapped in truth and illusion.

Related Source

The strange cast of characters and the allusive language of *Amy's Eyes* make it difficult to define a particular audience. It is definitely not for primary level, despite the pervasive Mother Goose quotations; it is too long and inferential. However, short chapters and high adventure makes this wonderful for reading aloud to fourth to sixth grades. It could also send them back to Mother Goose, perhaps even Baring-Gould's ***The Annotated Mother Goose*** (Bramhall House, 1962), to search out the historical bases for many of the rhymes. Complex character development could provoke thoughtful discussions of motives, reactions, and personalities. The constant and unexpected turns of events make this book the perfect context for using predicting skills. All in all, it should keep readers' imaginations stirred up.   B.B.

Language Arts,
Literature
Intermediate
Middle School

Related Source

176.   Konigsburg, E.L. *Up From Jericho Tel*. Atheneum, 1986. ISBN 0-689-31194-X, $13.95. Ages 10-up.

ALA Notable Book

In this fanciful mystery, the spirit of the dead actress, Tallulah, turns two willing children invisible to find the Regina Stone, a necklace that was taken from her neck after she had died. Jeanmarie and her new friend, Malcolm Soo, use their invisibility as a cover as they check up on Tallulah's old street friends: Nicolai, the ventriloquist; Emmagene, the sweet young folk singer; Patrick Henry Mermelstein, the magician; and Widdup, the butler. Along the way, Jeanmarie and Malcolm, both with hopes of someday becoming famous, learn much about the pathway to success and what it takes to be a star. Well-written with strong characterizations, this adventure is lightly humorous and will undoubtedly please Konigsburg fans.

A magician and ventriloquist are featured in this story as street performers. An in-depth look at either profession could make an interesting classroom activity. Have the students begin with background on famous performers and their training, and a general overview of acting as a career. Next, students could try their own hand at either performing magic or throwing their voices. "How to..." handbooks or beginner's kits offer information to help students get started. Finally, a semi-professional (or a very good amateur) could be invited to the class to perform and to answer questions.   L.S.

Drama, Language Arts
Intermediate
Middle School
Junior High School

177.   Lester, Julius, reteller. *More Tales of Uncle Remus: Further Adventures of Brer Rabbit, His Friends, Enemies, and Others*. Illustrated by Jerry Pinkney. Dial, 1988. ISBN 0-8037-0420-8, $14.89. All ages.

ALA Notable Book

In his second lively collection of Brer Rabbit stories, Lester retells thirty-seven more rollicking tales from the African-American tradition so identified with the fictional Uncle Remus. As they have for generations, the escapades of Ol' Brer Rabbit will entertain and enlighten audiences of all ages. Readers will discover Brer Rabbit's sentimental side when, in "Brer Rabbit Falls in Love," he visits Miz Meadows but just sits there and sighs. They can laugh along with the animals when finally "Brer Rabbit Gets a Little Comeuppance." The dialect in Lester's retellings has the ring of authenticity, as well as the humor and sense of today. Pinkney's full-page color illustrations add to the fun of the adventures.

Black Studies, Literature
Primary
Intermediate
Middle School
Junior High School

In his instructive introduction, Professor Lester discusses the importance of the Uncle Remus tradition. He rejects the concept that these tales represent exclusively a reaction to slavery. He says "Whether we are black or white, slave or free, child or adult, Brer Rabbit is us." In the spirit of this point of view, Brer Rabbit can be studied as a traditional literary trickster. Introduce students to the motif of the trickster character by sharing stories from other cultures, for example, Coyote in Native American stories, Reynard the Fox in European stories, and Anansi in West African and West Indies tales.   L.B.

178.   Lester, Julius, reteller. *The Tales of Uncle Remus*. Illustrated by Jerry Pinkney. Dial, 1987. ISBN 0-8037-0271-X, $15.00. All ages.

ALA Notable Book

Though there are many volumes of "Uncle Remus stories," Julius Lester has made them all obsolete (except, perhaps, to literary scholars). In these 48 retellings of the 263 original tales Joel Chandler Harris wrote down and published nearly a hundred years ago, Lester captures perfectly the rhythms and melodies of the storyteller in contemporary dialect that matches the humor and wit of the stories themselves. The result is no small achievement. As he did in his highly successful and appealing *Black Folktales* (Grove, 1970) and *The Knee-High Man and Other Tales* (Dial, 1972), Lester selects stories for fast action, true humor, and strong imagery, and then simply tells them in print. The reader is virtually compelled to use the intonations and style of the storyteller as the book is read aloud. Lester has created a valuable contribution to American folklore and a resounding literary triumph.

Related Sources

Black Studies,
Storytelling
Primary
Intermediate
Middle School
Junior High School

Related Source

In her introduction to this collection, Augusta Baker, one of America's great storytellers, emphasizes the importance of the "heard story." Lester maintains that the stories live "only if they flow through your voice." Truly these stories must be heard, told by a caring reader or by a storyteller who loves them enough to share his or her retelling with a group. Nancy Schimmel's *Just Enough to Make a Story* (Sisters' Choice Press, 1978) is a useful guide for novice storytellers who would like to make one of these stories their first effort.   H.M.

179.   Levoy, Myron. *The Magic Hat of Mortimer Winter-green*. Harper & Row, 1988. ISBN 0-06-023842-9, $11.89. Ages 8-12.

Joshua and Amy Baines were two orphaned children who lived with a physically and mentally abusive aunt. On a summer day when a wacky magician with a magical hat comes to town, they decide to escape the abuse and run away to their grandparents. The children travel from South Dakota to New York City, experiencing all sorts of wild adventures. Levoy captures the feelings of an abused child in a sensitive and subtle way. He allows the reader to feel empathy for the characters without feeling pity. Readers will discover that Joshua and Amy are strong characters who determine their own fate.

The travel–adventure side of this book could be developed into an interesting social studies project. Students could pick their favorite time period and write their own traveling adventure. By studying the lifestyles, current events, and hardships of that period, students could identify and discuss the kinds of problems people at that time or place would have had to overcome, e.g., "If you were in your log cabin trapped by an angry bear, what would you do?" or "If you were in a wagon train under attack, how would you get away?" By picking a period in American history—perhaps by lottery or with a partner in a project for pairs—they can do background reading in reference books, historical fiction, and nonfiction in order to become sufficiently "expert" to create believable stories.   D.M.A.

Language Arts,
Social Studies
Primary
Intermediate
Middle School

180.   Lord, Bette Bao. *In the Year of the Boar and Jackie Robinson*. Illustrated by Marc Simont. Harper & Row, 1984. ISBN 0-06-024003-2, $9.89. Ages 8-12.

In 1947 Shirley Temple Wong and her mother arrive in Brooklyn, N.Y., to join Mr. Wong, who immigrated earlier to establish a home for his Chinese wife and daughter. Shirley's adjustment to a foreign country—to a new neighborhood and school, to a new language, and to new customs—makes a poignant and often humorous story, reflecting the experience of any child who moves to a new house or neighbor-hood. It could be the story of any immigrant child, yet Shirley Temple Wong is Chinese and her thinking and outlook are bound to her old world traditions and beliefs. The author, who is wife of the American ambassador to China and herself a Chinese immigrant, captures perfectly the joys, frustrations, and fears of Shirley's ultimate triumph in this remarkable book for middle graders.

The study of immigration can be fascinating to upper elementary students. There are scores of books that focus on different immigrant experiences, e.g., Clifton's *All Us Come Cross the Water* (Holt Rinehart and Winston, 1973), Vineberg's *Grandmother Came from Dworitz* (Tundra, 1969), and the "Coming to America" series published by Delacorte. Yep's *Mountain Light* (Harper & Row, 1985), which tells of Chinese immigration at the turn of the century, might be useful to compare with the story of Shirley Temple Wong. The

ALA Notable Book

Asian-American Studies,
Multicultural Studies
Intermediate
Middle School

Related Sources

topic could be easily extended to the study of each student's family history of immigration. Fourth or fifth grade is not too soon to start.   H.M.

181.   Lowry, Lois. *Anastasia has the Answers*. Houghton Mifflin, 1986. ISBN 0-395-41795-3, $12.95. Ages 9-12.

Sixth in Lowry's Anastasia series

Picture Anastasia wearing a royal blue gym suit, unsuccessfully trying to climb a rope while being observed by all her classmates and her favorite teacher. This is one of the embarrassing dilemmas that faces Anastasia in her sixth adventure. Interspersed with the challenge of learning to climb the elusive rope, Anastasia attacks each of her "problems" as a journalist would approach an article—using who, what, why, when, and where to examine each situation. Lowry also provides Anastasia's first and final drafts of these fantasized newspaper articles. Needless to say, the rope climb is accomplished, but how, where, when, and why it occurs must be read to be appreciated.

Social Studies, Language Arts Intermediate Middle School

Related Source

Many children will be able to relate Anastasia's plight with the rope to a challenge that they have faced in their own lives. They can discuss their situation and solution, comparing it to Anastasia's. This is an excellent opportunity to introduce children to the "Kids Did It" feature in *National Geographic World* which reports on children's unusual achievements. Students may want write their own "Kids Did It" article describing a success story about themselves—an achievement they have truly experienced or one they would like to reach.   B.C.

182.   Lowry, Lois. *Rabble Starkey*. Houghton Mifflin, 1987. ISBN 0-395-42607-9, $12.95. Ages 10-up.

In this heart-warming story set in a small Appalachian town, twelve-year-old Rabble Starkey, given the Biblical name Parable Ann to stave off trouble, has had her share. She and her mother were deserted by her father when Rabble was one month old and her mother only fourteen. Life has been hard, but things change when Rabble's best friend's mother becomes mentally incapacitated and the Starkeys move in with the Bigelows: Veronica, her little brother Gunther, and Mr. Bigelow. Rabble's mother assumes the role of Mrs. Bigelow and, to Rabble and the Bigelows, something like a family is formed. That year their lives are changed forever. Lowry's characters are realistic and readers are made to care deeply about them in this story about the nature of families and the value of growth, change, and love.

Language Arts Intermediate Middle School

In chapter six, Rabble's teacher introduces her students to a thesaurus and a wealth of words and a love of language open up to Rabble. After reading this chapter aloud, discuss ways they can improve their writing by avoiding the repeated use of the same words or phrases. Students can be challenged to rewrite a paragraph replacing some of the words with others from their thesaurus. Urge students to continue to find interesting new words to spice up their written work.   J.P.

183. MacLachlan, Patricia. *The Facts and Fictions of Minna Pratt*. Harper & Row, 1988. ISBN 0-06-024117-9, $11.89. Ages 8-12.

Minna is a budding cellist in search of her vibrato. Her mother is an author of children's books in pursuit of truth. As Minna's friendship with fellow musician Lucas grows, she can't help comparing his orderly, fact-filled life to the random chaos of her own. She wishes her mother would concentrate less on the notes she tacks above her typewrite, e.g., "Facts and fictions are different truths." and more on cooking, cleaning, and laundry. However, as Minna grows to learn more about Lucas's family, her mother, and herself, she better understands that truth is often more valuable than fact. Through Minna and her off-beat family, MacLachlan has created characters that should be especially appealing to students wrestling with intellectual dilemmas of their own.

Minna's mother was inspired as a writer by the thought-provoking quotes she collected. By providing a bulletin board and a stack of index cards for students, they can display quotes, thoughts-for-the-day, and ideas they find interesting. Sources like Bartlett's *Familiar Quotations* (Citadel Press, 1983) and Byrne's *Six Hundred Thirty-Seven Best Things Anybody Ever Said* (Fawcett, 1985) are useful additions to the classroom library. During time set aside for journal writing, give students the opportunity to respond to the posted quotes that cause them to think in new ways. Occasionally give students the opportunity to share their ideas and questions in a whole class discussion. K.L.M.

ALA Notable Book

*Language Arts
Intermediate
Middle School*

Related Sources

184. MacLachlan, Patricia. *Sarah, Plain and Tall*. Harper & Row, 1985. ISBN 0-06-024102-0, $8.89. Ages 8-10.

In this beautifully crafted brief story, Patricia MacLachlan sketches a portrait of a motherless prairie pioneer family and Sarah, who comes to join them as a mail-order bride from Maine. It is daughter Anna who remembers the songs which filled the house before her mother's death and she is delighted when Sarah writes, "Tell them I sing." She and the younger Caleb anxiously try to make Sarah welcome. Just as important as the authenticity of the story is MacLachlan's art of fully developing her characters in a direct and uncluttered style, which is at the heart of her work. This 1986 Newbery Award book is a gentle, touching picture of early prairie life.

Not only is *Sarah, Plain and Tall* an extraordinarily fine example of creative writing, but it also can be easily tied in with social studies units that focus on 19th century settlement in America's heartland. There have been a number of excellent companion books published recently, both fiction and nonfiction, that could make up a core of readings for such a curricular focus. Among them are Anderson's *Christmas on the Prairie* (Clarion, 1988); Freedman's *Children of the Wild West* (Clarion, 1983); George's *One Day in the Prairie* (Crowell, 1986); and Harvey's *My Prairie Year: Based On the Diary of*

*Newbery Award Winner
ALA Notable Book*

*U.S. History
Intermediate
Middle School*

Related Sources

Elenore Plaisted (Holiday House, 1986). This is also an appropriate opportunity to reintroduce Wilder's *Little House on the Prairie* (1935) and *Little Town on the Prairie* (1941) both published by Harper & Row.   B.S.J.

185.   Mark, Michael. *Toba*. Bradbury, 1984. ISBN 0-02-762300-9, $10.95. Ages 9-12.

Toba is a collection of nine quiet, finely drawn vignettes that illuminate the everyday life of the family of a loving, blind Jewish tailor in Poland just before World War I. Through Michael Mark's perceptive characterizations, readers can experience Toba's joys, her fears, and her dreams in such a way that they can sense the differences between then and now, between there and here. *Toba* will become special to those sensitive readers who grasp the timeless truths of these gentle stories and are moved by Michael Mark's rapport with the feelings of children and the universality of human experience.

Language Arts
Intermediate
Middle School
Junior High School

This is an excellent book to begin helping children become more sensitive to their emotions and their responses to the familiar people and events in their everyday lives. The stories, which can and should be read aloud, will help children to understand that in the day-to-day there can often be found deep, personal meanings. As a writing exercise, students may choose to focus their writing on a brief, "small" episode or human characteristic and enlarge upon the moment or trait as deeply as possible. They may also select from their outside reading an episode or character description to share aloud with the class.   H.M.

186.   McHugh, Elisabet. *Beethoven's Cat*. Illustrated by Anita Riggio. Atheneum, 1988. ISBN 0-689-31364-0, $12.95. Ages 8-12.

Beethoven's Cat is a successful and entertaining personification of a typical house cat who is obsessed with the possibility of being a direct descendent of Ludwig van Beethoven's pet cat, Ludwig. Wiggy's obsession transforms him from a lovable, lackadaisical, obese cat into a self-centered, arrogant feline bent upon eating only fresh fish, just as Beethoven's cat had. McHugh's readers may find it difficult to keep from chuckling as they encounter page after page of dry humor as Wiggy comes to grips with his problem by seeking the advice of a veterinarian psychiatrist.

Social Studies, Science,
Language Arts
Primary
Intermediate

Reading *Beethoven's Cat* could be an appealing introduction to an integrated science and social studies activity. Students could choose a famous person and select an animal that they think would have made a good pet for that person. Then after researching both the person and the animal, students could develop a story from the characteristics of both. Students might also develop a story told completely in dialogue that would reflect the pet's personality and illustrate several humorous incidents taken from observations in real life.   A.M.B.

187.   Naylor, Phyllis Reynolds and Lura Schield Reynolds. *Maudie In The Middle*. Illustrated by Judith Gwyn Brown. Atheneum, 1988. ISBN 0-689-31395-0, $13.95. Ages 7-11.

Eight-year-old Maudie decides that the only way a middle child in a family of seven can be noticed is to go about the business of being good. She discovers this is not easy, since one bad action can cause her parents to forget all the good she accomplishes. Readers will empathize with Maudie's struggle for attention that sometimes seems unattainable. At the same time they can applaud the never-give-up attitude that leads to her eventual personal satisfaction. Naylor's portrayal of a young girl's honesty in dealing with her many feelings makes this book a worthwhile addition to all libraries.

As a follow-up to exploring Maudie's insecure feelings, a personal inventory might be developed by each student. On a sheet of paper, children can record to whom they are special and why. This list may include friends, family members, and/or people in the community who may be dependent upon them. When this list is completed, they may want to share it with a small group or with the whole class, giving others a chance to consider and evaluate relationships they may not have thought about when preparing their own list.   J.T./A.M.M.

Social Studies
Primary
Intermediate

188.   Newman, Robert. *The Case of the Watching Boy*. Atheneum, 1987. ISBN 0-689-31317-9, $12.95. Ages 8-12.

Andrew Tillett, boy detective, is back. This time he is asked to do a little undercover work for the headmaster of his school. Of course, this turns out to be far more complex than simply watching a schoolmate who has been acting strangely. Suddenly, Andrew finds himself in the middle of a kidnapping and international intrigue. As he did in his other Andrew Tillett mysteries, Robert Newman writes with clarity without giving away too much of the mystery too soon. His characterizations are a special strength: each book is full of a variety of well-delineated villains, scoundrels, innocents, and eccentrics.

Seventh in Newman's
Andrew Tillett mysteries

The turn-of-the-century London setting is vividly brought to life by Robert Newman in the seven books of his Andrew Tillett series, partly because he uses authentic names of London streets, shops, and hotels. An interesting project might be for small groups to read one of the books and then trace the action in it on a large street map of London. A local travel agent might be able to supply the map as well as some descriptive travel brochures that would help children visualize the setting. A single map could be placed upon a bulletin board and different colored yarn could be tacked up to trace each mystery. Pictures from the travel brochures could also be displayed to identify locations in the book(s) in which they appear. These might encourage readers to learn more about London at the turn of the century, as well as read other books in Newman's series. Both may lay the groundwork for enjoying Sherlock Holmes mysteries as they get older.   M.A.C.

Social Studies
Intermediate
Middle School

Related Source

189.   Paterson, Katherine. *Come Sing, Jimmy Jo*. Dutton, 1985. ISBN 0-525-67167-6, $12.95. Ages 9-12.

ALA Notable Book

Paterson has created a near-perfect blending of theme, character, and place in this story of an Appalachian family. The Johnsons are all country singers who reach the "big-time" chiefly on the merits of eleven-year-old Jimmy's talent. Deeply attached to his grandma who taught him what he knows about singing, Jimmy leaves her to join the tour with the rest of the family. He must overcome his fear of crowds and cope with hordes of admirers. More importantly, he is forced to explore his feelings about his daddy, a competitive mother, a "real" father, and a variety of school friends. Paterson examines varying capacities of human beings to offer love and friendship. Compassion overflows in her telling as she builds an understanding of emotional ties that goes beyond blood and color of skin. The Appalachian setting created by Paterson is one of the best in children's literature.

Music,
Social Studies,
Language Arts
Intermediate
Middle School
Junior High School

Paterson has given us a sense of the "roots" of country music as well as of the hard work and chance which lead to success as a performer. Music fans and/or critics could profit from the picture portrayed here. The underlying theme of human gifts to be shared with others suggests multi-dimensional analyses. Thus, this book would be good to read to a class at Christmas time or at some other "giving" time of the year to stimulate substantive activities and discussion of gifts of the heart and person.   A.P.N.

190.   Paterson, Katherine. *Park's Quest*. Lodestar, 1988. ISBN 0-525-67258-3, $12.95. Ages 10-up.

More than anything, eleven-year-old Parkington Waddell Broughton the Fifth wanted to know about the man whose name he carried. But Park's mother was strangely silent about her husband and his death in Vietnam. Park's quest for answers to a myriad of questions led him to the Vietnam War Memorial and, ultimately, to his grandfather's farm. Paterson's engaging story, interspersed with parallel scenes from Knights of the Round Table adventures, presents the difficult subject of Vietnam veterans fathering racially-mixed children. However, Park's easy acceptance of the discovery that his uncle's Vietnamese stepsister, to whom Park has been referring as "geek," is actually his half-sister lacks the shock and pain that such a discovery would seem likely to cause most children.

Language Arts,
Literature,
Social Studies
Intermediate
Middle School
Junior High School

Related Sources

This book may be effective to stimulate thinking about personal quests among intermediate graders. You can begin by creating a learning center entitled "Quests," which might include pictures of the Vietnam War Memorial, racially-mixed children, and Knights of the Round Table pictures and posters. Include books on the war, such as Hauptly's *In Vietnam* (Atheneum, 1985), which includes a useful bibliography of additional, as well as books on King Arthur and the quest for the Holy Grail—Sutcliff's *The Sword and the Stone* (Dutton, 1981) would be excellent for this purpose. Students could discuss the nature and purpose of quests, create original quest tales, and discuss contemporary quests—even list the kinds of individual quests they realistically would like to undertake that year or by some point in their lives.   L.B.

191.   Pendergraft, Patricia. *Miracle at Clements' Pond*. Philomel, 1987. ISBN 0-399-21438-0, $13.95. Ages 10-up.

Few first time authors write with the decisiveness of style and meticulous plot structure as Patricia Pendergraft has in her story of three children who find an abandoned baby and place it on the porch of the kindly town spinster. Thirteen-year-old Lyon and his friends live in fear that the baby's real mother will reappear, the spinster will lose her "gift from God," and they will be caught by J. Edgar Hoover's FBI. But this is only part of Lyon's problem. His loving but frequently absent father has returned, and Lyon finds the prospect of another separation more painful than the last. Pendergraft's characters are completely believable as the small town kids caught between childhood fantasies and the realities of growing up. Her story is fast-paced, and even the most reluctant reader will find it hard to resist her style of writing and her portrayal of such a touching subject.

"'Iffen you been out froggin' in this weather, I've been out callin' hogs!' Aunt Esther blasted in my face..." Dialect like this is skillfully used by Pendergraft to delineate her characters. The expressions used by the characters and the descriptions of events and characters by Lyon, the young first person narrator, are charming and add comic relief to a serious subject. Students might enjoy leafing through the book to find their favorite examples of this. These can be listed on the chalkboard and discussed in terms of meaning and how they add color and authenticity to the story. Regional expressions and colloquialisms can be discovered in a good thesaurus. Finally, students can rewrite a bland passage supplied by the teacher and bring it to life through the judicious use of authentic dialect or local idioms.   L.A.B.

*Language Arts
Intermediate
Middle School
Junior High School*

192.   Pinkwater, Daniel. *The Moosepire*. Illustrated by the author. Little, Brown, 1986. ISBN 0-316-70811-9, $12.95. Ages 8-12.

The Moosepire is Daniel Pinkwater's third book about the Blue Moose. This one opens with a hilarious interview between Pinkwater himself and Sir Charles Pacamac, the World's Champion Samovar Crasher and stereotypic crusty English gentleman. It seems that the Blue Moose solved the riddle of the Moosepire who was terrorizing the isolated town of Yellowtooth, and Sir Charles never bothered to find out what happened. Thus Pinkwater journeys north to find out for himself. He discovers the Blue Moose's notes in the public library and what follows is that account. The book is short, fast-paced, and likely to bring a giggle—and a tantalizing puzzle: how did pictures of the Blue Moose that were just taken happen to be the ones that started his whole investigation? The answer is as outrageous as Pinkwater himself!

Why not have a Daniel Pinkwater Festival in the school library?

Young fans could create posters from his zany illustrations or from scenes in his books. A short biography could be researched and posted for all those who wonder about the man behind the humor. "Pinkwater Performances" could include readings and skits selected from his books or written by the students as further adventures. A report of the activities would surely be appreciated by Pinkwater himself, who can be contacted through his publisher, Little, Brown & Company, 34 Beacon Street, Boston, MA 02106.   M.A.C.

193.   Pollack, Pamela, compiler. *The Random House Book of Humor*. Illustrated by Paul O. Zelinsky. Random House, 1988. ISBN 0-394-98049-2, $14.99. Ages 7-11.

What could be more fun than compiling the best laughs in children's literature? Pollack has gathered a history of humor to do just that, including such great authors as Mark Twain, E. Nesbit, and Beverly Cleary, to name but a few! The thirty-four selections, most excerpts from longer works, succeed in balancing the classic with the contemporary. Though the collection seems to get off to a slow start, it is arguably a book for picking and choosing, not necessarily meant to be read cover to cover. Additionally, Zelinsky's zany black and white pencil illustrations enhance the humor and add cohesiveness to the array of selections. Though not everyone may agree on what is humorous, all are likely to get some giggles indulging in the stories.

Because humor is a matter of personal taste, students are likely to think of favorite funny pieces that Pollack overlooked. After sharing selections with the class, ask each of them to bring in a short story or chapter to add to a classroom book of humor. Transcribing their selections would provide a great opportunity to develop word processing skills on the school computers. Fill a three-ring notebook with their choices and have students design a cover. During the extra minutes that often occur during the school day share selections from both "Books of Humor" with the class.   K.L.M.

194.   Rappaport, Doreen. *The Boston Coffee Party*. Illustrated by Emily Arnold McCully. Harper & Row, 1988. ISBN 0-06-024825-4, $10.89. Ages 4-8.

In 17th century Boston, not only was tea scarce, coffee, too, was precious. In a twist on the legendary Boston Tea Party, Rappaport shapes an authentic account into an entertaining and feminist story of the women of Boston taking just action against a greedy merchant who has "locked up 40 barrels of coffee in his warehouse," waiting for prices to rise. Abandoning their army sewing, women and girls devise and carry out an effective plan to "relieve" Mechant Thomas of his coffee. This "I Can Read" book is an engaging, humorous, and suspenseful story presented through the eyes of young Sarah and her little sister, Emily. McCully's watercolors detail much of Boston's everyday life, from gathering eggs to making jam. The last page includes a quotation from one of Abigail Adams' letters to John Adams describing this historical event.

The wealth of detail, both in the text and in the illustrations, suggests a myriad of investigations into home life in Colonial America: cooking, sewing, games, caring for animals, shopping, and other everyday activities. Ann McGovern's *If You Lived in Colonial Times* (Four Winds, 1964) and Jean Fritz's *Why Don't You Get a Horse, Sam Adams?* (Coward, 1974) and *And Then What Happened, Paul Revere?* (Coward, 1973) provide accurate views of Boston during the Revolutionary War era. Children should be encouraged to compare life then and now through these and other appealing nonfiction works for primary grades. Miriam Bourne's fictional *Nabby Adams' Diary* (Coward, 1975) offers a child's point of view about that same historical time and place.   B.B.

*U.S. History
Primary
Intermediate*

Related Sources

195. Rappaport, Doreen. *Trouble at the Mines*. Illustrated by Joan Sandin. Crowell, 1987. ISBN 0-690-04446-1, $10.89. Ages 8-12.

At the turn of the century, many mine workers endured much suffering during their attempts to unionize. The story of such a strike and the leadership of the union organizer "Mother Jones" is presented from the perspective of the miners' wives and daughters in *Trouble at the Mines*. This short, illustrated work, using the techniques of fictionalized history, portrays the realities of management tactics, such as evictions from company housing, as well as the anguish of families torn apart over whether to be a scab or to strike.

There are alternatives to round robin reading of the basal social studies textbook that are both manageable and educationally sound. One alternative involves the use of trade books that are historically accurate, that deal with significant social/political events, and that are appropriate to be read aloud. This is one of those books with characters who effectively teach children an important aspect of what they need to know to be "culturally literate" about early attempts to unionize.   J.F.A.

*Social Studies
Intermediate
Middle School*

196. Richler, Mordecai. *Jacob Two-Two and the Dinosaur*. Illustrated by Norman Eyolfson. Knopf, 1987. ISBN 0-394-98704-7, $10.99. Ages 6-10.

Jacob Two-Two, the boy who has to say everything twice to be heard by his large family and who previously grappled with the Hooded Fang, is back. This time it is Dippy, a real live (and not very bright) Diplodocus, who challenges Jacob Two-Two's creative energies. Professor Wacko Kilowatt and Canadian Prime Minister Perry Pleaser are the new adversaries: they are out to exterminate Dippy so that Pleaser can become a national hero. It is up to Jacob Two-Two to escort Dippy to safety (and, hopefully, a mate) in the Rocky Mountains of British Columbia. Richler's writing is fast-paced and pokes fun at everything. It is also full of kid-appealing earthy humor. This is likely to

*Second in Richler's
Jacob Two-Two series*

become a real favorite with the lower elementary grade readers.

Students might enjoy tracing Dippy's and Jacob Two-Two's path as they make their way across Canada. Straight pins, some yarn, and a National Geographic map of the country would be ideal for this purpose. They can then learn as much as they can about the Canadian Rockies, and discuss whether this area is remote enough for Dippy to hide himself from civilization. The journey across Canada is reminscent of Sheila Burnford's classic *The Incredible Journey* (Little, Brown, 1965); though the characters and the route are quite different, Burnford's realistic animal adventure may be an excellent follow-up book for those seeking more serious reading.   M.A.C.

197.   Roberts, Willo Davis. *Sugar Isn't Everything*. Atheneum, 1987. ISBN 0-689-31316-0, $12.95. Ages 9-up.

Amy had never heard of diabetes. Her craving for sweets, fluids—anything edible—led to weight loss, headaches, and eventual collapse. A supportive family experienced grief, anger, and then acceptance of Amy's condition. Learning to cope with and to continually monitor blood-sugar levels, making strict dietary changes, plus educating family and friends was almost more than she could handle. Meeting other diabetics and seeing how people in her life cared about helping her gave Amy new strength. This appealing and thought-provoking book informs young people of the very real aspects of diabetes, perhaps made more real by the author's insights as a diabetic.

This book is excellent for a science or health unit on diabetes. The glossary and the material from the fifteenth chapter on anger and adolescents' reactions can be reproduced. This provides an instructional base for discussing the disease, its symptoms, and normal reactions when people discover it is a lifetime condition. A speaker from the American Diabetes Association (1-800-ADA-DISC) will provide further information and answers to students' questions. Finally, a film, such as "Josh" or "No Sugar Coating" would be an appropriate conclusion of the study. For further information, students and teachers can contact the American Diabetes Association, Inc., National Service Center, 1660 Duke Street, Alexandria, VA 22314).   R.M.K.

198.   Rocklin, Joanne. *Dear Baby*. Illustrated by Eileen McKeating. Macmillan, 1988. ISBN 0-02-777320-5, $12.95. Ages 8-12.

Farla is in the sixth grade when her mother announces that she and her new husband, Charlie, are going to have a baby. Farla experiences tumultuous and conflicting emotions about this event. Her mother and her sixth grade teacher suggest that she write letters to the unborn baby to express her feelings. Farla's letters sound like a journal as she tells the baby about the happenings in her life. She also tells the baby how it is developing according to a book her mother got her and how Charlie is coming with the photographic ABC's he is making for the nursery.

Social Studies
Primary
Intermediate

Related Source

Health Education
Intermediate
Middle School
Junior High School

Related Source

Rocklin, who is a clinical psychologist, is attuned to the concerns of a typical sixth-grader who is undergoing some family change. Through Farla's story, she suggests an effective therapy for such children that they can easily emulate. Farla's changing attitude toward the baby is heartwarming and suggests that, even though life brings changes, things have a way of working out.

For those teachers who encourage students to keep journals, this book suggests a new twist: making the journal in letter form. Because letters are written *to* people, children are more directed in their writing than if they are simply asked to write down their thoughts or chronicle their day. To start students off in this venture, make blank books as a class project. Use beautiful fabric remnants or scraps sent from home for the covers. Hand sew the pages together. Glue the cover material to cardboard that has been cut slightly larger that the open pages. Attach the pages to the cover by centering them in the cover and gluing the end pages down.   M.A.C.

Language Arts
Intermediate
Middle School

199.   Rylant, Cynthia. *A Fine White Dust*. Bradbury, 1986. ISBN 0-02-777240-3, $11.95. Ages 11-13.

Pete came under the spell of the Preacher Man in the summer of his thirteenth year. His submission was so complete that he prepared to leave the love and security of his home and friends to go on the road with this man who changed his life so completely in a few short days. Pete's search for religious meaning in his "ordinary" life is movingly and sensitively portrayed. Cynthia Rylant proves why she is one of today's finest writers of poetry, short stories, picture story books, and short novels for young people. In *A Fine White Dust* she combines an understanding of human emotions and a gift for clarity and imagery in her writing to create her most evocative work.

Newbery Honor Book
ALA Best Book

Religious questioning and indecision has been the subject of many books for middle grade readers. Suzanne Newton's *I Will Call It Georgie's Blues* (Viking, 1983) is among the most powerful in exploring the turmoil within the family of a minister. Lost amid extraneous controversy is the central question of religious identity by a young girl in Judy Blume's *Are You There God? It's Me, Margaret* (Bradbury, 1970). Louise Fitzhugh's *The Long Secret* (Harper & Row, 1965) should also be included in any list of such books for study and discussion by middle grade readers.   H.M.

Social Studies
Intermediate
Middle School
Junior High School

Related Sources

200.   Sanders, Scott R. *Hear the Wind Blow*. Illustrated by Ponder Goembel. Bradbury, 1985. ISBN 0-02-778140-2, $14.95. Ages 10-up.

Many of us hear or sing a traditional ballad such as "John Henry," "Frog Went A-Courtin'," or "Sweet Betsy from Pike" and imagine a story behind the verses of it. Academician-folk singer-story-teller Scott Sanders imagined such stories and wrote about 20 of America's best-loved traditional ballads in this witty, fresh, and entertaining collection of stories to read aloud (or learn to tell). Sanders's stories are filled with action, outlandish characters, and enough exaggeration and hyperbole to tickle the funny bone of the most hardened listener. Those wishing to sing the verses that are included will have to seek the music elsewhere— Alan Lomax's *Folk Songs of North America* (Doubleday, 1960) is a good place to begin.

Related Source

Music, Social Studies
Intermediate
Middle School
Junior High School

Related Source

Teachers would not be remiss for urging their students to try their hand at writing "the story behind the song." While popular songs occasionally have sufficient story line for this purpose, clearly the rich store of folk music is a more appropriate place to begin. There are dozens of collections of traditional ballads (with music) in every library with songs that easily parallel areas of study, especially topics in social studies and/or science; *Folk Song in the Classroom* (140 Hill Park Ave., Great Neck, NY 11021 [516-466-8546]) is an outstanding quarterly publication that would be invaluable for such projects. Sing the songs as a group, talk about how each might have originated, discuss the songs' characters, settings, and historical periods. Then share the different written versions that will inevitably result.   H.M.

201.   Schwartz, Alvin, compiler. *All Of Our Noses Are Here*. Illustrated by Karen Ann Weinhaus. Harper & Row, 1985. ISBN 0-06-025288-X, $9.89. Ages 4-8.

The silly Brown family is back in this collection of five easy-to-read noodle tales from around the world. In the title story, the family members are unable to count themselves correctly until they finally stick their noses into the mud and then count the holes. Children will chuckle over the jokes and enjoy being smarter than the noodles. The humorous and gentle pictures complement the simple text perfectly. This is an excellent book to encourage independent reading by even the most reluctant reader.

Related Source

Literature,
Social Studies
Primary
Intermediate

Related Sources

This book and Schwartz's *There is a Carrot in My Ear* (Harper & Row, 1982) are fine introductions to American noodlehead tales in versions young children can read independently. Children may be interested to learn that stories of foolish folk exist in most oral traditions around the world. To compare these similarities of theme and characters in such stories, teachers may want to read aloud from *Noodles, Nitwits, and Numskulls* by Maria Leach (World, 1961) and *Noodlehead Stories From Around The World* by M.A. Jagendorf (Vanguard, 1957).   A.S.

203.   Schwartz, Alvin, compiler. *Fat Man in a Fur Coat and Other Bear Stories*. Illustrated by David Christiana. Farrar, Straus & Giroux, 1984. ISBN 0-374-32291-0, $10.95. Ages 8-up.

Alvin Schwartz is one of the busiest collectors of American folklore working today. Through his many well-researched and appealing collections of stories, rhymes, sayings, and superstitions, young people have discovered the richness and diversity of our oral tradition that remind us of our common social history and homegrown customs. **Fat Man in a Fur Coat** is a potpourri of fact and fiction, of stories real and legendary, about bears—and people. Each story is concisely and interestingly told in a style that encourages elaboration by a teacher–storyteller. The appendices include a description of the stories' sources and an extensive bibliography .

This is an excellent collection to read aloud: each selection averages less than five minutes in length and the emphasis is always on action. Many of the stories are perfect for storytelling, especially the section of tall tales titled "No Ordinary Bears." For a whole group project, the class might create their own compilation of stories centering around some theme (e.g., weather, the ocean, creation, etc). During the school year children can gather materials from a wide variety of sources, evaluate them, and select the best to be "published" as an anthology for the school library. Schwartz's book can serve as a model for this effort.   H.M.

Storytelling, Literature All Grades

202.   Schwartz, Alvin, compiler. *In a Dark, Dark Room and Other Scary Stories*. Illustrated by Dirk Zimmer. Harper & Row, 1984. ISBN 0-06-025274-X, $9.89. Ages 4-8.

Folklorist Alvin Schwartz has gathered seven well-known American folk tales and retold them for beginning readers in this attractive addition to Harper & Row's popular "I Can Read" series. The stories are mildly eerie and scary, though Dirk Zimmer's colorful illustrations give each an oddly humorous, not-to-be-taken-seriously quality. This is an excellent contribution to the growing body of fine "chapter books" for those just learning to read independently.

ALA Notable Book

These stories are excellent as a source for beginning storytellers: the versions are terse, permitting the teller to elaborate by adding details or modifying the story to fit the occasion or the teller's personality. For example, "The Night It Rained" is a version of the well-known "Vanishing Hitchhiker" tale that can be successfully adapted for older audiences or changed to fit a particular time or place. Try telling it as a first-person tale told about something that happened to you or to someone you know.   H.M.

Storytelling All Grades

204.   Seidler, Tor. *A Rat's Tale*. Illustrated by Fred Marcellino. Farrar, Straus & Giroux, 1986. ISBN 0-374-36185-1, $12.95. Ages 9-12.

Tor Seidler, acclaimed for **Terpin** (Farrar, Straus and Giroux, 1982), has created a memorable hero in Montague Mad-Rat who will join Stuart Little, Ralph, and other favorite literary rodents as a rat to admire. Montague's Central Park family is shunned by respectable rat society because they work with their paws and actually have contact with humans. Uncle Mooney sells his engraved gold rings to an art dealer, and it is that connection that Montague uses to save the high-

Related Source

society wharf rats and his new love, Isabel Moberly-Rat, from extinction. His heroism wins him respect, Isabel, acclaim for his own art work, and, most importantly, self-recognition of his own worth as a rat of value. This whimsical, gently humorous story, strongly evocative of New York City, is elegantly enhanced by Marcellino's tongue-in-cheek pencil illustrations. The fast moving plot should keep readers involved to the last page.

Literature,
Social Studies
Intermediate
Middle School

This is a story of values to be explored by intermediate readers: honest work and self-expression vs. mere acquisition of objects to create a "rich and famous" image. The tight plot with its quirky turns could be analyzed for its story structure. Companion books to compare for themes and characters might include George Selden's *The Cricket in Times Square* (Farrar, Straus & Giroux, 1960), William Steig's *Abel's Island* (Farrar, Straus & Giroux, 1976) and E.B. White's *Stuart Little* (Harper & Row, 1945).   B.B.

Related Sources

205.   Service, Pamela F. *The Reluctant God*. Atheneum, 1988. ISBN 0-689-31404-3, $13.95. Ages 9-13.

As a young teen, Lorna prefers digging in ancient Egyptian ruins with her archeologist father to anything else. Always ready to imagine and speculate about what she finds, her mind wanders back to the ancient peoples and their culture, the divine rights of their kings, and the absolute power of their gods. When she discovers an ancient royal tomb, her life is transformed into a different time and place for this adventure tale when she meets a prince who has been entombed in a state of suspended animation for 4,000 years! Service's well-written and imaginative story has plenty of action and builds upon the theme of the existence and immortality of the gods of all peoples and all cultures.

Ancient History,
Language Arts
Intermediate
Middle School
Junior High School

The Reluctant God will add life to classes or units on ancient history, especially the study of ancient Egypt. Here is an opportunity to nurture children's natural curiosity about hieroglyphics. Provide each student with a "stone tablet" (clay that will harden). Encourage them to write their individual names and create personal messages in the "secret code" of hieroglyphics. Stolz's *Zekmet, The Stone Carver* (Harcourt Brace Jovanovich, 1988) is a good companion book that illustrates the use and meaning of some hieroglyphics.   S.J.S.

Related Source

206.   Shannon, George. *Stories to Solve: Folktales from Around the World*. Illustrated by Peter Sis. Greenwillow, 1985. ISBN 0-688-04303-8, $11.75. Ages 8-10.

This is an anthology of fourteen riddle-mysteries collected from various cultures, including Germany (the Grimms' "Three Rosebushes"), fables from Aesop ("A Drink for the Cow"), and tales of King Solomon ("Two Mothers" and "Which Flower"). Most of the riddles are one or two pages long with the solution immediately following. Each provides children with a provocative problem to think about and attempt to solve. Peter Sis's black and white pointillistic illustrations help younger readers visualize the problems.

Children who enjoy reading Sobol's Encyclopedia Brown mysteries may look forward to this book as well, and for the same reasons. These folktale "riddles" are good brain teasers requiring careful observation and logic. Further, each could be used as an attention-grabber at the beginning of the day or period to get the class settled and thinking, especially in a math class where sequential thinking, logic, and verbal discrimination are needed. Thoughtful choice of an individual story may lead directly in to the lesson. *Unriddling* by Alvin Schwartz (Lippincott, 1983) contains more of this type of material and can also be used in the same way.   H.M.

*Math, Science,
Language Arts
Primary
Intermediate*

Related Source

207. Sharmat, Marjorie Weinman. *Nate the Great Stalks Stupidweed*. Illustrated by Marc Simont. Putnam, 1986. ISBN 0-698-202-6, $10.95. Ages 6-9.

Can you spare a nickel? Did you say, " Yes?" Well, step right up and buy a superweed—complete with a certificate of ownership and money back guarantee. Oliver bought his weed from Rosamond, but the mystery begins when this super specimen disappears. Never fear! Oliver engages Nate the Great (super detective) and his trusty pup Sludge to root out this riddle! Marjorie Sharmat's story line, vocabulary, and style make this a backyard adventure beginning readers should find enjoyable. Yellow and green chalk drawings by Marc Simont match the mood and humorous tone set by Sharmat. Story and illustrations work in tandem to deliver chuckles in this well-paced, primary "who-dun-it."

Not many kids are willing to pay a nickel to adopt their own weed, especially because there are so many growing in the backyard which are absolutely free. Whether a plant should be called a weed or a wild flower often depends on the use we make of it. An inexpensive illustration of "one man's trash is another man's treasure" could use dandelions, small flower pots, and potting soil. Children could then transplant spring dandelions from their school yard into individual pots. A card accompanying the plant might say "Spectacular Secret Salad Ingredient" and include a simple recipe for tossed salad using clean, snipped dandelion greens. A simple salad dressing recipe might be printed by the children and included with this dandy gift, completing the simple Mother's Day present to Mom or Grandmother.   G.G.

*Science, Language Arts
Primary
Intermediate*

208. Singer, Marilyn. *Where There's a Will, There's a Wag*. Illustrated by Andrew Glass. Henry Holt, 1986. ISBN 0-03-005747-7, $11.95. Ages 9-12.

The story of our heroine, Sam Spayed, a talking dog who is more intelligent than her master, is a humorous imitation of the early radio detective shows of the 1940's. Sam's not so bright master, the detective Philip Barlowe, blunders into comical mystery situations in which Sam must use her superior dog-powers to effect a rescue and solve the mystery. This episode involves a cat named Snoogums who has inherited an estate of twenty million dollars and a larcenous nephew who wants control of the money. Only Sam has the necessary experience and know-how to unravel the mystery.

Drama, Music,
Reader's Theater
Intermediate
Middle School

Using the style of early radio detective shows as is suggested by the book, students could divide into groups and write their own scripts for a radio show. When the scripts are completed, the students could devise sound effects, assign parts, and produce a tape recording of their show. The tape then could be played for the rest of the class. An alternative could be a performance of the radio show as if it were being taped in a studio. Old recordings of radio detective shows could be researched and listened to before beginning this project.   R.M.G.

209.   Smith, Doris Buchanan. *Return to Bitter Creek*. Viking Kestrel, 1986. ISBN 0-670-80783-4, $11.95. Ages 8-12.

ALA Notable Book

Lacey is leaving Colorado and going home to a place she had never known. When she was a baby, her unwed mother fled from their Appalachian mountain home to avoid having Lacey become the legal ward of her domineering maternal grandmother. Lacey is twelve now, and her mother's boyfriend has taken a job at Bitter Creek, the very place Lacey's mother left. The characterizations in this novel are strong and fully developed, portraying vividly the people who want the young girl's love: a possessive grandmother; a cousin who is thoroughly indoctrinated by the grandmother; David, her mother's blacksmith boyfriend, who wants to "meld" the family together again; and Lacey's mother, torn between running away from conflict and standing up for her family. The descriptions of the mountain setting show how closely related prose and poetry can be.

Art, Math
Primary
Intermediate
Middle School

Mountain crafts are central to Lacey's life: David is a blacksmith, her mother makes things from leather, and her grandmother quilts. Young people who are accustomed to buying blankets in a store may be fascinated by traditional crafts like quilting. Making a quilt can be a lot of fun and easier than it may seem. From a book or a guest speaker from a local quilting group students can learn about patterns and materials and choose a favorite design. Integrate math skills by having the children calculate how much material is needed to make the chosen pattern. Discuss what complex shapes of material are used in the pattern and how many of each shape they would have to make to produce a certain size quilt. The quilt can be made of scraps from home or from home economics classes. The finished quilt can be donated to the school for display or sold at a school fund raising event.   J.J.S.

210.   Snyder, Carol. *Ike and Mama and the Seven Surprises*. Illustrated by Charles Robinson. Lothrop, Lee & Shepard, 1985. ISBN 0-688-03732-1. $11.75. Ages 8-13.

Fifth in Snyder's
Ike and Mama series

Twelve-year-old Ike Greenberg, soon to have his Bar Mitzvah, rescues a stray dog from certain death. When his Mama learns of his deed, she tells him a saying her mama from Russia once told her: "Such a deed would bring seven surprises before sundown on the day you are a man, some of the surprises you will get, some you will give." Ike listens in disbelief, all the while wondering how so many wonderful things could happen within the next five weeks. The most wonderful surprise that Ike could wish for would be for his ill father to attend his Bar Mitzvah. Deep in his heart he knows his father will never recover in time. The story of Ike and the days leading to his Bar Mitzvah is so extremely well-written, with finely-developed characters and dialogue, that it is easy for the reader to become immersed in the lives of Ike and his family. Snyder has artistically created a story that exudes family traditions, devotion, unity, and love.

This book serves as a valuable basis for the discussion of the Bar Mitzvah. With many Jewish traditions and customs surrounding the Bar Mitzvah, a rabbi from a local synagogue could be asked to speak to the class and explain this important day; a student who has had, or is about to have, his Bar Mitzvah may retell his experiences. Students may be interested in the author's other Ike and Mama books including *Ike and Mama and Trouble at School* (1983) and *Ike and Mama and the Block Wedding* (1979), published by Lothrop, Lee & Shepard.   C.G.T.

*Jewish-American Studies
Primary
Intermediate
Middle School*

Related Sources

211.   Stolz, Mary. *The Explorer of Barkham Street*. Harper & Row, 1985. ISBN 0-07-025976-0, $9.89. Ages 9-11.

There's no justice! If it wasn't for daydreaming and true-life adventure books, the big gray rut which makes up Martin Hasting's existence would swallow him alive. Very enjoyable and thoughtfully written, this book chronicles a young boy's climb from his infamous days as "the Bully of Barkham Street" to the respect and friendship of neighbors and kids his own age. All Marty asks is a chance to prove himself to his family and, most importantly, to himself. Though he longs to be an explorer, he learns that by proving himself in small ways, greater adventure and self-confidence are within his grasp. The author gives a sensitive portrayal of Marty's character. Other titles in Stolz's "Barkham Street" series include *A Dog on Barkham Street* (Harper & Row, 1960) and *The Bully of Barkham Street* (Harper & Row, 1963).

*Third in Stolz's
Barkham Street series*

The conquest of Antarctica and the heroic lives of explorers are themes Martin Hastings dearly loved, themes other children might want to read more about. Admiral Richard Byrd's account of his exploration of that continent can be found in his *Alone* (Island, 1984). Milton Lomask's *Exploration—Great Lives* (Scribner's, 1988) is a collection of exciting accounts of brave men who made great sacrifices in the exploration of our planet. After reading a numer of these biographies, students might assume the role of one of these explorers and write a log of his or her explorations.   G.G.

*Social Studies,
Language Arts
Intermediate
Middle School*

Related Sources

---

212.   Stolz, Mary. *Quentin Corn*. Illustrated by Pamela Johnson. Godine, 1985. ISBN 0-87923-553-5, $11.95. Ages 8-12.

Mary Stolz is a writer of some daring and great imagination. In *Quentin Corn* she tells of a pig who learns of his imminent transformation from healthy porker to succulent barbecue and escapes this terrible fate disguised as a young man! Despite some obvious drawbacks, Quentin, as he names himself, manages a week in the world of humans, fooling everyone but the children he gets to know and endearing himself to the adults for his good manners and willingness to work hard. Any messages or moral are lost amid the humor of the improbable situations that develop. Stolz makes everything work so well, including a satisfying ending, that one gladly accepts the book's outrageous premise and simply enjoys watching Quentin maintain his unlikely disguise. This is a rare treat by a master storyteller.

Literature
Intermediate
Middle School

Related Sources

There are many stories and tales in which animals are given human qualities that would be appropriate and enjoyable extensions to share with younger audiences as a follow-up to *Quentin Corn*; E.B. White's *Charlotte's Web* (Harper & Row, 1952) and *Stuart Little* (Harper & Row, 1945) come to mind quickly, though for different reasons. This would also be a fine opportunity to read Hans Christian Andersen's "The Emperor's New Clothes" and discuss the parallels that are apparent. Whatever activities or books that may follow, *Quentin Corn* should be heard read aloud for its delicious humor.   H.M.

213.   Sutcliff, Rosemary. *Flame-Colored Taffeta*. Farrar, Straus & Giroux, 1986. ISBN 374-32344-5, $11.95. Ages 9-12.

The English seacoast village of Somerley Green had always been home and haven to smugglers, especially in the mid-18th century. Local folks knew to be suspicious of strangers, not knowing if they were spies for King George looking for smugglers or if they were loyal to the exiled Bonnie Prince Charlie. When twelve-year-old Damaris discovered a seriously wounded young man in the woods near her cottage, she put personal danger aside to help save his life and help him in his ultimate flight to safety. Rosemary Sutcliff paints a clear and accurate, as well as exciting, portrait of historical England, allowing the reader live through the past aided by one who knows its events and people. This is first-rate fiction created by one of literature's finest and most respected historians.

Related Source

Literature,
Social Studies
Intermediate
Middle School
Junior High School

Those who have read Bette Greene's *Summer of My German Soldier* (Dial, 1973) will be struck by the several parallels between the two stories: young girls risking severe punishment to help a man in some danger; young men in trouble for their political beliefs; social outsiders whose assistance is crucial to the men's survival and safety; and major political-military conflicts as the background to both stories. These and other points of contrast and comparison make the two books excellent for literature study by middle school readers.   H.M.

214. Taylor, Mildred. *The Friendship*. Pictures by Max Ginsburg. Dial, 1987. ISBN 0-8037-0418-6, $11.89. Ages 7-11.

ALA Notable Book

Related Source

Mildred Taylor has, since *Song of the Trees* (Dial, 1975), painted sharp, often grim, portraits of growing up in the South two generations ago. *The Friendship* is a penetrating sketch of an unlikely relationship between an elderly Black man and a white storekeeper whose life the Black man saved years before in a childhood incident. In this brief episode, as stirring and as taut as any found in short story literature, the two play out their conflict to its inevitable and tragic end. As usual, Taylor's sense of place and time are unerring, and her characterizations are sharp and sure.

Students will be moved to discuss not only what led up to the last scene, but also what may follow. Such discussion can and should be confined to the characters and the historical setting. Rather than a quickly assigned writing activity, pursue this discussion in depth over a longer period of time to permit reflection, background reading, family discussions, and an exchange of impressions in class. The writing could take the form of an "epilogue" perhaps written by one of the children— now an adult—who witnessed that tragic day in 1933.   H.M.

Black Studies, Language Arts Intermediate Middle School Junior High School

215. Taylor, Mildred. *The Gold Cadillac*. Pictures by Michael Hays. Dial, 1987. ISBN 0-8037-0342-2, $11.95. Ages 7-11.

Related Sources

The Gold Cadillac is not the long-awaited sequel to *Roll of Thunder, Hear My Cry* (Dial. 1976) and *Let the Circle be Unbroken* (Dial, 1981). This new novella cannot and should not be compared with her more complex and emotional histories of America's recent past. Rather, in 34 tautly written pages, Toledoan Mildred Taylor recalls a brief family episode when her father came home with a new 1950 Coupe deVille, gold colored inside and out. During a trip back to Mississippi to visit family, the children encounter for the first time Southern racism of the 1950's: segregated drinking fountains and public bathrooms, "Colored Not Allowed" signs, and local police suspicious of Blacks in new cars. Taylor's writing is sparse and crisp, perfect for the younger audience and the emotional level, as well as for reading aloud. Readers of this brief story will have the opportunity to understand the attitudes of the times in which their parents grew up.

The trip from Toledo to Mississippi is detailed enough to follow on a road map. Younger children, individually or in groups, can trace the route described in the story using yarn or a felt tip pen on a regional road map. Older children might want to compare the route taken by the family in 1950 before the interstate highway system with how that same trip be completed today: How many more miles might the trip have been in 1950? How much longer might the trip take then when the road conditions, highway speeds, and traffic, are taken into account? What other factors make travel today more pleasant?   H.M.

Black Studies Primary Intermediate Middle School

216. Uchida, Yoshiko. *The Happiest Ending*. Atheneum, 1985. ISBN 0-689-50326-1, $10.95. Ages 8-12.

Twelve-year-old Rinko is an American with Japanese roots. In an effort to retain her heritage, her family provides special language instruction and maintains close contact with others from Japan. Rinko struggles with one custom in particular—that of arranged marriages. She feels the arranged marriage between Teru, a friend of her family, to an older man is wrong and that Teru should instead marry a handsome young man Rinko knows. Through a number of experiences related to her family, to Teru, and to her language instructor, Rinko begins to realize the intricacies of relationships and love, and begins to "grow up." Other books about Rinko, *A Jar of Dreams* (Atheneum, 1981) and *The Best Bad Thing* (Atheneum, 1983), may also be enjoyed by intermediate readers.

The Happiest Ending provides an excellent opportunity for a project researching family roots, focusing not just on where the family lived before coming to this country, but also on what customs, traditions, and beliefs have been handed down through several generations. Be sensitive to the fact that the project could be difficult for students from one-parent families or families who are far from the "family homestead" and allow plenty of time for correspondence between the student and relatives. *My Backyard History Book* by David Weitzman (Little, Brown, 1975) is an invaluable source book for projects of this kind.   L.M.H.

217. Van Allsburg, Chris. *The Mysteries of Harris Burdick*. Illustrated by the author. Houghton Mifflin, 1984. ISBN 0-395-35393-9, $14.95. Ages 8-up.

This is a deliciously strange book, one designed to evoke a wide variety of unpredictably diverse responses from readers of all ages. We are told in the introduction that a mysterious (and fictional) artist and writer, Harris Burdick, left a series of puzzling pictures and captions with a publisher and then promptly disappeared. The fourteen exquisite drawings by Caldecott medalist Van Allsburg are presented in no particular order to tingle the reader's imagination. Yet each establishes a curious premise—sometimes humorous, sometimes frightening—for the incomplete and "missing" stories. This is a book to return to again and again.

Here is an opportunity for young people of all ages to create a completed story based upon the "story starters" that the pictures and captions provoke. The writing can focus on either finishing the story, or writing about what might have happened that led up to the point of the illustration and its caption. Each is certain to confound and stimulate the imagination, and the possibilities of written responses are endless. Comparing individual stories will confirm the range of creative thinking within the group. A parallel writing/art activity is creating a new picture with a caption for an unwritten story.   H.M.

218. Voigt, Cynthia. *Tree by Leaf*. Atheneum, 1988. ISBN 0-689-31403-5, $13.95. Ages 9-13.

Speer Point was a wild, lonely bit of coastal Maine in 1920, an obliging place for twelve-year-old Clothilde to hear "the Voice." Father is back from World War I, disfigured in body and bitter in mind; Mother sits in the parlor, embroidering, unable to take charge; brother Nate has disappeared with school friends that July; Clothilde is left to grope for ways to restore the family's wholeness. Wandering the beach alone, "the Voice" and her four wishes to right the family's wrongs come true in unexpected ways. In a dramatic departure from her Tillerman saga, Voigt illuminates a child's dreams and hopes. Her prose is evocative with details of place and time. More important, sensitive readers will be led to care deeply about this family whose story will linger in the mind, particularly with an epilogue suggesting the tale's truth. The emphasis here is not on taut dramatic action, but on the workings of adults scarred by their past and of a child's powerful imagination.

The magic of this book resides in the questions left unanswered, notably "the Voice" and what it represents, and why Clothilde was chosen to hear it. References are made to others who have heard voices: Joan of Arc and Socrates. Older readers may find this a fascinating area to explore. For all ages, the concept of wishing and receiving should lead to intriguing discussions, especially after reading Aiken's *The Moon's Revenge* (Knopf, 1987) and Bill Brittain's *The Wish Giver* (Harper & Row, 1983). Students can keep a private journal for one week, particularly noting those situations they would wish to change and the possible consequences.   B.B.

Literature, Language Arts Intermediate Middle School Junior High School

Related Sources

219. Weller, Frances Ward. *Boat Song*. Macmillan, 1987. ISBN 0-02-792611-7, $12.95. Ages 8-12.

Each summer, Jonathan Ayer's family spends four weeks at his grandmother's house on the New England coast. Here Jonno meets Scotsman Rob Loud, a colorful and heroic World War II veteran, who walks the beach playing his beloved bagpipes. The music and the man capture Jonno's heart and imagination. As a sensitive and quiet twelve-year-old, Jonno feels the pressure of trying to measure up to the expectations of his analytical and competent father, finding communication with him impossible. With intuitiveness and clarity, Weller has written about the thought processes and emotions of a young boy reaching out for self-assurance and independence, and his struggle to find his place in the family.

Rob's bagpipes have been an essential part of his life. He tells Jonno interesting tales of the vital role bagpipes have played in Scotland's history. Students may want to learn more about this instrument—how it works, its history, and where and how it is used today. Recordings of the music of the bagpipes can be played to the class to understand and appreciate the styles and kinds of music that traditionally is played on these instruments. Two albums are "The Pipes of Scotland," featuring various pipe bands, and "Highland Bag Pipes"

Music, Social Studies Intermediate Middle School

by Schumas and MacNeill, both of which are likely to be found at a public library. To add to the Scottish-Gaelic atmosphere, read aloud from *Gaelic Ghosts* (1964) or *Heather and Broom* (1960) by Nic Leodhas, published by Holt, Rinehart and Winston.   S.J.S.

220. Wosmek, Frances. *A Brown Bird Singing*. Lothrop, Lee & Shepard, 1986. ISBN 0-688-06251-2, $10.25. Ages 8-12.

The memory of the soft, warm brown bird singing reminded Anego, a nine-year-old Chippewa, not to be afraid. She remembered her mother's smile and the music of her words. After her mother died, Anego's father brought her to live with the Veselkas, promising to come back for her when he could. But that was many years ago and now even the memory of the brown bird singing cannot still he fear that he is coming to take her away from the family and the life that she has come to love. Anego's story as a Native American living with an Anglo family is well written and filled with warmth, humor, and sensitivity.

Native American Studies
Primary
Intermediate
Middle School

Related Sources

Anego becomes part of the Anglo world through living with the Veselkas, but when her father sends her some moccasins, she is surprised at the realization that she is indeed a Chippewa. *A Brown Bird Singing* should help reinforce in students the universality of the human race. Older readers and adults will find this same theme represented in *Eyes of Darkness* by Jamake Highwater (Lothrop, Lee & Shepard, 1985), Hal Borland's *When the Legends Die* (Harper & Row, 1963), and *The Man Who Killed Deer* by Frank Waters (Ohio University, 1942).   J.P.

221. Wright, Betty Ren. *Ghosts Beneath our Feet*. Holiday House, 1984. ISBN 0-8234-0538-9, $10.95. Ages 9-12.

Katie hopes that she and her "family," shattered by her step-father's death, will be healed by staying with her invalid "uncle" and caring for him. Instead, her step-brother seems to be pulling further away from them and is in trouble with the law. Besides, Katie has been listening to legends about ghosts in the old mines and has even seen a ghost-girl several times who has warned her of danger. No one will listen until it is almost too late. These events lead to a breathtaking climax and, much to her surprise, Katie's initial hopes for pulling the family together are realized. What started out very unlike a mystery is about as close to a believable ghost story as one could find. The tension within a family on the verge of breaking apart is interwoven throughout with hopes for a brighter future shining through at the end because of the mystery. The two plots are skillfully combined.

Social Studies,
Language Arts
Intermediate
Middle School

Since much of *Ghosts Beneath Our Feet* depicts loneliness— of a neglected senior citizen, a distraught widow, and misdirected teenagers—perhaps an inspirational follow-up activity could involve the students in a program designed to provide companionship for those who are alone. Students could become pen pals with retirees or could visit a nursing or retirement home on a regular basis. They will be amazed, as

Katie was, at how much retirees or seniors have to offer if we would but listen. Students could tape record interviews with older persons as a social studies lesson in local history. Schwartz's ***When I Grew Up Long Ago*** (Lippincott, 1978) demonstrates how oral history can stir the imagination and effectively teach today's reader about the not so distant past.   H.A.F.

Related Source

222.   Yep, Laurence. ***The Curse of the Squirrel***. Illustrated by Dirk Zimmer. Random House, 1987. ISBN 0-394-88200-8, $1.95. Ages 7-9.

The Curse of the Squirrel is one of Random House's new "Stepping Stone" books, a series designed to bridge young readers from basals to chapter books. Each book is 64 pages long, has readable type and many illustrations; the books have chapters and are written and illustrated by established authors and illustrators. Such talents as Laurence Yep, Clyde Robert Bulla, Susan Shreve, Dirk Zimmer, Sue Truesdell, and Susan Saunders are among those who have contributed to this effort to lure young readers to the pleasures of independent reading. Yep demonstrates his versatility as a writer by showing that he can write an interesting tale in this form. ***The Curse of the Squirrel*** is a story of a mighty hunting dog who is plunked into the role of the hunted. There is humor and adventure in his story, as well as some values to provoke thought. Dirk Zimmer's combination of textured, cartoon-style pen and ink drawings and silhouettes extend the images begun in Yep's text.

When the moon is full, Howie, the dog in ***The Curse of the Squirrel***, turns into a giant squirrel because of the bite and curse of a monster squirrel. After reading about Howie's adventures, students might enjoy seeing how two other authors had some fun creating vampire animals. They can be led to ***The Moosepire*** by Daniel Pinkwater (Little, Brown, 1986) and ***Bunnicula*** by Deborah and James Howe (Atheneum, 1979). These books will challenge, but not frustrate, children who are just beginning to read chapter stories.   M.A.C.

Language Arts Primary

Related Sources

223.   Yolen, Jane. ***Commander Toad and The Dis-Asteroid***. Illustrated by Bruce Degen. Coward, McCann & Geoghegan, 1985. ISBN 0-698-30744-5, $7.99. Ages 5-8.

Many younger readers will applaud the return of Commander Toad, brave and bright, bright and brave, and his hardy ship, Star Warts. This time he and his stalwart crew (including Mr. Hop and Jake Skyjumper) are off to rescue an asteroid whose swollen bean crop has plugged up the drains and caused a severe flood. There are plenty of puns to make the going fun, and Degen's amusing illustrations maintain the humor in this latest in Yolen's popular series of space spoofs.

With some adult direction, students could turn this into a reader's theater play to perform for the class. It requires six characters and a narrator. Younger children may need the help of an adult or an upper

Reader's Theater Primary Intermediate

grade student to work out the parts for the script. The other Commander Toad books should be available as well so that other groups of students can perform separate reader's theater productions thus involving everyone.   A.S.

224.   Yolen, Jane. *The Devil's Arithmetic*. Viking Kestrel, 1988. ISBN 0-670-81027-4, $11.95. Ages 10-14.

Empathy is the ability to project oneself into the feelings and experiences of another. It is a quality that Hannah did not have as she faced with impatience the discomfort of another Passover seder with Grandpa Will, a Holocaust survivor. During the seder she goes to the front door and is transformed into Chaya, a young girl living in a Polish shtetl who soon faces capture and imprisonment in a Nazi death camp. There she is both victim of, and witness to, the tortures, atrocities, and despair that are her grandfather's memories. The emotional atmosphere is taut. Readers will vicariously experience the horrors Jews suffered during that period so that they, too, will gain both knowledge and understanding of the victims of history's darkest period. Yolen uses all her considerable artistic skills in creating a believable character. She maintains a clear sense of history for many of today's readers who, like Hannah, are too removed from that time to remember or care.

Holocaust Studies, Literature, Drama Intermediate Middle School Junior High School

Related Sources

The Devil's Arithmetic is a remarkable contribution to Holocaust literature for middle school readers. It also demonstrates the effective use of time-shifting as a means of putting oneself into the shoes of those who are misunderstood. Some other recent examples include Voigt's *Building Blocks* (Atheneum, 1984) and Hurmence's *A Girl Called Boy* (Houghton Mifflin, 1982). Encourage students who read one or all of these books to select a living, historical, or fictional character who might be an interesting subject for investigation. Search their early years to shed light on why they behave or think as they do now. Many students may find that working together to create a play dramatizing their findings would be a most effective way of reporting what they have read.   H.M.

225.   Yolen, Jane, editor. *Favorite Folktales from Around the World*. Pantheon, 1986. ISBN 0-394-54382-3, $19.95. All ages.

Thank goodness there remain writers of Jane Yolen's grace and genius who can tell stories with such respect for the beauty of language and sensitivity for the human condition as she displays in this remarkable volume. This 475 page volume is, most emphatically, not to be confused with other collections produced in earlier times for easy appeal and quick sale. Yolen's selections are organized around thirteen themes, such as "True Loves and False," "Heroes," "Shape Shifters," "Wonder Tales," and more. Collectively they show both cultural diversity and the universality of human behavior and belief. More than a reflection of the careful scholar that she is, however, the 160 stories are a wellspring of joy and pleasure for children from the pen and the heart of one of America's gifted writers and storytellers. This is meant for a year—or a lifetime—of reading, telling, and listening pleasure for young and old alike.

The benefits of regular storytelling or reading aloud to young children are well known and easily documented. Studies for generations have shown the gains made in language facility by younger children: reading scores improve, composing skills are expanded, critical judgment increases, etc. Secondary teachers must assert the same benefits are equally available to older children, provided the stories are appropriate in content and form for older audiences. The stories in *Favorite Folktales from Around the World* are that rich resource for junior and senior high school teachers, just as they are for elementary teachers and storytellers. Yolen's style is clear and evocative, never condescending. This should be on the desk of every high school English and social studies teacher, as well as the librarian.   H.M.

Multicultural Studies, Literature, Storytelling All Grades

226.   Yolen, Jane, Martin H. Greenberg, and Charles G. Waugh. *Dragons and Dreams*. Harper & Row, 1986. ISBN 0-06-026792-5, $11.89. Ages 10-up.

Dragons and Dreams is a challenging and lively collection of fantasy/science fiction short stories. Each selection is readable and short enough to be shared with children in one sitting. A fine array of authors has contributed stories, including such well-known writers as Jane Yolen, Zilpha Snyder, Patricia McKillip, Diana Wynne Jones, and Monica Hughes. Children should recognize familiar faces in several of the selections: the young wizards, Kit and Nita, from Diane Duane's *Deep Wizardry* (Delacorte, 1985), and the wise and powerful necromancer, Chestomanci, from Diana Wynne Jones's *Charmed Life* (Greenwillow, 1978). This entertaining volume also includes brief biographical sketches of each contributing author.

Related Sources

These easily understood tales are prefect for reading aloud, and they provide an excellent source for introducing young readers to several top-notch writers. Books by the various writers could be gathered in a reading center with the short stories from *Dragons and Dreams* as an introduction to each author's work. After sampling works by each author, students could choose their favorite writer to do an in-depth study. Biographical information can be gathered from reference books, magazines, and other sources, including writing to the author's publisher (who often has photographs in addition to other free publicity materials they are happy to send out). The biographical sketches, once created, could then be shared with others in the class.   M.O.T.

Author Studies Intermediate Middle School Junior High School High School

FICTION FOR
OLDER
READERS

FICTION FOR OLDER READERS

227. Alexander, Lloyd. *The Beggar Queen*. Dutton, 1984. ISBN 0-525-44103-4, $11.95. Ages 11-up.

Cabbarus, the former chief minister of Westmark, forces a brutal seizure of power, establishing himself as Director. In a desperate attempt to overthrow Cabbarus's peculiar form of government, the dethroned Queen Augusta, Theo, his "associates," and the citizens of Westmark rise in a show of resistance to put an end to the monarchy forever and to establish a republic. This concluding story in the Westmark trilogy is the strongest and most dramatic of the three. The characters are well-drawn and true to their original depiction in *Westmark* (Dutton, 1981), the story that began it all. *The Beggar Queen* is a satisfying ending to a very worthwhile series.

Although Alexander's portrayal of armed conflict is relatively low-keyed, readers will nevertheless gain some understandings of the horrible realities of war and its cost in terms of friendship and loyalty. Students also may begin to understand the nature of the war within oneself, a conflict that often proves to be the most difficult battle, a battle demanding tremendous courage and determination. Teachers can use this theme to focus discussion and writing activities on the problems people face when group pressures conflict with loyalties to family, to a friend, and to oneself.   N.S.R.

ALA Best Book

Third in Alexander's Westmark Trilogy

Related Source

Peace Studies, Language Arts Junior High School Middle School

228. Alexander, Lloyd. *The Drackenberg Adventure*. Dutton, 1988. ISBN 0-525-44389-4, $12.95. Ages 10-14.

This third Vesper Holly adventure finds Vesper as impetuous as ever as she accepts the Duchess of Drackenberg's invitation to her Diamond Jubilee. Vesper, her guardian Brinnie, and his wife Mary are caught up in a sinister plot to destroy Drackenberg's independence. They soon find themselves counter-plotting with a friendly band of gypsies, tracking down a priceless painting, and avoiding the sinister Dr. Helvitius. Like the previous Holly adventures, this is a thriller in the classic style: kidnappings, mysterious castles, daring deeds, all carried out at a breathless pace in an imaginary and romantic Middle European setting. Alexander's tight style, imagination, and likable, believable characters make this lots of fun for adventure lovers.

Readers may also want to enjoy the first two Vesper Holly books:

Third of a series of adventures featuring Vesper Holly

Related Sources

Social Studies, Music, Language Arts, Science Intermediate Junior High School Middle School

The Illyrian Adventure (Dutton, 1986) and *The El Dorado Adventure* (Dutton, 1987). As each of these books has its own imaginary international setting, students may enjoy inventing a "country" complete with a wild landscape, distinctive residents, and its own weather, coastline, etc. Such a country offers many possibilities for map-making, an invented history, legends, music, stamps, coinage, even a composed language—activities that can enrich all curricular subjects.   B.B.

229.   Alexander, Lloyd. *The Illyrian Adventure*. Dutton, 1986. ISBN 0-525-44250-2, $12.95. Ages 10-14.

ALA Notable Book

First of a series of adventures featuring Vesper Holly

Vesper Holly, a 19th century Indiana Jones, is Lloyd Alexander's most recent adventure heroine: absolutely fearless, resolute, sprightly, and possessing a great zest for life. Upon her father's death she takes up his effort to prove the truth of "The Illyriad," a mythic 12th century tale set in the miniature Adriatic kingdom of Illyria. She and Brinnie, her reluctant but competent guardian, set forth for Illyria and a mystery involving magical warriors, a country in revolution, corrupt police, and a reborn villain of supernatural powers. This is high adventure reminiscent of "Raiders of the Lost Ark," yet literate, humorous, and truly heroic. Middle grade readers should find this tale absorbing and entertaining. Vesper Holly is the sort of adolescent adventurer one hopes to hear more from in future stories.

Social Studies, Music, Language Arts Intermediate Junior High School Middle School

Writing fantasy requires creating an imaginary place that becomes real in every way, from its geography and cities to the ways the people live and work. Older students can begin with a map (as Alexander does in his fantasies) showing the boundaries of the country, its surface features, and its towns. Creating a clear picture of the people, their customs, and their social organization can come next. Some students may imagine what artists, dancers, or composers in the imaginary land would create. Others might describe housing, occupations, or write a "history" of the country. A fairly complete portrait of the imagined place and people should be done before writing a story set there.   H.M.

230.   Anderson, Joan. *1787*. Illustrated by Alexander Farquharson. Gulliver, 1987. ISBN 0-15-200582-X, $14.95. Ages 12-up.

Young Jared Mifflin has been "volunteered" by his uncle to become James Madison's aide during the Constitutional Convention taking place in Philadelphia in 1787. As a young man interested in politics, but also a young man in love, he is torn by the appointment. He fears he may have no time for anything other than the convention. However, his job as an aide actually brings him closer to the young woman he loves. In addition, it provides him—and the reader—with a preview of the developing Constitution and opens his eyes to the racial and social class biases that existed at that time. Anderson uses facts she gathered to develop a thought-provoking story, intertwined with a developing romance, that brings the Constitution alive.

1987 marked the 200th anniversary of our Constitution. For interesting historical insights about its history, *1787* is one book that should not be overlooked. Action in the book is fast-paced enough to permit an oral reading likely to hold the attention of most listeners. In addition, the practice of debate and compromise is clearly shown while the personalities of the delegates come forth in their actions and their words. Other appealing books for a wide range of readling abilities published this year on this topic are Jean Fritz's *Shh...We're Writing the Constitution* (Putnam, 1987), Doris and Harold Faber's *We the People: The Story of the United States Since 1787* (Scribner's, 1987), and Margot C. J. Mabie's *The Constitution: Reflections on a Changing Nation* (Henry Holt, 1987).   L.S.

*U.S. History, Government
Junior High School
Middle School
High School*

Related Sources

231.   Angell, Judie. *One-Way To Ansonia*. Bradbury, 1985. ISBN 0-02-705860-3, $11.95. Ages 12-up.

"I'm not running away from anybody," said Rose Rogoff, "I'm running to something." As she handed her last three dollars to the ticket agent, Rose knew she was buying more than a seat on a train. This was her ticket to independence. In this touching and personal account, based upon the memories of her grandmother's immigration to America, Judie Angell writes about Rose, a young girl who works hard and asks little of life except some beauty, music on Sunday, and the hope for a better tomorrow. This turn of the century tale is sobering in its depiction of economic as well as spiritual poverty. Angell paints a vivid, sometimes heartbreaking portrait of a heroine anyone would feel proud to call Grandmother.

One Way to Ansonia opens America's golden door and invites other young readers to follow their families' journey into our wonderful nation. In 1981 Delacorte published the "Coming to America" series with such titles as *Immigrants from Eastern Europe* by Shirley Blumenthal, *Immigrants from the Far East* by Linda Perrin, and *From Mexico, Cuba, and Puerto Rico* by Susan Garver and Paula McGuire. All are compatible with Rose Rogoff's story. Delacorte also provides a teacher's guide to accompany the paperback editions designed for classroom use. Milton Meltzer also has written of immigrant experiences in *The Chinese Americans* (Harper & Row, 1980), *The Hispanic Americans* (Harper & Row, 1982, and *The Jewish Americans* (Harper & Row, 1982).   G.G.

*Multicultural Studies,
U.S. History
Middle School
Junior High School
High School*

Related Sources

232.   Arkin, Alan. *The Clearing*. Harper & Row, 1986. ISBN 0-06-020140-1, $11.89. Ages 12-up.

Alan Arkin's *The Lemming Condition* (Harper & Row, 1976) ended with Bubber leaving home following the mass suicide of his fellow lemmings. To the possibility of staying, proposed by other survivors, Bubber answered with an emphatic "No!" and added that he wasn't sure where he was going, but he was sure of one thing: "I'm not a lemming anymore." Thus begins the story of Bubber's search for self-understanding. In a clearing, Bear, the father figure, encourages Bubber

*Sequel to
The Lemming Condition*

and a widely diverse gathering of animals (a duck, a boa constrictor, a cougar, a crow) to find the "lion," or essence of being, in each of them. This is a very philosophical and sophisticated novel for young adults: the reader is drawn to new perspectives on old questions of what is real, what is truth, and what is knowledge. The discussions among the animals show Arkin's genius for presenting in fine humor the "paradoxes within paradoxes" in our lives.

The Clearing should be required reading in every high school. It is a humorous introduction to philosophy, while it comfortably explores human behavior. It is powerful and demands discussion. Other animal fantasies for older readers include Adams's *Watership Down* (Macmillan, 1974), Kennedy's *Amy's Eyes* (Harper & Row, 1985) and, of course, Orwell's classic allegory, *Animal Farm* (Harcourt Brace, 1946).   E.A.H.

Literature
High School

Related Sources

233.   Baehr, Patricia. *Falling Scales*. Morrow, 1987. ISBN 0-688-07208-9, $11.75. Ages 12-up.

Thea has problems and often cannot see things clearly enough to handle them effectively. With a drunken father and a mother overly-involved with her boss, more home responsibilities are piled upon dependable Thea. Her refuge is her clarinet, which leads to both Mr. MacGraw's acceptance of her into his own orchestra ensemble and meeting Marilyn. Soon best friends, their good times are overshadowed by Marilyn's obsessive infatuation with MacGraw. MacGraw's own obsession becomes evident when Thea turns to him for comfort, and in the guise of providing it, he sexually abuses her. Betrayed by Marilyn when she reveals the situation, Thea finds refuge unexpectedly from another person. This is a compelling story in which complex situations are portrayed realistically. Thea's courage at the end, contrasted with her inabilities at the beginning, shows strong character growth. As a person finally in control of her life, Thea makes a positive role model.

The clarinet is Thea's solace, the only thing that takes her mind off what is happening in her life. Many times young people bury themselves in something in order to deal with or to avoid uncomfortable situations. Two other books about a young woman involved in some sort of activity to handle problems are Woolverton's *Running Before the Wind* (Houghton Mifflin, 1987) and Terris's *Nell's Quilt* (Farrar, Straus & Giroux, 1987). Students might choose to read one of these three books. Then, as a large group, they can discuss whether the activities of these young women in the books are done in order to deal with or to avoid problems. Students might also share strategies they find effective in dealing with stress or anxiety in their lives.   L.S.

Related Source

Literature, Social Studies
High School

234.   Bates, Betty. *Ask Me Tomorrow*. Holiday House, 1987. ISBN 0-8234-0659-8, $12.95. Ages 12-up.

Paige Truitt, a fifteen-year-old Maine boy, must decide how to tell his father that he does not want to take over the family's apple orchard business. However, after befriending thirteen-year-old Abby Winch, a visitor who sees Maine from a fresh perspective, Paige realizes that the decision to stay or go is his own and that leaving would not be as easy as he previously believed. This book is a charming and realistic look at the sometimes confusing life of a teenager who is faced with an important decision. The story's pace is as comfortable as the characters portrayed. There are beautiful descriptions of the New England countryside as well that should not be overlooked.

This novel could be an effective introduction to a unit on problem-solving or decision-making skills. A good resource book for classroom activities illustrating problem-solving techniques is Stephen Tchudi's *The Young Learner's Handbook: A Guide to Solving Problems, Mastering Skills, Thinking Creatively* (Scribner's, 1987). After becoming familiar with the techniques, students could write about an important decision that they've had to make. What did they do to help them make the decision? Did they make the right decision? Did the choice they made work out for the best? What techniques could they have used that they might not have known about at the time? Fictitious situations that are pertinent, such as alcohol and substance abuse, career and college choice, or sexual responsibility, could be the focus of further group practice. The students could apply what they have learned to a current problem in their lives.   M.H./M.A.C.

Related Source

Family Life, Literature
Junior High School
High School

235. Beatty, Patricia. *Charley Skedaddle*. Morrow, 1987. ISBN 0-688-06687-9, $11.75. Ages 10-14.

Take a tough New York street kid, a member of the Bowery Boys gang, plop him into the Union Army in the position of drummer boy, and what happens? Plenty, but not what the reader might guess. Beatty's extensive research makes the adventures in *Charley Skedaddle* entirely believable. Even though the story opens with Charley exhibiting a street gang mentality, he is still such a vulnerable and likable young man that the reader feels his loneliness on the troop ship, his horror when he encounters the real war, his revulsion when he shoots a Rebel, his guilt when he "skedaddles" from the battle, and his blossoming under the tutelage of an old mountain woman, Granny Bent. Beatty's text moves smoothly along, providing indelible images of Civil War times both in the city and in the remote mountains, as well as provoking thought about the nature of men when they become involved with war. Similar to Stephen Crane's *Red Badge of Courage* (Modern Library, 1942) but with a very different hero, this fast-moving novel may supplement that classic for many readers.

In the author's notes at the back of the book, Beatty describes the research that she did which added so much authentic detail to her story. Using this as an example, history teachers can encourage students to write an account of a fictional character who lived during a time period they are studying. Students should be encouraged to do as much research as is needed to make their story believable and to give attention to details that characterize successful historical fiction. The stories do not have to be long, but they should make the setting vivid.   M.A.C.

Related Source

U.S. History, Literature
Middle School
Junior High School

236.   Bonham, Frank. *Premonitions*. Holt, Rinehart and Winston, 1984. ISBN 0-03-071306-4, $11.95. Ages 12-up.

In a persuasive blending of the occult with realism, Bonham has told a gripping story of two teen-agers: the sixteen-year-old girl-shy Kevin, editor of his high school newspaper, and a French classmate, Anni, who is clairvoyant but reluctant to admit it. Anni's brother, Dante, also a high school student, had died under mysterious circumstances. Kevin takes it upon himself to investigate Dante's death. In the process, he learns a great deal about Dante, Anni, and himself. Bonham's writing is straightforward and the action never slows in this appealing mystery.

This slim novel is multi-layered in discussion-provoking situations. Included are the problems of shyness, withdrawal, popularity, cliques, trust, cruelty, abuse, parental influence, teacher–student relationships, sibling rivalry, and teen-age suicide. Indeed, there are so many different problematic episodes that nearly every young person can relate to one or more of them. Small group discussions can focus on how realistically or fully Bonham develops each "problem."   F.M.H.

237.   Bridgers, Sue Ellen. *Permanent Connections*. Harper & Row, 1987. ISBN 0-06-020712-4, $12.89. Ages 12-up.

Trouble follows seventeen-year-old Rob like a "sniffing dog." When he leaves New Jersey to visit relatives in the hills of North Carolina, he is successful at finding trouble again. Rob is ashamed of his family and is unable to make friends. As he continues to alienate himself from those who care most, he seeks comfort in drugs and alcohol. Ultimately, he learns that his loved ones form the "connection" between himself and the rest of the world. Although the mood of the story is overwhelmingly dismal, exquisite characterization draws the reader into the lives of this troubled family. This is a powerfully-written, intense book that is likely to appeal mainly to the older, more mature reader.

An especially sensitive novel, *Permanent Connections* offers insight into the causes and effects of drug and alcohol abuse. Enlightening classroom discussions could result from exploring the reasons why Rob felt dependent on these substances. The consequences of this dependency, in terms of his emotional health and his relationships with others should also be stressed. Most important, students should recall what alternatives were available to Rob. The class may reflect upon the role that drugs and alcohol play in their own lives. As a group, ask them to list the reasons for substance abuse, the consequences of such abuse, and effective strategies for saying "No."   H.M.

238.   Brooks, Bruce. *The Moves Make the Man.* Harper & Row, 1984. ISBN 0-06-020698-5, $12.89. Ages 12-up.

Jerome Foxworthy ("Jayfox") is cool and confident on the basketball court, as well as in life. When he is selected to be the token Black to integrate all-White Chestnut Street Junior High School, he meets Bix

River and so begins a friendship as off-balance and unpredictable as Bix. What starts out as a sports book (which it is, in part) and a story of interracial conflict (which it is, in part) becomes ultimately a piercing dissection of human behavior and mental illness that grips the reader through to the final desperate scene. This 1985 Newbery Honor Book is written with humor, some realistic language (though never offensive), sharp insights into human relations, and human compassion that never talks down to the reader.

Older students may be encouraged to look again at the literature of school desegregation, especially *Lions in the Way* by Bella Rodman (Follett, 1966), as well as the history of school bussing and the civil rights movement. Equally important is the exploration of mental illness and emotional abuse, which may be related to recent increases in teenage suicide and runaways. Several themes dealing with the fragility of personal and group interactions can be discussed and developed in formal writing activities.   H.M.

Related Source

Multicultural Studies, Literature High School

239.   Brooks, Bruce. *Midnight Hour Encores*. Harper & Row, 1986. ISBN 0-06-020710-8, $13.89. Ages 12-up.

ALA Best Book

Sibilance T. Spooner, abandoned by her mother at birth, is now sixteen years old and a musical prodigy on the cello. Having lived only with her father, whom she calls Taxi, Sib erroneously gives herself credit for her self-sufficiency. When she finally asks Taxi to take her to meet her mother, their journey from Washington, D.C. to San Francisco provides her with insights into her father's and mother's past. She learns much about her father and the strong role he played in her early development, and is provided with the reasons for her mother's abandonment. Upon arrival in California, Sib reveals another reason for wanting to go to San Francisco: a cello audition that can lead to a scholarship there and the necessity of leaving her father to live with her mother. The heart-wrenching decision she must make and the manner in which she makes it provides a dramatic conclusion to the intertwining facts revealed previously in the story. Newbery Honor Book-winner Brooks has told an emotionally challenging story that will intrigue readers and linger in their minds long after the reading is done.

Sibilance is a somewhat typical teenager, yet she has a deep love for the cello and cello music. Use this opportunity to expose students to various types of music, especially those featuring the cello. Coordinate with the music teacher and obtain recordings of classic pieces of music ranging from jazz, rhythm and blues, and soft rock to classical, country and western, etc. Play selections from these categories. Encourage students to listen to the music with an open mind. Reassure them that they do not have to like it, only to try to appreciate the talent involved. Discuss how the music makes them feel, if they like or dislike it and why, and whether they can distinguish the various instruments and styles. To show your open-mindedness, be sure to play music you normally do not listen to and discuss its good qualities and the interconnections of forms and styles among all musical genres.   L.S.

Music, Literature High School

240.   Clements, Bruce. *The Treasure of Plunderell Manor*. Farrar, Straus & Giroux, 1987. ISBN 0-374-37746-4, $12.95. Ages 12-up.

Lovers of gothic romance should enjoy *The Treasure of Plunderell Manor* for its setting in a darkly foreboding English mansion and its cast of clearly good and evil characters. It is the story of Laurel Bybank, a fourteen-year-old orphan, who goes to Plunderell Manor to become a personal ward of Alice Plunderell. At seventeen, Alice is about to come of age and inherit the manor. Laurel finds that Alice is held a virtual prisoner by her aunt and uncle. She also discovers that there was a motive in their hiring her: they plan to use her to find the treasure of Plunderell Manor and then destroy both her and Alice. Clement's clear and descriptive writing makes for an enjoyable reading adventure. The girls' solutions are clever and their male champions heroic. One in particular, Harold Pomfret-Watkin, is a humorous stereotype of the "perfect" English gentleman, albeit one whose wealth comes from industry. Lord and Lady Stayne also add a light touch to the story, with their constant bickering and klutzy conniving.

Literature, Language Arts High School

Teens who have not been exposed to the gothic novel can be introduced to it via *The Treasure of Plunderell Manor*. Then they can read some of the novels of Victoria Holt, Phyllis Whitney, Mary Stewart, and Joan Aiken as other outstanding modern examples. After reading a variety of these books, students can work in small groups to determine their characteristic structures or elements. These can be listed and compared on the chalkboard. Students may enjoy taking those elements and developing an outline for their own gothic.   M.A.C.

241.   Cormier, Robert. *Beyond the Chocolate War*. Knopf, 1985. ISBN 0-394-87343-2, $11.95. Ages 12-up.

Sequel to The Chocolate War

Robert Cormier's powerfully realistic *The Chocolate War* (Pantheon, 1974) has been acclaimed by critics and young adults for its searing portrait of conformity, manipulation, and undercurrents of violence centered at fictitious Trinity High, a parochial boys' school in western Massachusetts. The characters and plot established eleven years ago are extended here: we are witness to further attempts by the Vigils, a secret gang at Trinity led by villainous Archie Costello, to terrorize students and faculty alike. Cormier successfully maintains control of the large cast of characters and the several plot twists as the Vigils seek to disrupt Fair Day, the climactic end-of-the-year school celebration. Cormier displays his mastery of fast-paced, tightly-structured narrative, realistic dialogue, biting characterizations, and his true sense of moral issues faced by today's teens. Though the language is appropriately rough at times and the events are seldom pretty, Cormier's sequel is a compelling story that cannot and should not be ignored.

Literature High School

Related Source

Here is a gripping novel that consciously reveals the darker side of human experience, reminiscent, as is *The Chocolate War*, of Golding's *Lord of the Flies* (Coward-McCann, 1962). Enough parallels between these two works exist (e.g., relative absence of adult/parental influence, "ordinary" appearing characters, the certainty of violence ready to burst forth, et al.) to warrant pairing them for discussion and/ or written assignments. Fundamental to both works are questions regarding the inherent nature of human behavior and the validity of both authors' assumptions about the pervasiveness of evil.   H.M.

242.   Cresswell, Helen. *Moondial*. Macmillan, 1987. ISBN 0-02-725370-8, $13.95. Ages 10-14.

Minty Kaye knows there is something unusual about the big house across the road when she hears ghostly children's voices crying for help. Through the mysterious powers of a sundial/moondial she is transported into time and meets two abused children from separate time periods; Tom, a kitchen boy who is physically abused, and Sarah, who suffers mental abuse at the hands of her nurse. Minty realizes she is the one who holds the key to release the children from their abuse, to enable Tom and Sarah to "run free forever in moontime." Though the ending is a bit contrived, *Moondial* is full of mystery and suspense, and will keep most readers captivated.

One of the strong points of this book is the prologue, which is extremely well-written and sets up the mystical tone for the story. Discuss with students why a prologue is included in some books and share other examples to include a variety of genres. After reading the prologues to students, discuss how they set the mood for the stories, how imagery was used, and how the authors made use of descriptive words. Students could then write their own prologues, either for a book which doesn't have one or for one of their own.   K.B.B.

Language Arts
Junior High School
High School

243.   Crossley-Holland, Kevin. *British Folk Tales: New Versions*. Orchard, 1987. ISBN 0-531-05733-X, $22.95. Ages 10-up.

Kevin Crossley-Holland's latest book will make the avid collector or even the occasional reader of folklore jump for joy. This collection captures the charm and the mystery surrounding the British Isles. The author has taken tales that we all know, like "Jack and the Beanstalk," and retold them with a hilarious and often biting emphasis on character development. Mixed with oft-told tales are more obscure but no less enjoyable poems and folk tales native to Ireland, Scotland, and England. Some of the stories are sad, some are eerie, but all are written with the fresh perspective and skilled craftmanship that have made Crossley-Holland an award-winning writer. This is a masterful collection guaranteed to please even finicky readers.

This volume contains scholarly sources, comments upon the tales, and a glossary. Students might find it entertaining to make a trip to the library to investigate the sources of the stories and to see how much they have changed in the retelling process. The oral tradition of storytelling is being sustained and revived by caring people who realize the importance of the story in all cultures. Teachers should encourage students to select a story from this collection to read aloud to the class using expression

ALA Notable Book

Speech, Drama,
Literature
Middle School
Junior High School
High School

worthy of the tale. Before these performances, provide students with some instruciton on and examples of good techniques, and encourage them to practice.   L.A.B.

244.   DeFord, Deborah H. and Harry S. Stout. *An Enemy Among Them*. Houghton Mifflin, 1987. ISBN 0-395-44239-7, $13.95. Ages 10-14.

It is Christmas, 1776, in Reading, Pennsylvania, and young Margaret Volpert finds that her family cannot remain insulated from the war that is affecting their future independence. Her brother John has already enlisted in the Continental Army and another brother, Jacob, is following suit. Meanwhile, Christian Molitor, a Hessian mercenary, has survived a difficult ocean crossing to do his duty for his king and fight on the side of England. The paths of Margaret and Christian cross and cross again as the war stretches on. Through it all, each grows in understanding of the meaning and cost of freedom. This first young adult novel by historian Harry S. Stout and writer Deborah DeFord reminds *Related Source* one of the similar and very successful collaboration of James and Christopher Collier in *My Brother Sam is Dead* (Scholastic paperback, 1985). *An Enemy Among Them*, rather than examining conflicting loyalties within a family, deals with the effect of the war upon non-English colonists, such as the fictional German Volpert family. It contains a fast-paced blend of adventure, romance, family feelings, and the harsh realities of war.

History teachers can make effective use of books like *An Enemy Among Them* and *My Brother Sam is Dead* to help students look beyond the facts and events of a period in history to the realities of people who lived through them. Individuals in some historical situations had conflicting loyalties, and had to make decisions that could mean life *U.S. History* or death to themselves and their families. In some cases, their course of *High School* action impacted upon the future course of the entire country. History and *Junior High School* social studies teachers can develop a series of quesitons to aid students in viewing historical events in this way. What if the non-English colonists had refused to become involved in the conflict with King George III? How would you feel sending your child off to war? What happens when two friends join opposite sides and meet each other face to face in battle? What would happen if the women and children were in charge of policy making? Discussing the less obvious but nonetheless real issues of history not only brings students to the dry bones facts of events, but also brings them to higher level thinking that will aid them when they face such decisions themselves.   M.A.C.

245.   de Jenkins, Lyll Becerra. *The Honorable Prison*. Lodestar, 1988. ISBN 0-525-67238-9, $14.95. Ages 12-up.

Jenkins's quietly eloquent and beautiful writing is in stark contrast to the suffering and violence of this gripping and fast-moving story. Teenager Marta and her family are placed under house arrest in a military camp in a Latin American country because her ailing journalist father wrote of government atrocities. Written in the first person, her story chronicles the day-to-day events of her life. As she watches her father fade away, she and the reader realize that suffering small indignities daily can erode the spirit and break the body as surely as any beating or bullet.

The First Amendment of the U.S. Constitution guarantees freedom of the press for Americans. A worthwhile project would be for students to research the history of a free press in America and the role that the press has played (and continues to play) in the shaping of our consciousness. Further research can determine the role of the press in other countries. High school students may be interested in the rules and laws governing high school newspapers, including court cases challenging local school policies. A useful source to begin with is Louis Ingelhart's *Press Law and Press Freedom for High School Publications* (Greenwood, 1986). In addition to keeping up with current newspaper articles, *The Reader's Guide to Periodical Literature* would yield articles in magazines that should be an equally useful for identifying student resources.   L.A.B./M.A.C.

Government
Junior High School
High School

Related Sources

246. Doherty, Berlie. *Granny Was a Buffer Girl*. Orchard, 1988 (1st Am. ed.). ISBN 0-531-05754-2, $12.95. Ages 10-up.

Author Berlie Doherty has captured British history, dialect, and culture realistically and convincingly in this 1986 Carnegie Medal winner. *Granny Was a Buffer Girl* remembers and celebrates the good and bad times shared by Jess and her close-knit family through a series of colorful individual flashbacks that flow from memory to memory, present to past. Personalities and events such as the sad death of brother Danny, Granny Dorothy's work as a buffer girl in the Sheffield cutlery factories, and the clandestine Catholic-Protestant courtship of Grandpa Jack and Grandma Bridie make Doherty's story understandably human and worthwhile.

Carnegie Medal Winner

Because *Granny Was a Buffer Girl* is full of rich characterizations and entertaining anecdotes, teachers might ask students to "adopt" a favorite character from the story, compile information about him or her from the text, and write their own "embedded story" or episode in that character's life. A portrait of the charcter could be drawn by a student artist to use as the frontispiece for each new "chapter." These chapters could be compiled as a companion book for those who might read Doherty's original.   J.B.R.

Language Arts, Art
Intermediate
Middle School
Junior High School

247. Evernden, Margery. *The Dream Keeper*. Lothrop, Lee & Shepard, 1985. ISBN 0-688-04638-X, $10.25. Ages 12-up.

Becka, faced with her parents' possible separation, discovers her great-grandmother's early life in Poland—how she dealt with the hardships of shtetl life and why she subsequently was able to come to America. As the reader is drawn to the great-grandmother's story, Becka's becomes secondary. In the end, by knowing her heritage, Becka gains strength to face the unknowns in her own life and to be a "dream keeper." Readers may easily be captivated by the contrast of two very different generations and cultures. This book realistically shows the universal struggles of growing up, taking responsibility, and facing changes.

Jewish-American Studies,
U.S. History
Junior High School
High School

Related Sources

Along with many books written on Jewish immigration and the Holocaust, this book lends insight and background to the earlier plight of Polish Jews in 1910. Other books that would complement this topic for students are **Grandmother Came From Dworitz** (Tundra, 1978) by Ethel Vineberg and **Isaac Bashevis Singer, The Story of a Storyteller** by Paul Kresh (Lodestar, 1984). **Taking Root** by Milton Meltzer (Farrar, Straus & Giroux, 1976) provides a good resource for teachers. The heritage and convictions of any immigrant group, coupled with the final thrill of reaching "free" land—America—are amplified in each of these books.   M.B.C.

248.   Fahrmann, Willi. **The Long Journey of Lukas B.** Bradbury, 1985. ISBN 0-02-734330-8, $13.95. Ages 12-up.

In 1870s Prussia work is scarce and a debt is owed to the local baron; if it is not paid promptly Luke's grandfather must forefeit his home and business. Thus, fourteen-year-old Luke travels with this grandfather, a master carpenter, and a skilled crew from their rural village in Prussia to work in America for two years. They plan to return to Prussia much richer and repay the debt. Throughout their travels, Luke matures and becomes a skilled member of the crew. However, his main concern is to trace his father's earlier movements across this same area. This story is expertly written in three separate segments that flow into a coherent recounting of their journey from Prussia through 19th century America, and finally their return home.

U.S. History
Middle School
Junior High School
High School

Only Luke and his grandfather return to their villiage. The rest of the crew decides, for various reasons, to make America their home. Immigration during this period was not an unusual happening. The crew members' decisions could provide a basis for discussion and an exploration of factors that make immigration necessary or desirable. Students could also construct a map of Luke's travels from his village in Prussia to his route in America and his trip home.   R.M.G.

249.   Fleischman, Paul. **Coming-and-Going Men**. Illustrated by Randy Gaul. Harper & Row, 1985. ISBN 0-06-21884-3, $10.89. Ages 11-up.

Related Source

Those who have read the 1983 Newbery Honor book, **Graven Images** (Harper & Row, 1982), will be delighted to know that Paul Fleischman has again given us a collection of skillfully-crafted spectral tales set in the past. The year is 1800 and the setting is the village of New Canaan, Vermont. Four itinerant peddlers pass through this village and each must confront illusion in one form or another. From Mr. Cyrus Snype, the silhouette cutter who wrestles with superstition, to Jonathan Wardwell, the neophyte peddler of dyes who dispels Ida's delusion of doom, we have four intriguing tales. Fleischman proves he is a master stylist who can create believable fantasy that is spell binding.

Read aloud, these tales are spooky enough to hold a group riveted in attention. Additionally, librarians are often asked for books that deal with the mores and the daily lives of a certain period in history. Since these stories contain detailed descriptions of life and customs in the year 1800, they would fill that need. A companion book could be Carol Carrick's *Stay Away From Simon* (Clarion, 1985), which is a poignant story of life on Martha's Vineyard in 1830.   M.E.M.

U.S. History
Middle School
Junior High School

Related Sources

250.   George, Jean Craighead. *Water Sky*. Harper & Row, 1987. ISBN 0-06022198-4, $11.98. Ages 12-up.

As Lincoln Stonewright set out for Alaska, he knew nothing of the Eskimo belief that when a whale is ready to die it "gives itself" to someone to be killed so that the Eskimo people may live. Living at an Eskimo whaling camp, Link develops a profound respect for the culture of these people and learns that a whale is "coming to him," though he finds that he cannot, ultimately, kill it. This realization and his relationship with Upkik, an Eskimo girl, help him see why his dream of being like an Eskimo can never be. Newbery Award-winner Jean George again skillfully weaves Eskimo tradition and folklore with modern technology and the dilemmas of drugs and government intervention in this powerful and moving tale of a young man and his desire to belong to two different cultures.

A major topic of concern throughout the book is the government's restriction that limits the number of whales Eskimos are permitted by law to kill. As a topic for formal debate, one group could take the Eskimo's position, another the view of environmentalists. One source of information is *National Wildlife Magazine*, especially the April-May, 1978, and the November-December, 1978, issues. Additional information on the International Whaling Commission may be obtained by writing to the National Wildlife Federation, 1412 16th Street, N.W., Washington, DC   20036.   K.B.B.

Native American Studies,
Contemporary Affairs.
Science
Junior High School
High School

Related Source

251.   Hamilton, Virginia. *Junius Over Far*. Harper & Row, 1985. ISBN 0-06-022195-X, $11.89. Ages 12-up.

In *Junius Over Far* Virginia Hamilton has characteristically written a multi-layered novel full of vivid imagery and dialect. It is at the same time a mildly suspenseful mystery, a character study of three generations, and a comment on the aging process and how family support can dignify it. Grandfather Jackabo is a Caribbean "island mahn" who decides to return to his beloved Snake Island. When his letters to Damius, his Americanized son, and Junius, the grandson who emulates him, become confusing and full of references to pirates, Damius and Junius become concerned and travel to Snake Island to make sure Grandfather Jackabo is all right. There they solve the mystery of the strange disappearance of Burtie Rawlings, Jackabo's old enemy and distant white relative, with whom he had been living in uneasy truce. There also Damius ultimately comes to accept what Junius and Jackabo have always known: that the "Caribbee," in spite of the depressing contrast between rich and poor that drove him away, is an undeniable part of his heritage. This is thought-provoking reading from one of this country's finest and most honored writers.

When Damius and Junius find Jackabo ragged, hungry, and toothless, his face wet with tears of relief that they have finally come, they embrace him and set about restoring his dignity. They find his false teeth, they feed him, and they give him love. Young adults who may be witnessing aging grandparents can explore the options families have in caring for an aging person, both today and historically. The students might also grapple with what they imagine their own lives will be like in old age. Faced with the options they discover in their research, they can discuss their individual choices and their rationales.   M.A.C.

Black Studies,
Social Studies
Junior High School
High School

252.   Hamilton, Virginia. *A White Romance*. Philomel, 1987. ISBN 0-399-21213-2, $14.95. Ages 13-up.

When Colonel Glenn High School starts bussing in white students, the last person Talley Barbour expects to befriend is blonde-haired Didi Adair. Yet they share a common love of running, and their friendship grows in spite of their differences and Talley's father's objection to the friendship. When Didi becomes involved with a punk rocker druggie, Talley jokingly refers to their relationship as a "white romance." Though she was able to see the faults of Didi's relationship with Roady, she loses sight of reason when she falls for Roady's friend David, who is a drug pusher. Hamilton writes with stark honesty and poignancy as she describes Talley's first love and the pain which results in a love based upon superficial need. Hamilton writes her story in dialect which adds to the authenticity of the characters and setting. Through Talley's first person narrative, via Hamilton's skilled pen, the reader is able to actually feel Talley's thoughts and experiences as someone carried away with a careless love. Some readers may object to sexual passages, but these are handled to reflect Talley's innocence.

Two chapters within the book are devoted to a rock concert, from standing in line for long hours to the loud and sometimes rowdy finish. These two chapters can be read aloud to students, noting Hamilton's exquisite attention to detail so that the reader is able to grasp what it is like to be there. Discuss with the students the sensory words used and how they make the reader feel. Brainstorm a list of topics for students to write about: an athletic event, either as participant or observer in the stands; a laundromat on a weekend; or any other event which evokes strong awareness of the senses. Then make five separate lists, one for each of the senses, and fill in with as many words as possible that appropriately describe their topic. These words can be used as a resource when students write their description of the event.   K.B.B.

Black Studies,
Literature
High School

253.   Harlan, Elizabeth. *Watershed*. Viking Kestrel, 1986. ISBN
0-670-80824-5, $12.95. Ages 12-up.

Noel has a great idea: he wants to pester a crotchety farmer by
flooding some of the farmer's fields. Noel's brother, Jeb, who is his
best friend, refuses to get involved but doesn't attempt to dissuade Noel.
The tragic outcome and the permanent effects of the prank, not only on
Noel's family but on the whole community, are chilling. The relationship between the brothers is especially touching, since two tragedies
could have been avoided if the brothers had talked about their feelings.
Instead, one poor choice leads to another for Noel, and he commits suicide because he can't envision life becoming better again. This subject
matter and Jeb's physical relationship with his girlfriend, though dis-
creetly discussed, make *Watershed* inappropriate for younger readers.
Nevertheless, it is a well–crafted portrayal of loving siblings and a family during a crisis.

Watershed is a book about making responsible decisions and facing the consequences of those decisions. Noel and Jeb, as main characters, make most of the decisions, but their parents, their younger brother, and others also influence the outcome of the story by ways they decide to respond. Divide the class into small groups (4-5 students) and
assign each group one character (more than one group can have the same
character). First, have each group go through the book and list the
choices that character made during the story. Then have the group think
of alternative decisions that the character could have made and hypothe-
size the possible outcome of the suggested option. Finally, have each
group draw a flow chart showing what the character actually did and
what the character could have done. Emphasize that everyone has options—some constructive, some destructive—in their lives, and perhaps
Noel would have avoided major mistakes had he understood all his options.   J.J.S.

*Family Life,
Social Studies
Junior High School
High School*

254.   Hartling, Peter. *Crutches*. Translated by Elizabeth D. Craw-
ford. Lothrop, Lee & Shepard, 1988 (1st Am. ed.). ISBN 0-
688-07991-1, $11.95. Ages 10-up.

Crutches, by Peter Hartling, is a translation from the German. Mr.
Hartling felt compelled to share this story, which is very close to being
an autobiography. His father, who was anti-Nazi, was drafted into the
German army and died in a Russian prison. Later, his mother committed
suicide, leaving him to survive with only his sister as family. Thomas,
in the book, has also lost his father for similar reasons and has become
separated from his mother. His benefactor and friend is a man called
Crutches because he lost his leg in the war. Thomas attaches himself to
Crutches, and both try to return to Germany. Their deep friendship and
survival needs result in an adventure and tell of humanity toward others
during a time of great adversity.

This book would add a new dimension to a unit on World War II.
Young people can read about the Jewish struggle for survival in books
like *The Endless Steppe* by Esther Hautzig (Crowell, 1986) and *The*

ALA Notable Book

Related Sources

Holocaust Studies
Middle School
Junior High School
High School

Upstairs Room by Johanna Reiss (Crowell, 1976). *Crutches* is the story of a gentile in that horrible era of human history. Reading it may stimulate students to research the lives of other gentiles who became entangled in Hitler's web, either because they were sympathetic to the Jews or were drafted into the Nazi army. An obvious example is Baron Von Trapp, whose story was made into the musical "The Sound of Music." Students may want to view this movie and then read Maria Trapp's

Related Source

The Story of the Trapp Family Singers (Doubleday, 1957), comparing the way two different story forms present the impact on the Von Trapps of the Nazi invasion of Austria.   V.H.S.

255.   Heuck, Sigrid. *The Hideout*. Translated by Rika Lesser. Dutton, 1988 (1st Am. ed.). ISBN 0-525-44343-6, $13.95. Ages 11-up.

Taken to a German orphanage in the last year of World War II, a young girl only remembers her first name, Rebecca. Having a Jewish name and dark features, she is taunted by peers who call her "Gypsy Child." Rebecca's consolation is her secret knowledge of Sami, an older boy hiding in a nearby cornfield. He imaginatively takes her to more peaceful realms, where the bombers (personified as Rebmob the dragon) are controlled. Although the novel ends abruptly, the children's resourcefulness in coping with the horrors of war is remarkable.

Rebecca chooses to ignore the fact that she saw a human face in the cockpit of a plane attacking her. Facing a dragon is one thing; facing a human being is another. Discuss the human flaws that generate war and find examples in the book. The misuse of power is seen in the cruelties of the orphanage children and of the Nazi soldiers. Sami helps Rebecca understand warlike mentality by engaging her in a war in their fantasy kingdom of Cornpeace. Staging a "mock war" in the classroom, perhaps modeled after Jean Merrill's *Pushcart War* (Scott, 1964) or Dr. Seuss's *The Butter Battle Book* (Random House, 1984), and discussing the resulting feelings might help students address the issue of avoiding conflict in their personal lives.   Y.D.S.

Peace Studies,
Holocaust Studies
Middle School
Junior High School
High School

Related Sources

256.   Highwater, Jamake. *Eyes of Darkness*. Lothrop, Lee & Shepard, 1985. ISBN 0-688-41993-3, $13.00. Ages 12-up.

The late 1800s were pivotal years for Native Americans everywhere, especially those People of the Plains whose lives were changed forever by the massacre at Wounded Knee. Jamake Highwater plunges the reader immediately into the turmoil and changes faced by the People whose lands and life were taken by the forces of a larger and better armed white culture. Yesa is brought up in the traditions of his people, yet is forced to attend schools and learn the religion of the whites whom he has vowed to war against. In the end, his intelligence leads him to university and medical school allowing the fulfillment of his pledge to help his people by using the white man's medicine. The ironic conclusion to this fast-paced and authentic fiction honors the image of Native

Americans—indeed all people—who stand against the tyrannies of an oppressor.

Eyes of Darkness compares favorably with such classics as Hal Borland's *When the Legends Die* (Bantam, 1972) and Frank Waters' *The Man Who Killed the Deer* (Swallow, 1942), representing literature about the Native American caught between the changing, traditional world of his/her people and the domination of European America. This theme is crucial in the study of literature about all minority groups struggling to retain their cultural identity in a society that seems to be bent upon absorption. A useful source of books for use with units on multicultural literature is Rudman's *Children's Literature: An Issues Approach* (Longman's, 1984).   H.M.

Related Sources

Native American Studies
Middle School
Junior High School
High School

Related Source

257.   Highwater, Jamake. *I Wear the Morning Star*. Harper & Row, 1986. ISBN 0-06-022356-1, $11.89. Ages 12-up.

Part three of the "Ghost Horse Cycle" begins with Amana's young grandson Sitko being torn from her and placed in a foster home. Eventually taken in by his mother and her white lover, Sitko never stops dreaming of his native heritage. He sees the visions that Grandmother Amana taught him to see and discovers within himself the talent to preserve them as paintings. Troubled and confused by the inner struggle to "belong" and to be himself, Sitko withdraws into himself, living in the shadow of others, until forced to be on his own to reach for his own dreams. Highwater again succeeds in eliciting the reader's empathy for the plight of Native Americans, this time as they are pressured to become "Americanized." Though not as intense as *The Ceremony of Innocence* (Harper & Row, 1985), this book still causes reflection and leaves the responsibility of our ancestors' cruelty, thoughtlessness, and heartless actions weighing heavy on the consciences of the present generation.

Related Source

I Wear the Morning Star would be an appropriate lead-in to introducing a class to the art of North America, centering upon the American Indian. A local art museum may be able to provide some background information on the subject and a field trip may expose students to the types of art created by the country's first settlers. Highwater has written several books on the subject of American Indian art and artists that could be consulted, including *Arts of the Indian Americas* (Harper & Row, 1983) and *The Sweet Grass Lives On* (Harper & Row, 1980).   L.S.

Art,
Native American Studies
Middle School
Junior High School
Middle School

Related Sources

258.   Highwater, Jamake. *Legend Days*. Harper & Row, 1984. ISBN 0-06-022304-9, $10.89. Ages 12-up.

It is a time of transition for the Blood tribe, and it is a time of transition for the remarkable Amana. When the white man's sickness—smallpox—brings death to all but a handful of her people, eleven-year-old Amana has a powerful vision that fills her with warrior powers. Throughout her adolescence and early adulthood her bravery in the hunt

ALA Best Book
ALA Notable Book

First of Highwater's
Ghost Dance cycle

and in battle permit her survival; yet rigid sex role customs frustrate her real desires and embarrass her new family. Highwater sets this story of a girl's coming of age against the backdrop of the Northern Plains Indians' thwarted efforts to maintain their traditional ways in the early 1800s. The pace is balanced between action and reflection, and the events are authentic. Rich in symbol and imagery, *Legend Days* succeeds in placing the reader squarely in the time and place.

Here is a powerful work that offers a multiplicity of meanings to older readers upon which teachers may capitalize. It may be viewed as "pro-feminist," though its central theme of the search for personal identity is universal. It joins with Joyce Rockwell's *Long Man's Song* (Holt, Rinehart and Winston, 1975) and *To Spoil the Sun* (Holt Rinehart and Winston, 1976) as one of the few novels of Indian–White relations written for young people that looks at historical events from the victims' perspective. Any focus on Native American literature or multicultural studies will be enriched by this literary gem and the others in this "cycle" of stories about Amana and her descendants.   H.M.

Women's Studies
Native American Studies
Junior High School
High School

Related Sources

259.   Hinton, S.E. *Taming the Star Runner*. Delacorte, 1988. ISBN 0-440-50058-3, $14.95. Ages 12-up.

ALA Best Book

As she does in her other acclaimed and widely read novels for adolescents, Hinton portrays a misunderstood and angry teenager who doesn't fit easily into a world perceived to be unsympathetic and uncaring; in other words, an outsider. In this latest variation on a familiar theme, Travis is sent to live with an uncle following an assault on his stepfather and short jail stay. He encounters unfriendly classmates and an uncle with marital problems. We are not surprised to learn that beneath his rage and hostility, Travis—like Tex, Ponyboy, and the others before him—is really a sensitive and caring young man who longs to be a novelist. His efforts to tame the wild horse Star Runner parallel his personal-social realities, but readers will get the idea anyway. Hinton's plot moves quickly with just the right amounts of romance and conflict. Her characters are easy to understand, appealing to the emotional needs of early adolescent readers, and have enough authenticity to garner wide appeal and reader enthusiasm.

Early teen readers should be drawn to the pathos of Travis's circumstances, just as they have been to the young people featured in Hinton's earlier books: *The Outsiders* (Viking, 1967), *Rumble Fish* (Delacorte, 1975), *That was Then, This is Now* (Dell paperback, 1980), and *Tex* (Delacorte, 1979). Here is an excellent opportunity for junior and senior high school literature teachers to focus on how an author delineates characters, and how the principle character embodies the social value(s) central to the story. The consistency of her writing and the similarities among her characters and their circumstances—plus their strong emotional appeal to early teen readers—make Hinton's novels ideal for closer study in literature programs. Films of her previous books are generally available at video rental stores or through the public library.   J.P./H.M.

Related Sources

Literature
Junior High School
High School

260. Hoover, H.M. *The Dawn Palace: The Story of Medea*. Dutton, 1988. ISBN 0-525-44388-6, $15.95. Ages 12-up.

ALA Best Book

Medea is a character out of Greek mythology who was considered a sorceress. She was married to Jason and betrayed by him. Hoover's depiction of Medea is sympathetic. We see her as a young girl, blinded by love, who sought to give comfort to her husband and children, but who was forced by circumsances of birth to take part in events of extreme brutality. One of the most interesting aspects of Hoover's story is that she explains scientifically some events of Medea's life around which myth grew. The "bulls of Hephaestus," for example, which Jason had to harness to sow the Field of Ares and win the Golden Fleece, were clever automatons driven by slaves hidden inside. Compared to sparse versions of the tale from anthologies of Greek myths, this one is detailed and compelling.

Reading *The Dawn Palace* may lead students to wonder about what things were available to people at the time of Medea. Hoover gives a short list in the back of the book which could start an investigation for others. Another area to explore is *perspective*. In the eyes of the Greeks, Medea was an evil sorceress one did not want to tangle with and a barbarian from a land far across the sea. Paradoxically, Medea's country, Colchis, was far more civilized and technologically developed than Greece. Medea brought better times to Corinth when she became Queen there by sharing the innovations common to Colchis. Students might select other "evil" people from Greek mythology and write short stories about some aspect of their lives from their perspective.   M.A.C.

Literature,
Language Arts
Junior High School
High School

261. Horwitz, Joshua. *Only Birds and Angels Fly*. Harper and Row, 1985. ISBN 0-06-022599-8, $11.89. Ages 12-up.

Related Source

If *A Separate Peace* had been set in the late 1960's instead of in World War II America, the result might have been similar to *Only Birds and Angels Fly*. This book is also the story of two boys who meet at a private school. One of the boys, Chris, is something of a flawed golden boy, and the other, Danny, is his faithful comrade. Instead of having war as a backdrop, the issue that eventually separates the friends is drugs. While Chris becomes enmeshed in the drug culture of the late 60's, finally dying in a drug-related incident, Danny realizes he must leave Chris's world in order to live. Excellent writing and characterizations make an otherwise predictable plot an interesting character study, showing how people can grow apart despite years of shared experience.

Although the most obvious way to use this book might be as a character study and a chance to examine how literature portrays relationships between friends, another use would be to have the students read both *A Separate Peace* and *Only Birds and Angels Fly*. Students can not only discuss not only the similarities, but also the differences, being sure to emphasize those that are related to the time settings. Especially note that even though there are strong similarities between the major characters, the similarities are as much in how the character functions

Drug Education,
Literature
Junior High School
High School

within the context of the relationship as in their actual character. After the students are familiar with both books, have them write a short adaptation of the general themes and relationships found in both books geared towards the 1980's.   J.J.S.

262.   Howker, Janni. *Isaac Campion*. Greenwillow, 1987. ISBN 0-688-06658-5, $10.25. Ages 10-up.

ALA Best Book

It is rural England in 1901, and for as long as twelve-year-old Isaac can remember, the Campions have been enemies of the Lacys. When Isaac's older and favored brother is accidentally killed taking a dare from Dick Lacy, Isaac's father is enraged. Heartbroken, Isaac must come to terms with his own grief—a confrontation complicated by the ever-widening chasm between Isaac and his father and the economic necessity of quitting school to work in the family's horse business. Isaac's inner struggle between family duty and his dreams is textured with complex human emotions; his empathy for both man and beast is especially powerful. The easy, flowing dialect present in 96-year-old Isaac's reminiscent narrative further intensifies the character development.

*Literature,
Language Arts
Middle School
Junior High School*

In detail, and with clarity and openness, Isaac tells of his thoughts, emotions, and the daily work he has to do throughout a period of a few months. Reading excerpts aloud from *Isaac Campion* could be an introduction to journal writing. Over a period of several weeks, encourage students to write down their personal thoughts and emotions, their interactions with family members, or the activities they do each day. If they stick to one main theme, they may discover a pattern of growth in one area of their lives. Included in their journal could be a childhood memory that, for various reasons, remains clear in their minds.   L.B./S.J.S.

263.   Hughes, Monica. *Sandwriter*. Henry Holt, 1988 (1st Am. ed.). ISBN 0-8050-0617-6, $12.95. Ages 12-up.

The Desert of Roshan is the backdrop for this mystical fantasy. A mysterious old woman called "Sandwriter" leads the young Prince Jodril and Princess Antia to the magical caves beneath the Great Dune. Their journey is threatened by the evil Eskoril, who yearns to learn about and exploit the powerful secrets of the underground water and fuel reservoirs. Hughes successfully blends mystery and adventure with an unusual setting and plot to refresh and intrigue the reader. Rich descriptions of camel caravans and ancient palaces delight the senses and transport the reader to the imaginary islands of Kamalant and Roshan.

*Drama,
Reader's Theater
Middle School
Junior High School*

Because the action and dialogue of Hughes's story lend themselves well to dramatization or reader's theater, students may enjoy staging certain scenes from *Sandwriter*. Pages 111-116, for example, tell the legend of how the secret waters of Roshan were discovered. By using sheets for costumes, recorded sitar music, a darkened room, and flashlights covered with colored cellophane, students can capture the desert setting and bring the story to life.   J.B.R.

264.   Hurmence, Belinda. *Tancy*. Houghton Mifflin, 1984. ISBN
0-89919-228-9, $11.95. Ages 11-up.

Considering the limited availability of appealing fictional material
for young adults concerning the Civil War, *Tancy* should be given consideration. Much as the Collier brothers did in their historical novels,
Hurmence weaves a dramatic tale of the turbulent Reconstruction period.
Tancy, formerly a favored house slave, ventures out into the unknown
world of freedom. In a ramshackle village of former slaves, she has a
less-than-warm reunion with her mother, who had been mysteriously
sold when Tancy was a baby. Tancy is a strong woman who makes it
her business to chronicle the feelings of former slaves as they become
accustomed to their newfound freedom.

February is a month to celebrate Black history. Teachers of junior
and senior high school social studies may want to bring some of that
history to life by introducing their students to *Tancy* and to Hurmence's
1982 novel, *A Girl Called Boy* (Clarion, 1982), in which a middle-
class black girl is time-warped back into slavery. Thus, she gets a taste
of what slavery would really have been like. Another excellent choice,
which could make this a "trilogy," is Virginia Hamilton's *Magical Adventures of Pretty Pearl* (Harper & Row, 1983). All three novels
are provocative and vividly written and should generate an empathetic
discussion of times our nation should never forget. Julius Lester's *To
Be A Slave* (Dial, 1968) offers firsthand accounts of those days by
those who lived them.   L.P.B.

*Black Studies
Intermediate
Middle School
Junior High School*

Related Sources

264.   Irwin, Hadley. *Kim/Kimi*. McElderry, 1987. ISBN 0-689-
50428-4, $12.95. Ages 12-up.

Irwin's absorbing book realistically presents a teenager's struggle
for "wholeness." Thoroughly Americanized sixteen-year-old Kim Andrew, born Kimi Yogushi, is half American and half Japanese and was
adopted with a half brother. Her search for information about her Japanese father, who died before her birth and who was disowned by his
family for marrying an American woman, leads her to California. Here
she makes the shocking discovery of the existence of Japanese-
American prison camps during World War II. When she travels to Lake
Tule, site of the concentration camp where her father and his family
were imprisoned, Kimi begins to understand her missing half. This
book's deeply moving human dimension promises students a powerfully emotional experience.

At one point Kim recalls studying World War II. "My American
history book was seven hundred pages long" and there was "one sentence about relocation camps—nothing about concentration camps." Unfortunately, Kim's statement is all too true. Irwin's factual account of
the Japanese–American camps makes this a timely and appropriate book
to supplement a textbook study of World War II. Use Jeannie Wakatsu-
ki Houston's autobiography, *Farewell to Manzanar* (Bantam,
1974), which chronicles her life during and after her imprisonment, or
Journey to Topaz by Yoshiko Uchida (Scribner's, 1971) as com-

*Asian-American Studies,
U.S. History
Middle School
Junior High School
High School*

Related Sources

panion books. Older readers and teachers can gain an in-depth historical understanding of those times from *Personal Justice Denied: Wartime Relocation and Internment of Japanese-Americans During World War II* (Revisionist, 1984).   L.B.

266.   Johnson, Annabel and Edgar. *A Memory of Dragons*. Atheneum, 1986. ISBN 0-689-31263, $13.95. Ages 12-up.

America is poised at the brink of a second civil war. A small group of high-tech terrorists backed by Arab oil money conspires to cause the western states to secede and form a new country under their control. Eighteen-year-old Paul Killian, a creative, non-political science whiz with a dark personal past, is drawn into an intriguing web of events and relationships that threaten his life and the lives of those he has come to love and trust. The Johnsons have created a story set in the near future that successfully combines fast action, mystery, and easy-to-know characters in a story that raises questions of political and social importance for young adult readers. The result is an engrossing futuristic adventure that should have appeal to younger and older teens alike.

Contemporary Affairs
Junior High School
High School

A central issue in the story is that serious political upheaval often occurs when there is a scarcity of natural resources. The histories of the Middle East (water and oil) and the American Southwest (water and mineral deposits) support this thesis vividly. Social studies teachers can use *A Memory of Dragons* to introduce students to "What if..." history (What if there were no shortage of water in the Middle East? What if environmental concerns always overrode the public demand for oil/coal/uranium, seal skins?). Taken a step further, students can study "What can happen..." history (What can happen if endangered species are not protected by law? What can happen if nuclear power is/is not permitted to develop?) Ultimately, class discussions or formal debates can focus on "What should..." value questions in response to the complex political-social issues that each student will face throughout his or her lifetime.   H.M.

267.   Johnston, Norma. *The Potter's Wheel*. Morrow, 1988. ISBN 0-688-06463-9, $11.95. Ages 12-up.

Laura Blair's grandmother is a hard act to follow, especially for Laura's mother, whose response is avoidance. Grandmother Serena's latest project is a restoration of her family's village into a museum site. As the family gathers to celebrate its opening, Laura, who appears to be as strong a character as her grandmother, becomes involved with a variety of gifted but troubled relatives. Laura's innocent acceptance of her mother's absence due to a writing assignment in London is shattered when she learns the real truth about her parents' failed marriage. Thus, she finds herself drawing strength from those who had been depending upon her. This is a moving novel, rich in characterization and sense of place. The emotional climate is especially well drawn; the reader feels deeply the suffering of Laura when she learns that her family is not the safe haven she has believed it to be.

Who in our lives has the power to stimulate us to do our best or cause us to feel that we can never measure up? As a journal writing assignment, junior high or high school students might explore the question of influence. They can discuss the different characters in Johnston's book and their response to Serena as a starting point for orienting their thinking. Their journal entries should concern an individual who affects them strongly. They should also be encouraged to examine their feelings about that person to determine if their response is externally or internally motivated, and if there is any action they can or want to take to change their relationship with that person. As an activity that probes feelings, the students' right to privacy should be respected, and they should be allowed to share only on a volunteer basis.   M.A.C.

*Language Arts
Junior High School
High School*

268.   Kherdian, David. *Bridger: The Story of a Mountain Man*. Greenwillow, 1987. ISBN 0-688-06510-4, $11.75. Ages 12-up.

Around a campfire, under a sky swept with stars, young Jim Bridger's story begins. The first person narrative allows young readers to trap and trail along with his famous mountain man as he reveals his vision of America's Great Plains. The strength of this factually-based historical novel lies in the fine characterization of Bridger and the sparse, determined writing style which forms the backdrop for this reading adventure. Realistic in content, Kherdian chronicles the difficult life of Bridger and contemporaries such as Mike Fink. As he did in *Finding Home* (Greenwillow, 1981) and the Newbery Honor Book, *The Road From Home* (Greenwillow, 1987), Kherdian gives his readers healthy respect for the difficulties his characters faced and overcame just to stay alive and make their way in this world.

Related Sources

Bridger could be an effective vehicle to expand students' understanding of folk tales and tall tales and their relationship to American history. Because Mike Fink is portrayed in an uncomplimentary light, students might find it interesting to question why heroes are important to a nation, and if these heroes are truly larger than life. Harold W. Felton's *Mike Fink–Best of the Keelboatmen* (Dodd, Mead, 1960) and James C. Bowman's *Mike Fink* (Little, Brown, 1957) paint their hero in the brilliant light of exaggeration which we usually associate with tall tales. The first part of the 19th century, because it was an era of expansion and westward growth, seemed to be an especially fertile time for the creation of tall tales. Studying them and their sources would give students a broader view of life during this rough-and-tumble period in western American history.   G.G.

*Literature, U.S. History
Middle School
Junior High School*

Related Sources

269.   Korman, Gordon. *Don't Care High*. Scholastic, 1985. ISBN 0-590-33322-4, $10.95. Ages 12-up.

Paul Abrams cares. His new friend Sheldon Pryor cares, too. But it seems that no one else at Don Carey High School even notices that the school exists. They cannot even get anyone to run for student body president at "Don't Care" High. Then Paul, who has just moved to this rather different school, and Sheldon, who is also new, concoct a totally implausible scheme for getting the most apathetic character in the school elected president. When the success of this well-intentioned hoax exceeds Paul's and Sheldon's expectations, they wonder how far they can go to raise school spirit without getting caught. Amazingly enough, they are never discovered, and the twists and tangles they go through to make the situation work out are inventive and quirky. The author has made an unlikely situation and preposterous characters totally believable through a finely-honed combination of good writing and an excellent sense of plot development.

Since enthusiasm in general, and school spirit in particular, are frequently regarded as "uncool" among some adolescents, this book presents an excellent opportunity to discuss the purposes and implications of school spirit. After a short discussion introducing the topic, have the students write a position paper, taking a stand on whether they feel school spirit is important or not. If students do not mention that some people gain a sense of identity through their affiliation with a school (on the pro side) or that the school is merely an institution, something required of everyone (on the con side), be sure to bring those points up for the class to consider.   J.J.S.

Language Arts
Junior High School
High School

270.   Korman, Gordon. *Son of Interflux*. Scholastic, 1986. ISBN 0-590-40163-7, $12.95. Ages 12-up.

ALA Best Book

Gordon Korman has written twelve books since age eleven and is as funny as columnist Dave Barry. *Son of Interflux* is the story of Simon Irving, a corporate brat, and his rebellion against Interflux, a giant company that only makes parts of things—zipper teeth, suitcase hinge pins, etc.—a company led by his father, Cyril. Simon's rebellion takes the form of Antiflux, a "company" consisting of the disgruntled students of Nassau Arts High School of Literary, Visual and Performing Arts. Antiflux gains a stranglehold on Interflux through purchasing a thin strip of neglected land that is essential to Interflux's new building project. As the corporations play cat and mouse with each other, Simon and his father call a truce at home, united in plots to avoid Mrs. Irving's latest fad diets. Also, Simon, a promising painter, is struggling to adjust to Querada, his brilliant but psychotic painting teacher, who expresses his reactions to his student's work by throwing chairs out the window and literally hitting the ceiling with his 6'8" body. Korman's zany characters are unforgettable, yet human, and his humor is delicious.

Literature,
Language Arts
Junior High School
High School

Related Sources

What turns an ordinary story into sidesplitting humor? The use of language, characterization, plot setting? High school students can be encouraged to discover what makes humor tick through an analysis of *Son of Interflux* and other humorous novels, such as William Goldman's *The Princess Bride* (Ballantine, 1984). Students can then work in small groups to take a skeletal story and turn it into a tale guaranteed to provoke laughter, or at least an amused smile.   M.A.C.

271. Lasky, Kathryn. *The Bone Wars*. Morrow, 1988. ISBN 0-688-07433-2, $12.95. Ages 12-up.

One usually thinks of the 1870s in the American West as the time when Native Americans were fighting to keep the last remnants of their land from an endless tide of settlers, the time of Custer and Little Big Horn. At the same time and in the same area, however, there was a battle of a very different kind going on: a competition among archaeologists for the bones of prehistoric creatures. Lasky places two boys from diverse backgrounds into this colorful setting: Thaddeus Longsworth, an orphan whose prostitute mother was murdered when he was only five, and Julian DeMott, a young British aristocrat whose father is a renowned scholar with opinions his son cannot condone. The boys' adventures are exciting, leading the reader not only into the history of early paleontological efforts in the U.S., but also into a better understanding of Indian affairs at the time. Lasky's presentation of Native Americans is sympathetic and respects not only their culture, but also their precarious position during those times.

The discovery of the first complete fossil, that of an ichthyosaurus in 1811 by twelve-year-old Mary Anning, marked the beginning of modern exploration for dinosaurs. Few dinosaur books, however, have focused upon the history of paleotology, save for a brief description of her find. *The Bone Wars* sheds a new light on this era, especially as Lasky has so skillfully interwoven it with its social and political context. It is, therefore, recommended for high school teachers of science and history as a vehicle for integrating their curricular areas and for helping students gain a more complete understanding of the American West in the decade following the Civil War.   M.A.C.

Science, History
Junior High School
High School

272. Lasky, Kathryn. *Home Free*. Four Winds, 1985. ISBN 0-02-751650-4, $13.95. Ages 12-up.

Home Free accurately portrays the efforts to reintroduce the bald eagle to the Quabbin wilderness of Massachusetts. But is this merely a nature story? Certainly not. It is a marvelous mixture of realistic fiction and fantasy. The construction of the Quabbin Reservoir in the 1930s literally caused four communities to cease existence. Fascinated by the effects of such a loss of place and identity, the young protagonist, Sam, discovers an implausible link between the submerged towns and mysterious autistic teenage girl, Lucy Swift. Deeply involved with the program to bring back the eagles, Sam also witnesses an unbelievable mutuality between the silent girl and the largest of the noble birds. The secret of Lucy Swift holds the key to preserving the Quabbin wilderness and luring the eagles home. Though all elements of the story are strong, the impressive style of her prose makes for an exhilarating reading experience.

This book is filled with detailed information concerning the bald eagle and methods used by naturalists for encouraging nesting. It examines the bitter controversy among differing philosophies concerning land use. *Home Free* could be an excellent complement to a science class study of endangered species and conservation. Here is an excellent op-

Science
Junior High School
High School

portunity to integrate the language arts with other subject areas and use children's trade books rather than texts for purposes of instruction.   M.O.T.

273.   Lasky, Kathryn. *Pageant*. Macmillan, 1986. ISBN 0-02-751720-9, $12.95. Ages 12-up.

ALA Best Book

Bits and pieces of the four years that Sarah Benjamin is enrolled in Indianapolis's most exclusive girls' school are presented in this well-written, thought-provoking story of Sarah's coming of age in the early 1960s. In addition to everyday problems, her teenage life is complicated by the annual Christmas pageant in which she must always be a shepherd; Aunt Hattie's moving in to recover from eye surgery as her sister leaves for college, rescuing a pregnant violinist in a blizzard; and finally, Kennedy's assassination. Moved by this last tragic event, Sarah reaches her breaking point, resulting in an insightful discovery of self which allows her to finally assume control of her life. Lasky has packed *Pageant* with honest emotions, sensitivity, and humor. She has successfully captured the inner turmoil of a confused and lonely adolescent girl trying to come to terms with herself and the direction in which life is taking her. Lasky provokes sympathy for Sarah as readers relate to her struggles and eventual success.

U.S. History
Junior High School
High School

The "New Frontier"—Kennedy's plans for the country—is often mentioned in *Pageant*. This book could be used as a springboard in a social studies class studying Kennedy's brief term in office. Break the class into groups and have each group research a particular aspect of the Kennedy years. For example, one group could gather information about the election, another on Kennedy's foreign policies, another on his domestic policies, etc. Each group could then prepare both a written report (to copy and share with classmates) and an oral report. After the oral presentations have been given, the class could speculate on how things might have been different if Kennedy had not been shot. Discussion should be based upon the available facts that have been gathered and students' assessment of those facts.   L.S.

274.   Lawrence, Louise. *Children of the Dust*. Harper & Row, 1985. ISBN 0-06-023738-4, $12.50. Ages 12-up.

ALA Best Book

A nuclear war might not mean the end of all life, but it would certainly create a radical change from what we now accept as civilized standards. Many types of "mutations" may occur. Written in three sections covering three generations of an English family, this chilling futuristic novel depicts the possibilities of survival, the physical destruction, the degeneration of survivors, the evaluation of old philosophies, and the type of new society that might be allowed to emerge. Through her vivid descriptions of emotional trauma, the author subtly evokes the need for a strong reassessment of political motives and social values.

This book could be explored for its wide variety of social/political ramifications. It lends itself easily to personal introspection about what we value and appreciate, including what we would not want to see wasted or lost in any way. Students can speculate about the possible changes that would occur and the forms of government that might emerge as communities that survive nuclear war attempt to resume civilized coexistence. For comparison, books that have dealt with developing governmental forms are Orwell's *Animal Farm* (Harcourt Brace Jovanovich, 1954), Golding's *Lord of the Flies* (Putnam, 1978), and Shute's best-seller, *On the Beach* (Morrow, 1959).   M.G.C.

*Peace Studies
Junior High School
High School*

Related Sources

275. Lawrence, Louise. *Moonwind*. Harper & Row, 1986. ISBN 0-06-023734-1, $11.89. Ages 12-up.

Bethkahn, an astral being from beyond the solar system, is stranded on Earth's Moon and secretly must call upon the help of Gareth, a visitor from Wales, to repair her starship so she may return to her home on Khio Three, nine thousand light years away. Gareth's disenchantment with his Earthlife and his willingness to believe in Bethkahn's existence lead him to his agonizing "permanent solution, the final freedom." As she does in her award-winning *Children of the Dust* (Harper & Row, 1985), Lawrence creates a spellbinding adventure story rich in human emotion, while posing questions crucial to the survival of the race. This is a remarkable blend of gripping action, gentle romance, and the futuristic imagination of an outstanding science fiction writer.

Related Source

At the beginning of the story, Bethkahn wakens from a cryogenic sleep of ten thousand years. The present technology of freeze-sleep is in its infancy and experimentation continues. Older readers may wish to learn more about current theory and technology, and the prospects of future applications. Their findings could easily lead to discussion or writing about the human benefits (e.g., reviving cancer victims when a cure is available), potential disadvantages (e.g., adjusting to a radically different social order or technology), and ironies (e.g., being younger than one's descendents).   H.M.

*Science
Junior High School
High School*

276. Lawrence, Louise. *The Warriors of Taan*. Harper & Row, 1988. ISBN 0-06-023737-6, $12.89. Ages 12-up.

In this fantasy of societies learning to live together, the rebellious Prince Khian of Taan shuns the sisterhood and leads his warriors out of Fen-havat into battle against the destructive Outworlders. Learning that extinction is inevitable, Khian retreats against his father's will. He listens to Eleana, the eventual Reverend Mother, and the inexplicable Leith, forming an alliance with the sisterhood and the feared but gentle non-human Stonewraiths. Prince Khian is imprisoned by his father while Eleana goes forth to negotiate with the Stonewraiths. Good wins over evil as Prince Khian and Elena lead the people of Taan to victory. Louis Lawrence weaves an entertaining and provocative story in which women must demonstrate great cunning and courage in battle as well as gentle and nurturing spirits.

In small groups, students could discuss the social, political, eco-

Women's Studies
Junior High School
High School

nomic, religious, and military aspects of society represented by the sisterhood, the warriors, and the Stonewraiths. Then, using a flow chart or storyboard, students could write examples of each aspect of society as discussed in the book. Finally, they could review these aspects in American society. As an end project, individual students could write an article discussing American society and how to use positive ideas from *The Warriors of Taan* to form an "ideal" society, including ways to implement their ideas.   C.E.L.

277.   L'Engle, Madeleine. *Many Waters*. Farrar, Straus & Giroux, 1986. ISBN 0-374-34796-4, $12.95. Ages 12-up.

ALA Best Book

Companion to L'Engle's
Time Trilogy

Religious imagery and historical events converge in this complex fantasy. Older readers should find in *Many Waters* something old and something new. Meg and Charles Wallace's twin brothers Sandy and Dennys accidentally "tesseract" through time to the eve of the Great Flood. They are befriended by members of Noah's family and live through the turbulent days preceding the building of the ark. Readers can gain an often frank glimpse of social living patterns in Biblical times and the events leading up to the building of the ark. In addition, it is the story of the coming of age of the twins who are mere decorations in L'Engle's other books. The sensual feelings of the boys toward the temptations of the beautiful Tiglah and of Noah's youngest daughter, Yalith, are made as important to the story as the conflict between Noah and his father, Lamech, or the mystery of the *nephilim* who coexist with humans. There is a generous mixture of the fantastic, of powerful human emotions, and of a great religious mystery in this new masterwork by one of America's most honored writers.

Related Sources

Author Studies,
Literature
Junior High School
High School

Many Waters is an addition to L'Engle's Time Trilogy, which includes *A Wrinkle in Time* (1962), *A Wind in the Door* (1973), and *A Swiftly Tilting Planet* (1978), all published by Farrar, Straus & Giroux. Though each of the books stands on its own as a finely crafted story, collectively they represent the story of family who combine scientific thought with fundamental human values. All four books are worthy of close reading and discussion by a class or a group. Teachers and librarians should encourage young people to learn as much as possible about the author's background and range of interests to provide greater insights into her writings. The period of study might be culminated with an interview by telephone conference call if it can be arranged through contacting her publisher.   H.M.

278.   Levitin, Sonia. *The Return*. Atheneum, 1987. ISBN 0-689-31309, $12.95. Ages 10-up.

ALA Best Book
ALA Notable Book

Desta is a young Ethiopian Jew determined to fulfill her deceased family's dream of life in Israel. Separated from her family's friends, she and her younger sister travel through dangerous territory often without food and water, to become part of "Operation Moses," the recent, real-life airlift of Ethiopian Jews. Levitin writes a simple, eloquent account

251

of their journey. The language is clear and colorful with touches of Ethiopian and Jewish philosophies and folklore woven into the story.
Through careful exposition this book manages to explain the plight of
the Jews without sounding preachy or maudlin. Levitin's writing takes
the reader to another world that is hard to imagine. No child should miss
this opportunity to travel with her.

Older children can examine the problems Jews have faced throughout history and discuss why they have so often been forced out of areas
where they have settled. Students could research the basis for the current
Arab and Israeli conflict and have a debate with one group of students
representing Arab interests and another group Jewish. The July, 1985,
issue of *National Geographic Magazine* has a still timely article, "Israel:
the Search for the Center" with useful information on the history of the
Jews' present land disputes. Look in the May, 1983, issue of *National
Geographic Magazine* for the article "Ethiopian Revolution in the Ancient Empire" that discusses the "Falashas" or Black Jews.   L.A.B.

*Contemporary Affairs,
Multicultural Studies
Middle School
Junior High School
High School*

Related Source

279.   MacLean, John. *Mac*. Houghton Mifflin, 1987. ISBN 0-395-
43080-1, $12.95. Ages 12-up.

Written as first person narrative, Mac is the story of a fifteen-year-
old boy who leads a normal life until something happens that drastically
changes his personality. As Mac tries to deny the incident, the reader is
unsure of what really happened to him, but is given hints and clues as
his pain and anger leak out from behind the controlled facade. When
Mac finally alienates his family, friends and girlfriend, he is referred to
Mrs. Resnick, a school counselor who gradually draws out the painful
secret that Mac had been sexually abused by a doctor during a physical
examination. Strong language is used at times, yet is appropriate to the
content. Brutally shocking and revealing, *Mac* is one story which will
not easily be forgotten as readers feel Mac's rage and humiliation as he
slowly comes to terms with what has happened to him.

Sexual abuse is a sensitive topic, and books such as *Mac* may provide bibliotherapy for students who are in this agonizing situation and
have become silent victims; it may help those who know a victim to better understand their friend's fear and anguish. Other books on this same
topic with girls as the main character are Hermes' *A Solitary Secret*
(Harcourt Brace Jovanovich, 1985) and Irwin's *Abby, My Love*
(Atheneum, 1985). Teachers, guidance counselors, and librarians can
help victims of sexual abuse by letting *all* children know what local resources, such as children's services boards, are available for them when
they don't know where else to turn.   K.B.B.

ALA Best Book

*Family Life
Junior High School
High School*

Related Sources

280.   Magorian, Michelle. *Back Home*. Harper & Row, 1984.
ISBN 0-06-024104-7, $13.89. Ages 12-up.

Now that the war in Europe is over, twelve-year-old Rusty has returned to England to rejoin her family and must adjust to a pattern of life
different from that of her five years in America. She finds it difficult to

ALA Best Book

feel close to her mother and younger brother, who was born while she was away. When her stiff and distant father returns from his tour of duty, she is sent off to a girl's boarding school where she truly suffers for her American ways. Michelle Mogorian has created a powerful and moving portrait of a young girl's struggle for acceptance and of a family torn by separation. Her characters are believable and vivid; her story is complex, coherent, and fast-moving. In spite of occasional mild profanity, it is a masterful story that ranks with the very best books of 1984.

The portrait of boarding school life offers many opportunities to contrast the rules, traditions, and programs of the British public (private) school with American schools. Further, Magorian's first book, the award-winning *Good Night, Mr. Tom* (Harper & Row, 1981), both critically praised and widely read, also centers on the evacuation of children in England during World War II. Readers may be curious about how this large-scale movement was carried out, and could discuss how such a program might be carried out in this country under similar circumstances.   H.M.

Related Source

*English History
Junior High School
High School*

281.   Mazer, Norma Fox. *After the Rain*. Morrow, 1987. ISBN 0-688-06867-7, $11.75. Ages 12-up.

ALA Best Book

Grandpa Izzy was stubborn and ill-tempered. The family's Sunday visits were unpleasant to fifteen-year-old Rachel. When the doctor confided to her parents that Izzy had a terminal disease and only two to three months to live, things changed. Rachel took him for after-school walks and they talked. Within weeks Izzy was hospitalized and a determined Rachel stayed by his side until his death. Mazer treats the family's emotions before, during and after Izzy's death powerfully and sensitively. Her vivid characterization of Rachel contrasts the pain of growing up with the powerful impact of different forms of love.

An unusual aspect of this book is its use of third person, present tense narration. Junior high students might benefit from a review of first and third person narration of literature. Reading aloud from *After the Rain* demonstrates that the third person, present tense narrator is an outside observer, one who tells the story as it happens. To practice writing from this point of view, have students select a page from a story of their choice. Be sure they recognize the point of view used. Then ask them to rewrite the selection as a play-by-play narration. Students can work in peer-critique groups to prepare final revisions.   R.M.K.

*Language Arts
Junior High School
High School*

282.   McKinley, Robin. *The Hero and the Crown*. Greenwillow, 1984. ISBN 0-699-02593-5, $11.75. Ages 12-up.

Newbery Award Winner

*"Prequel" to
The Blue Sword*

In 1982, both readers and critics praised Robin McKinley's high fantasy adventure, *The Blue Sword* (Greenwillow, 1982); it was voted a 1983 Newbery Honor Book. It is filled with action, magic, and morality in language that is enriching and beautiful to the ear. In *The Hero and the Crown*, the 1985 Newbery Winner, McKinley returns to the mythical kingdom of Damar sometime before *The Blue Sword*, where the agents of evil again threaten the Damarians. Aerin, the daughter of the king and his witchwoman from the north, must battle Maur, the last of the great Black Dragons, to possess the fabled Blue Sword. In the final battle, Aerin must defeat the archdemon Agsded to seize the Hero's Crown, the source of power to Damaria kings. The story gathers momentum to a crashing conclusion. Fantasy readers will not be disappointed in high drama, powerful magic, and acts of great daring.

There is, unfortunately, not a long history of literary female characters who think and act in "heroic" or "assertive" ways. Aerin joins a growing list of courageous and daring girls/young women in children's and young adult literature: e.g., Meg Murry (L'Engle's Time Trilogy), Biddie Howe in Lord's *Spirit to Ride the Whirlwind* (Macmillan, 1981), and Amana in Highwater's *Legend Days* (Harper & Row, 1984). By studying the qualities that make male *and* female characters successful, students can learn those values and behavior that are the basis for true heroism.   H.M.

*Women's Studies
Literature
Junior High School
High School*

Related Sources

283.   McKinley, Robin. *The Outlaws of Sherwood*. Greenwillow, 1988. ISBN 0-688-07178-3, $12.95. Ages 12-up.

Tales of the outlaw Robin Hood began with bards and storytellers long before the first written version appeared in the 12th century. McKinley's feminist version is a brilliant addition to the legends of Robin Hood—who he was, what he did, and what his fate was. In McKinley's retelling we find that women are both helpmates and willing soldiers against the evil Sheriff of Nottingham. After she wins the archery contest staged to lure Robin into a trap, Marian nearly dies from a sword wound she receives in the skirmish that follows; Cecily cuts short her hair and fights as "Cecil" alongside Little John, the man she loves; Sibyl and Marjorie also survive the life and death battle against Guy of Gisbourne and his mercenaries. McKinley's writing is polished and lyrical without diminishing the action and heroics that are the heart and soul of this centuries-old hero tale.

Older readers may be surprised to learn of the many versions of this familiar tale and how it has changed over the centuries as it was adapted to different social and political climates. McKinley's brief "Afterword" provides some explanations and encourages further reading. Curious students can begin with Howard Pyle's 1883 classic *The Merry Adventures of Robin Hood* (periodically reprinted by Scribner's) and the Errol Flynn movie version it inspired. Another popular version is Paul Creswick's *Robin Hood*, beautifully reissued in 1984 with N.C. Wyeth's illustrations (Scribner's).   H.M.

*ALA Best Book
ALA Notable Book*

*Language Arts
Junior High School
High School*

Related Sources

284.   Murphy, Shirley Rousseau. *The Ivory Lyre*. Harper & Row, 1987. ISBN 0-06-024362-7, $12.89. Ages 12-up.

Murphy's second book in the Dragonbards Trilogy takes up where *Night Pool* (Harper & Row, 1986) left off. Tebriel, a young bard, along with his dragon, Seastrider, and three other dragons, battle the

*Sequel to Murphy's
Night Pool*

Powers of the Dark. With their magical ability to sing goodness and light into the hearts of those enslaved by the Dark, Tebriel and Seastrider incite small revolts throughout the land. Realizing he needs help, Tebriel seeks to engage the assistance of an underground resistance movement in the city of Dacis. Murphy's mystical tale is woven with strong, convincing characters and a believable plot as Tebriel struggles to fortify justice and virtue in a land slowly being consumed by wicked and corrupt powers. Readers who enjoy high fantasy will find *The Ivory Lyre* filled with action, powerful magic, and the ultimate triumph of good over evil.

Literature
Junior High School
High School

Students who enjoy fantasy may be interested in exploring the role of dragons in literature. In *The Ivory Lyre*, dragons are portrayed as good creatures who help mankind to battle the forces of evil. In *Dragonsinger* by Anne McCaffrey (Bantam, 1977) the fire lizards, or dragons, are comparable to those in *The Ivory Lyre*. As a contrast, in Ursula LeGuin's Earthsea Trilogy (published by Bantam) dragons were feared by the common people yet had power equal to the wizards. The dragons in Jane Yolen's Pitdragon Trilogy (published by Delacorte) also invite comparison.   K.B.B.

Related Sources

285.   Myers, Walter Dean. *Scorpions*. Harper & Row, 1988. ISBN 0-06-024365-1, $12.89. Ages 12-up.

Newbery Honor Book
ALA Best Book
ALA Notable Book

Jamal is a twelve-year-old with plenty to be afraid of: teachers who intimidate him, school bullies, police, drug dealers, and the familiar dangers of an impoverished Harlem neighborhood. To make it worse, his brother, Randy, expects him to take over as leader of the Scorpions while he is in prison for a robbery. When he gets a gun from one of the Scorpions, Jamal learns he has the power to protect himself and to avenge past humiliations. He also finds things out of control and his life filled with more turmoil than he can handle. Myers's characters are portrayed with all the realism the story and the setting demand, yet with insight that gives them depth and humanity and makes the reader care. The setting and the constant undercurrent of violence makes this contemporary story as gripping and immediate as today's headlines.

Related Sources

City gangs are not new either as urban blights or as topics for teen novels, though few are done as well as *Scorpions*. Haskin's historical perspective *Street Gangs, Yesterday and Today* (Hastings, 1974) examines this familiar and often dangerous phenomenon. Bonham's *Durango Street* (Dutton, 1965) and *Viva Chicano* (Dutton, 1970), and S.E. Hinton's still-popular *The Outsiders* (Viking, 1967) remain worthwhile reading, though the stakes and the level of violence have grown in the decades since these earlier teen novels were written. With reports of new outbreaks of gang violence in many cities, reading and discussing novels that focus on the individual as a gang member can be helpful to personalize the headlines for young people and give them a more complete understanding of otherwise impersonal and distant newspaper accounts.   H.M.

Contemporary Affairs
Junior High School
High School

286.   Namovicz, Gene Inyart. *To Talk in Time*. Four Winds, 1987. ISBN 0-02-768170-X, $11.95. Ages 10-14.

Childhood shyness can be devastating to the development of some children. Namovicz's engaging book sensitively explores Luke's shyness, a disability so severe it makes him a virtual mute. He speaks only to his family, one trusted friend, Jo, and Mrs. Bessemer, a sensitive, caring woman who nurses wounded wildlife. But when a sick fox infects Mrs. Bessemer's dog with the dreaded rabies virus, Luke painfully and gradually overcomes his paralyzing shyness. He must "talk in time" to find and warn a kind stranger also infected with the deadly virus. Namovicz's outstanding character development of Luke, plus the factual, vivid portrayal of the terror of rabies, make this book authentic and compelling reading for older readers.

Many people think that the rabies virus is always transmitted through a bite by a rabid animal foaming at the mouth. This and other common misconceptions about the disease are addressed in this book. Have students research rabies and report their findings to the class. Discuss discrepancies in findings. Make a bulletin board listing the actual symptoms of rabies and various ways the disease is transmitted. Mrs. Bessemer's dog was infected with rabies because she had neglected to have it immunized. Invite a game protector to talk to the students about controlling rabies in the wild and about safety in handling wildlife. Contact your local park district for help in setting up speakers.   L.B.

*Science,
Health Education
Middle School
Junior High School*

287.   O'Dell, Scott. *The Road To Damietta*. Houghton Mifflin, 1985. ISBN 0-395-38923-2, $14.95. Ages 12-up.

Playboy Francis Bernardone had a reputation for being where the parties were, where the girls were. He was the object of Ricca di Montanaro's first crush, which turned into an obsession. A familiar enough story, but Francis Bernardone later became Saint Francis of Assisi. Based upon thorough research, award-winning author Scott O'Dell relates the drastic metamorphosis of the wealthy, fun-loving boy into Saint Francis through a fascinating fictional narrative by Ricca, who is loosely based on a real person, Angelica di Rimini. O'Dell does not always paint a complimentary picture of Francis, either before or after his religious transformation, but the final impression O'Dell leaves with the reader is one of a multi-faceted person, not just a saint.

European history teachers should take notice of this book. Although technically fiction, it is based upon O'Dell's vision and knowledge of 13th century Italy and is rife with images and references from that period. Students frequently remember and understand history better when presented in a fictional form, so reading and discussing this book in conjunction with a unit on Italian history would be educationally appropriate. The question of how accurate O'Dell is, and how many times he invoked literary license to replace factual error, could lead students to further research.   J.J.S.

*History, Literature
Middle School
Junior High School*

288.   O'Dell, Scott. *The Serpent Never Sleeps: A Novel of Jamestown and Pocahontas*. Houghton Mifflin, 1987. ISBN 0-395-44242-7, $15.95. Ages 10-up.

In *The Serpent Never Sleeps* Scott O'Dell has woven a fictional character, Serena Lynn, into the facts surrounding the settlement of Jamestown and the involvement of Pocahontas with that settlement. This is a story that has been told many times, and O'Dell appears to have done his research as well as anyone. It is his point of view that is so unique here. The story is told through the eyes of Serena, who was not excited about being at Jamestown, and who was not convinced that the English settlers should even be there. Through the eyes of this young and spunky heroine, enlightened moderns can see the settlers encroaching upon Indian land, demanding corn for the release of hostages, brutalizing captives, and being too lazy or "gentlemanly" to plant the crops that were essential to the colony's survival. Serena's questioning is believable because her background is court-connected. Indeed, the variety of characters presented by O'Dell constantly remind the reader that people of the same time and place setting are not necessarily of one mind. O'Dell manages to do this with out appearing to be biased toward any one faction, and he does it with a hefty measure of adventure.

Related Sources

Literature, U.S. History
Middle School
Junior High School

An interesting project might be to compare *The Serpent Never Sleeps* to *The Double Life of Pocahontas* (Putnam, 1983), a biography by Jean Fritz. Then students could list the aspects of *The Serpent Never Sleeps* which are fact and those which are fiction. They can discuss how the story might have been different if the main character had been someone other than Serena. Some students might want to take this one step further and research a different time and place setting in which to place a character such as Serena. The resulting stories could be shared with the entire group.   M.A.C.

289.   Paulsen, Gary. *The Crossing*. Orchard, 1987. ISBN 0-531-05709-7, $11.95. 12-up.

ALA Best Book

Gary Paulsen always challenges his readers to live through adventures that test one's physical and psychical strengths. The result is a reading experience that appeals to those who want action, as well as to those who seek insight into the human condition. For Manuel Bustos, a young Mexican orphan living on the mean streets of Juarez, getting across the Rio Grande to the United States is the only hope he has for escaping hunger and constant fear. His chance encounter with Sgt. Robert Locke, an army veteran seeking escape from his nightmares of the Vietnam War in the cheap bars of that border town, begins an unlikely relationship that ends abruptly in the death of one and life for the other. Paulsen's human and social portraits are incisive, realistic, and compelling, though laden with despair. *The Crossing* combines vigorous action with a glimpse of the dark side of life.

Both legal and illegal immigration from Asia and Latin America, especially Mexico, have created economic and social problems for this country that remain unresolved. As a nation of immigrants, many view the recent immigrations and illegal immigrants with mixed feelings. Here is an excellent opportunity for students to better understand the issues of both sides: the needs of the immigrant and the interests of the United States. There are scores of books, both fiction and nonfiction, that will help young adults appreciate the complex history of our nation's growth. Yep's *The Serpent's Children* (Harper & Row, 1984) and *Mountain Light* (Harper & Row, 1985) and Geras's *Voyage* (Atheneum, 1983) show the hardships of earlier immigrant groups. Russell Freedman's *Immigrant Kids* (Dutton, 1980) captures in photographs the conditions faced by turn-of-the-century children arriving here from Europe. Because of the abundance of literature materials and the central role of immigrants in American history, *Immigration* is an excellent theme for combining these two disciplines.   H.M.

*Contemporary Affairs
Junior High School
High School*

Related Sources

290.   Paulsen, Gary. *Dogsong*. Bradbury, 1985. ISBN 0-02-770180-8, $11.95. Ages 12-up.

Fourteen-year-old Russel was unhappy with himself and with the modernization of his small Eskimo village. It was the kind of deep down-in-the-gut feeling when one knows that something isn't right, but just doesn't understand why. His father was aware of Russel's restlessness and did not know how to help him, but Oogruk would. Oogruk saw into Russel; he knew of his needs and thoughts and what Russel needed to do. Oogruk spoke of songs and journeys from the old time, and how no one did that now. And before Russel knew what he was saying, he said, "I will get a song, I will be a song." Using vivid imagery, intermixed with powerful symbolism, Paulsen eloquently writes of Oogruk's teachings and of the unification of Russel's spirit with the sled dog's during his mystical and majestic journey over ice, tundra, and time. His beautifully crafted words become a song of the soul and heart, of peace and contentment, that lures the reader into the journey.

*Newbery Honor Book
ALA Best Book*

Reading *Dogsong* aloud on a cold and blustery day would provide the perfect experience for students to fully savor the rich imagery Paulsen uses so generously. This could then serve as the beginning of a social studies unit on Eskimos. Students could investigate how Eskimos traditionally survive freezing temperatures, explore their customs and legends, and discuss how the modernization of villages has affected their lives. Other books on the same topic or theme include Scott O'Dell's *Black Star, Bright Dawn* (Houghton Mifflin, 1988), Jean George's *Water Sky* (Harper & Row, 1987) and books by Arnold Griese and James Houston. For personal reading, teachers might enjoy Hans Ruesch's *Top of the World* (Pocket Books, 1977) for its high adventure and broad exploration of traditional Eskimo life.

*Native American Studies
Middle School
Junior High School
High School*

Related Sources

291.   Paulsen, Gary. *Hatchet*. Bradbury, 1987. ISBN 0-02-770130-1, $12.95. Ages 11-13.

Brian Robeson's dramatic story of surviving 54 days in the northern Canadian wilderness is a gripping, tautly-crafted adventure story that

*Newbery Honor Book
ALA Notable Book*

will nail readers to their seats. When the pilot of the single engine plane in which Brian is a passenger has a heart attack, the thirteen-year-old survives the crash when he manages to guide the plane onto an isolated lake. More than a tale of physical survival in the unfamiliar environment of nature—though that in itself is an achievement of the boy's ingenuity that readers will cheer—Paulsen challenges our beliefs about ourselves and about the complexity of our contemporary life. That we are provoked to think about profound and social issues while being highly entertained is Paulsen's achievement. This is a clear example of fine writing for any audience.

Related Sources

Literature
Intermediate
Middle School
Junior High School

The theme of survival has attracted writers and appealed to readers for centuries, well before the universal popularity of Robinson Crusoe. For middle grade readers books like Sperry's *Call it Courage* (Macmillan, 1940), O'Dell's *Island of the Blue Dolphins* (Houghton Mifflin, 1960), and Mowat's *Never Cry Wolf* (Little, Brown, 1963)—even Steig's humorous and fanciful *Abel's Island* (Farrar, Straus & Giroux, 1976)—have many points of comparison with *Hatchet*. Students can form interest groups to read one or several of these books. Whole class activities that follow can easily include charting points of similarity and differences among these five and other stories that the teacher and class might include.   H.M.

292.   Paulsen, Gary. *The Island*. Orchard, 1988. ISBN 0-531-05749-6, $13.95. Ages 11-14.

ALA Best Book

Just when fourteen-year-old Wil Neuton was beginning to feel comfortable as a teenager growing up in Madison, Wisconsin, his father's new job takes the family into the woods in the northern part of the state. In exploring this new area, Wil discovers a tiny island in Sucker Lake where he spends several days and nights closely observing his surroundings and keeping a journal of his thoughts. In the process he probes his own personality and his understandings of family and friends. It is an inward journey of self-discovery that is brilliantly conceived and convincingly written with wit, sincerity, and quiet images that are riveting. Though it does not have the high drama of his earlier *Tracker* (Bradbury, 1984) or *Hatchet* (Bradbury, 1987), *The Island* is perhaps the most eloquent literary offering by one of this country's best and most popular writers for young people.

Related Sources

Language Arts,
Literature
Junior High School
High School

Wil writes in his journal what he observes while on the island as a means of understanding what is around him, as well as himself. These short essays can be read with the class. Together discuss the imagery and layers of meanings they suggest. For a similar assignment, ask the students to isolate themselves for a hour or so—for example, in a quiet room, in a treetop, or in a corner of a park—focusing upon a small occurance or image and enlarging upon it as Wil did so well in the story. Save each effort and compare them with those in *The Island*. Repeated attempts spaced judiciously throughout the school year will result in more success and greater student satisfaction.   H.M.

293. Paulsen, Gary. *Tracker*. Bradbury, 1984. ISBN 0-02-770220-0, $9.95. Ages 11-14.

ALA Best Book

For the past three seasons, John and his grandfather have gone deer hunting together in the woods near their northern Minnesota farm. This year will be different: John will have to go alone because grandfather is dying of cancer. John's two-day hunt becomes his quest to make peace with death—of the doe he tracks and his grandfather's. Paulsen's writing is rich in forest images and creates binding tension. However, what emerges as lasting is the realization of the mystery of death as part of life. *Tracker* will haunt the reader and make an indelible mark that lasts beyond the final page.

This is a story for reading aloud to permit time to savor the rich imagery and the finely drawn characterizations and to absorb the emotion as the story builds to a final climax. It is also an ideal book to illustrate the fact that individuals with different backgrounds respond in a variety of ways to the same literary work. Though the first week of the local deer season is a timely opportunity to share this book with a class, the questions *Tracker* poses will lead to discussion that will range far beyond this annual ritual.   H.M.

*Literature
Intermediate
Middle School
Junior High School*

294. Pendergraft, Patricia. *Hear the Wind Blow*. Philomel, 1988. ISBN 0-399-21528-X, $14.95. Ages 10-up.

Twelve-year-old Isadora Clay dreams of becoming a famous dancer someday, like the one she was named after, the one whose faded picture still occupies a place in her mother's picture album. Yet, growing up in rural Sweetwater Valley presents her with a very different reality. First, she must cope with the teasing and antics of Haskell Moore, a hooligan with a terrible home life. Then her best friend, Maybelle, decides she is going to go to the church revival, even though her fanatic father has banned her from doing so. Maybelle sits outside the revival in the freezing cold and becomes ill. Isadora and her family watch as she gets worse and even try to intervene when they see that her father will get no help to save his daughter. Pendergraft's use of dialect was stronger in *Miracle at Clements' Pond* (Philomel, 1987), but this is still a credible, moving story that touches the heart. The characters are well-developed and real, drawing the reader into feelings of amusement, anger, pity, and fear. Readers who appreciate both action and contemplation of some of the inequities in life should find *Hear the Wind Blow* a source of personal satisfaction.

Related Source

Sometimes things are done in the name of (or in spite of) religion that do not seem to follow the basic ideals of the faith. Examples of this can be found in the news almost daily—the fall from grace of certain TV evangelists, world terrorism backed by religious leaders in the Middle East, the Irish Protestant/Catholic "troubles," etc. Several thought-provoking books have come out in recent years that handle this delicate issue sensitively and fairly, yet realistically. Besides *Hear the Wind Blow*, students may want to take a look at *A Fine White Dust* by Cynthia Rylant (Bradbury, 1986) and *God's Radar* by Fran Arrick

*Contemporary Affairs,
Social Studies
Middle School
Junior High School*

Related Sources

Related Sources

(Bradbury, 1983). In addition, nonfiction materials, such as *Voices of Northern Ireland* (Gulliver, 1987) and *Voices of South Africa* (Harcourt Brace Jovanovich, 1986) both by Carolyn Meyer, look at the complex issues dividing those countries and how they affect their young people.   M.A.C.

295. Pinkwater, Jill. *The Disappearance of Sister Perfect*. Dutton, 1987. ISBN 0-525-44278-2, $13.95. Ages 10-14.

Jill Pinkwater, in *The Disappearance of Sister Perfect*, has managed to explore the very serious issue of cults with humor that may cause readers to laugh until they hurt! The family of Sherelee Holmes is so typically American that it is tragic. Yet, how many parents *really* know what is going on in their children's lives and how many *really* listen to their children? Sherelee Holmes is very concerned about her sister's behavior. Using Sherlock Holmes's (whom she claims is her great-great grandfather) approach, she discovers that her sister is about to join the Temple of Perfection. One crazy episode follows another, leading to her sister's rescue. Involved in all this mystery and adventure are a loyal friend, Joan; a butler named George who drives like a madman; several members of the Temple of Perfection; and four dogs.

Related Source

Social Studies
Middle School
Junior High School

This book could be effectively contrasted with *People Might Hear You* by Robin Klein (Penguin, 1985) which also deals with the issue of cults, but more in a more serious tone. The two books can be discussed and the issue of cults can be defined and researched. How are cults different from "non-cult" religions? What is their appeal? Why are they successful? How are they dangerous? Teachers may want to focus discussion on Pinkwater's use of humor to approach serious subject matter and ask which was more effective: Klein's serious tone or Pinkwater's lighter touch?   V.H.S.

296. Posell, Elsa. *Homecoming*. Harcourt Brace Jovanovich, 1987 (1st Am. ed.). ISBN 0-15-235160-4, $14.95. Ages 12-up.

This compelling novel, based upon the author's childhood, takes readers to Russia during the Bolshevik Revolution and leaves them with indelible images: the murdered Jewish doctor and his wife floating face up in the well; Mama's protruding belly as she slowly starved so that her six children could eat; Koznikov screaming his hatred of Papa to defenseless Mama; and the dark bowels of the wagon the children hid in as they escaped to Poland. These and other images return to haunt the reader long after the book is closed. Posell's writing is straightforward and her perspectives are true to the nature of her child narrator, young Olya, who represents Posell herself. The characters are convincing as they illustrate both human frailty and family compassion.

Related Source

Homecoming will be a fine addition to collections on Jewish life in the Soviet Union, the Russian Revolution, and the Holocaust. It has a happier ending than *The Diary of Anne Frank*, yet still provides opportunities for students to explore their values concerning human rights, family responsibility, parental sacrifice, feeding the hungry, class systems, and/or communism versus capitalism. These issues are central to this book and others like it. Discussion in a comfortable, accepting atmosphere among students who are informed or are seeking and informed position. Students may choose one of these issues to debate, making sure to research their respective sides thoroughly.   M.A.C.

Jewish-American Studies,
Holocaust Studies
Middle School
Junior High School
High School

297.   Rinaldi, Ann. *The Last Silk Dress*. Holiday House, 1988. ISBN 0-8234-0690-3, $15.95. Ages 12-up.

Lovers of historical fiction should thrill to the adventures of fourteen-year-old Susan Chilmark as she copes with family difficulties and the ups and downs of the Confederacy in Civil War Richmond. The story is based upon the true account of a Confederate surveillance balloon made from the donated silk dresses of Southern women. Ann Rinaldi has created a character, Susan Chilmark, who is largely responsible for both the making and the capture of the balloon. Susan's Rhett Butler-like brother, Lucien, is estranged from their somewhat ineffectual father and abusive mother. Through him Susan learns to question the fundamental issues over which the Confederacy was formed. Her new understanding about the hypocritical lives of even her own family changes her from a manipulative Southern belle into a woman of conviction, if an immature one who does not always think about the consequences of her actions. Rather than romanticizing or glorifying the Civil War South, Rinaldi forces readers to look at the harsh realities of that unhappy era in U.S. history. At the same time, she provides entertaining escapades and an engagingly human heroine.

ALA Best Book

What can one person—especially a young person—do to help in times of crisis? Much more than he or she might think. Students can brainstorm various types of problems—world hunger, war, drought, abusive parents, accidents, et al.—and list ways an individual could make a contribution towards solving the problems. Finally these suggestions could be evaluated in terms of the consequences of them to the individual and society. Students may want to research and submit to similar analyses efforts towards solving problems that have been in the news, such as live aid concerts or the child in New York City who brought food and clothing to street people.   M.A.C.

Social Studies,
U.S. History
Junior High School
High School

298.   Rinaldi, Ann. *Time Enough for Drums*. Holiday House, 1986. ISBN 0-8234-0603-2, $12.95. Ages 12-up.

The Revolutionary War is coming to Trenton, New Jersey, fifteen-year-old Jemima's hometown. Family conflict arises because part of Jem's family is loyal to England, while others, including Jem and her parents, are Patriots. Jem's strong will gets her into trouble with her parents and her Tory tutor. Later, however, her determination gives her the strength to manage as her family begins to disintegrate when the War enters her life and her home. As a pleasant way to learn history, *Time*

Enough for Drums has enough action to keep the reader moving eagerly through the historical descriptions. The "Author Notes" give more historical details of the Revolutionary War.

U.S. History
Junior High School
High School

This book could be used to add human dimension to the study of the American Revolution. The descriptions of George Washington and the Battle of Trenton could easily motivate the students to find out more about them and the War in general. The book could also be used in conjunction with *My Brother Sam is Dead* by James Lincoln Collier and Christopher Collier (Four Winds, 1974), which tells about the Revolutionary War from a young boy's viewpoint, or DeFord and Stout's fictional *An Enemy Among Them* (Houghton Mifflin, 1987), which shows how the War might have affected a German immigrant family. These books lend themselves to comparing and contrasting an event from different perspectives.   J.E.M.

Related Sources

299.   Rochman, Hazel, compiler. *Somehow Tenderness Survives: Stories of Southern Africa*. Harper & Row, 1988. ISBN 0-06-025023-2, $12.95. Ages 12-up.

ALA Best Book

There is precious little tenderness found among the ten stories in this moving and evocative collection of short stories about contemporary life in southern Africa. Behind statistics and news headlines are the emotions and daily personal struggles of those bound together in that troubled area. These are difficult problems powerfully brought to life by writers, both white and black, who were born or raised there. The stories show how apartheid (an Afrikaans word meaning separateness, pronounced "apart hate") affects every aspect of life. The stories tell of punishments for loving someone of another color and for standing up to a gang of white bullies; of the loneliness and pain of a mixed-race teenager and of a black whose only privacy is the sanctuary of a public toilet; and of the guilt of a white who knowingly sacrifices his self-respect to conform to white supremacist ways. The kaleidoscope of images is not pretty, and there are often frightening echoes of America at other times. However, the stories demonstrate the power of literature to illuminate world events that have been dehumanized by typical media reporting.

Contemporary Affairs,
Literature
High School

The cultural and political history of sub-Sahara Africa is, at best, given only superficial treatment in schools. Some textbooks still call it "The Dark Continent" in reference to our knowledge of this complex area. Educated adults often refer to Africa as a country. Those who read or hear these stories will be compelled to ask themselves, "How did this come to be?" "How can one person do something like that to another human being?" "What's being done to stop it?" "What can I do?" There is no better time for social studies and/or English teachers to initiate an intensive study of pre-colonial African cultures, the period of European colonization and domination, and the transition from post-colonial to independence than with today's headlines: rioting in South Africa and its "homelands"; Nelson Mandela and Bishop Desmond Tutu; American citizen protests over apartheid; institutional investments in companies "doing business" in South Africa—the list is much longer. To misunderstand the significance of these events thousands of miles from our country is to deny the humanity of those whose voices cry out to us from penetrating, yet often overlooked, stories like those in *Somehow Tenderness Survives*.   H.M.

300.   Ruckman, Ivy. *No Way Out*. Crowell, 1988. ISBN 0-690-04669-3, $11.89. Ages 11-up.

Nineteen-year-old Amy, her fiance Rick, her eleven-year-old brother Ben, and several friends are hiking through the Zion Narrows in Utah. The Narrows is a thin canyon carved out by the North Fork of the Virgin River over millions of years. An unexpected rainfall causes a potentially deadly flash flood in the canyon. All members of the group have to work hard to stay alive as they try to hike out of the canyon (from which any other type of rescue is impossible). This is a survival story, well told in a realistic and adventurous fashion. Through the experience, Amy and several other characters discover, in a very natural way, more about who they are and what is meaningful in their lives.

Students can use *No Way Out* as a starting point in researching actual weather statistics about Zion Canyon in Utah and the conditions under which flooding would occur. This can lead to a focus upon floods in general and flash floods in particular. Using a program like "Bank Street School Filer," students can build a data base of information on floods in different parts of the country. Data such as the frequency of floods, severity of damage, weather conditions, and topography can be recorded on the data base. Students can then be asked to compare and contrast this data and choose a location other than Zion Canyon as the basis for writing about a flood, a survival story in which the characters make discoveries about themselves.   G.B.

*Science
Middle School
Junior High School*

301.   Sanders, Scott, R. *Bad Man Ballad*. Bradbury, 1986. ISBN 0-02-778230-1, $14.95. Ages 12-up.

Set in the 1800's, *Bad Man Ballad* chronicles the search for the bearman—a giant, hairy being now commonly referred to as "Bigfoot"—and the events subsequent to finding him. Ely Jackson is a young man simply curious about the beast, Owen Lightfoot is an attorney wanting to see justice done, and Rain Hawk is a French-Indian woman who understands the giant; this is the odd trio who feel driven to find the bearman. Once they do find him, Ely and he became blood brothers, and he meekly follows Ely back to his home in Roma, Ohio. There Owen attempts to arrange a fair trial for the bearman, who has been accused of murder. Only Rain Hawk knows the true story of what actually happened. The townspeople, however, are not interested in truth and justice; spurred by their own fear and insecurity, and engulfed by rumors, they only want the beast destroyed. Sanders tells this story well, with powerful imagery and with a humanitarian view toward the beast. Empathy is felt for all involved and the sense of injustice is vivid.

After reading this book, an in-depth study can be done to learn more about the existence of a "bearman." Have interested students delve

ALA Best Book

into articles in magazines that contain information about alleged sightings and people's experiences with the creature. They could also see what accounts exist in literature, both fiction and non-fiction; Alvin Schwartz's ***Fat Man in a Fur Coat and Other Bear Stories*** (Farrar, Straus & Giroux, 1984) is an excellent source. Students can then use their findings to write a fictional story about such a creature, basing their story upon the facts they have found. The stories can then be shared with the rest of the class, and also sent to Scott Sanders, c/o Bradbury Press, 866 Third Avenue, New York, NY 10022.   L.S.

302.   Sleator, William. ***The Duplicate***. Dutton, 1988. ISBN 0-525-44390-8, $12.95. Ages 10-16.

Sixteen-year-old David often forgets that he is supposed to do something dull and makes another commitment to do something fun, like go on a date with Angela. When he finds Spee-Dee-Dupe, a mysterious duplicating machine, he "duplicates" himself. He quickly discovers that having a duplicate causes more problems than it solves and the reader is treated to amusing scenes regarding double laundry, alternating family meals, and dates with Angela. However, the tone turns dramatically serious when distrust causes Duplicate A to duplicate once again creating Duplicate B. The ensuing power struggle and progressive mania compels the reader to the fatal conclusion of this spellbinding tale.

Students might like to explore what it might be like to have a duplicate by using a theater activity called "The Mirror." Students need to have plenty of floor space. After splitting up the class into pairs, have students face each other as if looking into a mirror. With one student identified as the leader, the "duplicate" must mimic the leader's every movement so well that an observer could not be able to tell which is the leader. Then allow the other partner to become the leader. Switch back to the original leader and have the partner expand the leader's movements. Alternate leaders again. Finally, tell the class that neither partner is the leader, that each is free to move at will, but both must still imitate the other's action. This enjoyable exercise encourages careful observation, ease in body movement, and anticipation of behavior.   L.B.

303.   Spiegelman, Art. ***Maus***. Illustrated by the author. Pantheon, 1986. ISBN 0-394-74723-2, $8.95. Ages 12-up.

The plight of European Jews during Hitler's reign of terror is shown in all its horror as acclaimed cartoonist Art Spiegelman creates a cat-and-mouse world where the Jews are the mice and the Germans are cats. In this unusual memoir of his parents' experiences in Germany up to their imprisonment in Auschwitz in 1944, Spiegelman uses the improbable medium of the cartoon strip to tell his father's story of the good days before the Nazis, the growing tide of anti-Semitism, and the rise of Hitler. Surprisingly, the result is moving and successful. For some young adult readers, *Maus* may be the most effective means to understand that historical period. The biting dialogue between the father and son shows a complex family and a bittersweet realationship between the two that is an emotional struggle for each. Do not be put off by the cartoons. In spite of a medium usually associated with laughs, this is a very forceful and convincing approach to history and to human relations.

Personal accounts of the Holocaust are available from many sources and in many forms. Meltzer's *Never To Forget* (Harper & Row, 1976) set the standard as a moving and readable history based upon a compilation of letters and interviews. The Council on Interracial Books for Children (1841 Broadway, New York, NY 10023 [212] 757-5339) and the Anti-Defamation League of B'nai B'rith (823 United Nations Plaza, New York, NY 10017 [212] 490-2525) are two excellent sources of films, bibliographies, records, tapes, and other media that can be purchased or borrowed for study in secondary schools.   H.M.

Related Source

*Holocaust Studies
Junior High School
High School*

304.   Stolz, Mary. *Pangur Ban*. Illuminated by Pamela Johnson. Harper & Row, 1988. ISBN 0-06-025862-4, $13.95. Ages 12-up.

Pangur Ban is a white cat, the pet of Cormac, son of a ninth century Irish farmer. Cormac does not want to follow in his father's footsteps: his desire in life is to draw. The only way for him to do so is to enter the local monastery. With his cat beside him, he finally gets to fulfill his dream, though this is interrupted by Viking raiders. This story, about the difficult choices one must make in life to follow a calling, was stimulated by a poem, "Pangur Ban," written by an anonymous monk on the parchment pages of a missal he was transcribing. Stolz was intrigued by this poem about how eagerly the monk and his cat both go about their respective jobs. Through Cormac she creates the answer to her own questions about who the young man was and what his life was like. The story is beautifully told and leaves indelible images of a simpler, yet perhaps more restrictive, way of life.

Few career options were open to Cormac: he could be a farmer or a monk. After reading Pangur Ban, students can discuss careers and what one must do to enter certain professions. What education must one have? What obstacles can stand in a person's way? What stereotypes exist about the profession? How much money can a person expect to make in the profession? What are the chances of "making it big" in the profession? How have opportunities in this profession changed over time? Students can each select a specific profession to research and report findings back to the whole class. In that way, the class will acquire a broader perspective about careers than they might if they went about the research on their own. A handbook could result, which could be given to the guidance counselors. M.A.C.

*Social Studies
Junior High School
High School*

305.   Sullivan, Mary Ann. *Child of War*. Holiday House, 1984. ISBN 0-8234-0537-0, $10.95. Ages 10-up.

Thirteen-year-old Maeve lives in Northern Ireland amidst the war between neighbors. Children are involved in the anger, violence, and vengeance found every day. One day, Maeve's little brother is killed by one of the soldiers and Maeve retreats into a fantasy world. She is bullied into becoming involved with the rebel children who shortly kill someone. Maeve moves in and out of her fantasy world trying to deal with the present, but not wanting to believe all that she sees around her is true. Many of the events depicted in the book are based upon actual incidents. This gripping story of a young person's attempt to survive physically and emotionally in a war is as familiar and immediate as yesterday's headlines.

Discussing war and its impact on "innocent" bystanders could be an important topic for young people. Are bystanders innocent? Can a person be held responsible for events around them? Is it true that "if you're not part of the solution, you're part of the problem?" What can one person do to stem a swelling tide of violence and hatred? Is it enough to "just say 'No?'" The implications of these questions and of our responses to them extend to the everyday events in which we all find ourselves enmeshed. Other books that could be used in conjunction with this are Vinke's *The Short Life of Sophie Stoll* (Harper & Row, 1984) Kome and Crean's *Peace* (Sierra Club, 1986) and Myer's *Voices of Northern Ireland* (Gulliver, 1987).   B.C./H.M.

306.   Terris, Susan. *Nell's Quilt*. Farrar, Straus & Giroux, 1987. ISBN 0-374-35504-5, $12.95. Ages 12-up.

In 1899, women had few, if any, choices. Financially unable to follow in her grandmother's footsteps to further women's rights, Nell makes the only choice she can—marry cousin Anson. The decision made, eighteen-year-old Nell's spirit is broken. Once determined and industrious, she now bides her time embroidering on Grandmother's crazy quilt, endlessly creating new patterns. As she becomes weaker due to her strange and sudden insistence upon foods that are white, the quilt becomes her obsession and only solace. Her very essence drained, Nell resigns herself to the mundaneness of the quilt, symbolic of her future life as Anson's wife. This intense and complex story will intrigue readers as they witness Nell's bizarre metamorphosis. The injustice of her limited options due to the time period in which she lives resounds throughout this thought–provoking book. Presented in journal form, Terris purposefully shifts the viewpoint from Nell's narrative to third person when Nell resigns herself to her fate and begins her transformation.

Nell longs to go off to college, but that is not an acceptable option for her family. In her time, college was for men and only wealthy women could attend only certain institutions. Use these facts to spur a discussion of how the lack of education was a disadvantage to a woman at the turn of the century. Bring the discussion to the present by considering ways in which women are still limited, not only educationally, but also by society's expectations and traditional sex roles. One area that could be considered is the political arena, where women's inexperience can be directly linked to society's previous rejection of this as an acceptable field for women. This can be tied in with Nell's aspiration to be like her grandmother, a woman who fought for women's rights.   L.S.

Peace Studies
Junior High School
High School

Related Sources

ALA Best Book

Women's Studies
Junior High School
High School

307. Thomas, Karen. *Changing of the Guard*. Harper & Row, 1986. ISBN 0-06-026164-1, $10.89. Ages 12-up.

Change is inevitable, but Caroline attempts to fight it by withdrawing into the past. When Maddy, a new girl in town, is drawn to Caroline's poetry, a unique friendship develops. Maddy appears to be buoyant, self-confident, and vivacious—an exact opposite of Caroline. Only as each girl shares her past does it become apparent that they have a common struggle. Sorting through their idealized memories, they begin the endeavor to drop their guard/defenses against the present. Thomas has interwoven several personal and social problems related to change: death, grandparents' senility, working mothers, unemployed fathers, drugs and step-mothers.

The teenage years are ones of great turbulence for a variety of reasons. A group of students could create a "Dear Abby" advisory panel. They might begin with problems identified in this story, and then submit questions about real student issues for review. As the panel offers suggestions, the class's task is to debate if the answers are too pat—easier said than done—or realistic solutions. Through this type of discussion, students can explore the options open to them in their immediate or similar situations   M.B.C.

Family Life
Junior High School
High School

308. Tolan, Stephanie S. *The Great Skinner Getaway*. Macmillan, 1987. ISBN 0-02-789361-8, $12.95. Ages 12-up.

Take one motor home and add two average parents, four kids (various sizes), two cats, and one large dog. Shake well over bouncy back roads, squeeze together for an entire summer, and what do you have? Nothing but trouble! Fifteen-year-old Jennifer Skinner documents her family's "sometimes disastrous" summer vacation, while trying to decide whether togetherness is really a very good idea. Although the camping escapades are fairly predictable, Tolan's first-person writing style is true to life and full of honest-to-goodness teenager talk. Situations and locations are clearly described and entertaining as well. Previous books in Tolan's popular series include *The Great Skinner Strike* (Macmillan, 1983) and *The Great Skinner Enterprise* (Four Winds, 1986).

Third in Tolan's
Skinner Family series

Related Sources

Everyone knows it is more fun to visit a vacation spot than to read about it—so why not hop aboard an imaginary motor home and "visit" vacation spots class members have discovered on their family journeys? As part of American geography, children could be travel guides, "experts in residence," on locations they have visited throughout the fifty states. They could narrate a mini-tour by sharing postcards, historical souvenirs, or photos of their vacations. *Stringbean's Trip to the Shining Sea* by Vera Williams (Greenwillow, 1988) shows how this might be approached. A map showing a motor home crossing America could grow as different states were visited by the class. Unfamiliar geographic areas should become more real as boys and girls share their adventures crossing the U.S.A.   G.G.

Social Studies
Middle School
Junior High School

Related Source

309.   Voigt, Cynthia. *Come a Stranger*. Atheneum, 1986. ISBN 0-689-31289-X, $13.95. Ages 11-up.

Cynthia Voigt demonstrates in *Come a Stranger* why she is acknowledged as a master of character study, in addition to offering older readers thoughtful entertainment. Mina is on the verge of young womanhood, a transitional time for which she is understandably unprepared and unsure of herself. When she is rejected by a prestigious ballet school, she is not sure whether it is because she is physically awkward or because she is Black. When she returns home to the small town and her loving family she sorts out her emotions toward her family and friends; toward the summer minister, Reverend Tamer Shipp; and about herself. The friend of Dicey who played such an important role in *Dicey's Song* (Atheneum, 1982) now has the opportunity to tell her story in this fifth installment of Voigt's brilliant anthology of the Tillermans and their friends. It is a story of lasting value and worth the reading.

Related Source

Beginning with *Homecoming* (Atheneum, 1981), Cynthia Voigt has enlarged her cast of characters in *Dicey's Song*, *A Solitary Blue* (Atheneum, 1983), *Runner* (Atheneum, 1985), and now *Come a Stranger*. To better understand time and place relationships among the five books, students can develop a Tillerman family tree to show the relationships of characters to each other: a line and chart diagram would suffice to keep the growing cast of characters straight. Students may also want to develop a time-place map showing where the characters came from, when they lived, and where they met other characters. Not only will the reading become a hunt for clues to making the maps and charts, but will help students understand the new characters as they inevitably appear in forthcoming books.   H.M.

Related Sources

Black Studies, Literature Middle School Junior High School High School

310.   Voigt, Cynthia. *Jackaroo*. Atheneum, 1985. ISBN 0-689-31123-0, $14.95. Ages 10-up.

Cynthia Voigt, so successful with her perceptive studies of the Tillerman family, has created a bleak, gray medieval landscape where the legendary swashbuckler, Jackaroo, rides forth to protect the people against the oppressions of hard times and cruel noblemen. Gwyn, the sixteen-year-old innkeeper's daughter, spirited and independent, does not believe the tales of Jackaroo though she sees all around her the need for such a protector. Following her experiences with a travelling Lord and his son, her discovery of a hidden package, and her friendship with Burl, the family servant—plus a series of exciting and dangerous adventures—Gwyn's story comes to a surprising and satisfying conclusion.

Literature Middle School Junior High School High School

Comparison of the Jackaroo legend to stories of Robin Hood or Zorro are natural and easy. The whole concept of the strong individual fighting the forces of evil on behalf of a weaker person or group has found its way into movies ("My Bodyguard") and TV ("The Enforcer") in addition to a whole host of comic book heroes from Superman to Captain Marvel. Students might want to try their hand at rewriting an episode from one of these stories as a newspaper article that might have appeared at the time of the story. In the case of Jackaroo or Robin Hood, it could be rewritten as a ballad sung by a travelling minstrel or shouted by the town crier.   L.M.H.

311.   Voigt, Cynthia. *Sons From Afar*. Atheneum, 1987. ISBN 0-689-31349-7, $13.95. Ages 12-up.

It had been six years since they had been abandoned and, with their sisters Dicey and Maybeth, came to live with their Grandmother (see *Homecoming* [Atheneum, 1981]). In all that time, James and Sammy Tillerman have not thought a great deal about their father, a man they never knew who walked away from the family years earlier. To fifteen-year-old James, however, learning about his father is now crucial to better understanding himself. Though he cares little for what they might learn, twelve-year-old Sammy goes along for the adventure that takes the boys from the quiet of the Maryland countryside to the squalor of the bustling Baltimore waterfront. Voigt's characterizations are as sharply defined as in her previous books; she takes her readers beneath the surface of human behavior to probe the spirit and emotions of characters about whom we have come to care a great deal. This sixth volume of the Tillerman saga will be welcomed by those interested in fine writing and believable characters.

How much a child inherits from a parent sparks James's interest to know his father. Older students may find their curiosity piqued by the debate over the importance of genetic inheritance versus social and environmental influences in determining personality, intelligence, success, etc. Issac Asimov's *How Did We Find Out About Our Genes?* (Walker, 1983) and Harry Sootin's biography, *Gregor Mendel: Father of the Science of Genetics* (Vanguard, 1958), explain how the study of genetics began. Asimov's *How Did We Find Out About Our Human Roots?* (Walker, 1979) introduces the environmental side with creationism, geological discoveries, and natural selection. Preparing for a formal debate on "Nature vs. Nurture" will help to clarify the issues, if not resolve the dispute.   H.M.

312.   Voigt, Cynthia. *The Runner*. Atheneum, 1985. ISBN 0-689-31069-2, $11.95. Ages 12-up.

With the skills of a master portraitist, Newbery medalist Cynthia Voigt once again has drawn a penetrating portrait of a family torn apart through misunderstanding and conflict. For readers charmed by *Homecoming* (Atheneum, 1981), the 1983 Newbery Award-winning *Dicey's Song* (Atheneum, 1982), and last year's Newbery Honor Book *Solitary Blue* (Atheneum, 1983), *The Runner* will be welcomed for its insight into another branch of the Tillerman family tree: Samuel (Bullet) Tillerman, son of Abigail and uncle to Dicey. The story deals with Bullet entering manhood in the 1960s and suffering, as did his brother and sister before him, his father's insensitivity and rejection. Though he is a loner in high school, he discovers himself through what

ALA Best Book

Sixth in Voigt's Tillerman Saga

Science, Literature Middle School Junior High School High School

Related Sources

ALA Best Book

Fourth in Voigt's Tillerman Saga

Related Sources

he does best, cleanest, and fastest: cross-country running. This helps defend him against family betrayal and the turbulence of the 1960s. The emotions are powerful and believable in this tightly-written novel.

The destiny of school sports programs—both intramurals and inter-scholastic sports—is periodically questioned by school administrators, faculty, parents, and the community. To some adults and students, par-ticipation in a sport is glamorous; for most who do participate only hard work, dedication, and sacrifice lead to success. Few books for teens fo-cus on the mental and physical discipline required by an "unglamorous" sport like cross-country running. With running gaining in popularity in all age groups, this could be a good opportunity to discuss the advantag-es and dangers of this sport. Magazines like *Runner's World* will keep readers informed about current activities and trends.   L.P.B.

Physical Education, Literature
Middle School
Junior High School
High School

Related Source

313.   Wilkinson, Brenda. *Not Separate, Not Equal*. Harper & Row, 1987. ISBN 0-06-026482-9, $12.89. Ages 10-up.

In this short, powerful novel, Malene Freeman's adoptive parents decide that she should be one of the six "Negro" students to desegregate Pineridge High in 1965. Through Malene's story, readers get as close as possible to the concerns and fears of these teenagers who are not only dealing with their own growing-up problems, but must deal with "adults" from a southern town who are against integration. Written largely in dialogue, Brenda Wilkinson has also included authentic dialect that adds realism and characterization to this story that will be a fine ad-dition to factual accounts of integration and the American Civil Rights Movement.

This story is helpful to read and discuss anytime during the year when dealing with attitudes of people. Not all of the situations reflecting attitudes are racially oriented. One memorable scene involved remini-scences with an old first grade teacher who grouped her children for reading according to height rather than ability: "Seem like teachers would've known how bad that (grouping high, medium, and low) had to make a slow person feel!" Older students can discuss their feelings about tracking students in junior and senior high school and debate the merits of such a grouping system.   B.C.

Black Studies,
Multicultural Studies
Intermediate
Middle School
Junior High School

314.   Yep, Laurence. *Dragon Steel*. Harper & Row, 1985. ISBN 0-06-026751-8, $12.89. Ages 12-up.

Magic abounds in this sequel to *Dragon of the Lost Sea* (Harper & Row, 1982), which opens with a "popular dragon ballad," Yep's clever way of telling his readers what went on before. *Dragon Steel* continues the story of Shimmer, a dragon princess who is trying to right a great wrong—the destruction of her homeland, the Inland Sea. Yep has created a fantasy world, both in and out of the sea, that is in-credibly rich in imagery: the dark, deep water dragon habitats, for exam-ple, are lighted by glowing worms that produce stronger light when stroked. There is also an amazing cast of characters, including the Lord

Sequel to Yep's
Dragon of the Lost Sea

of Flowers, who "woke to the songs of creation;" Monkey, who is as boastful and ingenious as his kind often are in folklore; spiky-haired Indigo, in whom Shimmer sees herself as a young outcast; and Thorn, a young man whose loyalty to Shimmer has now brought him through two novels. Yep created these characters as finely-tempered as dragon steel, so they will be ready to brave the "biggest foolishness of all"— war between humans and the dragons to restore the Inland Sea.

Authors who write fantasy are often loathe to leave the worlds they have imagined: one book leads to two and then three. Students may want to explore other fantasy trilogies, chronicles, or series, like those of Alexander, Tolkien, and LeGuin. Allan Eckert and Robin McKinley are authors who, like Yep, have started what will probably end as trilogies with *The Dark Green Tunnel* (Little, Brown, 1984) and the Damar books (published by Greenwillow). Students may wish to write to these authors to ask them about their fascination with their created worlds. Students may also enjoy making up a fantasy world in which to set a story. The requirements are that every detail must be thought out in advance and there must be logical internal consistency. Perhaps the students, too, will become "hooked" on the images in their minds and will strive to be more effective at conveying those images to others through language.   M.A.C.

Asian-American Studies, Literature Junior High School High School

Related Source

315.   Yep, Laurence. *Mountain Light*. Harper & Row, 1985. ISBN 0-06-026759-3, $11.89. Ages 12-up.

In this sequel to *The Serpent's Children*, master storyteller Laurence Yep continues the story of Cassia, the freedom fighter. This time, however, we see Cassia through the eyes of Squeaky Lau, a young man from the neighboring village which Cassia's village has been feuding with for generations. Squeaky is a perfect foil for the over-serious Cassia: he has coped with life's hardships by clowning. Through their growing relationship, each learns to take on some of the character traits of the other, thus balancing their somewhat lopsided personalities. Eventually, Squeaky gets up the courage to make the dangerous journey to America, where he discovers that the brutal realities of China cannot be outdistanced by a broad ocean. Indeed, old problems are compounded by a new culture. Laurence Yep has kept the high quality of *The Serpent's Children* in *Mountain Light* while also broadening and deepening the reader's understanding of the Chinese and Chinese-American experience.

Yep's technique of creating a sequel from a different character's viewpoint could be an interesting area for students to study. After reading both *The Serpent's Children* and *Mountain Light*, the students could look at the works of other authors to see whether they play with viewpoint in their sequels. Cynthia Voigt did this when she wrote *A Solitary Blue* (Atheneum, 1984), in which some of the events of *Dicey's Song* (Atheneum, 1983) are retold through the eyes of Jeff. Finally, older students can experiment with this technique by writing two parallel/companion short stories.   M.A.C.

Sequel to Yep's The Serpent's Children

Asian-American Studies, Literature Junior High School High School

Related Sources

316.   Yep, Laurence. *The Serpent's Children*. Harper & Row, 1984. ISBN 0-06-026809-3, $12.95. Ages 12-up.

Yep presents a rebel family devoted to driving the Demons (the English) out of 19th century China. Cassia and Foxfire want to do this in different ways. Their father's struggle to accept this is a strong theme, and the influence of the deceased mother's stories is effectively interwoven. Yep masterfully illustrates the complexities of the situation in China at that time through both unsavory and admirable characters, and through detailed descriptions of harsh living conditions and ingenious attempts to stave off starvation. He also gives us a deeper understanding of the Chinese culture and shows the realities of immigration to America from the Chinese perspective. Waves of immigrants suddenly become real individuals with a common humanity.

Asian-American Studies, U.S. History Junior High School High School

Related Source

Use this as part of an exploration of immigrants to America, why they came, the cultures they left behind, etc. Children who have moved in the lifetimes can begin to understand the concept of immigration from the immigrant's point of view, which is invaluable in promoting understanding of our multicultural society. Making weed soup in class would allow students to "taste" the daily struggle for survival faced by Cassia's family. Jean Craighead George's *Wild, Wild Cookbook* (Crowell, 1982) is a good source for recipes. This may lead to a study of world hunger and an investigation of the nutritional value of rice and other staple foods of third world nations.   M.A.C.

317.   Yep, Laurence. *The Tom Sawyer Fires*. Morrow, 1984. ISBN 0-688-03861-1, $10.75. Ages 10-up.

Companion to The Mark Twain Murders

Laurence Yep demonstrates his versatility as a writer in *The Tom Sawyer Fires* and its companion, *The Mark Twain Murders* (Four Winds, 1982). Both are nothing like *The Serpent's Children*. *The Tom Sawyer Fires* is a romp—action-packed and full of colorful characters, including the Duke of Baywater, a teenaged street urchin who likes to think he is of royal parentage; Tom Sawyer, ace firefighter when San Francisco most needed them; Mark Twain, a wise-cracking, not-yet-famous newspaperman; and Major St. John, a dangerous Confederate saboteur. These characters, and some equally delightful minor ones, move the reader through a variety of fiery situations, as the tension mounts toward the inveitable confrontation with the diabolical Major. The situations are authentic, and the reader can learn much about San Francisco in the 1860s, the firefighting techniques used there, and about early photography methods—all in a fast-paced novel.

Author Studies Intermediate Junior High School High School

This book, as well as *The Mark Twain Murders*, could be used to introduce children to Samuel Clemens's life and work. Children might like to speculate about why Laurence Yep chose to write about some already-famous characters. They might want to write Laurence Yep (c/o William Morrow and Co., 105 Madison Ave., New York, NY 10016). History teachers will also find that this is one of those books that present quite painlessly a clear picture of what life was like in a particular time and place.   M.A.C.

318. Yolen, Jane. *A Sending of Dragons*. Delacorte, 1987. ISBN 0-385-29587-1, $14.95. Ages 12-up.

After escaping the revolt on Austar IV and bonding with the dragon who died to save him, Jakkin develops the ability to telepathically communicate with dragons and with the people he discovers living underground. This primitive society has learned the secret of making metal, a commodity nearly as precious on Austar IV as life itself. The final volume of the Pitdragons trilogy comes to an exciting and thoughtful climax that will thrill and satisfy both first time readers and those who have read the first two books: *Dragon Blood* (Delacorte, 1982) and *Heart's Blood* (Delacorte, 1984). Yolen's vision of this futuristic society is fanciful, yet terrifyingly real and compelling. Her characters—both human and dragon—are convincing and refreshing. This is the conclusion to a major work by one of our most gifted and most honored writers.

Dragons have played a major role in mythology, especially in that of China. The fabled creature has been pictured in a variety of forms and has been associated with the forces of both good and evil. Students can study the earliest beliefs about dragons in different cultures and how they were portrayed from tales in which dragons are prominent. Students might begin with *A Book of Dragons* by Leonard and Hosie Baskin (Knopf, 1985) or *Dragons and Unicorns: A Natural History* by Paul and Karen Johnsgard (St. Martin, 1982).   H.M.

Third in Yolen's Pitdragon Trilogy

Related Sources

Literature Junior High School High School

Related Sources

319. Yolen, Jane. *Children of the Wolf*. Viking, 1984. ISBN 0-670-21763-8, $11.95. Ages 12-up.

The discovery of two feral children, girls who have been raised by a family of wolves, changes the lives of a fourteen-year-old Indian orphan, Mohandas, and the Reverend Mr. Wells, the English missionary who runs the Christian orphanage near where the girls were found. Mohandas is given the task of teaching the girls the necessary language and social skills for their survival in the world of humans. The challenges to Reverend Wells are helping local villagers to accept the two girls as human and bringing the girls into the family of God's creation. The story of this remarkable event is has action, an exotic setting, and is always thought-provoking.

Whether read aloud to a class or read individually, older readers may want to want to learn more about the historical facts upon which this story is based. They may wish to explore encyclopedia references to the discovery of feral children by J.A.L. Singh near the Indian village of Godamuri in 1920, parts of Dr. Singh's personal account, *Wolf-Children and the Feral Man* (Harper, 1942), or Charles Maclean's *The Wolf Children* (Hill and Wang, 1978).   H.M.

Science Middle School Junior High School

Related Sources

POETRY
FOR
ALL AGES

POETRY

320. Adoff, Arnold. *Greens*. Illustrated by Betsy Lewin. Lothrop, Lee & Shepard, 1988. ISBN 0-688-04277-5, $10.88. Ages 6-10.

Related Source

Move over Mary O'Neill! Not since *Hailstones and Halibut Bones* (Doubleday, 1961) has an American poet had so much fun with color! This volume of poems about "green" is a bargain at $10.88, and, one hopes, is the start of a series. Adoff plays with space, rhythm, and rhyme so that each poem is a treat for both the eyes and the ears. His topics range from objects found in nature to an old green truck stuck in the mud. Sketchy watercolored drawings by Lewin add a child-like exuberance to the visual display of the poems themselves. The book is dedicated: "For/ Ker/ Mit/ The/ Frog/ With/ This/ Kiss/ And/ Hug/ For/ Being/ Green/ And/ For/ His/ Green Song/ Live Long."

Children can't help but be stimulated to look at the colors in the world around them after reading such poetry as Adoff's and O'Neill's. Encourage them to choose a color and focus upon it for a day or a week, recording in a notebook sights and thoughts related to the color. The notes can be made into poems modeled after either Adoff's or O'Neill's. O'Neill's structure is more defined and may, therefore, appeal to younger children as a model; older children may enjoy playing with spacing, rhythm, and rhyme as Adoff does. They may find that using a computer word processing package allows them to try different spacing more easily. The results should certainly be displayed in the library or classroom for everyone to savor.   M.A.C.

Art, Language Arts
Primary
Intermediate

321. Adoff, Arnold. *Sports Pages*. Illustrated by Steve Kuzma. Lippincott, 1986. ISBN 0-397-32103-1, $10.89. Ages 8-12.

Perhaps it takes a poet to put into words the doubts and the dreams, the fears and the joys athletes in all sports feel when on the track, field, rink, or in the gymnasium. Arnold Adoff has captured perfectly many private thoughts and recognizable emotions of young people in a variety of sports settings: the reflective soccer goalie wondering why he/she is standing alone in the hard-driving rain; the baseball catcher ("I am always heavy..."); or the equestrian ("Dear Horse:/ you want this apple./ and I/want that/ competition cup.") This is a collection for individual reading, and reflecting, and remembering. Each selection speaks directly to anyone who has played any sport.

There is such grace, vigor, and emotion in athletic competition that it is a wonder more attention has not been paid by poets to the individual athlete and to sport. Older students could be encouraged to put together a class or school anthology of outstanding sports poetry. The search might start with Thayer's "Casey at the Bat," Martin Gardner's *The Annotated Casey at the Bat* (University of Chicago, 1984), Arnold Adoff's previously published *i am the running girl* (Harper & Row, 1979), or *American Sports Poems* by R.R. Knudson and May Swenson (Orchard, 1988). Most selections, however, will be found within more general anthologies. The collected poems can be gathered together in book form and illustrated with drawings or photographs of the students in uniform or in action. The bound book should be catalogued and placed in the library.   H.M.

322.   Bauer, Caroline Feller, editor. *Rainy Day: Stories and Poems.* Illustrated by Michele Chessare. Lippincott, 1986. ISBN 0-397-32105-8, $10.89. Ages 7-10.

Three stories, twenty-three poems, four sayings, three activities, five facts, a three-page bibliography, and an index all about rain comprise this grand collection. Theme story hours are commonplace, but storyteller Bauer has prepared a theme book and it is a good one. The stories are "Cloudy with a Chance of Meatballs," "The Jolly Tailor," and "When the Rain Came Up from China." The poems are by Lillian Moore, Rebecca Caudill, John Ciardi, Karla Kuskin, Langston Hughes, and Eve Merriam, to name a few. Almost every page is illustrated in gray, rain-like tones and humorous interpretations of the text. The format should appeal to six- to ten-year-olds, but any age could enjoy the content. Each story is preceded by a short paragraph introducing its origin and genre. Students do not have to like rain to love this book.

The various approaches to rain should motivate students to learn weather lore, to conduct science experiments, to search for more information to verify what is there, or to use a bibliography or an index. The book as a whole would be good for teaching point of view—some like rain, some do not; some see metaphor in rain, some look for ways to escape it. A discussion of feelings or writing poems about feelings may be a good follow-up to this useful classroom resource.   A.P.N.

323.   Bauer, Caroline Feller, editor. *Snowy Day: Stories and Poems.* Illustrated by Margot Tomes. Lippincott, 1986. ISBN 0-397-32177-5, $10.89. Ages 7-11.

Caroline Feller Bauer has put together more than just a book of poetry with *Snowy Day: Stories and Poems.* She has included three stories from diverse cultures that are also related to snow, some activities to try, and some recipes. This makes her book an easy resource for an integrated, seasonally-related unit. The quality of the poems and stories is high: selections are by well-known authors such as

Isaac Bashevis Singer, Yoshiko Uchida, Myra Cohn Livingston, Eve Merriam, X.J. Kennedy, and John Ciardi, and others. Margot Tomes's black and white, half-tone illustrations vary appropriately with the subjects, and they successfully and charmingly convey the different cultures represented.

Snowy Day: Stories and Poems could be used at the start of an integrated unit on winter. Its advantage over some of the other winter books available is its primary focus on poetry. This makes it a useful companion to *Exploring Winter* by Sandra Markle (Atheneum, 1984), *Winter Barn* by Peter Parnall (Macmillan, 1986), and other similar books. Students may enjoy finding other winter poems or writing their own. Teachers may, after enjoying this integrated unit, become intrigued with integrated teaching in other areas and develop additional units to share with colleagues.   M.A.C.

*Science,
Language Arts
Primary
Intermediate
Middle School*

Related Sources

324.   Behn, Harry. *Crickets and Bullfrogs and Whispers of Thunder*. Illustrated by the author. Harcourt Brace Jovanovich, 1984. ISBN 0-15-220885-2, $11.95. Ages 4-8.

Harry Behn has rightfully earned the praise of critics and the delight of children who have heard and read his poetry for the past thirty-five years. His lyric and fanciful poems remind us to find beauty in the natural world around us and in the imaginative world within. Lee Bennett Hopkins has thoughtfully selected fifty of the poet's finest works and organized them into three sections: "Poems of the Seasons," "The World of Fantasy," and "The World Through a Child's Eye." This is a collection that teachers and librarians everywhere should have close at hand to share with children regularly.

The axiom that children should hear poetry read—to savor the sounds of words, to feel the rhythms of phrases and sentences, and to enjoy the images of the poems—is evident in Harry Behn's work. There is no need here for elaborate introductions or follow-up activities. The imagery and sense of wonder that the poems create work their magic by reaching out to each listener directly.   H.M.

*Literature,
Language Arts
Primary
Intermediate*

325.   Demi, compiler. *Dragon Kites and Dragonflies*. Illustrated by the author. Harcourt Brace Jovanovich, 1986. ISBN 0-15-224199-X, $14.95. Ages 4-8.

This collection of traditional Chinese nursery rhymes was adapted and illustrated by Demi, who drew upon primary resources and upon materials from earlier in this century. The rhymes are delightful. Some are about objects that children everywhere can identify—fireflies, kites, frogs. Others will expand children's experience by exposing them to things unique to the Chinese culture—silk worms, the Great Wall of China, a camel-backed bridge. The rich illustrations are simple line drawings colored with bright watercolors. An abundance of red, traditional costumes, and architectural details contribute to the cultural expression of the folklore.

During the study of China, upper elementary students may find ***Dragon Kites and Dragonflies*** to be a surprisingly interesting and quite useful resource in a social studies class. An activity that would focus them on cultural universals would be to examine each poem for elements suggestive of any culture and those elements that are purely Chinese. These could be charted and confirmed through research in other sources. Doing this with the nursery and childhood rhymes of other cultures would reinforce the idea that some themes and language forms are the same for all peoples.   M.A.C.

Social Studies,
Literature,
Language Arts
Primary
Intermediate

326.   de Regniers, Beatrice Schenk, et al., editors. *Sing a Song of Popcorn*. Illustrated by nine Caldecott Medal artists. Scholastic, 1988. ISBN 0-590-40645-0, $16.95. All ages.

ALA Notable Book

Related Source

Nineteen years ago Citation Press issued a poetry anthology with the optimistic title ***Poems Children Will Sit Still For*** (1969) edited by Beatrice Schenk de Regniers, Eva Moore, and Mary White. *Sing a Song of Popcorn* is only a slightly revised version with a more playful title and illustrations that should be cause for celebration. Maurice Sendak, Marcia Brown, Trina Schart Hyman, Arnold Lobel, Leo and Diane Dillon, Margot Zemach, Marc Simont, and Richard Egielski create the magic that children will be drawn to again and again in this beautifully designed tribute to the marriage of words and images. This is an attractive volume, one that will easily appeal to the eye. Unfortunately the poetry selections do not match the verve and delight of the illustrations and what might have been cause for great celebration is simply old (ordinary) wine in a new (beautiful) bottle.

In her introduction de Regniers properly points out the importance of hearing the poems—they can only be fully appreciated if read aloud. Her advice on how to read poetry aloud is the same advice the Duchess gave Alice: "Take care of the sense, and the sounds will take care of themselves." Older students can be encouraged to prepare an audiotape to accompany this volume for the personal pleasure of younger children. Background music can be selected to fit the words and images of each poem.   H.M.

Speech,
Literature, Music,
Language Arts
Primary
Intermediate

327.   Esbensen, Barbara Juster. *Words with Wrinkled Knees*. Illustrated by John Stadler. Crowell, 1986. ISBN 0-690-04505-0, $11.89. Ages 7-12.

As the names of the twenty-one animals parade before the reader, Esbensen creates images and feelings that each name evokes: "P E N G U I N/ Best-dressed word in the world atlas!" or "An evenly balanced/ word W H A L E/ it floats/lazily on the page..." or "The word comes shambling in/ bristling/ with a thousand pens/ fiercely attached/ P O R C U P I N E." Esbensen's images are sharp, often surprising, always fresh, and never condescending. She entices her audience to stand back and reappraise familiar animals from a poet's perspective. John Stadler's black and white illustrations add the right complement of images and textures to this gifted poet's third collection. The result is a series of delights to return to again and again.

Like collecting stamps or baseball cards, collecting poems on a specific topic can be a very satisfying and rewarding activity in which children may engage over a long period of time. Browsing through anthologies becomes worthwhile if the purpose is to expand one's collection. Esbensen's animal poems could become the starting point for each child in class to put together his/her collection of, for example, penguin poems. The poems could be handwritten, typed, or computer printed and presented with appropriate illustrations. The anthology should be preserved in a sturdy, attractive book format suitable for adding to a library collection (and be sure to add it to the card catalog).   H. M.

Science, Literature, Language Arts Primary Intermediate

328. Fisher, Aileen. *When it Comes to Bugs*. Illustrated by Chris and Bruce Degen. Harper & Row, 1986. ISBN 0-06-021822-3, $11.89. Ages 4-8.

"Beetle folk beneath the grass/ must get scared when mowers pass,/ and go darting helter-skelter/ looking for an air-raid shelter." Fisher's clever verses about life from an insect's perspective are amusingly illustrated by the Degens. The pictures and the poems lean toward the fanciful, which younger readers or listeners should find appealing. Although some of the poems are witty, the quality varies greatly in this selection. Still, Mrs. Beetle's retreat from winter (she "nestled down and went to sleep/ and slept till April came") and the ladybug who encounters five hills (a child's toes) are appealing poems that should stimulate the imaginations of many younger children.

Children generally enjoy poetry, often having been introduced to rhyme and rhythm through Mother Goose and Dr. Seuss, but many lose the love of poetry when forced to analyze it in school. This book and Fisher's other books, as well as verse by poets like Dorothy Aldis, David McCord, and Eve Merriam, can be used with early elementary pupils to help them make the transition from Dr. Seuss-style verse to other forms. Poetry is often best understood and appreciated when it is made an integral part of the classroom by reading poems each day, either at a regularly scheduled time or at a time to fit the topic; encourage students to read or recite favorite poems, too. The group might like to make a class list of the poems they most enjoyed. Teachers can take requests for that day's selection so the students can re-hear favorites.   J.J.S.

Science, Literature, Language Arts Primary

329. Fleischman, Paul. *Joyful Noise: Poems for Two Voices*. Illustrated by Eric Beddows. Harper & Row, 1988. ISBN 0-06-021853-3, $11.89. All ages.

From the cover to the decorative end papers, these unusual poems by an author known for his prose are pure delight. Expressive images tumble down the pages in side by side "parts," intended by Fleischman to be read aloud "by two readers at once...meshing as in a musical

Newbery Award Winner ALA Best Book ALA Notable Book

duet." This arrangement is perfectly suited to the poems' subjects: insects, both familiar and lesser known. From water boatmen to book lice, these tiny creatures come amazingly alive in both words and pictures. The highly informative content is echoed in Beddows's finely-drawn pencil illustrations; not only are they biologically authentic, but they convey just enough subtle humor to personify each type. Fleischman succeeds admirably in avoiding the sentimental by creating sharp, precise images.

While a good bit of these poems' content and allusions is more appropriate for older students, there are plenty of selections for younger children to play with and enjoy. Fleischman states that the poems are to be read aloud, making this an intriguing addition to a classroom's reader's theater resources. Give students plenty of practice time and some coaching to help them find the rhythm and feel easy with the matching lines. Performances need not be limited to literature units; this poetry is a natural for science study. Students can be challenged to find examples of many of the insects depicted and to do further research on the more arcane insects so appealingly presented.   B.B.

Speech, Drama, Literature, Science Intermediate Middle School Junior High School

330. Forrester, Victoria. *A Latch Against the Wind*. Illustrated by the author. Atheneum, 1985. ISBN 0-689-31091-9, $8.95. Ages 12-up.

Victoria Forrester has written and illustrated a collection of poems that is vibrantly alive and concentrates on the delights of an everyday world. In "Pines" she uses rhyme to evoke an almost eerie sensation: "There lives a spirit/ In the pines/ Ancestral as the shore,/ Both evergreen/ And ever-grey/ And almost evermore." In "Sunset" and other selections she uses a lyrical rhythm to create and sustain a mood. In each of her poems she uses only a few well-chosen words like light brush strokes to enthrall her audience with her vision of our world—economy and understatement powerfully evoking images that ring true.

This collection of poetry is for every young person or adult who has ever thought poetry had to be stuffy or boring. These poems speak *to* young people, rather than *at* them. Forrester has given teachers, parents, and librarians an ideal source to help us all view our everyday worlds with new eyes. Like a scientist who examines the smallest details, this collection could be an effective springboard for helping students realize that poetry, beauty, and significance can be found in something as simple as bird tracks. Reflective, open-ended group discussion can expand children's awareness of the beauty of our language and their worlds, large and small.   N.S.R.

Science, Literature Intermediate Middle School Junior High School

331. Glenn, Mel. *Back to Class*. Photographs by Michael J. Bernstein. Clarion, 1988. ISBN 0-89919-656-X, $13.95. Ages 12-up.

With *Back to Class*, Glenn has written a third book about high school. He began with *Class Dismissed* (Clarion, 1982) and won a

Christopher Award in 1987 for *Class Dismissed II* (Clarion, 1986). These poems are about fictional students and their teachers, but are based upon Glenn's own experiences as a high school teacher. Glenn says that "any resemblance to actual persons is purely intentional in the artistic sense." And resemble they do: this collection acts as a mirror of the soul of today's high school. The concerns, aspirations, inadequacies, family problems, peer pressures, and frivolities of these people trapped together in a building all day under the guise of learning are touchingly painted in vibrant emotional colors. This book should be in every high school library to remind everyone there—teachers and students alike—that we are all individual human beings struggling to make sense out of our world and what life has brought us. Bernstein's black and white photographs add a sense of reality to the fictional characters, extending the human dimension.

Related Sources

The poems by children collected by Richard Lewis in *Miracles* (Simon and Schuster, 1966) and Kenneth Koch in *Rose, Where Did You Get That Red?* (Random House, 1973) are powerful in their imaginary and emotional insights into the lives of young people. Students can be encouraged to keep a small blank book with them to write thoughts, impressions, and feelings while the images are fresh. Shared weekly, the best can be reworked and polished for publication in a class or school literary annual as a supplement to the high school yearbook.   M.A.C./H.M.

Related Sources

*Literature, English
Junior High School
High School*

332. Greenfield, Eloise. *Under the Sunday Tree.* Illustrated by Mr. Amos Ferguson. Harper & Row, 1988. ISBN 0-06-022257-3, $19.95. All ages.

Under the Sunday Tree is a special collaboration. The paintings in bold color and design are powerful graphic primitives, reflecting artist Mr. Amos Ferguson's native Bahamas. The poems, by respected author Eloise Greenfield, were created to complement the pictures, the reverse of the usual order of book making. Her ability to do this so successfully is a tribute to her great talent. Through subjects ranging from fishing to Sunday strolls, this team has brought the Bahamas to life for readers of all ages. Even the primary typeface used for the text complements the naive art and the uncluttered poetry, and contributes to the island feeling.

ALA Notable Book

Connecticut Public Television made a half hour documentary about Ferguson and his work that received a nomination for an Emmy. It may be possible to borrow a copy of this and/or other documentaries through your local public television station, public library, or video store to show to older students. After viewing the documentary(ies), students might enjoy making one themselves. They can select a local artist as the subject of their film. Then they can research that individual, develop interview questions, and film an interview with the artist using a camcorder. The end product should focus on the artist's life and his or her work, both finished and in progress. The most workable arrangement for this activity may be to divide into small teams of two or three. If this is done, the project need not be limited to one artist.   M.A.C.

*Art, Literature
Intermediate
Middle School
Junior High School
High School*

333.   Hayes, Sarah, editor. *Clap Your Hands: Finger Rhymes*. Illustrated by Toni Goffe. Lothrop, Lee & Shepard, 1988. ISBN 0- 688-07693-9, $12.88. Ages 1-6.

Related Sources

This delightfully illustrated collection of traditional finger rhymes ranks with Marc Brown's *Finger Rhymes* (Dutton, 1980) and *Hand Rhymes* (Dutton, 1985) for a number of reasons. First, the selection is excellent. All 23 rhymes are appealing, easy to follow, and sure to entertain and surprise the younger set. Second, Goffe's watercolor and pen-and-ink drawings not only illustrate the poems, but also cleverly incorporate the directions for the hand movements. Finally, the cartoon-style characters should especially draw children's attention as they are multiethnic children often dressed in open-faced animal costumes. The overall effect of the text and pictures is warm and playful, making finger rhymes a pleasure for everyone.

Language Arts Primary

This book would be a wonderful resource for preschool and primary teachers, for parents, and for librarians conducting story hour. The rhymes and accompanying movements are easy to learn and are likely to distract a fussy toddler or a nervous story hour novice. Teachers and storytellers can keep these handy to regain the straying attention of a group of antsy youngsters as well. Parents will find that a stock of activities needing no supplies except fingers can turn such ordeals as waiting at the doctor's office or being confined during a plane ride from nightmares into happy shared experiences. Simplicity often works wonders with children, and these rhymes are perfectly simple.   M.A.C.

334.   Hopkins, Lee Bennett, editor. *Best Friends*. Illustrated by James Watts. Harper & Row, 1986. ISBN 0-06-022561-0, $11.25. Ages 5-8.

Hopkins has compiled a humorous and touching collection of poems about friendship by such noted writers as Langston Hughes, Myra Cohn Livingston, Judith Viorst, and others. With poems that evoke images ranging from anger and sadness to adventure and just plain fun, children will identify with the wide range of emotions experienced by the young people in each selection. Appealing watercolor illustrations provide additional feeling to the already expressive poems.

Language Arts Primary Intermediate

This book would be a good introduction to simple poetry collections that intermediate students might enjoy making and sharing with their best friends. Then, as they deal with such emotions as anger, sadness, and joy throughout the year, direct them to their poetry books to help them express their feelings. Primary teachers may want to make one class anthology, allowing younger children to discuss poems they hear each day and select those they would like to hear again. As either group begins to understand that poetry is an effective way of communicating emotions and feelings towards others, they can be encouraged to write poems as a way to express their own feelings toward their family and their friends.   C.A.Y./M.A.C.

335. Hopkins, Lee Bennett, editor. *The Sea is Calling Me*. Illustrated by Walter Gaffney-Kessell. Harcourt Brace Jovanovich, 1986. ISBN 0-15-271155-4, $14.95. Ages 9-12.

Seashore images that are swift and sharp remain clear even after this brief anthology is put aside. From sand castles and shells to sandpipers and starfish, familiar objects are woven into a tapestry of shore life that makes us feel relaxed, thoughtful, and serene: "Sand white—sea blue,/ and nothing you really have to do." There is also the wonder of discovering new images and rediscovering those that may have been forgotten: "A seashell is a castle/ Where a million echoes roam,/ A wee castle,/ A sea castle,/ Tossed up by the foam..." Hopkins's selections are varied and always have the younger child in mind. Walter Gaffney-Kessell's blue and white illustrations are evocative of the colors and textures of water and sand, complementing the selections perfectly.

Here is a timely opportunity to create an interest table or corner in a classroom or library with items collected from family vacations to the shore. Each poem from *The Sea is Calling Me* can be displayed with a miniature scene of a sand castle, dried starfish or seaweed, a variety of shells, driftwood, a model lighthouse, etc., created by children or teachers. Other books—both fiction and nonfiction—about the seashore should be on a nearby bookshelf to catch the interest of students who want to learn more.   H.M.

Art, Science, Language Arts Primary Intermediate

336. Janeczko, Paul B., collector. *The Music of What Happens: Poems That Tell Stories*. Orchard, 1988. ISBN 0-531-05757-7, $14.95. Ages 12-up.

Narrative poetry is likely the most appealing form of verse for all ages, either because narrative satisfies a need for closure, or because it rejects the formality and distancing of ritualized language structures. A new anthology of story poems is, therefore, a joyful occasion, especially one compiled by Janeczko, high school teacher and poetry editor for *English Journal*. His selections are contemporary, fresh in form and image, and appropriately challenging to high school students. The topics range from early loves and families (Mark Jarman's "The Gift" and Wing Tek Lum's "My Mother Really Knew Him" are sharply affecting) to history (especially moving is Erika Mumford's "The White Rose: Sophie Scholl 1921-43"). Throughout this diverse collection rings the simple truth of Jared Carter: "The purpose of poetry is to tell us about life." Janeczko has successfully followed that declaration in this sterling collection for young adults.

There is a good deal of emotional imagery throughout *The Music of What Happens* that deserves a second reading, quiet reflection, and opportunities to respond and probe at length personal meanings with others. "Teaching" a poem can be enhanced through discussion not only with other students and the teacher, but also with poets and anthologists. Writing to Paul Janeczko (c/o Orchard Books, 387 Park Avenue South, New York, NY 10016) to ask about how he went about putting together the collection, where he looked, or why he chose the ones he

ALA Best Book

Author Studies, Literature Junior High School High School

did can add greatly to understanding individual poems. Contacting the individual poets can offer further insights; Janeczko may be able to help here. Teachers, librarians, or students can also invite members of a local writing group to share insights about these and other works by contemporary poets.   H.M.

337.   Janeczko, Paul B., editor. *Pocket Poems*. Bradbury, 1985. ISBN 0-02-747820-3, $8.95. Ages 12-up.

Paul Janeczko has selected 120 short modern poems by eighty American poets, including Maya Angelou, Archibald MacLeish, Ogden Nash, John Updike, and William Carlos Williams. Most of the poets, however, are less well known writers whose works offer young readers a twentieth century perspective on timeless themes ranging from locomotives to lasagne to love. Janeczko has both an eye and an ear for what the young adult reader of poetry is likely to understand and enjoy. There is a poem for every reader in this collection.

While this collection nicely complements the traditional textbook study of twentieth century literature, much of the poetry expresses emotions understandable to older readers. Read a variety of the selections aloud, encouraging students to freely respond in a non-critical classroom climate. Louise Rosenblatt, in *The Reader, The Text, and The Poem* (Southern Illinois University Press, 1978), reminds us that the meaning of a poem depends upon the background experiences of the reader/listener. Hearing the variety of responses that result in class discussions should broaden and deepen a student's undertanding of individual poems and of poetry as an art.   M.J.H./M.A.C.

338.   Kennedy, X. J. *Brats*. Illustrated by James Watts. Atheneum, 1986. ISBN 0-689-50392-X, $11.95. Ages 8-up.

No run-of-the-mill brats here! Each is extraordinary for her or his mischief-making, whether it is tossing little brothers into clothes dryers, gluing a pig to the kitchen ceiling, or skinny-dipping in fabric shrinker. Each (usually) suffers consequences equal to the occasion: "Louise, a whiz at curling hair,/ Sneaked up on a snoozing bear,/ Left its fur all frazzly-frizzly./ My, but its revenge was grisly!" Not to be taken seriously, each of the 42 verses in this collection by one of America's favorite poets is a treat guaranteed to blow the blahs from the grayest day. James Watts' occasional black and white illustrations add just the right dash of wit to the outrageous humor of Kennedy's poem-jokes.

Kennedy usually uses a simple four-line form like the one above. Children will be tempted to try their hand at creating a "brat" of their own, and will draw inspiration from the poet's son, Josh, whose own effort is included as an acknowledgement in the beginning of the book. All each student needs is her or his personal do-it-yourself poet's kit: a sharp pencil and plenty of blank paper. Then stand aside and watch the verses flow.   H.M.

339. Kennedy, X. J. *The Forgetful Wishing Well*. Illustrated
by Monica Incisa. Atheneum, 1985. ISBN 0-689-50317-2,
$9.95. Ages 9-up.

"I'll put my bat cape on and creep/ Downstairs and switch the TV
on," says Amanda Rose to herself when her father complains that she is
watching too much TV. Children will recognize their own experiences
in these poems. The 70 poems offer ample variety on such topics as
growing up, animals, people, family matters, wonders of the world, the
city, and holidays. There is no nursery flavor here, no sentimental pap.
Amusing but not superficial, these poems will link children to their inner
selves and nourish their imaginative spirits and sense of wonder.

Adults who enjoy poetry can usually recall someone who regularly
and generously read or recited poetry to them while they were growing
up. Often it is a teacher or librarian whom we remember fondly and with
respect. To help children find the same pleasures from poetry, reading
poetry to children should meet these conditions: (1) it should be read
daily, as much a part of the day as recess or spelling; (2) reading poems
should be practiced so that your sense of the poem's meaning and feeling is communicated; and (3) poems should be shared for the pleasure
of the poem, not to test listening comprehension.   M.E.M

*Literature
Intermediate
Middle School
Junior High School*

340. Koch, Kenneth and Kate Farrell, editors. *Talking to the
Sun*. Henry Holt, 1985. ISBN 0-03-005849-X, $18.95. All
ages.

At first glance, one is almost overwhelmed by the sheer beauty of
this book. Illustrated with photographs of paintings and objects from the
Metropolitan Museum of Art, the poetry shares the spotlight with art.
However, the poems have been chosen well and the selections, both familiar and rarely seen, are appropriate to a broad range of ages and
tastes. Arranged chronologically, the poems vary from ancient chants to
modern verse. Koch and Farrell make thoughtful, useful comments that
offer insights to all who will spend time with this remarkable book.

This book could be very useful in a classroom. The art prints provide a study in and of themselves; many could also be used as a stimulus for creative writing. The poetry collection provides some unusual selections for reading and discussion. The chronological arrangement also
lends itself to correlation with social studies units. This is an extraordinarily useful book that should be a lasting contribution to the school or
home library.   B.S.J.

*Art, Literature,
Social Studies
Intermediate
Middle School
Junior High School
High School*

341. Lewis, Richard. *In the Night, Still Dark*. Illustrated by Ed
Young. Atheneum, 1988. ISBN 0-689-31310-1, $13.95. All
ages.

"The Kumulipo" is the Hawaiian creation chant which not only
chronicles the genealogy of Hawaiian kings, but also was chanted after
the birth of each royal child to meld the new life with the first stirrings

of life itself. *In the Night, Still Dark* is an abridgment of the original 2000+ line chant focusing upon the Hawaiian people's traditional concept of evolution and the emergence of daylight. The text is simple and poetic: "In this the darkest night, in this the darkest sea,/ After the coral was born, there came the mud-digging grub,/ and its child the earthworm." Ed Young's artistic interpretation of the chant is haunting. Oil pastel drawings on textured black background, like that darkest night in the beginning, have a quality so luminous that they almost shimmer in the darkness and create the feeling that one is really there in that murky time before daylight came to the world. This is a wonderful collaboration, pictures and text joining as did new life with old with the chanting of "The Kumulipo."

Social Studies,
Literature
Intermediate
Middle School
Junior High School

The beginning of the world and its creatures has been the subject of controversy for many generations. *In the Night, Still Dark* provides an excellent opportunity for older students to take a look at this subject from a specific cultural viewpoint. Students can read other versions of creation in Virginia Hamilton's *In the Beginning* (Harcourt Brace Jovanovich, 1988); in "The Creation," James Weldon Johnson's powerful and evocative poetic retelling of Genesis; or Darwin's theory of evolution. Then they can search the folklore section of the library for additional creation stories from other cultures, including *In the Beginning: Creation Myths Around the World* by Maria Leach (Funk and Wagnall's, 1956), the book Lewis used in writing *In the Night, Still Dark*. The study might enrich students' understandings of the importance and diversity of beliefs about creation that could help clarify persistent controversies about the origins of human beings.   M.A.C.

Related Sources

342.   Little, Lessie Jones. *Children of Long Ago*. Illustrated by Jan Spivey Gilchrest. Philomel, 1988. ISBN 0-399-21473-9, $13.95. All ages.

Seventeen poems about rural life in the early 1900's depict a diversity of scenes: a buggy ride, going barefoot, jumping ditches, watching wood being cut for the woodpile, or filling the wood box. Strong, bold chalk illustrations enhance the poems' imagery. Though all children shown are Black and evoke strong images of Little's southern childhood, the poems themselves have universal appeal. The poems may be read aloud successfully even to the very young, as the word-pictures are vivid: "Silky ribbons long and green" are corn plant leaves; Grandma's glasses are "pretty and thin and clear/ With long gold arms that hug your ears;" The images are sharp visions of a bygone era.

Social Studies, Science
Primary
Intermediate
Middle School

Few children of today—whether from urban or rural neighborhoods—know much about that simple but hard life before electricity, super highways, tractors, or automobiles, when wood was fuel for both cooking and heating homes and when kerosene lamps furnished the only light at night. Invite an elderly resident to describe those early days in your community and answer the questions children will have. Read the poems and let the children suggest what things are still the same today and which are no longer extant.   F.M.H.

343. Livingston, Myra Cohn. *Celebrations*. Illustrated by Leonard Everett Fisher. Holiday House, 1985. ISBN 0-8234-0550-8, $14.95. Ages 5-8.

Award-winning poet Myra Cohn Livingston celebrates with feeling sixteen important days on the calendar. These feelings are echoed in Leonard Everett Fisher's richly-textured and striking, full-color paintings. From Halloween's "Green cat eyes in midnight gloom" to "A birthday wish is right," memories and moods are artfully blended in this delightful book. This is another welcome creation by these two collaborators who gave us *Sky Songs* (1984) and A *Circle of Seasons* (1982), both published by Holiday House. Of the latter book a reviewer said, "Neither the poet nor the painter has ever done better." However, in *Celebrations* they have!

Related Sources

Teachers can show students the bright, full-of-feeling paintings and ask them to express their poetic ideas for each picture through word gatherings, a group poem, or individual creations. This can be done with each picture before or after hearing the poem, whichever way the teacher feels best stimulates the use of simile, metaphor, analogy, and even occasional rhyme. An excellent companion book that prompts a different set of follow-up activities is Byrd Baylor's *I'm in Charge of Celebrations* (Scribner's, 1986).   M.E.M.

Art, Literature
Primary
Intermediate

Related Source

344. Livingston, Myra Cohn. *Higgledy-Piggledy: Verses and Pictures*. Illustrated by Peter Sis. McElderry Books, 1986. ISBN 0-689-50407-1, $10.95. Ages 8-12.

Higgledy-Piggledy is the perfect boy—so perfect that the narrator wishes him ill: "Higgledy-Piggledy/ takes out the garbage./ He whistles and sings/ when he's doing his chores./ He dries all the dishes;/ he washes the windows./ (And I'd like to use him/ for mopping up floors!)" Thus, page by page, Higgledy-Piggledy's virtues are extolled and bemoaned. Peter Sis illustrates each page with humorous pen and ink drawings made entirely of dots. At the top of each page we see good old Higgledy-Piggledy and at the bottom what is wished upon him! This little book works—it is funny, warm, and real.

Higgledy-Piggledy can be used to provoke discussion about "perfect" people. Is anyone truly perfect? Why are such people resented? Should we look for fatal flaws in them or accept them for what they are? Do "perfect" people have feelings of inadequacy just like the rest of us? School-aged children from elementary through high school daily grapple with peer acceptance, both their own and that of others. Our perceptions of people, whether accurate or not, can really color our relationships. Perhaps *Higgledy-Piggledy* can, in a light-hearted way, bring some understanding of self and others to students. An exercise which may promote this would be for students to make a chart headed by two columns entitled "How do I perceive myself?" and "How am I perceived by others?" Sharing these in a trusting environment could really open some eyes. Bernard Waber's *Nobody is Perfick* (Hough-

Social Studies, Literature
Primary
Intermediate

Related Source

ton Mifflin, 1971) is a humorous companion collection of short stories on the same topic of human perfection.   M.A.C.

345.   Livingston, Myra Cohn. *Sky Songs*. Illustrated by Leonard Everett Fisher. Holiday House, 1984. ISBN 0-8234-0502-8, $14.95. Ages 5-10.

Following *A Circle of Seasons* (Holiday House, 1982), this poet and artist collaboration has created a celebration of the sky through day and night and changing weather. The texts of fourteen poems are printed directly on full double page spread paintings in acrylic on textured paper. Both the poetry and the art deliver images so strong that the heavens seem to rest in the reader's hands. The paintings' colors, textures, and shapes are so vivid and palpable that the poems often seem overwhelmed. The book's strength is its imaginative personification of the sky as both a vast power and a victim.

Social Studies, Art, Literature Primary Intermediate

Younger children should respond to the strong images in words, colors, and shapes; they may be challenged to create their own "sky book" (or "star book" or "earth book"). Older children also might want to do the same activity, and may also want to investigate how various cultures have envisioned the sky, moon, stars, sun, etc. as part of their folklores. These collections can be illustrated by original drawings or from pictures gathered from discarded magazines from home or the library.   B.B.

346.   Livingston, Myra Cohn. *There Was a Place and Other Poems*. McElderry Books, 1988. ISBN 0-689-50464-0, $9.95. Ages 8-12.

It is difficult to recommend a volume of poetry that is as unrelenting as this one in portraying the emotional maelstrom faced by many children as their families are torn apart by divorce, separation, and loneliness. Yet, Livingston's brief sketches evoke images and emotions that go to the heart of what is left behind when their lives are shattered, and they are denied the emotional security they need to grow healthy. Stepfathers, new boyfriends for Mom, runaway parents who can't be forgotten, the dilemmas of shared custody—all are the result of what Livingston calls "circles broken." These brief but poignant sketches will move even the most cynical to ponder the future of those caught in a society of changing family patterns. The unfortunate fact is that many children already know too well the truth of the poems.

Family Life, U.S. History Intermediate Middle School Junior High School

These are poems to be shared aloud and discussed for their emotional veracity and social realities as understood by students. The collection can appropriately be central to a more extended focus on "The Family" as a topic of historical study. Many good works of historical fiction, as well as biographies, diaries, and other nonfiction, attest to the difficulties faced by many generations of families through our nation's history, often complicated by poor medical, social welfare, and educational facilities, hostility toward immigrants, and an indifferent legal system.

Learning how other children and families were and are able to persist—
even to succeed—may help children and their families view their futures
more optimistically.   H.M.

347.   Merriam, Eve. *You Be Good & I'll Be Night: Jump-
            on-the-Bed Poems*. Illustrated by Karen Lee Schmidt.
            Morrow, 1988. ISBN 0-688-06743-3, $12.88. Ages 3-7.

This buoyant collection of nursery-style poems is for an audience
younger than many of Merriam's previous works. Still, the language
play that characterizes her style is very visible: "You be saucer,/ I'll be
cup,/ piggyback, piggyback,/ pick me up./ You be tree, I'll be pears,/
Carry me, carry me/ up the stairs./ You be Good,/ I'll be Night,/ tuck
me in, tuck me in/ nice and tight." Rhythm is the strong suit here: the
poems literally make one want to "jump-on-the-bed." Schmidt's realistic
watercolor drawings, sometimes soft and sometimes vibrant, complement the variety of moods.

Literature Primary

Primary children might enjoy a pajama party day at school. They
could wear their coziest pajamas (teachers too!) and bring their favorite
stuffed animal. Nursery rhymes from modern authors like Eve Merriam,
as well as from traditional sources could be shared. Some other modern
day nursery rhyme collections include Jack Prelutsky's *Ride a Purple
Pelican* (Greenwillow, 1986) and Clyde Watson's *Father Fox's
Pennyrhymes* (Crowell, 1971). These also contain ebullient illustrations by Garth Williams and Wendy Watson respectively. The pajama
party would not be complete without popcorn and jumping on a bed—or
perhaps a mini-trampoline instead!   M.A.C.

Related Sources

348.   Metropolitan Museum of Art. *Go In and Out the Window:
            An Illustrated Songbook for Young People*. Illustrat-
            ed with works from the Metropolitan Museum of Art. Henry
            Holt, 1987. ISBN 0-8050-0628-1, $19.95. All ages.

Music and art serve the same master: to evoke images that touch our
emotions so that we more fully know ourselves and our world. By
bringing the two together here, the effects of both are enhanced. The 61
familiar songs selected and arranged on the pages of this handsomely
designed and luxurious volume stand harmoniously with the beauty of
the art which has been attractively reproduced. The piano arrangements
are easy enough for beginners, and there are guitar chords as well. This
is gorgeous for looking through, for playing, and for singing together.

ALA Notable Book

Music written down has no life for most readers. What is missing—sound—can be supplied by students armed with portable tape recorders and blank tapes. Many libraries have recorded versions of the
songs in the book. Students could produce a tape on which the songs
are presented in the same order as they appear in the book; this would
make the book complete. Older students could also record the text that
explains the art work so that younger children could better enjoy *both*
the art and the music.   H.M.

*Speech, Art, Music,
Literature
Middle School
Junior High School
High School*

349.   Morrison, Lillian. *Rhythm Road: Poems to Move To*. Lothrop, Lee & Shepard, 1988. ISBN 0-688-07098-1, $11.95. Ages 9-up.

Lillian Morrison has collected a provocative anthology of poems representing movement and action for intermediate and older readers. As Morrison points out in her preface, the poets suggest movement in several different ways; by accent and beat, length of lines, pauses, and careful selection and arrangement of words and phrases. The book is divided into chapters which include "The Twirl and the Swirl" (poems to dance to), "At the Starting Line" (the feel of sports), "The Rusty Spigot Sputters" (TV and technology), and others in which students will be able to associate everyday objects or events with the common element of movement. Though some of the poems are "older," many are contemporary, and this combination in an anthology lends new and different ways of looking at a poem, old or new. This balance is at the heart of the book's strength and appeal.

Speech, Drama, Literature
Intermediate
Middle School
Junior High School

Because of the read-aloud nature of these poems, students should be provided the opportunity perform them, either in small groups, individually or in pairs. After a discussion on how the author used different ways to suggest movement, students could select a favorite poem from this anthology or from Morrison's other book, *Sprints and Distances: Sports in Poetry & the Poetry in Sport* (Crowell, 1965). Another book of poems especially selected for their read-aloud potential is Paul Fleischman's *Joyful Noise* (Harper & Row, 1988). If a video camera is available, students could record someone or something which represents the movement in their poem while the poem is read in the background. These could all be collected onto one tape as "poetry videos" to be given to the school library.   K.B.B.

Related Sources

350.   Prelutsky, Jack. *My Parents Think I'm Sleeping*. Illustrated by Yossi Abolafia. Greenwillow, 1985. ISBN 0-688-04019-5, $10.95. Ages 6-9.

These fourteen light verses capture perfectly a sleepless young boy's nighttime activities after the good-nights have been said and the bedroom door has been shut. Jack Prelutsky, whose *New Kid on the Block* (Greenwillow, 1984) continues to delight children of all ages, is alternately comic, thoughtful, mischievous, wistful, ironic—and always in perfect tune with children's feelings. Yossi Abolafia's drawings match the moods and expressions of each poem. Parents should appreciate having this book recommended for gift giving; it can be enjoyed by young and old alike for many years.

Related Source

For the younger child, nighttime is filled with mystery and wonder. Writers have written countless stories and poems in which children have found pleasure and delight. Teachers can do few things better than to simply allow children to talk and ask questions about their feelings and fantasies about the night to help them understand and gain a greater sense of security and self-assurance. These poems will serve to begin such discussions.   H.M.

Social Studies
Primary

351.   Prelutsky, Jack. *The New Kid on the Block*. Illustrated by James Stevenson. Greenwillow, 1984. ISBN 0-688-02272-3, $12.88. All ages.

Dear Shel,

Watch Out! There's a new kid on the block who's threatening your title of America's favorite children's poet. And no wonder! His poems are as zany and outrageous as yours. Most of them speak about food, eating, or putting things in your mouth, just as yours do. Kids laugh right out loud at his occasional, slightly scatological poems, just like they do when they hear yours. Kids who have memorized every one of your poems and crave something new are going to snatch up Jack Prelutsky's *The New Kid on the Block* just as they did *Where the Sidewalk Ends* (Harper & Row, 1974) when it first came out. On second thought, don't worry. There's plenty of room on the block for you both.

Yours truly,
H.M.

ALA Notable Book

Language Arts, Literature
Primary
Intermediate

Related Source

352.   Prelutsky, Jack, editor. *Read-Aloud Rhymes for the Very Young*. Illustrated by Marc Brown. Knopf, 1986. ISBN 0-394-97218-X, $14.99. Ages 3-8.

"Happy" best describes this successful collaboration between one of America's most popular poets and one of the finest illustrators of books for young children. Both know what touches children, what brings them pleasure. Both know how to present words and images that appeal to young audiences. The large format and whimsical drawings showcase the best works of the finest poets who have ever penned lines for young listeners. The indices of titles, poets, and first lines make it easy to find personal favorites each time children request a repeat performance. This is an especially excellent value for parents seeking a useful book for sharing with children at home; both teachers and librarians should appreciate the selections and organization of this outstanding resource.

An added bonus in *Read-Aloud Rhymes* is the introduction by Jim Trelease. His plea is a rationale for greater emphasis on giving children many regular listening experiences as a foundation for becoming more fully literate. "Simply put, if the child has never heard the word, the child will never say the word; and if you have neither heard it nor said it, it's pretty tough to read it and to write it." Trelease's widely read *Read Aloud Handbook* (Penguin, 1985) effectively develops this thesis in non-technical language with many useful examples and suggestions for parents and teachers. Librarians and teachers should encourage colleagues and parents to read and discuss Trelease's ideas. Together all can work to make sharing literature with children, both at home, in the library, and at school, a more natural and frequent part of every child's day. The result will more like be a child who looks forward to reading and, ultimately, a more literate adult—the goal of everyone who works with children.   H.M.

Literature, Language Arts
Primary
Intermediate

Related Source

353.   Prelutsky, Jack. *Ride a Purple Pelican*. Illustrated by
Garth Williams. Greenwillow, 1986. ISBN 0-688-04031-4,
$13.00. Ages 2-up.

Related Source

In *Ride a Purple Pelican* Jack Prelutsky has created a brand-
new set of nursery rhymes with all of the elements that have made the
traditional ones endure—rhythm, rhyme, imagery, language play, and
an effective blending of the familiar with the nonsensical and the magical. Garth Williams, so well known for his soft drawings in *Charlotte's Web* (Harper & Row, 1951) and the Laura Ingalls Wilder
books, has illustrated each poem with a full-page, full-color painting.
He uses an effective technique of accenting the main portion of the painting by outlining it in India ink, while leaving the background unout-
lined. His pictures are as charming as usual and should stay fixed in the
imaginations of children as firmly as Prelutsky's words and imagery.

While *Ride a Purple Pelican* is certainly a book to be shared on
a parent's or grandparent's lap at bedtime, it could also be used with
older children in the classroom. These poems truly imitate traditional
Mother Goose rhymes. Older students may wish to analyze just how

*Literature, Language Arts
Primary*

Prelutsky used language to accomplish this. For starters, he used interesting, real place names such as Saskatchewan, Delaware, Kalamazoo,
and Albuquerque. He also created names and phrases that roll off the
tongue, like Timble Tamble Turkey, Buntington Bunny, and Jilliky Jol-
liky Jelliky Jee. Finally, students may wish to apply their new-found
knowledge in writing nursery rhymes of their own.   M.A.C.

354.   Prelutsky, Jack. *Tyrannosaurus Was a Beast*. Illustrated
by Arnold Lobel. Greenwillow, 1988. ISBN 0-688-06443-4,
$11.88. Ages 4-up.

Just when you wondered if the world needed another dinosaur
book, along comes the court jester of children's poetry with a poet-view
of these "terrible lizards" that hold perennial fascination for young people. The fourteen poems, each decorated by Lobel's expressive watercolors, describe both familiar and lesser-known dinosaurs from a contemporary viewpoint. Each selection is properly rooted in basic scientific
knowledge as well as in the wonder of a child's imagination. Prelutsky
also knows what young people want to hear: "Allosaurus liked to eat,/
and using teeth and talons,/ it stuffed itself with tons of meat,/ and
guzzled blood by gallons." Not all are as graphic in their descriptions,
but each is no less appealing. These selections are for the pure enjoyment of sharing together, making this slim volume a worthy addition to
a library or classroom.

Dramatizing poetry is an activity that young people often respond to
with enthusiasm, especially if they can do the planning and performance

*Science, Drama,
Language Arts
Primary
Intermediate*

together in small groups. After sharing and discussing the poems in *Tyrannosaurus Was a Beast*, have two or three students select one or
more poems for dramatizing. Discuss with all the groups what makes a
good dramatization and what planning is needed. Give enough time both
in class and outside school to rehearse and to prepare any costuming, in-

cluding creating dinosaurs. The final performances can be videotaped for the school or community library.   H.M.

355.   Ryder, Joanne. *Inside Turtle's Shell and Other Poems of the Field*. Illustrated by Susan Bonners. Macmillan, 1985. ISBN 0-02-778010-4, $10.95. Ages 7-10.

Inside Turtle's Shell is a stimulating collection of 41 poems that portray the meadow and its creatures from the morning on through to the nighttime. Turtle is 100 years old on this day between the seasons, and we follow him as he goes through his special day observing his fellow meadow creatures. Susan Bonners's black and white detailed illustrations depict the flora and fauna of the meadow with close-up realism. This attractive and appealing book should be a welcome addition to science programs as well as to the general library of classroom collection.

Poetry featuring animals is as old as Mother Goose and will long remain a popular topic for children. Though some of Ryder's poems are authentic, others are whimsical like those of Edward Lear and Ogden Nash; still others are thoughtful like those in de Gasztold's *Prayers from the Ark* (1962) and *The Creature's Choir* (1965), both translated from the Spanish by Rumer Godden and published by Viking. The wide range of types, approaches, and forms of poetry featuring animals makes possible an integrated language arts–science unit on zoo animals, pets, or farm animals; or on insects, birds, or mammals, etc.; or on animals of a particular environment—the jungle, the backyard, a tidal pool, et al. How poets know and understand animals and their living conditions is as appropriate and valid a viewpoint as those who understand them scientifically.   H.M.

Related Sources

Social Studies, Science, Language Arts
Primary
Intermediate
Middle School

356.   Rylant, Cynthia. *Waiting to Waltz: A Childhood*. Illustrated by Stephen Gammell. Bradbury, 1984. ISBN 0-02-778000-7, $10.95. Ages 10-14.

A happy pairing of poetry and illustration gives us a remarkable evocation of childhood. This cycle of 30 poems vividly expresses in journal-style language the feelings, longings, and events of a girl growing up in a small town: "For a year had/ a best friend named Randy./ Japanese American/who liked to play Tarzan." Strong images poignantly convey universal feelings and thoughts of childhood, at the same time creating an appealing portrait of a unique girl in the process of becoming. Gammell's pencil drawings masterfully illuminate the poet's spirit in an impressionistic style in keeping with the tone of selections. This is reflective and touching memoir that deserves to be in every classroom and widely shared.

The selections in this collection are directly from Cynthia Rylant's personal experiences growing up. Some will provoke an immediate response or may prompt questions about the poem or about the poet. Some will take longer for their full impact to be felt. While the selections

ALA Notable Book

Author Studies, Literature
Intermediate
Middle School
Junior High School

can be enjoyed for the universality of feeling and imagery, knowing something of the author's life can help to illuminate the poem and, therefore, the experience of the poem. Students can write to her at Orchard Books, 387 Park Avenue South, New York, NY 10016.　　　B.B

357.　Service, Robert. *The Cremation of Sam McGee*. Illustrated by Ted Harrison. Greenwillow, 1987. ISBN 0-688-06903-7, $13.00. Ages 8-up.

ALA Notable Book

Ted Harrison's richly colored and stylized illustrations bring to life the classic ballad of Sam McGee's bitter death and surprising resurrection, as well as give readers a glimpse of the Yukon Territory during the glory days of the Klondike Gold Rush. Service's story is the harrowing tale of a solitary man battling the Arctic cold to fulfill his promise to cremate his friend, Sam. Harrison lives and teaches in the Yukon, and he succeeds in capturing the vastness and beauty of his area. Since much of the poem is based upon both fact and myth of that turn-of-the-century era, Harrison provides a brief historical and biographical explanation with each picture. The reader will gain a deeper appreciation of Northern Canada, adding another dimension to an already exciting visual event.

Language Arts
Intermediate
Middle School
Junior High School

This story could easily be the subject of a newspaper headline; it certainly could be rewritten in the form of a news story. A short review of the five "W's"—who, what, where, when, and why—might be helpful for students. To aid in starting the students on their "rewrite," bring in news articles and examine them in class. The students can begin by answering the five "W's" of poem first, then outlining their story before writing. When finished, they may want to add a different ending telling what happened to Sam McGee.　　　H.M.

358.　Siebert, Diane. *Mojave*. Illustrated by Wendell Minor. Crowell, 1988. ISBN 0-690-04569-7, $13.89. Ages 4-8.

Compare this poetic description of the desert with the bland writing of social studies basal textbooks: "Here Joshua trees, in mighty stands,/ Spread twisted arms and sharp, green hands/ Above the tortoises who sleep/ Within the shade, then slowly creep/ Across my rocks, in armored domes..." Siebert understands and demonstrates current thinking in social studies: we should not restrict ourselves to social scientists if we wish to gain insight into contemporary social and scientific phenomena. The author and illustrator have given social studies teachers an excellent resource for comprehending the desert world. This is a fine example of the principle that oversized and picture books can and should be used with middle grade students.

Science, Social Studies,
Language Arts, Music
Intermediate
Middle School
Junior High School

Social studies or science units often culminate with a program after school or in the evening for parents and the community. As one of the presentations, the illustrations in *Mojave* could be photographed, reproduced as slides, and projected on a large screen while a group of students recites the poetry accompanying the paintings. Also, appropriate background music can be found and played as part of this slide presentation. Those schools with videotaping facilities can prepare a permanent copy of the program for later viewing by other classes.   J.F.A.

359.   Thayer, Ernest Lawrence. *Casey at the Bat*. Illustrated by Patricia Polacco. Putnam, 1988. ISBN 0-399-21585-9, $13.95. Ages 5-10.

This books marks the one hundredth anniversary of the ballad "Casey at the Bat." Polacco uses an expressionistic cartoon style in her paintings that captures the emotional tension of the story. Her facial expressions are particularly notable: each person, even those in the stands, is a distinct individual. Cleverly, Polacco visualizes the poem in a context that tells the reader that this is little league and that Casey is an overconfident kid whose sister gets him to the game just in time for his famous strike out. The umpire, who has greeted him with a "murderous look in his eye," turns out to be his father. "Sorry, Casey," he says at the end, "but I calls 'em the way I sees 'em." Casey admits that he was "struck out fair and square" and they all go home to supper! This edition is remarkable and certainly worthy of representing the one hundredth anniversary of the poem.

In addition to taking a look at other illustrators' versions of this narrative classic—e.g., Wallace Tripp's (Coward, 1980) and Paul Frame's (Prentice-Hall, 1964)—students would enjoy hearing or reading the numerous "sequels" found in *The Annotated Casey at the Bat: A Collection of Ballads About the Mighty Casey*, edited by Martin Gardner (University of Chicago, 1984). After exploring the various portrayals of Casey through the years, give students the opportunity to present the infamous slugger in yet a different light. Attempting their own narrative poems should seem much less threatening when their subject is such a familiar character!   M.A.C.

Related Sources

Language Arts, Art, Literature
Intermediate
Middle School
Junior High School
High School

360.   Tripp, Wallace. *Marguerite, Go Wash Your Feet*. Illustrated by the author. Houghton Mifflin, 1985. ISBN 0-395-35392-0, $15.95. All ages.

Children (and adults) who have enjoyed Tripp's *Granfa Grig Had a Pig* (Little, Brown, 1976) and *A Great Big Ugly Man Came Up and Tied His Horse to Me* (Little, Brown, 1973) will relish his new collection of humorous verse and comic drawings. Though this volume is shorter than his previous efforts, it is no less engaging. Each page is a visual feast to be searched through for every last morsel of caricature and visual pun. For example, Emily Dickinson's four-line "I'm Nobody! Who Are You?" is set on a two-page illustration that includes Winnie the Pooh, Howdy Doody, Chicken Little, and dozens of characters for the youngest audience. The same drawing includes Fay Wray (her legs, anyway), Charlie Chaplin, Robinson Crusoe, and others for those of us who will do the reading.

Like the "Hidden Pictures" in *Highlights Magazine*, readers of all ages are drawn to Tripp's illustrations for the tantalizing puzzles they of-

Related Sources

Author Studies, Art
Intermediate
Middle School
Junior High School

fer. They are the bait that draws readers to the diversity and wit that are hallmarks of the verse he selects. Teachers and librarians might take the opportunity to feature his works and offer prizes to those who can find the most characters who have appeared in Tripp's books. Verification can be either based upon photos, or by writing to Wallace Tripp, c/o Houghton Mifflin Co., 2 Park Street, Boston, MA 02108.   H.M.

361.   Turner, Ann. *Street Talk*. Illustrated by Catherine Stock. Houghton Mifflin, 1986. ISBN 0-395-39971-8, $11.95. Ages 10-up.

"There's a new beat/ in the street/ kids practicin' days/ out of sight/ to get it right explode/ onto the square..." Thus begins "Breakin'," Ann Turner's poem about break dancing from *Street Talk*, a poetic celebration of life in New York City. There are upbeat poems, like "Breakin'," as well as thoughtful, quiet poems about city people, old and young and often poor. Many of the poems present city life from a young person's viewpoint. For example, in "Hello, Graffiti" the child describes the comfort graffiti gives to him (or her) down in the otherwise dark, scary subway. Catherine Stock's black and white linocut prints present a montage of city sights and the people who live there.

Local History
Intermediate
Middle School
Junior High School

Related Source

After sharing the poems in *Street Talk*, teachers or librarians may encourage older students to write poems about their environments. To prepare for this, students may want to take a long walk around their community and take note of things about which they could write that would really characterize where they live. They can also be encouraged to remember things or people that really stuck in their minds when they were younger, perhaps from a child's perspective. Cynthia Rylant's *Waiting to Waltz* (Bradbury, 1984) might be an excellent additional resource. The final poems could be illustrated and compiled into a book and presented to the mayor, to the neighborhood's city council representative, or to the neighborhood library.   M.A.C.

NONFICTION
FOR
ALL AGES

NONFICTION

362. Abells, Chana Byers. *The Children We Remember*. Photographs from the archives of Yad Vashem. Greenwillow, 1986. ISBN 0-688-06372-1, $10.88. All ages.

The impact of the Holocaust on Jewish children is dramatically communicated in this short photo-essay. The language used is straightforward and not complex, yet the strong images and stark realism of the presentation of Holocaust themes makes this work perhaps too graphic for many younger children. Nevertheless, the agony and anguish of this period remain in the memory of many, and the message to "never forget" is important to help young people confront and understand. Abells's brief text complements the moving photographs of children caught in Hitler's evil scheme.

For older children, the photographic images will serve as a foundation for reading histories and fictionalized accounts of the Holocaust. Atkinson's *In Kindling Flame* (Lothrop, Lee & Shepard, 1985) and *The Short Life of Sophie Scholl* by Hermann Vinke (Harper & Row, 1984) are excellent biographies of young people growing up during Hitler's reign. Perhaps even more powerful to share with young people as a companion book is *...I Never Saw Another Butterfly* (McGraw-Hill, 1964) which contains poetry and drawings produced by Jewish children held at Theresienstadt Concentration Camp between 1942–1944. H.M.

Related Sources

Holocaust Studies,
Literature
Intermediate
Middle School
Junior High School

363. Adler, David A. *Martin Luther King, Jr.: Free at Last*. Illustrated by Robert Casilla. Holiday House, 1986. ISBN 0-8234-0618-0, $11.95. Ages 8-10.

Designed for younger readers, this is an easily understood look at the events that chronicle the life of Martin Luther King, Jr. From the Jim Crow laws and the prejudices King felt as a child, to the March on Washington and his "I Have a Dream" speech, Adler has presented a readable and factual biography. He also manages to appeal to the reader's sense of justice and to elicit support for the plight of Blacks by allowing the truth of the unfairness and the social realities to speak out clearly. Combined with ink wash illustrations portraying all aspects of King's life, this book delivers a simple yet powerful message of peace and civil rights. A listing of important dates provides a useful reference.

Black Studies,
Multicultural Studies
Middle School
Intermediate

Related Sources

Most young people know no more about King than that his birthday gives them a day off from school. Even less is known about other civil rights leaders, so this book can be a starting point in exposing children to great leaders of our time. ***Martin Luther King*** (1985) by Nancy F. Shuler, part of Chelsea House's "World Leaders: Past and Present Series," has additional information. Jules Archer's ***You Can't Do That To Me: Famous Fights for Civil Rights*** (Macmillan, 1980) could also be used to introduce children to civil rights workers and leaders. Emiglio's ***Civil Rights Struggle: Leaders in Profile*** (Facts on File, 1979) may provide background information the teacher can share about others active in the civil rights movement.   L.S.

364.   Adler, David A. ***Thomas Jefferson, Father of our Democracy: A First Biography***. Illustrated by Jacqueline Garrick. Holiday House, 1987. ISBN 0-8234-0667-9, $12.95. Ages 8-10.

The young reader discovers in this book that Thomas Jefferson was an inventor, musician, farmer, lawyer, architect, statesman, founder of the University of Virginia, U.S. President and Vice President, and, above all, author of the Declaration of Independence. This honest account of his life gives details of Jefferson's parents and family, boyhood, schooling, political career, marriage and children, and his personal dilemma about owning slaves. Adler's writing style is interesting and he includes facts that should appeal to the intended audience. A chronological listing of Jefferson's accomplishments and the events in his life enhances this very useful, easy-to-read biography and helps readers place Jefferson's accomplishments in time. Interspersed throughout the text are thirty black and white watercolor and pencil illustrations.

U.S. History
Intermediate
Middle School

Here is an opportunity to explore adjectives that describe personal charcteristics. Print the letters THOMAS JEFFERSON vertically on a paper's left margin. List words that children suggest describe this remarkable man, beginning with each letter; for example: T—tall, truthful, tolerant, talented; H—handsome, honest, humble, hard-working. This could be done as an individual student assignment or as a class project by writing the words on the blackboard. A bulletin board could be developed from this which could be decorated with student drawings illustrating various aspects of Jefferson's life.   F.M.H.

365.   Aliki. ***How a Book is Made***. Illustrated by the author. Crowell, 1986. ISBN 0-690-04498-4, $12.89. Ages 8-up.

The mystery of how a book becomes a book is revealed by Aliki in technically accurate, yet understandable step-by-step explanations. Accompanied by humorous cat-people illustrations, the text follows the book making process from the author's idea for the book, to the part that the publishing company plays in the many stages the manuscript must go through to be published in its final form. Promotion and publicity for the book is also discussed, including reviewing and how a book gets to the bookstore. Though somewhat technical at times—the explanation of how the artwork is color separated, for example—the book portrays the book making process accurately, giving credit to the many people in addition to the author who are involved.

A logical use of this book is as a reference when students are making their own books. Have students first write their story, edit it, and put into a final draft. Next decide how many pages will be needed and make a dummy copy of how the book will look when finished, including rough illustrations. Choose paper for the actual book, fold it in half, and add end papers by folding two pieces of construction paper over the inside pages. Stitch these papers together using strong thread or dental floss, both starting and ending on the outside piece of construction paper. The story can now be copied in final form onto the paper and illustrations added where appropriate, following the design of the dummy book. A cover for the book can be made by covering cardboard (slightly larger than the inside pages) with wrapping paper, contact paper, or other paper that has been decorated and then laminated. Fold the cover in half and place the sewn pages, which now contain the story, into the middle. Glue the outside end papers to the cardboard with white glue or contact cement. The book is now complete.   L.S.

Art, Language Arts
Primary
Intermediate
Middle School

366.   Ames, Lee J. ***Draw 50 Beasties and Yugglies and Turnover Uglies and Things that Go Bump in the Night.*** Illustrated by the author. Doubleday, 1988. ISBN 0-385-24625-0, $12.95. Ages 8-up.

Lee J. Ames, a veteran of Walt Disney Studios, has created a whole series of "Draw 50" books. This is but the latest. The idea behind these is that being able to successfully draw interesting characters through step-by-step copying is an incentive to children just getting started with drawing. Ames's other books have included such subjects as holiday decorations, monsters, famous cartoons, athletes, and motor vehicles. This one has all sorts of creative creatures that are sure to appeal, especially to the many intermediate-aged "artists" who are interested in monsters, mythology, and robots.

A teacher could use Ames's books to make an art center in the class. Provide "Draw 50" books on several different topics—available in paperback for only $4.95—so children can have a choice . Also provide plenty of white paper, soft leaded pencils, and kneadable erasers. Children rarely need directions to follow the step-by-step drawing procedures. The teacher can go through one of the drawings with the class as a whole on the chalkboard or the overhead with the children working at their seats. This would allow opportunity for discussion and direction about drawing procedures. After that, children should be able to take off on their own. When they have learned to draw some of the figures, they can be encouraged to draw short cartoon strips with captions and/or conversation bubbles. The final results could be shared with the class and displayed in the library.   M.A.C.

Art
Intermediate
Middle School
Junior High School
High School

367.   Anderson, Gretchen, editor. *The Louisa May Alcott Cookbook*. Little, Brown, 1985. ISBN 0-316-03951-9, $10.95. Ages 8-12.

Get out the pots and pans, line up the ingredients, and prepare for an afternoon of cozy kitchen fun with *The Louisa May Alcott Cookbook*, written expressly for the readers of *Little Women* and *Little Men*. Charming, homespun illustrations and vignettes from Alcott's books combine to give children a total experience of what life was like in the March household. Authentic recipes—coded from easy (one star) to more difficult (three stars)—rely on "old-fashioned" ingredients such as molasses or rye flour, so check the pantry before tying up those apron strings. Nine-year-old Gretchen Anderson compiled this delightful, "do-able" theme cookbook for other young cooking enthusiasts.

Boys and girls alike might enjoy playing chef with the unusual 19th century recipes geared to their own tastes. Special interest groups, such as Brownies or Saturday educational enrichment programs, could enjoy an afternoon in the kitchen with the March sisters. A useful reference page is included by Gretchen Anderson listing Louisa May Alcott's books for children. Selected chapters from Alcott's works could be re-written as a series of short plays and presented for a special parents' evening. After the final curtain, the guests could be served story-inspired treats, made with love by the actors themselves. An entire evening devoted to mid-19th century life could be built around classroom studies and the personal accounts found in Louisa May Alcott's books.   G.G.

368.   Anderson, Joan. *The First Thanksgiving Feast*. Photographs by George Ancona. Clarion, 1984. ISBN 0-89919-287-4, $12.95. Ages 7-12.

The First Thanksgiving Feast was photographed at Plimoth Plantation, a living history museum of 17th century life in Plymouth, Massachusetts. Living history museums attempt to present a picture of life as it was at a specific time and place. This is done through close attention to detail and careful research. The people at these museums, called interpreters, speak and act as the people who lived there would have. Anderson literally had to learn to speak the language of the Plimouth Plantation interpreters before she wrote a word. She also noted that the descendents of the Wampanogs, the native people who helped the Pilgrims, today gather at Plymouth Rock on Thanksgiving for a National Day of Mourning because they believe the first Thanksgiving feast marked the beginning of the end of their original way of life.

Traditional school celebrations of Thanksgiving often promote faulty history, misconceptions, and ethnocentrism. This book would be an excellent vehicle not only to present children with a living view of the past, but also to stimulate their thinking about how not everyone involved in change is necessarily happy about it. Lively discussion is almost inevitable when exploring the rights of different interest groups in almost any historical context.   M.A.C.

369. Anderson, Joan. *Pioneer Children of Appalachia*. Photographs by George Ancona. Clarion, 1986. ISBN 0-89919-440-0, $12.95. Ages 7-10.

The teaching of social history in the elementary school should be enhanced by the many fine photographs and informative text that capitalize on the living history museum of Fort New Salem. Two appealing "pioneer" youngsters visit their grandparents and this story line is used to inform the reader about aspects of pioneer life including making soap, hunting, basket making, and candle making, as well as quilting bees and harvest festivals. Ancona's photographs clarify the text and help make readers feel they are present at that historical moment.

In living history programs individuals assume the appearance and lifestyle of those who came before us. Some museums, rather than using guides, have their interpreters dress in appropriate costume to perform the activities of the historical period and then answer the visitor's questions. A more recent development is to invite visitors to play the role of pioneers for a day or a weekend. A number of museums with pioneer schools encourage teachers to use museums for a living history program with students. For one day, children read the books and experience the pedagogy of the prior century.   J.F.A.

U.S. History
Primary
Intermediate

370. Anderson, Joan. *A Williamsburg Household*. Photographs by George Ancona. Clarion, 1988. ISBN 0-89919-516-4, $15.95. Ages 8-11.

A Williamsburg Household is a chronicle of that colonial city in 1770 centering on two families: the white homeowners and their slaves. Rippon, a young slave, endures the endless drudgery experienced by slaves, the whippings, and the constant threat of being sold and separated from his family. Ancona's color photographs permit the reader a closer look at the characters and their eighteenth century surroundings. The Company of Colonial Performers authentically interpret the characters and events of the story.

Because of the abundance of dialogue, a play could be adapted by the students for performance during Black History Month or for a study of colonial America. The students can make simple props and costumes with the help of Ancona's photographs. Reading the book, discussing it as a group, and producing the play should promote a deeper understanding of the injustice of one human being owning another. *Nettie's Trip South* by Ann Turner (Macmillan, 1987) is an excellent companion book for this age group.   K.I.

Black Studies,
U.S. History
Intermediate
Middle School

Related Source

371. Angelou, Maya. *All God's Children Need Traveling Shoes*. Random House, 1986. ISBN 0-394-52143-9, $15.95. Ages 12-up.

In her newest book, actress-poet-dancer-author Maya Angelou continues the biographical narration which began with her earlier book,

ALA Best Book

Sequel to
I Know Why the Caged
Bird Sings

Women's Studies
High School

I Know Why the Caged Bird Sings (Random House, 1970). To read this book is to discover a person who is passionate, colorful, energetic, and forever rushing forward to meet life and its challenges. Angelou's journey to Africa is a search for her beginnings, and it becomes a journey of revelations about her son, about Africa, and about her own niche in life.

Angelou's family life, from its intimate beginnings to the extended family and the relationships shared with friends and acquaintances, presents an important view of a large segment of our American culture. Mature readers will gain an historical perspective of the era covered, as well as an in-depth understanding of a cultural group often portrayed in a less admirable light. This most recent book can be used as a starting point; students can then return to her earliest account and trace Angelou's life to the present. Perceptive readers well be able to contrast her narrative style with other biographies and autobiographies included in the literature curriculum.   R.M.G.

372.   Anno, Mitsumasa. *Anno's Sundial*. Illustrated by the author. Philomel, 1987. ISBN 0-399-21374-0, $16.95. Ages 9-up.

Before clocks, the shadow cast by the sun across a stick or tower or stone monolith served the ancients in their quest to measure time. In his first book in pop-up format, Anno demonstrates clearly and explains in detail the science that underlies creating sundials and solving such related problems as hemisphericity, cloudy days, true north versus magnetic north, and solar time versus clock time. The illustrations and the pop-up format perfectly demonstrate the concepts found in the very readable text. The result is a sophisticated appreciation of the science of measuring time for older readers.

Art, Math
Intermediate
Middle School
Junior High School

Related Sources

In addition to the models present in this highly useful format, there are clear directions for making several types of sundials. Students should be encouraged to design sundials for decorative as well as functional purposes. Having basic materials available in the classroom or the library will be helpful in getting projects started. Additional sources of information about construction and decoration include Stoneman's *Easy to Make Wooden Sundials* (Dover, 1982) and Earl's *Sun Dials and Roses of Yesterday* (Tuttle, 1971).   H.M.

373.   Archer, Jules. *Winners and Losers: How Elections Work in America*. Illustrated with photographs. Harcourt Brace Jovanovich, 1984. ISBN 0-15-297945-X, $13.95. Ages 12-up.

This is a useful book about presidential elections. Chapters on topics such as lobbyists, political parties, conventions, and third parties are made particularly interesting because of the repeated use of historical anecdotes. The book is neither bland nor particularly partisan: Nixon is labelled as vulgar, dishonest, and corrupt, while Eisenhower is described as warm, honest, sincere, and courageous. Although *Winners and Losers* was published in 1984, an unexpected event makes the following passage quite out of date: "No major political party has ever nominated a woman as a candidate for president or vice-president."

Grateful will be the junior high school student (or parent) who locates this work while preparing a report about presidential elections. Additionally, despite its sometimes cynical outlook, it argues for student involvement—addresses of The Young Democratic Club of America and Teen Age Republicans are provided. After describing the American Independent Party, the Communist Party, and the Socialist Workers Party, Archer advises: "Your local librarian will be able to help you contact third party national headquarters." Students can gain a broader understanding of our country's complex and occasionally colorful political spectrum by pursuing the author's suggestions.   J.F.A.

Government
Middle School
Junior High School
High School

374.   Armor, John and Peter Wright. *Manzanar*. Photographs by Ansel Adams. Times Books, 1988. ISBN 0-8129-1727-8, $27.50. Ages 12-up.

Whether called a "military necessity" or a "mistake of terrifically horrible proportions," over 100,000 Americans of Japanese descent were imprisoned in concentration camps from 1942-45. As this moving photo-history reveals, the tragedy was due to the combined effects of local bigotry, political ambition, and military incompetence. Manzanar, located in the dry desert just north of California's Death Valley, was the subject of a sympathetic book—long out of print—*Born Free and Equal*, written and photographed in 1944 by Ansel Adams. Armor and Wright include an extensive historical overview by John Hersey and draw upon government documents and Adams's 1944 photographs to give today's reader provocative and forthright insights into this bleak period in America. This is stimulating and readable history.

"Persons of Japanese lineage...alien and citizen alike" were, by Executive Order 9066, abruptly uprooted from their homes and allowed to take only what they were permitted to carry to a relocation center. Discuss with students what two possessions they would select to take with them if they were placed in a similar situation (pets had to be left behind). Discuss also the basis for their decisions. Older students will find a wealth of detailed information on the contributing events and consequences of this national shame in *Personal Justice Denied*, a Congressional report prepared by the Commission on Wartime Relocation and Internment of Civilians published in 1982.   H.M.

Asian-American Studies
Junior High School
High School

Related Source

375.   Ashabranner, Brent and Melissa. *Into a Strange Land*. Illustrated with photographs. Dodd, Mead, 1987. ISBN 0-396-08841-1, $12.95. Ages 10-up.

Among the 750,000 Southeast Asian refugees who have immigrated to our shores since 1975 are children who come unaccompanied by parents or other adults who would be responsible for them. Often sent out in the middle of the night alone and without prior knowledge, these children boarded rickety boats and braved the China Sea with strangers. If they were not caught by patrols, they arrived at crowded, lonely refugee camps in Malaysia, Thailand, or nearby islands, and hoped they would qualify to be accepted into a welcoming country. They knew it was unlikely they would ever see their families again. This dramatic book gives a simple, factual account of the varied reasons they left their countries. Biographies, photographs, and interviews with some of these refugees who made it to this country and with their foster American families make their stories come alive. While this is often a sad book, it is a testimony to the tenacity of the human spirit as one reads of their attempts to assimilate into our culture.

Asian-American Studies
Middle School
Junior High School

Related Sources

This book can act as a catalyst for discussion about the personal impact war has on families. Students can discuss and decide whether or not individuals, groups, and nations have a moral obligation to assist those who are hurt by our involvement in the affairs of their country. *National Geographic Magazine* (May 1980) contains an informative article on the Asian homeless, specifically those in camps in Thailand awaiting entry into this country. Students should do further research and update themselves on the current situation in Southeast Asia. Jamie Gilson's fictional *Hello, My Name is Scrambled Eggs* (Lothrop, Lee & Shepard, 1986), the story of a refugee boy from Southeast Asia, is an excellent companion book for reading aloud.   L.A.B.

376.   Asimov, Isaac. *Futuredays: A Nineteenth-Century Vision of the Year 2000*. Illustrated by Jean Marc Cote. Henry Holt, 1986. ISBN 0-8050-0120-4, $12.95. Ages 12-up.

In 1899, a commercial artist, Jean Marc Cote, was commissioned by a toy company to design a set of cigarette cards depicting the year 2000 for the *fin-de-siecle* celebrations throughout France. Unfortunately, the company went out of business before the cards could be distributed. However, they were brought to Isaac Asimov's attention and he reproduced many of them in *Futuredays*. The subject of each card is discussedd by Asimov, who, having the advantage of living near the year 2000, describes how much of each prediction was based upon things known in 1899 and how much became reality. Asimov's introduction to the topic of futurism is provocative.

Science, Social Studies
Middle School
Junior High School
High School

Related Sources

After reading *Futuredays*, many students will likely want to speculate about what the future will be like in 2100, one hundred years from now. They may want to research some of the technologies available now and predict where those technologies will lead. A series of picture postcards like Cote's could be drawn. Students may also want to read the novels of Jules Verne and H.G. Wells and discuss which of their science fiction concepts became reality and which were impractical. Finally, students may want to explore futurism as a career for, as Asimov suggests in his introduction, in both business and government, decisions must be made with an eye on the future.   M.A.C.

377. Atkinson, Linda. *In Kindling Flame*. Illustrated with photographs. Lothrop, Lee & Shepard, 1985. ISBN 0-688-02714-8, $13.50. Ages 14-up.

There are two enduring misconceptions surrounding the Holocaust: that the general populations of Europe and government leaders in Europe and the United States were unaware of the Nazi extermination of the Jews in Europe; and that Jews offered no resistance. This biography of Hannah Senesh serves to put such notions to rest. Based upon her diary and other materials from interviews and correspondence, this carefully-structured and penetrating biography tells of her youth in Budapest, her years on a kibbutz in Palestine, and her role as a British commando working behind German lines to save the lives of Hungarian Jews. Her senseless death at the age of 23 just before the end of the war underscores the ruthless disregard for human life that was Nazi policy. This is a tragic yet uplifting story of true heroism and human courage of the highest order.

To study the Holocaust is to study the history of hatred. As Milton Meltzer says in the preface to his provocative history, *Never to Forget: The Jews of the Holocaust* (Harper & Row, 1976), "That it happened once...means it could happen again. Hitler made it a possibility for anyone. Neither the Jews nor any other group on earth can feel safe from that crime in the future." Bibliographic materials, films, teaching units, videotapes, and other curricular materials and teaching resources are widely available for use with all grade levels. An excellent place to begin is to write or call the state or national offices of the Anti-Defamation League of B'Nai B'rith.   H.M.

Related Source

Holocaust Studies,
Literature
Junior High School
High School

378. Bell, Ruth, et al. *Changing Bodies, Changing Lives* (rev. ed.). Illustrated with photographs and drawings. Random House, 1988. ISBN 0-394-56499-5, $19.95. Ages 12-up.

The first edition (1981) of this widely respected source of information on teenage health and sexuality has been updated to keep up with current research, changes in the legal system, and new approaches to dealing with social problems facing young people today. Prepared by hundreds of individuals and groups across the country, *Changing Bodies, Changing Lives* is one of the small but growing number of sources that teenagers can rely on for candid and straight answers to questions on all aspects of sex and sexual relations, including homosexuality, rape and incest; emotional health, including suicide, drugs and alcohol; and physical health care, including pregnancy, birth control, and disease. Schools, community organizations and, most of all, parents should welcome this valuable and indispensable compendium of up-to-date information about the most troublesome social problems faced today by young adults and by their parents and teachers.

Random House makes this book available at a discount to "clinics, groups, and organizations...offering health education and information to teenagers" at a cost of $5.99 for the hardback edition or $3.89 in paperback (other conditions are listed on the copyright page). Teachers and librarians, as well as parent and community groups, should be actively encouraged to take advantage of such an offer, making this resource available to as a wide an audience as possible. High school health education teachers should take the leadership in launching a drive to underwrite the project as a means of assuring that this resource, like others of its kind and quality, are used and discussed by teenagers. The consequences of misinformation or the absence of information about health risks is truly a matter of life and death.   H.M.

379.   Bjork, Christina. *Linnea in Monet's Garden*. Illustrated by Lena Anderson. R & S Books (available from Farrar, Straus & Giroux), 1987 (1st Am. ed.) ISBN 91-29-58314-4, $10.95. All ages.

This is the unique and innovative limited biography of impressionist painter Claude Monet through the eyes of a young girl who visits his home in Paris. Readers are treated to a trip through France as they travel with Linnea and her friend, Mr. Bloom. The book is lavishly illustrated with photographs of Monet's gardens, house, and family, pictures of his paintings, and illustrations by Anderson in soft watercolors that depict her interpretation of Monet's gardens as well as the youthful exuberance of Linnea. The life of Monet is told as a story for children, interspersed with Linnea's own experiences and thoughts as she learns about one of the world's great impressionist painters.

After children have read or listened to the book read aloud, it may inspire them to paint their own impressionistic picture. Bring in more photographs, books, or posters containing works by Monet, Degas, Renoir, or Pissarro and discuss what makes a painting impressionistic. Before the children begin to paint, remind them that their painting should be an *impression* of what they see. This could also be a good time to discuss how certain colors make them feel. Because most impressionist artists painted from life, why not have an outdoor painting session (no worry about paint spills!)? If the weather does not permit, set up several still lifes in the room that reflect a variety of media, light, and textures.   K.B.B.

380.   Booth, Jerry. *The Big Beast Book*. Illustrated by Martha Weston. Little, Brown, 1988. ISBN 0-316-10263-6, $14.95. Ages 8-12.

Books about dinosaurs outnumber those about nearly every other animal. There seems to be no end to the fascination they hold for readers of all ages. In this latest addition to the popular and well-respected Brown Paper School Book series, Booth demonstrates the many ways in which young people can learn more about these spellbinding creatures while enjoying creative activities that teach skills and concepts in math, composition, history, science, and the arts. The directions for these motivating and appealing activities are clear enough to be followed independently and are suitable for use in the classroom or at home. Booth has made learning challenging and interesting and, more important, rewarding. If textbooks were like this, the classroom would be a more inviting place for both teachers and young people.

Organizing instruction around a theme or topic is not a new idea, but for those who have never tried it, the topic of dinosaurs is a good place to begin. For one week, organize all instruction around the topic, using Booth's book as a guide for teaching ideas in all areas of the curriculum. The activities explore writing and mathematics skills, history and science, and there are lots of art activities suggested. Physical activities and games can be created by the class. For reading, one need only look through any library for scores of books at all reading levels and in all genres, including such diverse approaches as Adler's *The Dinosaur Princess and Other Prehistoric Riddles* (Holiday House, 1988), Lauber's *Dinosaurs Walked Here and Other Stories Fossils Tell* (Bradbury, 1987), and the poetry found in Hopkins's appealing *Dinosaurs* (Harcourt Brace Jovanovich, 1987) and Prelutsky's *Tyrannosaurus Was a Beast* (Greenwillow, 1988). Teachers who find this approach to instructional planning exhilarating can find many other topics around which to plan activities for a day, a week, a month, or longer.   H.M.

Science, Math, Art, Physical Education, History, Language Arts Primary Intermediate Middle School

Related Sources

381. Branley, Franklyn M. *Flash, Crash, Rumble, and Roll.* Illustrated by Barbara and Ed Emberley. Crowell, 1985. ISBN 0-690-04424-0, $11.89. Ages 4-8.

This very useful and versatile book is a good choice to read aloud and would be easy for children in the third grade to read. Branley, author of scores of books on a wide variety of science topics, provides clear, simple explanations about where rain comes from and what causes thunder and lightning. Children are presented with some new information, such as how to calculate the distance a storm is away from them. The text is accurate and logical, and includes safety tips about lightning. The illustrations are colorful, attractive, and visually support the text while providing clarity and understanding.

Teachers will find this book an informative and useful addition to their classrooms. Weather phenomena have held a fascination for people throughout all cultures. Studying rainstorm-related weather satisfies the curiosity and fears of many young people. *Flash, Crash, Rumble, and Roll* would be, for example, an excellent choice for children who are afraid of thunderstorms. On pages 17-19 are two useful experiments which provide a hands-on approach to understanding sound and light waves. The safety tips could be made into a bulletin board either during the thunderstorm season or in coordination with a science or weather lesson. This could follow a group reading of Mary Szilagyi's *Thunderstorm.* (Bradbury, 1985) or Mary Stolz's *Storm in the Night* (Harper & Row, 1988).   J.P.

Science Primary Intermediate

Related Sources

382.   Branley, Franklyn M. *Mysteries of Outer Space*. Illustrated by Sally J. Bensusen and with photographs. Lodestar, 1985. ISBN 0-525-67149-8, $10.95. Ages 10-14.

This is not about extraterrestrials and UFOs. Rather, Dr. Branley, an astronomer and author of over a hundred books for children, presents what scientists theorize and speculate about, or still do not know for certain, from the realm of space. In a crisp question-and-answer format he covers a wide range of topics from the "emptiness of space" to life in outer space, asteroids and other heavenly bodies. Some questions asked are: "What is time?"; "Is space moving?"; and "Is there an end to space?" Readers receive cautious answers. Photographs and diagrams add greatly to the clarity of the subject matter. This is a stimulating book for the neophyte and the science enthusiast; a brief list of books for further reading only whets the appetite.

*Science
Intermediate
Middle School
Junior High School*

What questions do older children wonder about related to space? Ask them. Those not answered in this book or by others in the class ought to be recorded for class research or study throughout the year. As answers are found, they, too, should be recorded. Questions not answered after a search over most of the school year could be submitted to Dr. Branley (write to him c/o Lodestar Books, 2 Park Ave., New York, NY 10002) or to a local scientist-author-scholar for his or her response.   H.M.

383.   Cartoonists Thanksgiving Day Hunger Project. *Comic Relief*. Illustrated with cartoons by Charles Schultz, Gary Trudeau, Milton Caniff, and others. Henry Holt, 1986. ISBN 0-03-009093-8, $5.95. Ages 8-up.

Cartoonists Charles Schultz, Gary Trudeau, and Milton Caniff were among the many organizers of recent relief projects in the United States and abroad. Their efforts, "The Cartoonists Thanksgiving Day Hunger Project," combined the talents of 175 artists to create cartoons focusing upon world hunger for the 1985 Thanksgiving Day issues of United States newspapers. The cartoon messages that day ranged from a gentle nudging of readers to straightforward pleas for people to care enough to take action. Following the newspaper publications of the comic strips, the book *Comic Relief*, with 179 of the Thanksgiving Day cartoons, was published and the profits from the book were designated for USA for AFRICA. *Comic Relief* is the result of a very successful collaboration of people who felt strongly about expressing their concerns.

*Art,
Contemporary Affairs
Middle School
Junior High School
High School*

This is a book that would work well to stimulate discussion on a variety of topics and in a variety of courses because world hunger involves political science, economics, geography, nutrition, sociology, and psychology, among others. After discussing the issues, students could begin collecting cartoons that relate to them, which would help them to realize that comic strips are not just for entertainment but often raise important questions. Students might also design their own cartoon strips relevant to issues in the classroom, school district, community, state, or nation. Books to accompany Comic Relief might include *BAAA* by David Macaulay (Houghton Mifflin, 1985), *Loaves and Fishes* by Linda Hunt and Marianne Frase (Herald Press, 1980), *The Hunger Road* by John Christopher Fine (Atheneum, 1988), and *Poverty* by Milton Meltzer (Morrow, 1986).   E.A.H.

384.   Chaiken, Miriam. *A Nightmare in History*. Illustrated with photographs and prints. Clarion, 1987. ISBN 0-89919-461-3, $14.95. Ages 10-up.

Related Sources

More than any other single resource for intermediate and high school readers, *A Nightmare in History* clearly and movingly chronicles the rise of anti-semitism world-wide, culminating in humanity's darkest period. As in Meltzer's *Never to Forget* (Harper & Row, 1976) for older readers, Chaiken lets the events and those who lived them speak directly to younger readers. Her ability to clarify complex issues and condense historical periods will help readers understand with insight and compassion both the broad sweep of Jewish history and the horror that was the Holocaust. Without being sensational, the carefully selected illustrations visually evoke the anguish of the victims and the setting in which from 1933–1945 they struggled against the forces of fascism and prejudice.

ALA Notable Book

Related Source

The extensive bibliography included—some sources are for young people, others for adults—is a beginning point for teachers and librarians who want to plan an expanded program of study on the Holocaust. It includes diaries, sources of archival materials, and song books, as well as fiction and history. For motion pictures, videos, pamphlets, teaching suggestions and instructional guides, and other materials, teachers can contact the state or national offices of the Anti-Defamation League of B'nai B'rith or the National Holocaust Memorial Center in Washington, D.C.   H.M.

Holocaust Studies, European History Intermediate Middle School Junior High School

385.   Chouinard, Roger and Mariko. *Amazing Animal Alphabet Book* Illustrated by Roger Chouinard. Doubleday, 1988. ISBN 0-385-24029-5, $12.95. Ages 4-8.

Unusual alliteration abounds in this imaginative picture alphabet book: "Anteater anticipating August" through "Orangutan ogling an overweight ostrich" to "Zebra zipping on his zoot suit." Every letter in the alphabet has equally outrageous alliterative descriptions. The mixed-media illustrations add to the fun: the "Yak on a yacht with his yo-yo" poses with dark glasses and a nautical cap, with a seagull balanced precariously on one horn, for example. Children should also enjoy finding the hidden letter on each page.

Primary children may not be as adept in alliterative activity as the authors of this book, but they can come up with simpler and similar descriptions for their own pets or the animals in the classroom. A single adjective is indicated rather than a whole phrase for the younger student: "dangerous dog," "delightful dog," "comical cat," or "curious cat." The

Language Arts Primary

classroom hamster, gerbil, mice, snake, or guinea pigs may be treated in the same way. Children may prefer using a pet's name: "Silly Spot," or "Famished Frisky." Vocabulary lists can be created from the descriptive words chosen, or pictures can be drawn by children showing their pets with these attributes.   F.M.H.

386.   Cleary, Beverly. *A Girl From Yamhill: A Memoir*. Morrow, 1988. ISBN 0-688-07800-1, $14.95. Ages 12-up.

ALA Best Book
ALA Notable Book

Looking back at her success as a writer, Beverly Cleary remarked that "children told me they liked my books because there isn't any description in them." It was a lesson in writing that she learned early, as related in this superb autobiography by one of our most beloved and enduring children's writers. Cleary followed that rule in writing this insightful and frank story of her life in Oregon during the Depression years, a life influenced by the distant love of a caring mother, frequent illnesses, and teachers who alternately frightened, belittled, praised, and befriended a young girl who sold her first story when she was in the third grade. Cleary's near-total recall of her childhood and her readable style, as comfortable and familiar as an old friend, make this personal history well worth reading by anyone who appreciates a moving story.

Author Studies,
Literature
Middle School
Junior High School

It has been said that art reflects life, and surely the stories and people she has written about are rooted both in Cleary's imagination and in her memory of life experiences. Junior high/middle school students can begin a study of the life–art connections in an author's works by reading both a biography or autobiography and the works of that author, noting life experiences that are the bases for characters, events, or settings in the author's books. Jean Little's recent autobiography, *Little by Little* (Viking Kestrel, 1987), is another fine resource to suggest to readers in this age group.   H.M.

Related Source

387.   Crews, Donald. *Ten Black Dots*. Illustrated by the author. Greenwillow, 1986. ISBN 0-688-06068-4, $11.88. Ages 2-5.

A popular counting book before the redesign and the revisions of the current edition book *Ten Black Dots* make it even more desirable. The emphasis remains "What can you do with ten black dots?" and as before, Crews makes the easily counted black dots, encompassed within familiar contexts, the focus of his stylized graphics. The most obvious change is that this book is twenty-five percent larger than the previous edition. Although the content of the illustrations remains the same, the addition of more details (stars with the moon), the move to more realistic colors, the updating of some of the objects (portable radio to jam box), and the improved logic (strings of the balloons hang downward) will enhance children's perception and comprehension of Crew's intent.

Teachers will find there are many uses for *Ten Black Dots* beyond the intended one of improving and developing counting skills.

Because the accompanying text, written in short couplets, is limited, the preschool child can quickly memorize the book and then "read" it independently. In addition to counting and reading, children can be directed to finding other circles in their environment. Their discoveries can then be drawn and described in their own version of "Ten Black Dots."   M.A.S.

388.   Dekkars, Midas. *The Nature Book*. Illustrated by Angela de Vrede. Macmillan, 1988 (1st Am. ed.). ISBN 0-02-726690-7, $12.95. Ages 8-12.

Subtitled "Discovering, Exploring, Observing, Experimenting with Plants and Animals at Home and Outdoors," this well-organized book is jam-packed with projects and activities for nature study: directions for constructing study equipment and your own museum, drying and preserving plants, feeding birds, building a tree house, using fruits and vegetables for science projects, and tracking animals. Many of the plans for projects include everyday items like the ubiquitous dandelion or bones left from a chicken dinner. Because this was originally published in the United Kingdom, there are a few references to plants not currently growing in our country, but most of the text refers to plant and animal life known to all.

Classroom teachers will find ideas galore to supplement the science curriculum in this thin volume. The most unusual experiment is "Grow the Soles of Your Shoes," which suggests scraping the soil—along with seeds picked up—from shoes which have been worn while walking in the woods, a field, or in town. The different kinds of plants which come up through careful nurturing and watering can be compared, charted, and mapped. The same experiment can be done with a plastic bag of soil from a garden shop, but it sounds like more fun with masking tape and children's own shoes.   F.M.H.

389.   Dewey, Jennifer Owings. *At the Edge of the Pond*. Illustrated by the author. Little, Brown, 1987. ISBN 0-316-18208-7, $14.95. Ages 6-10.

In delicate colored pencil drawings, Dewey masterfully captures life at the edge of a pond. Her lyric text is divided into "chapters" entitled "Daybreak," "The Surface of the Pond," "The Shoreline," "Deep Water," "The Pond Bottom," and "Nightfall." Each explores that particular aspect of pond life. The text makes use of wonderfully descriptive language such as "A whirligig beetle gyrates its way through a forest of stems,/ spinning a dizzy track across the surface." or "...Sinking lower and lower,/ the turtle falls through shimmery, sun-bright colors/ to faded, twilight shadows." This book would serve as an excellent supplement to any book on this topic as the reader gains a feeling, as well as information, about pond life through Dewey's narrative style. Her drawings of water and the creatures within are done so skillfully, one almost senses the gentle rocking motion of the water and the quiet beauty of the aquatic life. Readers are left wishing for more illustrations to go along with the text.

At the Edge of the Pond is a good example of how nonfiction can have an almost story-like quality because of its use of description. This book could serve as an effective introduction to an integrated unit on pond life as students are presented many scientific terms in a literary way. For example, when describing the concept of surface tension, Dewey explains that the water surface is firm, making it "...a floor to some, a ceiling to others." Using this concept, students can create dioramas using boxes and plastic wrap to represent the surface of the pond. Students can draw creatures that live above and below the surface of the pond, cut them out and place them appropriately in the diorama. Shore plants and animals can be painted in the background. A related writing activity would be to have students write their own story making use of descriptive phrases to capture the mood of their diorama pond and the life within.   K.B.B.

390.   Ehlert, Lois. *Planting a Rainbow*. Illustrated by the author. Harcourt Brace Jovanovich, 1988. ISBN 0-15-262609-3, $14.95. Ages 4-7.

"Every year Mom and I plant a rainbow." Ehlert's simple text and brightly colored pictures explore a flower planting season in an uncluttered and uncomplicated manner appropriate for young children. Including bulbs to plant in the fall and seeds to plant in the spring, the story concludes with summer flowers bursting forth in a brilliant rainbow colors. Ehlert familiarizes children with the names and pictures of many different flowers. But her strong point is in exposing her reader to the variety of wonderful colors found in a garden. Ehlert's paintings are clear, simple, and lush. By including individual pages of flowers in each particular color, she successfully builds her floral rainbow.

Planting a Rainbow could be used to encourage children to paint their own classroom rainbow. Such an activity begins by planting seeds or bulbs that will flower in a school yard or classroom garden plot. Then children could paint pictures of how they anticipate their particular flowers will look. When the paintings are dry, cut them out and arrange them in rainbow fashion on a large bulletin board. An alternative activity could be to encourage children to paint their own fanciful flowering plant, accompainied by a brief description of its height, how it smells, how to care for it, etc. Once again, arrange these in a display of rainbow colors.   S.J.S./H.M.

391.   Feldbaum, Carl B. and Ronald J. Bee. *Looking the Tiger in the Eye: Confronting the Nuclear Threat*. Illustrated with photographs. Harper & Row, 1988. ISBN 0-06-020415-X, $14.89. Ages   12-up.

In this provocative and well-researched book, the authors ask three questions: "What led human beings to develop the first bomb, and what drove us, after the devastation of Hiroshima and Nagasaki, to build the vast arsenals of today?" "How have the U.S. and other nations attempted to limit or eliminate these weapons, and why have we not been more successful?" and "What are our choices for the present, and what sort of future can we look forward to?" As in Mansfield and Hall's *Some Reasons for War* (Crowell, 1988), Feldbaum and Bee show various beliefs about war—including the popular perception of its inevitability, and the various personalities and circumstances that have led to the development and use of nuclear weapons. The authors include personal accounts of participants from the early stages of World War II and the Manhattan Project through the Cold War to present disarmament talks. According to the authors, "Looking the tiger in the eye" is to face the nuclear threat head on with an understanding of how this tiger has come to be and, with informed judgment, to decide how the threat of devastation can be eliminated. This is a compelling book that should be read for its rare insight into human behavior and motivation.

Related Source

Older students could develop a questionnaire for a series of interviews with family members, teachers, neighbors, and friends about issues raised in *Looking the Tiger in the Eye* and then compare perceptions reflected in their interviews with Feldbaum and Bee's research. They could also draw parallels to the photo-essay by Robert del Tredici entitled *At Work in the Fields of the Bomb* (Harper & Row, 1987). Recent news accounts of nuclear weapons manufacturing, such as the Fernald Feed Plant in Cincinnati or at Rocky Flats near Denver, would make for interesting additions to their research. After such investigation, encourage students to draw conclusions about the tiger and how to look it in the eye.   E.A.H.

Peace Studies, Social Studies Junior High School High School

Related Source

392. Fine, John Christopher. *The Hunger Road*. Atheneum, 1988. ISBN 0-689-31361-6, $12.95. Ages 10-up.

Children's thoughts on world hunger are disarmingly simple: they're hungry—let's feed them. John Fine offers a clear and unsettling history of how corrupt governments and civil wars have made it almost impossible to get the food and money that is collected to those who need it. As a mission volunteer in Ethiopia, Sahel, Indochina, the Congo, and the United States, Fine experienced first-hand the many problems causing world hunger. Each chapter is devoted to a certain locale and its inhabitants. The brief history of their plight, including black and white photographs, makes the problem take on a personal aspect that will undoubtedly move the reader. Though it is well-written, it comes alarmingly close to leaving the reader with a sense of hopelessness and helplessness. It is saved by a directory of relief organizations in the back of the book which may provide the motivated reader with a means of being helpful.

A class, or even the entire school, could select one of the organizations suggested by the author and write or phone to see how they can help fight world hunger. Additionally, they can write to UNICEF at 331 East 38th Street, New York, NY 10016 to obtain a publication that provides information on hunger and health problems of

Contemporary Affairs Middle School Junior High School High School

the world's children. One project that is at a level that children can understand is the Heifer Project International (P.O. Box 767, Goshen, IN 46526). This organization sends live animals to farmers around the world. Children everywhere can contribute by earning money to buy chickens, goats, rabbits, cows, or bees. When the animals reproduce, the recipient farmer passes a pair along to another farmer. The idea is so simple and effective that children understand it completely.   L.A.B.

393.   Fisher, Leonard Everett. *The Alamo*. Illustrated by the author. Holiday House, 1987. ISBN 0-8234-0646-6, $12.95. Ages 10-up.

Fisher's concise account of the history of the Alamo takes the reader from its beginning as a Spanish mission to its designation as a national Historical Landmark commemorating the courage of the 188 Americans who died defending it against General Santa Anna in 1836. Touching on the internal political strife in Mexico just prior to the Texans' struggle for independence, and then focusing upon the defenders themselves and the events taking place during the siege and subsequent battle, Fisher has made this period come alive for intermediate grade readers. The fate of the Alamo after the battle until 1905 when it was entrusted to the Daughters of the Republic of Texas and eventually made a Historic Landmark in 1960 completes this accurate, well-researched presentation. Numerous portraits, photographs, maps, drawings, and Fisher's familiar scratch board illustrations add fresh images to the informative text. A detailed index makes this book a useful source for learning about the Alamo.

The Alamo also provides a springboard for a general discussion about courage, self-sacrifice, and heroism—qualities displayed by the men and women who fought and died at the Alamo in the name of liberty and patriotism. Teachers may also want to have students write an imaginary account of the battle in the form of a diary or letter from one of the children in the fort who was spared by the Mexicans. Some children may also be interested enough in the characters and events introduced by Fisher that they can be encouraged to read more detailed biographies of Bowie, Crockett, and other Americans, as well as General Santa Anna.   B.J.S.

*U.S. History
Intermediate
Middle School*

394.   Flanagan, Dennis. *Flanagan's Version: A Spectator's Guide to Science on the Eve of the 21st Century*. Knopf, 1988. ISBN 0-394-55547-3, $18.95. Ages 12-up.

Students whose academic passions are absorbed by some area of science often are narrow in their focus in spite of a good mind and a probing curiosity about their subject. Flanagan, for 36 years the editor of Scientific American, speculates about the direction of current work in biology, astronomy, physics, and geology and the consequences of scientific endeavors into the 21st century. As a journalist interested in matters scientific, his essays have the ability to make comprehensible theories, concepts, and issues that are often beyond the ken of even the well educated layman. His range of scientific interests spans the history of the human race, and his insight on the human side of science is a perspective that future scientists must confront and understand.

High school science teachers and upper level high school students would benefit from opportunities to read and discuss the questions and issues raised in this book and others like it (e.g., the writings of Stephen J. Gould and Lewis Thomas). A science "club" or discussion group for faculty and students—for example, those in honors science sections—could meet at noon or after school as a legitimate extracurricular activity. By inviting area college teachers, doctors, or industrial and/or government scientists to serve as "visiting experts," the entire group benefits from the stimulation that comes from exploring a specialized topic in great depth. Such a program might encourage more promising students to take an interest in these fields of study.   H.M.

*Science
High School*

395.   Fleming, Alice. *The King of Prussia and a Peanut Butter Sandwich*. Illustrated by Ronald Himler. Scribner's, 1988. ISBN 0-684-18880-5, $12.95. Ages 7-9.

This short account of the Mennonites' immigration to America begins with a question: "Is there any connection between the King of Prussia and a peanut butter sandwich?" The question draws young readers into this well-written story illustrated with detailed, textured black and white drawings. The Mennonites were a peace-loving people who first immigrated to Russia, where they were given a one hundred year draft exemption. In the harsh climate of the Crimea, the Mennonites watched Turkish residents defy the natural order of planting to grow winter wheat. This method eliminated worry about dry conditions and insect and disease blights. When the one hundred year exemption was over, they found themselves moving on again, this time to the Kansas plains. Their first crop was harvested before a plague of grasshoppers ruined the crops of other local farmers, who soon followed the Mennonites' ways farming. Thus the Great Plains of Kansas became famous for its winter wheat, the wheat that is used to make flour for bread and peanut butter sandwiches.

The Mennonites were encouraged to move to America by a railroad company representative who was looking for settlers to live along his company's lines, and thus make use of the railroad as a means for getting crops to market and acquiring needed goods from other parts of the country. An interesting project might be to research the role that transportation has played in the settling and urbanization of our country, including ocean shipping, railroads, canals, airplanes, and interstate highways. *Timmy O'Dowd and the Big Ditch* by Len Hilts (Gulliver, 1988) is an example of a fictional, yet very informative, story set along the Erie Canal, one of the other modes of transportation that flourished during the 19th century period of westward expansion. Students could also trace the parallel growth of both canals and railroads on a map and a timeline.   M.A.C.

*U.S. History,
Multicultural Studies
Primary*

Related Source

396.   Foster, Sally. *Where Time Stands Still*. Illustrated with photographs by the author. Dodd, Mead, 1987. ISBN 0-396-09090-7, $13.95. Ages 7-11.

Recognizing that there are differences among Amish orders, Foster focuses on the Amish of one county in Pennsylvania and follows the children of one family in Lancaster County as they go to school, do chores, and play throughout the seasons of the year. Through her photo-documentary, Foster presents an honest look at the ways of these people who have maintained their basic traditions of simplicity in dress, transportation, and devotion to God for 250 years in America. An introduction to the book provides some background which traces the Amish from their early roots in 1525 to their arrival in the United States in the 1700s.

Multicultural Studies
Primary
Intermediate

The Amish of Ohio and other states follow somewhat the same traditions as those presented in the book, but there are subtle differences such as practicing "shunning" and curricular emphases in the public and private Amish schools. It would be most interesting to have non-Amish students develop a survey based upon the content of Foster's book and send it to Amish children in an Amish school. In Ohio there are many Amish public and private schools and a specific district to consider would be the East Holmes County School District. Teachers there have been very receptive to pen pal arrangements and would enjoy having their students complete a survey of this type. If students are interested in pursuing the idea of simple living, they might be introduced to the

Related Source

cookbook for children *Loaves and Fishes* by Linda Hunt and Marianne Frase (Herald Press, 1980), in which the emphasis is upon being good stewards of our resources so that all people might enjoy nutritious living.   E.A.H.

397.   Freedman, Russell. *Lincoln: A Photobiography*. Illustrated with photographs and prints. Clarion, 1987. ISBN 0-89919-380-3, $15.95. Ages 9-up.

Newbery Award Winner
ALA Best Book

Lincoln once said of himself: "Common-looking people are the best in the world; that is the reason the Lord makes so many of them." However, there is nothing common about our 16th president or historian Freedman's straightforward and readable "photobiography." Drawing widely from historical photographs, magazine prints, and other documents of the times, Freedman shapes a portrait of Lincoln that is clear, unadorned, and bound to be widely read. He lets the facts of Lincoln's life—his growing up years, his early days as an Illinois lawyer and politician, his wife and sons, the turmoil of his presidential years—speak for themselves, without romance or myth. The profusion of carefully chosen historical illustrations and the straightforward text make this 1988 Newbery Award winner a useful and lasting investment for both elementary and secondary school libraries.

Lincoln is one of the presidents about whom young people of every generation are often curious to know more. There are many materials for all reading levels available. By combining instructional time in English/

language arts, social studies/history, art, and music, teachers can set aside a one- or two-week period of intense study called "A Lincoln Read-In," during which biographies, historical stories, poems and songs, old newspaper articles and drawings, and other materials about Lincoln and his era can be read, discussed, and shared. The result will be a group who will probably know more about Lincoln than any other class in the country.   H.M.

*Literature,
U.S. History
Intermediate
Middle School
Junior High School*

398.   Fritz, Jean. *China Homecoming*. Photographs by Michael Fritz. Putnam, 1985. ISBN 0-399-21182-9, $12.95. Ages 10-up.

ALA Notable Book

With warmth and love, Jean Fritz describes her return to China, the country of her birth, and to the town in which she grew up. It is a new China, but there are old landmarks and endearing memories. In a way, this is a sequel to *Homesick: My Own Story* (Putnam, 1982). In other ways, it is a completely new and different book with photographs (by husband Michael Fritz) of China today with Jean Fritz, as a mature adult, pursuing her past. It is a poignant and touching story.

Included are a bibliography and an outline of Chinese history from 21st century B.C. to 1976. Jean Fritz's book can serve as a supplement to Asian studies and, in particular, a unit about present-day China. Ours is a mobile society; chances are that many students have moved away from their birthplaces or hometowns. Almost certainly, they have moved into different houses. A "homecoming," either real or imaginary, would make a good topic for a creative writing assignment. Encourage the students to examine not only what has or might be at their old home, but also how they have changed since they lived there.   F.M.H.

*Author Studies,
Social Studies,
Language Arts
Intermediate
Middle School*

399.   Fritz, Jean. *China's Long March*. Putnam, 1988. ISBN 0-399-21512-3, $14.95. Ages 10-up.

ALA Notable Book

Is anyone more qualified to write the story of China's greatest historical moment than Jean Fritz? She is not only a respected historian, but also was born in China (see *Homesick: My Own Story* [Putnam, 1982]) and recently returned to her place of birth to observe the social and political changes there (*China Homecoming* [Putnam, 1985; see preceding review]). In recounting the 6,000 mile journey of Mao and the Communist Army, Fritz not only leads the reader through the complex geography of interior China, but makes the reader feel the fears and frustrations, as well as the hardships and heroism, that make The Long March a political event of mythic proportions in China, as central to that country's past as the building of the Great Wall.

Related Sources

Even though there are maps at the beginning of chapters showing the route of the March, young people should be encouraged to gather current photographs of the areas along the route to better understand the difficulties of travelling there. These can be stretched across the room or down a school hallway marking the route to scale from beginning to end. In addition to movies, videotapes, and book materials listed in the

*Social Studies
Intermediate
Middle School
Junior High School*

bibliography, magazines such as *National Geographic* can help to complete a visual picture of the areas where this historic event took place.   H.M.

400.   Fritz, Jean. *Make Way for Sam Houston*. Illustrated by Elise Primavera. Putnam, 1986. ISBN 0-399-21303-1, $12.95. Ages 10-up.

Big and dramatic was the way Sam Houston did things. He was a born actor and costumed himself gallantly for all the roles he played— soldier, lawyer, congressman, governor. But foolish he was not, as proven by his sincere loyalty and patriotism to his country, the Constitution, and, most important to him, "his Texas," as he so often referred to it. Through Jean Fritz's informal yet insightful writing, the reader is drawn into a compassionate friendship with Mr. Houston and gains a deep respect for this massive, principled, and deeply caring founder of Texas.

Art, Math, U.S. History, Literature Intermediate Middle School Junior High School

Big was the way Sam Houston did things, so what better way to pay him tribute than to construct a big map of Texas to use in the classroom? Encompassing the subjects of art, math, and history, have students draw a large scale replica of Texas on cardboard or other thick paper. Mark important places of Houston's life on the map (use page 97 in text for reference). Other Texas cities and towns could be marked off as they are studied through textbooks or by reading biographies of other famous Texans.   L.S.

401.   Fritz, Jean. *Shh! We're Writing the Constitution*. Illustrated by Tomie dePaola. Putnam, 1987. ISBN 0-399-21403-8, $12.95. Ages 8-12.

With her usual flair for adding interest and color to factual information, Jean Fritz makes the writing of the Constitution come alive for young readers. Accurate details and amusing anecdotes about the delegates' lives allows them to be seen as real people rather than revered ghosts who dictated how the country should be governed. The spirited debate and compromise shows that even these politically-minded and learned men could not easily agree on how things should be done. Tomie dePaola's familiar style shows the Constitution writers free of the characteristic stuffiness normally associated with them. Lightly humorous but always factual, this is one book that should not be overlooked by even by middle school and junior high school history teachers.

Government, U.S. History Primary Intermediate Middle School Junior High School

Children in the suggested reading age are often very concerned with the notion of fairness. This sense of justice can be the basis of an activity where debate and compromise are required to reach a solution. An example of how this could be done might be in determining the class seating arrangement or organizing the room furniture. Ask students to form groups to propose the best plan. Each group should list their reasons for their choice. Next, allow members from each group to take turns telling why their choice is the best. Give each group several turns at speaking so they may also refute their opponents' reasons. After completion of the debate, inform students that they must determine the actual location by compromising—each side giving in to some of the others' ideas. When a consensus has been reached, follow through by rearranging the chairs and desks.   L.S.

402.   George, Jean Craighead. *One Day in the Alpine Tundra.* Illustrated by Walter Gaffney-Kessel. Crowell, 1984. ISBN 0-690-04325-2, $10.53. Ages 10-12.

The events of a day in the alpine tundra, namely Rendezvous Mountain in Wyoming, become a tale of suspense as a secluded no-man's land changes from a place of peace to one of violence and disruption. Jean Craighead George marvelously describes the land above the tree line on one mid-August day through the eyes of a young man alone on the tundra. Thus, the reader vicariously experiences changing weather patterns of blizzards, high winds, ice, lightning, and blazing sunlight. Walter Gaffney-Kessel's finely-textured drawings illustrate with appropriate detail not only the weather changes and action scenes, but also the creatures native to the tundra environment.

Older children primarily will use this book by naturalist Jean Craighead George as an excellent resource for the study of mountains and tundra ecology. They may also be drawn to some of her other books: *One Day in the Desert* (Crowell, 1983) describes the powerful changes that can occur in the desert environment and *The Wild, Wild Cookbook* (Crowell, 1982) describes ways to cook foods found in the wild. Students may want to research the natural environment in the area in which they live and/or consult a local naturalist about a food foraging field trip in a local wildlife preserve.   L.P.B.

Science, Social Studies
Intermediate
Middle School
Junior High School

Related Sources

403.   Gibbons, Gail. *Dinosaurs, Dragonflies and Diamonds.* Illustrated by the author. Four Winds, 1988. ISBN 0-02-737240-5, $13.95. Ages 5-8.

In her usual straightfoward manner, Gibbons has crafted a book showing behind-the-scenes activities at a natural history museum. The reader can study pictures explaining methods of identifying, preserving, and storing objects for exhibition, including the procedure for making a lifelike plastic snake from a dead rattlesnake mold. Other drawings show the varied exhibits of plants, animals, birds, insects, clothing, and jewelry. The colors are bold, and the text is brief. Scientists, museum guides and other personnel, as well as visitors, are shown to be of all ages, sexes, and races. An example of some perhaps unexpected startling historical facts with matching illustrations: "The first natural history museum in the U.S. was (built)...in 1773 in South Carolina."

Many children have never visited a real natural history museum. However, children themselves can create their own museum with rocks, fossils, shells, pine cones, acorns, bones, insects, bird's eggs, Indian arrowheads, animal fur—whatever they can gather and bring to class.

*Science
Primary*

After identification, each item on exhibit should be labeled neatly, perhaps color-coded on different card stock for different categories: earth science, botany, or zoology. Displays can be planned by the class showing background scenery, growth stages, etc. Other classes, parents, and administrators should enjoy and benefit from a visit to the children's natural history museum.   F.M.H.

404.   Gish, Lillian, as told to Selma Lanes. *Lillian Gish: An Actor's Life for Me!* Illustrated with photographs and drawings by Patricia Henderson Lincoln. Viking Kestrel, 1987. ISBN 0-670-80416-9, $14.95. Ages 7-10.

ALA Notable Book

Lillian Gish has been acting since 1902, when she was six years old. Her career has spanned traveling theatricals, silent cinema, the advent of "talkies," and on into full–color Dolby sound movies and home videos. *An Actor's Life for Me!*, however, is about her childhood in the theater, the survival years when she, her mother, and her sister Dorothy traveled from small town to big city playing in melodramas for $10-$15 per week each. The book is told in first person to Selma Lanes, who wrote *The Art of Maurice Sendak* (Abrams, 1985) and who has let Lillian Gish's personality shine through. The result is delightful, full of anecdotes and comments that reflect the age, experience, humor, and charm of the legendary actress. Photographs provided by Lillian Gish give the reader faces to place with the text and are a constant reminder that these were real little girls leading rather a hard life. Full color drawings depict scenes from the reminiscences that the old photographs can't. Together, text, photographs, and illustrations depict a lifestyle that exists no longer.

Related Source

*Social Studies, Drama
Primary
Intermediate
Middle School*

Lillian Gish's career was threatened at times by the Gerry Society, an organization designed to protect children from hard labor. Students might be interested in doing further research about child labor. Do the same laws pertain to young people today who are working in TV, movies, commercials, popular music, etc.? Under what conditions have children worked in the past? What laws protect children from exploitation? Under what conditions do children work today, both in our country and elsewhere? Should children be barred from working when family survival depends upon their income? What is required for young people to obtain a work permit? With so many young people seeking work today, knowing one's rights and restrictions is essential before entering the work force.   M.A.C.

405.   Goffstein, M.B. *A Writer.* Illustrated by the author. Harper & Row, 1984. ISBN 0-06-022142-9, $11.89. All ages.

Related Source

Those who enjoyed *An Artist* (Harper & Row, 1984) will be pleased to see this companion book that briefly and poetically describes the work of a writer. The ideas germinating in the writer's mind are compared to seeds planted in the soil that, with just the right care, sprout and grow. The language is simple and beautiful, as are the watercolor illustrations. The message of the book is simple and beautiful, matched by impressionistic watercolors of abstracted shapes in a soft pastel palette of colors.

Together, *An Artist* and *A Writer* could be used to stimulate some thinking about careers, especially careers in the arts. Young children may not ever have thought about the people who create the art we look at and the books we read. These books talk about the creative process in terms that can be understood intuitively as well as analytically. This may help children understand and respect these creative activities and approach them with more appreciation for the modes of thinking inherent in being an artist within any medium. Leo Lionni's *Frederick* (Pantheon, 1967) makes an excellent companion book.   M.A.C.

Art, Language Arts
Primary
Intermediate

Related Source

406. Goodall, John S. *The Story of a Main Street*. Illustrated by the author. McElderry, 1987. ISBN 0-689-50436-5, $14.95. All ages.

Through only detailed watercolor and pencil illustrations, Goodall "tells" the story of a main street in England from medieval to modern day. Students will be able to observe how a main street began with wattle and daub houses, a market cross, and a church and how each changed through time. Included are street scenes as well as interior views of different shops, showing alterations in transportation, costumes and customs and how architecture has changed to suit the needs of an ever-growing population. Goodall's unique format of full and half pages will keep readers turning the pages of this wordless picture story book again and again.

As part of a social studies unit, this book can be used by students to sharpen their skills of observation. Teachers could prepare a list of different concepts to look for, such as the ones mentioned in the above paragraph. Students could go on a "scavenger hunt" looking for ways in which time alters a main street. Students can also speculate on the types of business and industry illustrated by looking at the wordless signs hanging on the buildings. After groups have been given time to look through the book, a list could be written on the board based upon the students' findings. As a follow-up activity, pictures of the main street in their town could be compared as it has changed throughout the years. These may be obtained through the public library or local historical society. *New Providence: A Changing Cityscape* by Renata Von Tscharner and Ronald Fleming (Harcourt Brace Jovanovich, 1987) and *The House on Maple Street* by Bonnie Pryor (Morrow, 1987) are excellent companion books for younger readers.   K.B.B.

Social Studies
Primary
Intermediate

Related Sources

407. Hamilton, Virginia. *Anthony Burns: The Defeat and Triumph of a Fugitive Slave*. Knopf, 1988. ISBN 0-394-98185-5, $12.99. Ages 10-up.

In 1854, Anthony Burns escaped slavery in Virginia only to be arrested a few months later in Boston under the Fugitive Slave Act. His

ALA Notable Book
ALA Best Book

trial in that city brought the forces of pro-slavers and Abolitionists into legal and bloody conflict. Amid the historic events involving powerful political movements and famous names, Hamilton never lets the reader lose sight of the anguish of Anthony Burns. She reconstructs his life through well-drawn and carefully structured flashbacks to his days on the Sutter plantation. The slave's experiences are agonizingly portrayed so that the reader feels and responds to his treatment as he struggles just to survive, and to do so with his dignity intact. It is story deserving of the considerable skills of this very gifted writer.

In the *Afterword*, Hamilton challenges her readers to consider the relevance of Burns and/or the Fugitive Slave Act to today's readers: "What does a single slave out of millions like him...have to do with us—you, me—in this last decade before the year 2000?" For history teachers, this is the fundamental question upon which rests the *raison d'etre* for this area of study. Drawing parallels between the events recounted in this biography that helped shape our nation's history and moral perspective and the events in our recent past and in today's headlines can help young people value the essential purposes for knowing and being moved by their history.   H.M.

Black Studies, Government, History
Intermediate
Middle School
Junior High School
High School

408.   Harris, Jonathan. *A Statue for America*. Four Winds, 1985. ISBN 0-02-742730-7, $14.95. Ages 12-up.

A factual account of several Frenchmen's dream of sharing liberty with America, this book spans the time from when the seed of the idea was first planted in sculptor Frederick Bartholdi's mind to the recent centennial restoration of the statue. Where the idea originated, plans from conception to completion, and Americans' reactions and complaints, as well as financial concerns, anecdotes, and famous people's connections to the statue are revealed in Harris's in-depth report. This is a good resource for obtaining a more complete knowledge of the Statue of Liberty. An index is also provided to facilitate access to specific information. Black and white photographs and other historical pictures from various sources provide additional information and clarity to Harris's history.

Frederick Auguste Bartholdi used the *repousse* method—in which a design is hammered in relief—in constructing his statue. Art students at junior high or high school levels can research this technique which has been used in creating many famous statues, including the 17th century statue of St. Charles Bovromeo in Italy. A cumulative result of the research could be an original statue or replica of an existing one created using the *repousse* technique.   L.S.

Art, Social Studies
Intermediate
Middle School
Junior High School

409.   Hatchett, Clint. *The Glow-in-the-Dark Night Sky Book*. Illustrated by Stephen Marchesi. Random House, 1988. ISBN 0-394-89113-9, $9.95. Ages 8-12.

Beautiful oil paintings combined with a nontoxic ink which glows in the dark make this book one to have in every library and home. The book contains a series of star maps on two-page spreads. One page contains the simple star constellation diagrams, and the other has paintings showing the constellations as the creature or person that the ancient peoples imagined long ago. Each page is also bordered with additional labeled information about other things found in the night sky. A preface is included to explain how to use the book (the pages are "recharged" with a flashlight) and children are encouraged to use the book outside at night. Each page also includes at what time and on what day one can see that particular map in the sky. This book offers a truly hands-on science activity for children and provides an innovative and unique way for children to learn about constellations. Parents will appreciate having this at home for night sky viewing year round.

On the last page is a brief glossary that gives information about the constellations in the book. Because of this abbreviated format, children may want to know more about ancient Greek mythology and the constellations. This curiosity could initiate an integrated reading–science unit with students reading both the stories and legends associated with the constellations, as well as studying them scientifically, thereby bringing more breadth to both experiences. *The Glow-in-the-Dark Night Sky Book*, like any field guide, is only for identification. For additional background, children can read *Adventures of the Greek Heroes* by Mollie McLean and Anne Wiseman (Houghton Mifflin, 1961) *Gods, Demigods and Demons, an Encyclopedia of Greek Mythology* by Bernard Evslin (Scholastic, 1975) and *The Macmillan Book of Greek Gods and Heroes* by Alice Low (Macmillan, 1985).   K.B.B.

Science, Literature
Primary
Intermediate

Related Sources

410.   Heller, Ruth. *A Cache of Jewels and Other Collective Nouns*. Illustrated by the author. Grosset & Dunlap, 1987. ISBN 0-448-19211-X, $10.95. Ages 4-8.

In lush and vibrant colors, Heller introduces young children to collective nouns through the use of rhyming text and full page illustrations. Some common terms, such as a *bouquet* of flowers or a *bunch* of bananas, should be familiar to young children and will help in understanding what a collective noun is, as well as aid in learning lesser known terms such, as a *gam* of whales, a *kindle* of kittens, or a *drift* of swans. This book would be an excellent supplement to the English text when discussing the topic of nouns, as the brightly colored illustrations are hard to resist.

Using this book as an example, children can be encouraged to look up other collective nouns and find some that are not included in it. Another book which uses this concept in poetry form is *A Bundle of Beasts* by Patricia Hooper (Houghton Mifflin, 1987). Sharing it with younger children will also extend their knowledge of collective nouns. Students can work on illustrating their own collective nouns which could be made into a class book for everyone to enjoy. Older students may enjoy using as many collective nouns as possible in a single story or writing poems about collective nouns as Hooper did.   K.B.B.

Related Source

Language Arts
Primary
Intermediate

411. Heller, Ruth. *Kites Sail High*. Illustrated by the author. Grosset & Dunlap, 1988. ISBN 0-448-10480-6, $10.95. Ages 4-8.

Heller has a way with words that turns grammar into great fun. This time she has turned her attention to verbs. Combining evocative language to form melodic rhymes, she makes meaning of verbs that put dittos and worksheets to shame. Verbs show action: "Roses BLOOM/ and people RUN./ Pelicans FLY,/ Kites SAIL high." That's not all! She introduces linking and helping verbs, irregular tenses, moods, and more. Her rich illustrations seem to glow in the dark, and her flamboyant choice of words and images gives life to the power of language.

Language Arts
Primary
Intermediate

Verbs call for action, and so does this book. Invite students to act out vigorous verbs like skip, shimmy, slither, slide, or skate. Send them hunting through favorite books for different types of verbs that they can keep track of on charts. Also, encourage them to select favorites to include in their own writing. Allow them to come to terms with the variety of verb types naturally as they meet up with them in their own literature selections. Above all, keep the energy of Heller's book alive by not turning it into a drill and practice lesson.   K.L.M.

412. Henry, Joanne Landers. *Log Cabin in the Woods—A True Story about a Pioneer Boy*. Illustrated by Joyce Audy Zarins. Four Winds, 1988. ISBN 0-02-743670-5, $12.95. Ages 7-11.

From an unpublished memoir of boyhood days in the Indiana of 1832, the author has developed a month-by-month account of one year in the life of eleven-year-old Ollie Johnson and his pioneer family. The chores and tasks of daily survival are recounted: growing crops, clearing fields, going to school, etc. Special events, such as holiday celebration, barn raising, or treeing a bear, are included as well. These stories faithfully and authentically paint a portrait of the lives of early immigrant settlers in the midwest.

History
Primary
Intermediate

As the book is based upon childhood reminiscences, it might be interesting to read a chapter and have children ask one of their parents a parallel question, such as: What was your boyhood like? Tell me about your first boyhood job. How were schools different from today? If you had an accident as a boy, what kind of medical treatment did you receive? What was your home like when you were eleven? How were such holidays as Independence Day and Thanksgiving celebrated? The responses can be collected into individual student books and presented to each child's parents as a present for a special occasion.   J.F.A.

413. Hilts, Len. *Quanah Parker*. Gulliver Books, 1987. ISBN 0-15-200565-X, $12.95. Ages 8-12.

Hilts took the results of in-depth research and wrote an emotionally moving biography of the life of Comanche war chief Quanah Parker.

The reader is presented the Comanche viewpoints about the westward expansion in the 19th century, the intrusion into their lands and the wholesale slaughter of their food sources. The text is so descriptive that the reader expects to see illustrations that come to mind included in the book. This is a gripping biography which presents a perspective not always found in history textbooks.

This book can be used as a springboard for a game of "What if...History." This is a discussion problem-solving activity in which students are encouraged to speculate about what would have happened in the course of history if certain events had been different. What would have happened, for example, if the settlers and Native Americans had not resorted to violence in solving their disputes, if treaty rights had been vigorously enforced by both governments? After coming up with a list of "What if..." questions, students can discuss the possible changes in our history and current situation that might have resulted from a different course of action by our ancestors. The results can be presented in a written report or, as an alternative, as a flow chart showing the alternative paths of action and their likely consequences.   C.A.Y.

U.S. History
Intermediate
Middle School

414. Hirschfelder, Arlene. *Happily May I Walk: American Indians and Alaska Natives Today*. Scribner's, 1986. ISBN 0-684-18624-1, $13.95. Ages 10-up.

This is an essential volume for all libraries. In this contemporary portrait of Native American, scholar-writer Hirschfelder dispels the romantic ficitons and images that are so central to many textbooks, novels, and social studies curricula. Gone are the loin cloths, war ponies, and tipis. In their place are Levis, pickups and snowmobiles, condos and corporate headquarters. This straightforward compendium is perfect for those seeking information that is current about the social, economic, and political aspects of contemporary Native American life. Names of books and addresses of individuals and organizations that can provide additional information are included.

Students are often unaware of newspapers and news magazines that are aimed at particular ethnic groups across the country. Hirschfelder notes there are over 500 such publications written for and about Native Americans. She lists several, but students could consult a serials index at their school or public library for a more complete list. A letter requesting a sample copy of each could result in a detailed, composite picture of contemporary Native American life—the significant current issues, as well as a more complete understanding of the daily lives of Native Americans everywhere.   H.M.

Native American Studies
Intermediate
Middle School
Junior High School

415. Hoban, Tana. *I Walk and Read*. Illustrated by the author. Greenwillow, 1984. ISBN 0-668-02575-7, $10.50. Ages 3-7

As she has done in her previous books for very young children, Tana Hoban lets her photographs of familiar objects speak for themselves in this collection of colorful signs on businesses, traffic directions, cars, buses, and city buildings. Young children should recognize easily most of the words—"police," "phone," "fire," etc.—especially where the context of the word or phrase is clear. Children can be encouraged to become more observant as they walk or ride through their town, and to attempt to read familiar signs on their own.

Both younger and older elementary age children might want to create their own books of familiar signs after reading Tana Hoban's *I Walk and Read*. Younger children may take their illustrations from magazines; older children may want to use a camera as they create books on "Signs Around Our School," "Sports Signs," "Advertising," or some other collection organized around a theme. The possibilities are numerous, and the books "published" by the children can be added to the school or classroom library.   H.M.

Art,
Language Arts
Primary

416.   Hoban, Tana. *Look! Look! Look!* Photographs by the author. Greenwillow, 1988. ISBN 0-699-07240-2, $12.88. Ages 3-up.

In her most recent work, Hoban tickles the minds of her young audience, turning the known into the unknown with cleverly packaged color photographs. Each full-page picture is preceded by a jet black glossy page containing a small cutout frame. This enables the viewer to see only a portion of the full photograph. A collie, a ball of yarn, and a guitar are obvious when seen in their entirety. However, restrict the view of each of these to only a small portion and the viewer's imagination runs wild. Young and old alike will enjoy guessing what object lies within the frame before turning the page to see the total image. The greatest enjoyment will be sharing this book with others to discover what their imaginations will bring.

Students can create a class "Look! Look! Look!" book using crayons and black and white construction paper. A picture should be drawn on the white paper using the entire space. Cut a three inch square frame in the black paper and lay it over the finished picture. Students can have others try to guess what the total picture is before revealing the answer. Captions such as "What is this?" can be placed on slips of paper and pasted to the black pages. Answers can be written on the bottom of the picture page, making the art experience a reading and writing one as well. Pages should be bound with a cover to complete the project.   J.T.

Art,
Language Arts
Primary

417.   Irvine, Joan. *How to Make Pop-Ups*. Illustrated by Barbara Reid. Morrow, 1988. ISBN 0-688-0792-4, $6.95. Ages 8-12.

Irvine has developed this practical and amazingly easy-to-follow book for students and teachers interested in novel ways to illustrate or visually extend stories or poems. Reviving the art of using flaps, peepholes, cut-outs, and pop-ups that were popular in the 18th and 19th centuries—and are becoming popular again today—Irvine provides classroom-tested directions with never-fail sketches to guide the beginner step-by-step in creating a variety of pop-ups from simple to complex. There are push and pop-out ideas, fold and fit pop-ups, and push, pull, and turn pop-ups—and Irvine shows they are easy to make.

There are dozens of different types of books for all ages of readers published each year that are "paper engineered" toy books or pop-ups. Some are new versions of old favorites (Bemelmans's *Madeline*, for example, is in pop-up format by Viking Kestrel, 1987); some use the movable format to help explain concepts (*Anno's Sundial*, [Philomel, 1985]); some pop-ups are essential to the presentation (Van Der Meer's *The Pop-Up Book of Magic Tricks* [Viking, 1983]). Examples may be hard to find since libraries understandably tend not to buy books that will not endure constant use, but a few copies on display can show children how effective the finished book can be.   M.G.C./H.M.

Art
Primary
Intermediate
Middle School

Related Sources

418.   Isaacson, Philip M. *Round Buildings, Square Buildings, & Buildings That Wiggle Like a Fish*. Illustrated with photographs by the author. Knopf, 1988. ISBN 0-394-99382-9, $16.99. Ages 10-up.

"The bridge is gentle and quiet. Its smooth stone and delicate shapes speak to one another in soft voices. These voices—almost whispers—turn Mr. Pultney's bridge into a short poem." This is the kind of narrative Isaacson uses to describe the architectural wonders to be found in this world. Isaacson discusses building materials, color, design, windows, doorways, roofs, support structures, ornamentation, and overall impressions. Full-color photographs on glossy paper beautifully complement the lyrical text. This book is a treasure!

About new architectural forms, Isaacson says, "The new may seem strange at first, but if we are patient and willing to think about them, their wonder will appear." This could be taken up as a challenge by a class. After reading Isaacson's book, find other books on architecture, such as Sylvester and Wiemann's *Mythology, Archeology, Architecture* (Learning Works, 1982) and Harvey Weiss's *Model Buildings and How to Make Them* (Crowell, 1979). *Cobblestone Magazine* did an entire recent issue on architecture, and The Boy Scouts of America have a publication, *Architecture* (BSA, 1966), as well. With the help and inspiration of these resources, students might design their own building, perhaps a specific project of local importance, such as a new museum or recreation center. Indeed, a whole new town could be designed by students, each one selecting a specified building. A local architect might volunteer to critique the final projects.   M.A.C.

Art, Social Studies
Intermediate
Middle School
Junior High School

Related Sources

419.   Jakes, John. *Susanna of the Alamo: A True Story*. Illustrated by Paul Bacon. Harcourt Brace Jovanovich, 1986. ISBN 0-15-200592-7, $13.95. Ages 6-up.

This beautifully illustrated true story of the role of Susanna Dickinson in Texas's struggle for freedom from Mexico is authentic and quite readable. Readers will learn that the Alamo was defended by

Mexicans as well as Americans; that all surviving male defenders, except slaves, were murdered after the fort fell; and that General Santa Anna was indeed a villain. The end pages contain a map of Texas with important events and dates in the state's history indicated by the city where they occurred.

Spending one class period reading this oversized work aloud should bring alive an event that basal social studies texts tend to dully portray. After reading the book aloud, discuss the story and its illustrations. Later make the book available to interested students who might wish to study the helpful maps on the end pages or to examine the reproduction of Travis's "I shall never retreat or surrender" letter. This will provide a better teaching of history than what usually occurs in many fifth grade classrooms using the regular text. Some students may want to compare this account with that by Leonard Everett Fisher's *The Alamo* (Holiday House, 1987).   J.F.A.

U.S. History
Intermediate
Middle School

Related Source

420. Johnston, Ginny, and Judy Cutchins. *Scaly Babies: Reptiles Growing Up*. Morrow, 1988. ISBN 0-688-07306-9, $12.88. Ages 7-10.

This short book is packed with information about reptiles and their young. It consists of four chapters on snakes, lizards, crocodilians, and turtles respectively. Each chapter begins with general information and goes on to discuss one or more illustrative species. The photographs are outstanding. They are in full color and clearly depict the variety of life in the reptile world. The authors have researched their subject, relying upon a host of experts to answer questions and confirm facts. They have managed to present those facts so that they read like a story. The book itself is even nicely formatted, with glossy pages, red borders, and stencilled titles—a welcome source for young readers.

A trip to the local zoo or nature preserve is likely to yield a close look at one or more of the reptiles represented in *Scaly Babies*. Live animal demonstrations at these sites will help destroy misconceptions like "snakes are slimy" and enable children to use knowledge to overcome fear. Back at school, students can report what they have learned by creating a class story in this pattern: "I used to think…, but now I know…" This could be illustrated and displayed in the hallway to help other children learn the facts about reptiles. If the zoo has an "Adopt-An-Animal" program, the group might decide to participate as an on-going project throughout the year.   M.A.C.

Science,
Language Arts
Primary
Intermediate

421. Kellogg, Steven. *Aster Aardvark's Alphabet Adventure*. Illustrated by the author. Morrow, 1987. ISBN 0-688-07257-7, $12.88. All ages.

"Aster Aardvark had an aversion to the alphabet." So begins Kellogg's latest book. In a series of short alliterative scenarios, Kellogg creates an uncommon alphabet book that is a treat to both the ear and the eye. Frolicking animals—illustrated in gentle colors and clothed in rich detail—bound, dangle, flop, and hurl across the pages. They grin and giggle, displaying typical Kellogg smiles, as the reader "guffaws in glorious giddiness" right along with them. Each letter is explored with alliterative and artistic humor. Although young children may not understand all the words in the narratives, they are likely to be captivated by the joyous sounds of the language.

Language Arts
Primary
Intermediate
Middle School

This book can be used with other alphabet books to teach the name, form, and associated sounds of the letters of the alphabet. Its extraordinary value, however, is in Kellogg's clever use of alliteration. It can be used with older children to teach this concept. Even junior high school students will appreciate the humor and language usage. Some students will want to experiment with writing alliterative tongue twisters or writing their own narratives using predominantly one sound. Each day can focus on a different letter of the alphabet. An enjoyable companion book is Schwartz's *A Twister of Twists, A Tangle of Tongues* (Lippincott, 1972), which contains numerous tongue twisters and a story using only words beginning with the letter *S*.   L.B.

Related Source

422.   Kitzinger, Sheila. *Being Born*. Photographs by Lennart Nilsson. Grosset & Dunlap, 1986. ISBN 0-448-18990-9, $14.95. All ages.

Childbirth has been a mixture of curiosity, mystery, and wonder to young people, as well as the subject of myth, misinformation, and ignorance. Few books for children and young adults have ever been as successful as *Being Born* in providing straightforward information in non-technical language for a wide range of readers. Nilsson's spectacular medical photographs show with remarkable clarity the creation of a human life from the impregnation of an ovum to birth. Kitzinger's graceful narrative of the "journey each of us has taken" complements the photos in this outstanding book for school and home use.

ALA Notable Book

Parents who want to provide their children with accurate sex information are often frustrated in their search for appropriate resources, especially those with illustrations that are as instructive as the text. Teachers and librarians should work together to prepare a list of books, magazines, audio and video tapes, and film resources appropriate for primary, intermediate and young adult audiences that are available in local libraries. A good place to begin is by writing for recommended sources from the American Library Association.   H.M.

Science, Family Life
All Grades

423.   Kome, Penney and Patrick Crean, editors. *Peace: A Dream Unfolding*. Illustrated with photographs and paintings. Sierra Club, 1986. ISBN 0-87156-700-8, $18.95. Ages 12-up.

Peace is an overwhelming experience, one not to be missed for the power of its message and for the visual and emotional impact it can have on the reader. The editors have organized in this volume the most important writings related to peace—poetry, letters, prose, speeches, and technical articles—by individuals, governments, and organizations from widely varying cultures. The drawings, paintings, posters, and photographs are alternatingly sobering, provocative, and poignant. There is more in the 250 pages than can be absorbed in a sitting, yet one is compellingly drawn into this moving history of peace activities that have always been part of the social and political history of the human race. Every young person should have the right and responsibility to read what may have been the most important book of 1986.

There are literally hundreds of individual and group activities described or implied by the articles in *Peace*, so many that teachers and parents may need only to serve as a facilitator for students who wish to pursue an idea, a topic, or project. Pages 208-211 list some very specific activities for students to undertake. *The Lion and the Lamb Peace Arts Center* at Bluffton (Ohio) College is an excellent resource for young people to gather additional ideas, materials, and support, and to become involved in its sponsored activities throughout the year. For further information, contact Dr. Elizabeth Hostetler, Bluffton College, Bluffton, Ohio 45817   (419) 358-8015.   H.M.

Peace Studies, Art, Music, History, Language Arts All Grades

424.   Kramer, Stephen P. *How to Think Like a Scientist*. Illustrated by Felicia Bond. Crowell, 1987. ISBN 0-690-04563-8, $10.89. Ages 8-12.

This is a well-written book that introduces children to the scientific method as a means of answering many of life's everyday questions. Kramer presents three stories, each with a question for the child to think about. Each of the articles presents something that could happen and shows how a question can be answered by looking at the evidence. Each story takes the child through the steps of the scientific method: 1) Ask a question, 2) Gather information about the question, 3) Form a hypothesis, 4) Test the hypothesis, 5) Tell others what you have found. Kramer writes in an interesting, easy-to-read manner, and Bond's humorous illustrations add to the appeal of this book.

This could be an excellent resource for helping children with thinking/problem-solving skills. Each story is thought-provoking and presents several possible answers. After discussing the stories in the book, have your students think of their own questions. Then apply Kramer's five steps to discover the answers. Results could then be shared in a class presentation, or projects could be displayed in a "Discovery Fair."   J.P.

Science, Math Primary Intermediate Middle School

425.   Krementz, Jill. *The Fun of Cooking*. Photographs by the author. Knopf, 1985. ISBN 0-394-54808-6, $14.95. Ages 6-16.

This oversize cookbook displays the fun and adventure of cooking. There are nineteen boys and girls, ages 6–16, leading the reader around the store, the garden, and then into their kitchens. Krementz's photographs give the reader a feeling of being included in the preparation of each dish. The young people are aided by fathers, mothers, grand-mothers, siblings, and even pets. There is a large selection of recipes, including ethnic dishes, ranging from "Jill's Matzo Ball Soup" to "Jason's Doggie Biscuits" for man's best friend. This book also includes unique recipes like "Rena's Cucumber Sushi" and "Michele's Angel Hair Spaghetti." The large-print format is fairly easy to read and may be a good choice for upper grade students with reading problems. Anyone who picks up this book should be inspired to head for the kitchen to try some of these interesting recipes.

The major use for *The Fun of Cooking* is obvious: put children in the kitchen. This book can give home economics teachers ideas of new recipes to let students try and may give elementary teachers who have not tried cooking projects in their classrooms some exciting ideas. Many recipes can be prepared without fully equipped kitchens. A hot plate and/or a toaster oven brought from home are sufficient. Be certain to share the parts of the text where the children in the book talk about cooking, and always go over the safety instructions included in the front of the book before beginning any cooking project.   C.A.Y.

*Family Life,
Social Studies
Primary
Intermediate
Middle School
Junior High School*

426.   Kuklin, Susan. *Thinking Big*. Photographs by the author. Lothrop, Lee & Shepard, 1986. ISBN 0-688-05827-2, $10.88. Ages 6-9.

Eight-year-old Jamie Osborne is a dwarf and a member of Little People of America. With the loving encouragement of her family and the support of other LPA's, she is learning to adapt to a world much larger that her small physical stature. Yet, as we learn in this informative and touching photographic narrative, Jamie acts and thinks big. "I am like everybody else, just little," Jamie says. Young readers will learn the reasons for dwarfism, the problems dwarfs face, and the ways in which at least one young girl copes on a daily basis. This is an excellent resource for teachers and parents as well as for children in helping to understand the special needs and capabilities of a dwarf child.

There have been a wide range of book materials for children about young people with a variety of handicaps and physical abnormalties. The best of these resources are described and catalogued in *Bookfinder* (American Guidance Service, Circle Pines, MN 55014), an excellent resource available at most libraries. Teachers or parents seeking and evaluated listing of fiction and nonfiction titles about a specific "problem" area—e.g., drug abuse, loneliness, divorce, etc.—can easily find appropriate reading materials for all ages. It is a reference well worth knowing and using frequently.   H.M.

*Family Life,
Social Studies
Primary
Intermediate

Related Source*

427.   Lapham, Lewis H., et al.. *The Harper's Index Book*. Illustrated by Martin Avillez. Henry Holt, 1987. ISBN 0-8050-0396-7, $6.95. Ages 12-up.

Mark Twain is supposed to have once observed that there are "lies, damned lies, and statistics!" Nevertheless, we are a society that is both surrounded with and fascinated by numbers. *Harper's Magazine* each month prints a statistical "Index" that measures shifts in our culture. This volume presents without conclusions or comment "1,159 numbers that count" from past issues, from what we eat (1,417 pounds of food annually per person, 9 pounds of which are chemical additives) to the percentage of sixth graders who can't find the U.S. on a world map (20%) and the percentage of teachers who say they would not go into teaching if they had it to do over again (24%, up from 7.1% in 1965). This is fascinating "reading" for anyone interested in understanding patterns of our social fabric, frayed ends and all.

The library can be the center for an annual school project of gathering and recording similar numbers on social phenomena and events, both locally and nationally, throughout the school year. Topics or categories can be determined in advance, or they can be established at the end of the year. Each statistic should be succinctly stated and entered following a standard format and footnoted with its source for verification. At the end of the year, selections can be prepared for printing and distribution with the school yearbook or a section in the yearbook can include those statistics gathered before the publishing deadline.   H.M.

*Social Studies
Intermediate
Middle School
Junior High School
High School*

428.   Lasky, Kathryn. *Puppeteer*. Photographs by Christopher Knight. Macmillan, 1985. ISBN 0-02-751660-1, $10.95. Ages 8-12.

ALA Notable Book

Puppeteer describes the transformation of a creative idea into a magical puppet play, each step performed by Paul Vincent Davis. Writer Kathryn Lasky and photographer Christopher Knight narrate and photograph each step that Davis must take to make the puppets and produce "Aladdin and His Wonderful Lamp." Davis studied books on Persian and Oriental art to develop the right facial features and to learn about designing appropriate buildings, plants, animals, and clothing. The story and photographs show Davis making each body part, every puppet, and all of the scenery. After all of his work, Davis is finally shown producing and performing the play.

Puppeteer is an appealing and encouraging account of puppet theater production to read to a class prior to putting on their own puppet play. It shows students the many steps of careful, meticulous planning and preparations. The book could encourage students to take their time, not to rush to get it done. Since his puppets' heads are carved from wood and difficult to make, a helpful companion book is *Hand Puppets: How to Make and Use Them* by Laura Ross (Lothrop, Lee & Shepard, 1969).   K.L.W.

*Art, Drama,
Language Arts
Intermediate
Middle Schol
Junior High School*

Relatd Source

429.   Lauber, Patricia. *Dinosaurs Walked Here and Other Stories Fossils Tell*. Illustrated with photographs. Bradbury, 1987. ISBN 0-02-754510-5, $15.95. Ages 8-up.

ALA Notable Book

"Like entries in a diary, fossils tell of the earth's history. They tell of continents that move, of changes in the face of the earth, of past climates. They tell of many kinds of past life, including the dinosaurs that walked here long ago." Newbery Honor medalist Patricia Lauber tells about fossils through such fine, clear use of language. She also weaves stories as she describes how a gnat might have become fossilized in amber or a baby mammoth became perfectly preserved in ice, and how a sloth, a saber-toothed tiger, and a vulture ended up together in a tar pit in Los Angeles. The illustrations are photographs of fossils and fossil sites and paintings of prehistoric scenes printed on paper with a high quality glossy finish. This is a beautiful piece of nonfiction, a joy to read and to view.

Students might want to try some fossil hunting themselves after reading *Dinosaurs Walked Here and Other Stories Fossils Tell*. A local amateur or professional paleontologist can be contacted to speak about his/her speciality to a group and to act as a guide to promising sites. Students can photograph their findings, research them, and write up a description. They might want to illustrate the scenes they imagine took place as the animals/plants became fossilized.   M.A.C.

Science
Intermediate
Junior High School

430. Lauber, Patricia. *Tales Mummies Tell*. Illustrated with photographs. Crowell, 1985. ISBN 0-690-04389-9, $11.89. Ages 10-14.

ALA Notable Book

This fact-filled book defines a mummy as "any well-preserved body, whether animal or human," and proceeds to discuss both human and animal mummies that were formed naturally or man-made, with descriptions of how they were preserved. The clear photographs, used in conjunction with the text, help the reader to better understand what mummies are like. Other excellent features in this book are the suggestions for further reading and an easy-to-use index. Lauber demonstrates that much can be learned about the reasons for mummification, the steps involved in the process, and the cultures that practiced it.

Perhaps the most popular exhibit at most museums of art or history is the Egyptian Room or similar area that displays mummies. Teachers can call the museum's main phone number to make arrangements for a class tour. *Tales Mummies Tell* is an indispensable source of information to prepare a class for such a visit. Students may wish to combine their study of mummies with an exploration of ancient Egyptian mythology and culture.   H.M.

Social Studies
Intermediate
Middle School

431. Lauber, Patricia. *Volcano: The Eruption and Healing of Mount St. Helens*. Illustrated with photographs. Bradbury, 1986. ISBN 0-02-754500-8, $14.95. Ages 8-11.

Newbery Honor Book

Soon after the eruption of Mount St. Helens in May, 1980, and the formidable destruction that followed, nature began healing the rifts: life returned to the mountain. Filled with information, charts, diagrams, and incredible color photographs of before, after, and during the eruption, this 1987 Newbery Honor book should be accessible for a wide age range of readers. Benefits of volcanoes are spelled out—facts the reader does not often encounter. The role a geologist plays is convincing and enlightening. Above all, the reader can envision the actual volcanic eruption from Lauber's lucid descriptions, in addition to the carefully selected photographs. Perhaps most remarkable are the images of plant and animal life that survived the holocaust. This is a fine example of outstanding nonfiction. Textbook publishers can learn a great deal from Lauber's books and follow her examples of clear and interesting writing.

Other books on volcanoes abound, as well as audio-visual teaching aids. Traditionally, classes make their own volcanoes, which can still be a worthy project. Follow the basic instructions of building a cone-shaped figure with clay, leaving a crater on the top to be filled with a tablespoon of ammonium dichromate and cautiously putting a lighted match on top of the chemical. To round off their study of volcanoes, students also might enjoy reading two amusing fictional accounts of volcanoes: *Hill of Fire* by Thomas P. Lewis (Harper & Row, 1971) and *Finches' Fabulous Furnace* by Roger Wolcott Drury (Little, Brown, 1971) in which a family heats their home by a volcano until the dreaded eruption occurs.   F.M.H.

*Science
Primary
Intermediate
Middle School*

Related Sources

432.   LeShan, Eda. *Grandparents: A Special Kind of Love*. Illustrated by Tricia Taggart. Macmillan, 1984. ISBN 0-02-756380-4, $9.95. Ages 8-12.

In one generation, lifestyles appear to have changed abruptly. Eda LeShan, a gifted writer and family counselor, has written in this book and others about coping with these changes, as well as conflicts in family relationships that have been and probably always will be present between different generations: "Parents NEVER stop being parents and children NEVER stop being children, no matter how old they are." Although any offspring over 21 has learned that, intermediate grade children can benefit from knowing how that reality influences their lives.

Other more poignant realities affect children's lives. Following an after school discussion between a teacher and student about the loss of a family member or an impending separation, a teacher could offer the suffering child a copy of LeShan's *Learning to Say Good-Bye: When a Parent Dies* (Macmillan, 1976) or *What's Going to Happen to Me? When Parents Separate or Divorce* (Macmillan, 1978). Her newest book would also support advice given by the teacher during an after school conference prompted by a child asking questions about step-grandparents, grandparents moving in, and arguments between parents and grandparents.   J.F.A.

*Family Life,
Social Studies
Primary
Intermediate
Middle School*

Related Sources

433.   LeShan, Eda. *When Grownups Drive You Crazy*. Macmillan, 1988. ISBN 0-02-756340-5, $11.95. Ages 8-12.

The importance of communication is a persistent and central theme in the works by this widely respected counselor and author. Through numerous stories and anecdotes, LeShan addresses the frustrations of children caused by parents exhibiting inconsistencies and insensitivity.

She also deals with other adults who are significant in the lives of children, ranging from school crossing guards to the advertisers on children's television shows. She acknowledges the right of children to experience frustration, but she also suggests ways of dealing with one's feelings and problems that arise in family and school situations. This is an excellent book for families to read and discuss together.

The book should provide children with insight into the motivations of adults who are usually portrayed in a balanced if not always sympathetic manner. It is a perspective that preadolescents can accept. Because the issues deal with universal concerns organized into chapter subdivisions, the book is particularly recommended to teachers in grades 4–6 who wish to help children understand that they are not alone in their feelings, and that discussing concerns with parents often results in a solution to the problem.   J.F.A.

*Family Life,
Social Studies
Intermediate
Middle School
Junior High School*

434.   Lipsyte, Robert. *Assignment: Sports*. Harper & Row, 1984. ISBN 0-06-023908-5, $11.89. Ages 12-up.

Though Robert Lipsyte is well known to readers of young adult fiction as the author of the widely read *The Contender* (Harper & Row, 1967) and *One Fat Summer* (Harper & Row, 1977), he remains foremost a sportswriter. In *Assignment: Sports* he is at his best covering the famous (including Mickey Mantle, Muhammad Ali, Joe Namath, and others) and the lesser known (Yuri Viasov, John Pappas, and Olaf Olsen) stars in the galaxy of sports from baseball and boxing to weight lifting and fishing. His focus is always on going behind the headlines to uncover the human dimensions of the sport and of the athletes. These articles, from his work at *The New York Times* and on CBS's "Sunday Morning," are refreshingly bright and literate and leave the reader with a sharp portrait of the person and the sport.

Related Sources

These short biographical articles should find many eager readers among high school and junior high school students labelled "reluctant readers," especially if recommended by a gym teacher or coach. It might get those who are fantasicizing about a professional career in athletics thinking realistically about their futures. A local professional athlete might agree to an interviewed for an article for the school paper; he or she may even be willing to be a guest speaker to talk about their career plans, especially those they had when they were in school.   H.M.

*Physical Education
Intermediate
Middle School
Junior High School
High School*

435.   Lomask, Milton. *Exploration–Great Lives*. Scribner's, 1988. ISBN 0-684-18511-3, $22.95. Ages 9-11.

Milton Lomask's insightful, informative, and entertaining book about 25 geographical explorers should thrill history buffs and may recruit those students who do not see the value in learning about the past. From Columbus's seafaring adventures to Byrd's mind-numbing quest for the South Pole, Lomask provides personal, as well as historically significant, facts that keep this book exciting and quite readable. The subjects are organized alphabetically and black and white photographs enliven the text. A three-page chronology of important dates in the history of geographical exploration, as well as suggestions for further reading, are included.

Let students be their own geographic explorers. Each school neighborhood or community has its peculiar geographic features. Students can work together to develop a "Guide to Local Geography" resource for school and community use by focusing on prominent geographic, geologic, and climatic features of their area and their relationship to larger regional features. They should include any significant mineral deposits, important surface water features, and natural vegetation. Local nature preserves and parks have experts who can assist. Drawings and photographs can complement the written narrative. A videotape account filmed on location as well as "in the studio" is an exciting and effective alternative format for presenting what the class learned.   L.A.B./H.M.

U.S. History
Intermediate
Middle School

436.   Lukes, Bonnie L. *How To Be A Reasonably THIN Teenage Girl*. Illustrated by Carol Nicklaus. Atheneum, 1986. ISBN 0-689-31269-5, $12.95. Ages 12-up.

Rather than promising a quick, gimmicky way of losing weight, this book offers a plan that is sensible and sound. The author encourages young girls to eat three well-rounded meals each day, selecting food from each of the four main food groups. Her secret for losing weight is simply to count calories, choosing the correct amount from the examples and chart provided. Lukes writes directly to her reader, using humor and her own experience with a weight problem to plead her case for a *reasonable* weight loss program. She offers tips for getting through special occasions—Friday night get-togethers at the pizza place, slumber parties, eating in restaurants—without feeling guilty or giving up eating entirely. Stressed throughout the book is the importance of being realistic: aiming for too great of a weight loss is not only self-defeating, but it also can be dangerous if it develops into anorexia nervosa. The occasional line drawings enhance the author's humorous and successful approach to this serious matter.

Health Education,
Family Life
Middle School
Junior High School
High School

Many teenagers, both girls and boys, do not eat well-balanced meals. Girls, influenced by society's expectations of how a woman should look, often skip meals or go on fad diets in an attempt to become "cover-girl" skinny. Here is an opportunity to discuss with adolescents the importance of eating food from all main food groups to receive the proper amount of calories and nutrients. Use Chapter 15 from *How To Be A Reasonably THIN Teenage Girl* with the class to determine their FIO (Food Intelligence Quotient). Allow students to share other food facts/myths that they have been exposed to and discuss the validity of each. Invite a nutrition expert to speak to the class and to answer any questions students may have. Teachers might keep this book in mind to recommend to young girls and boys who may ask for help in dealing with a weight problem.   L.S.

437. MacDonald, Suse. *Alphabatics*. Illustrated by the author. Bradbury, 1986. ISBN 0-02-761520-0, $15.95. All ages.

Caldecott Honor Book

A 1987 Caldecott Honor Book, *Alphabatics* is an inventive and entertaining look at the 26 letters. It is a visual treat as well: bold graphic design in pure colors illustrates this alphabet book in which the letters tumble across each page gradually changing position until they become a something that starts with that letter. The letter "i", for example, flies up and away to become an insect, while "v" takes root to become vegetables. The fascination is not with what each letter stands for so much as with what acrobatics each letter goes through as it is visually transformed.

Alphabatics imight be useful to help children link the physical shapes of letters with their sounds. Children exposed to *Alphabatics* may, for example, mentally rotate a "p" into a plane to remember the /p/ sound. As a related art project which would extend this idea, give children letter cutouts. They can play with the positioning of these until they can visually connect the letter with a thing that begins with its sound. Younger children can be helped with this by first brainstorming words with each initial sound. Older children can use their dictionary to help them in their quest. Then they can trace around the letter cutout to illustrate the acrobatics it went through, modifying the letter as needed. Finally they can draw or cut and paste colored paper to illustrate the thing their letter turned into. The results could be made into posters and displayed in the classroom or library.   M.A.C.

Art, Language Arts
Primary

438. Madden, John *The First Book of Football*. Illustrated with photographs and drawings. Crown, 1988. ISBN 0-517-56981-7, $10.95. Ages 8-up.

"Whap! Bam! Smack! Thunk!" Flamboyant TV commentator and former NFL coach Madden makes this short (90 pages) guide to how the game is played as lively and entertaining as it is informative. He defines terms carefully and explains the fundamentals with clarity and his own brand of zany humor. Chapter titles, such as "The Guys with Neat Lockers: Offense" and "The Guys with Messy Lockers: Defense," introduce the basics of strategy and position requirements. Madden also makes clear the importance of personal characteristics and attitude required for success, in addition to physical strength or size. Reluctant readers will be drawn to Madden's insights and experience, just as millions of viewers are each week during the season. This could become one the library's most popular seasonal books.

While the book is not particularly suitable for whole class reading, it can serve more than the needs and interests of reluctant readers. The book may also be used by a parent with a child in conjunction with television viewing or seeing a game in person. The illustrations and diagrams can make watching the game more interesting and add to one's understanding the sport. Parents who wish to learn about the game of football in order to enjoy their time spent with the football fan or player child will find this a useful and enjoyable book.   G.E.C.

Physical Education
Intermediate
Middle School
Junior High School
High School

439.   Maestro, Betsy. *A More Perfect Union: The Story of Our Constitution*. Illustrated by Giulio Maestro. Lothrop, Lee & Shepard, 1987. ISBN 0-688-06840-5, $12.88. Ages 6-10.

ALA Notable Book

Many books on the Constitution exist and this one is aimed at elementary students. Handsome pictures abound, accompanied by easy-to-understand text. Additional information includes simplified summaries of Constitutional articles and amendments, plus a list of the signers and interesting facts. Projects suggested by the author for K-6 students are to print a colonial newspaper, to write a patriotic song, and to play a game, such as Eraser Tag, while constantly changing the rules, which would point out the necessity of having rules in our lives.

Related Sources

Government, U.S. History Primary

Since the 200th anniversary was celebrated in September, 1987, a wealth of material on the Constitution has become available. One of the best books is *Shh! We're Writing the Constitution*, by Jean Fritz (Putnam, 1987). Videos include *America: Inventing a Nation* (Time-Life), *Constitution at 200* (Guidance Associates, 1986), and *The U.S. Constitution* (six 30-minute segments hosted by Bill Moyers). A sound filmstrip set of merit is *America: Colonization to Constitution* (National Geographic, 1972).   F.M.H.

440.   Mansfield, Sue and Mary Bowen Hall. *Some Reasons for War: How Families, Myths & Warfare Are Connected*. Illustrated with historical art and photography. Crowell, 1988. ISBN 0-690-04666-9, $13.89. Ages 12-up.

What have been some of the reasons for warfare in our past? Who studies war? Why do we need to study war? Mansfield and Hall have successfully answered those questions and have drawn parallels between various kinds of warfare, family structures, and the way children are raised in various societies. They relate how these societies wage war, taking into account the political, economic, literary, and religious factors. Most important, they emphasize the psychological factors involved. From interesting vignettes in history and literature, they develop a definition of war and explore its beginnings. Finally, they discuss the fallacies in popular beliefs about war (for example, that war is part of human nature and is, therefore, inevitable). Mansfield and Hall end their book with a chapter of hope entitled "Building Ramparts of Peace," which emphasizes that people can make a difference, that with understanding we can eliminate the good guy–bad guy myths, and that with courage we can take unpopular, but necessary, positions to dispel those myths.

Peace Studies Middle School Junior High School High School

Related Sources

This book is important for students in history, sociology, psychology, and literature. The sources, index, and related readings suggest real integrity in author research and a commitment to provide for additional research by its readers. Students should not stop with Mansfield and Hall, but should read on and find out what others are saying. Older readers might consider *The Arms Race: Opposing Viewpoints* by David L. Beder, (Greenhaven Press, 1982),

Commodore Perry in the Land of Shogun by Rhoda Blumberg (Lothrop, Lee & Shepard, 1985), *Ain't Gonna Study War No More* by Milton Meltzer (Harper & Row, 1985), and Feldbaum and Bee's *Looking the Tiger in the Eye* (Harper & Row, 1988; see earlier review). They could compare these sources with their history or sociology textbooks to assess how different authors treat the topic of war and the reasons for it.   E.A.H.

Related Sources

441.   Markle, Sandra. *Exploring Winter.* Illustrated by the author. Atheneum, 1984. ISBN 0-689-31065-X, $11.95. Ages 8-11.

As a former science teacher, Markle has the experience and enthusiasm to write an activity book with stories, games, puzzles, and facts about winter. Using a format of short articles, Markle briefly explains interesting and varied facts, from the composition and preservation of snowflakes to how plants and animals adapt to this cold season and simple foods to prepare when children are stuck inside on a winter afternoon. The diagrams, charts, illustrations, and clear directions for experiments and winter games enhance this appealing book for school and family use.

Children, either individually or as a class project, could learn about other games, experiments, recipes, stories, pictures, local field trip possibilities, etc. Individual stories could focus upon personal or family recollections of "Our Most Unforgettable Winter." The results of all these activities could be compiled into a volume entitled "Exploring Our Winter" and catalogued in the school library.   A.H.

Science,
Language Arts
Primary
Intermediate

442.   Markle, Sandra. *Science Mini-Mysteries.* Atheneum, 1988. ISBN 0-689-31291-1, $12.95. Ages 8-12.

Sandra Markle's new book presents science experiments in an unusual style: in the form of short mystery stories. The reader must solve a puzzle, observe results, seek a solution, or answer questions. The instructions for each procedure and the equipment needed are clearly described, and the solutions are printed upside down at the conclusion of each of the twenty-nine activities, so they are handy after the student has tried each experiment. The scientific method universally observed is explained in five steps right on the first page. Black and white photographs or diagrams clearly depict the required materials or the activity in progress.

Any one of the twenty-nine experiments would be suitable for a class project, or they could be conducted at home. One way to organize would be to divide the class into groups of two or three children. Each group would choose an experiment and report on results after completion at home. One particular activity, "The Myterious Floating Egg," crosses into another currcular area: after the class, or small group, determines that added salt makes the egg float, it would be logical to begin research on the Great Salt Lake or the Dead Sea to identify the effects of concentrated salt water on swimmers or boats.   F.M.H.

Science
Primary
Intermediate
Middle School

443.   Marrin, Albert. *1812: The War Nobody Won*. Illustrated with prints, maps, and engravings. Atheneum, 1985. ISBN 0-689-31075-7, $12.95. Ages 9-up.

When studying the War of 1812, students usually learn about the burning of the White House, but few know that the U.S. earlier burned the Parliament Buildings in Toronto. They learn about impressment, but little about the cruelty of British Naval commanders. Marrin's complete yet succinct work provides much detailed information, plus many vignettes and biographical anecdotes that a teacher can use to give substance to the brief treatment of the War of 1812 in most school textbooks. The phrase "Negro sailors and soldiers" to describe the heroic deeds of Black men is somewhat balanced by the act of including such information that should be known by school children—especially those in inner city schools.

U.S. History
Intermediate
Middle School
Junior High School

This book is especially useful for preparing classes for field trips to such historical sites as Ft. Meigs (Ohio), Ft. McHenry (Maryland), or another location where the War of 1812 was fought. Such a trip will be much more meaningful if the teacher reads the applicable sections of the book to the class before leaving. Students can locate or identify on-site a place or object mentioned in the book. In addition, the maps and old prints can be enlarged for individual use or prepared for the overhead projector for use with large groups. A mural-sized map can be drawn using an opaque projector and mounted either in the classroom, in the library, or in a hallway.   J.A.F.

444.   Marrin, Albert. *The War for Independence: The Story of the American Revolution*. Atheneum, 1988. Illustrated with maps and prints. ISBN 0-689-31390-X, $14.95. Ages 10-up.

Although events on the frontier and Gates's defeat of Burgoyne are described, Marrin's military history of the revolution dwells on Washington's ability to prevent his army from being destroyed. Unlike the stilted accounts of the war so prevalent in high school history books, this author knows well how to tell a story. He underscores the meaning of significant events by dwelling on the human dimension. He also knows the value of using an anecdote and historical aside to make a point. For example, he points out that "Yankee Doodle Dandy" was originally used by the British to ridicule and taunt the colonists. Yet it was played by the American army at the surrender of the British at Saratoga. Similarly, he tells of the tears of the British at the surrender at Yorktown and Washington's emotions when he bid farewell to his troops. This is excellent historical writing for students of the American Revolution from middle school through high school.

Related Sources

This work completes Marrin's trilogy. His earlier works were *Struggle for a Continent: The French and Indian Wars* (1987) and *1812: The War Nobody Won* (1985), both published by Atheneum. Instead of students preparing the traditional research report on a historical individual or era, they might benefit from doing a study of a historian such as Marrin whose works deal with an era known by students and whose books are quite readable. Talented junior and senior high school students could discuss perspective ("How do you know he writes from the viewpoint of an American?"), his use of evidence ("How does the author use data to prove his points?"), and analysis of causality ("In the author's opinion what causes major events to happen? Does he attribute changes to individuals or events?").   J.F.A.

U.S. History
Intermediate
Middle School
Junior High School

445.   McCurdy, Michael. *Hannah's Farm: The Seasons on an Early American Homestead*. Illustrated by the author. Holiday House, 1988. ISBN 0-8234-0700-4, $12.95. Ages 6-9.

Through lyrical text and beautiful wood engravings, Michael McCurdy gives his readers a glimpse into the past. He follows young Hannah, an actual ancestor of his, through a year on Morgan Farm, which is McCurdy's home today. The reader is taken through winter's idle time when the only major chore is wood cutting and Grandfather has time to spin tales about how he cleared the forest to build Morgan Farm. Spring brings maple sugaring, plowing, and planting. This is the time, too, when the big barn is raised by neighbors using tools with "funny names such as 'gluts' and 'beetles.'" Summer is time for haying and fall for the harvest. October means cider making and apple drying. The book ends with the family's Christmas tradition, changing now as cut trees become commonplace. The wood engravings are lively and detailed, suitably evoking the early American setting.

After reading *Hannah's Farm* aloud, ask children to think about the chores their family does and how these change with the seasons. While many children today do not live as close to nature as do those on a farm, there are still seasonal activities, like lawn mowing and changing our wardrobes to suit the weather. Children's play even changes with the seasons. Make a bulletin board with a "Circle of Seasons" upon it. This can simply be a large circle divided into four season or twelve month slices. On a small square or circle of paper, children can draw pictures, complete with explanatory captions, to illustrate a seasonal activity. These can then be placed upon the appropriate section of the "Circle of Seasons." *A Circle of Seasons* by Myra Cohn Livingston and beautifully illustrated by Leonard Everett Fisher (Holiday, 1982) could extend the experience to include poetry and art.   M.A.C.

Science,
Social Studies
Primary
Intermediate

Related Source

446.   Meltzer, Milton. *Ain't Gonna Study War No More*. Harper & Row, 1985. ISBN 0-06-024200-0, $11.89. Ages 12-up.

Meltzer's very readable story of America's peace seekers picks up its title from the familiar spiritual, "Down By The Riverside." The primary contribution of this historical account is the clear reminder that opposition to violence and war is as American as the military actions themselves. Meltzer observes that the United States has participated in

ALA Notable Book
ALA Best Book

seven officially-declared wars and that in each of these there have been strong opposition movements, often spearheaded by religious and political pacifists. Meltzer's account provides a very helpful account of America's peace movements, with many fascinating human interest stories, but it is also clearly a partial account. Primary emphasis is given to the Quaker religious movement (Society of Friends) and the various vocal political movements which arose in times of crisis, with very scant attention to such groups as the Brethren and the Mennonites, which have, at least since World War II, provided the largest number of religious conscientious objectors in the United States. *Ain't Gonna Study War No More* is crucial reading for young people in this nuclear age when one more American war could well prove to be the last.

Meltzer's history fills a gap in American history collections for young people, and compels its readers to do more research. Students can write for newsletters or search out primary source materials from such places as the Peace Resource Center and Hiroshima/Nagasaki Memorial Collection at Wilmington (Ohio) College, the Center for Peaceful Change at Kent State University, and the Mennonite Historical Library at Bluffton (Ohio) College.   E.N.

Peace Studies
Middle School
Junior High School
High School

447.   Meltzer, Milton. *Mary McLeod Bethune: Voice of Black Hope*. Viking Kestrel, 1987. ISBN 0-670-80744-3, $10.95. Ages 7-11.

The newest addition to the "Women of Our Time" series is this sensitive, well-written biography of the Black educator and activist Mary McLeod Bethune. Meltzer tells the story of a poor girl from rural South Carolina whose life is a commitment to education. Her struggle as a child to acquire her own education foreshadows the challenges she meets in establishing what becomes Bethune-Cookman College. The book is replete with anecdotes about her challenges to racism, successful in part because of the organizational ability she demonstrated by forming The National Council of Negro Women. While rightly portraying the woman as the hero that she was, Meltzer does not hide other aspects of her life: she was divorced, overweight, and possessed what sometimes was an overwhelming personality.

A few years ago, Steve Allen produced a series of provocative programs for public television called "Meeting of the Minds." The format consisted of prominent individuals from different historical eras discussing philosophical issues. Their positions were predictable given their writings or achievements. If a teacher assumed the role of Steve Allen, the moderator of the program, and girls were assigned to be the characters from the "Women of Our Time" series, an interesting discussion might ensue regarding issues such as sexism, power, or personal conflicts that might occur when a woman assumes a leadership role. It would be particularly effective since this series includes not only historical figures, but also contemporary ones, such as Mother Teresa, Martina Navratilova, and Diana Ross.   J.F.A.

Women's Studies,
Black Studies
Intermediate
Middle School
Junior High School

448. Meltzer, Milton. *Rescue: The Story of How Gentiles Saved Jews in the Holocaust*. Harper & Row, 1988. ISBN 0-06-024209-4, $12.89. Ages 12-up.

Children need to know that there exists in the spirit of humans an ability to rise above seemingly insurmountable forces. Children can read about the courage of ten gentle heroes of the Holocaust in *Rescue*. Meltzer, a man worthy of this challenge, has written an important book that records the exploits of well known "Righteous Ones," as well as those whose heroic acts are less recognized.

There is a current emphasis on "writing across the curriculum." This valuable work facilitates that goal in social studies. It can be particularly effective to have children record their reflections after experiencing an emotional stimulus, such as reading this book or hearing a chapter read to them. Following discussions with a parent or significant others, students could write an introspective essay dealing with the following kinds of questions: Would someone in my family have been a "Righteous One?" Would I want them to be? For what or for whom would I volunteer to risk my life or my family's lives? If America needs heroes, our children need to explore what it is that makes one heroic. *Rescue* could make that happen in your classroom.   J.F.A.

ALA Best Book
ALA Notable Book

Holocaust Studies,
Middle School
Junior High School
High School

449. Meltzer, Milton. *Starting from Home: A Writer's Beginnings*. Illustrated with photographs. Viking Kestrel, 1988. ISBN 0-670-81604-3, $13.95. Ages 12-up.

Starting with his parents' emigration from the Ukraine and moving through their early years in America, Meltzer sets the stage for this partial, yet insightful, memoir of his first seventeen years. We learn of his insatiable search for knowledge and what he uncovered as part of that search. We meet people who influenced him greatly because they survived difficult times and dared to make a difference, and they challenged Meltzer to do the same. Adolescent readers today are fortunate to have the opportunity to learn from Meltzer about his personal journey and the world that influenced and gave shape to his ideas. Meltzer enjoys the status of being an award-winning author of histories and biographies for the intermediate and adolescent reader. Now he has added another fine work of art to his body of literature.

There is a growing collection of biographies, memoirs, and autobiographical works on authors of literature for young people. Students might read several such books for analysis and comparison, seeking out those people, events, and experiences that motivated writers, as well as influenced what they chose to write about. Such works include Jean Craighead George's *Journey Inward* (Dutton, 1982), Jean Fritz's *Homesick: My Own Story* (Putnam, 1982), Beverly Cleary's *A Girl from Yamhill* (Morrow, 1988; see earlier review), and Roald Dahl's *Boy: Tales of Childhood* (Farrar, Straus & Giroux, 1984). Addison Wesley publishes an excellent series of autobiographies by such familiar and award-winning artists of children's books as Trina Schart Hyman and Margot Zemach.   E.A.H.

Author Studies,
Literature
Middle School
Junior High School
High School

Related Sources

450.   Meyer, Carolyn. *Voices of Northern Ireland: Growing Up in a Troubled Land*. Gulliver Books, 1987. ISBN 0-15-200635-4, $15.95. Ages 12-up.

Related Source

This is not a cursory, one-sided look at what the natives call "The Troubles" in Northern Ireland. Carolyn Meyer, who also wrote *Voices of South Africa* (Harcourt Brace Jovanovich, 1986), researched her subject and then traveled throughout Northern Ireland for six weeks talking with Protestant and Catholic teens, their parents, and the people who work with youth programs. She even talked with some teens taking part in Channels of Peace, an exchange program designed to mix Protestants and Catholics in a neutral territory, both before and at the end of their trip. The end result is as depressing as the incessant rain that fell upon Meyer during her entire visit. She concludes that the roots of "The Troubles" are twisted in history, politics, and economics and the people seemed unwilling, or unable, to compromise. The few lights piercing the haze of depression, usually made by people devoting their lives to promoting peace, are worth noting. Meyer's anecdotal style is easy to read and yet manages to convey information clearly. She is cautious throughout, careful to label personal comments as such and to alert the reader when she thought the young people she was interviewing were putting her on.

Contemporary Affairs
Middle School
Junior High School
High School

Students should find themselves asking what it is about Northern Ireland that makes a solution to "The Troubles" seem so impossible. They will also undoubtedly draw parallels to various "troubles" America has had to deal with, particularly racism. While American problems still abound, citizens of this country do not live under a constant threat of violence. Factors that may account for this difference include the size of the countries, the number of alternative churches, the amount of good farmland, the availability of employment, and the personalities of people who immigrate vs. those who stay put. After thorough discussion and further research, students might engage in some creative problem solving about Northern Ireland and evaluate the results in light of all they have learned.   M.A.C.

451.   Munro, Roxie. *The Inside-Outside Book of Washington, D.C.* Illustrated by the author. Dutton, 1987. ISBN 0-525-44298-7, $12.95. All ages.

The bright, oversized, detailed drawings of Washington landmarks in this book—including Kennedy Memorial Stadium and Georgetown row houses—will provide children with a pleasing introduction to our capitol's built environment. The Library of Congress, The Supreme Court, The Lincoln Memorial, The Bureau of Engraving and Printing, The Organization of American States, The White House, and The United States Capitol are shown as the title suggests: one page has an interior view and another the exterior view. Words are restricted to identifying the buildings. The adult reader will appreciate the after page with additional information about each building.

"What is Washington?" For those literal-minded six or seven-year-olds the answer "the seat of our government" is not sufficient. Munro provides the teacher with a way of helping the young child understand that it is a city with impressive, monumental buildings where important things happen and where tourists visit. It is also the President's home from which he is interviewed on TV. Primary teachers should appreciate having an appropriate method of teaching children about our nation's capital.   J.F.A.

Social Studies
Primary
Intermediate

452.   Murphy, Jim. *Guess Again*. Illustrated by photographs of patent drawings. Bradbury, 1986. ISBN 0-02-767720-6, $12.95. All ages.

This is the equally successful sequel to Murphy's *Weird & Wacky Inventions* (Crown, 1978). Here, as in the first volume, the reader is given a drawing from a patent applicaiton along with brief clues (i.e., the date or general use of the invention) and is then asked to choose its identity from among four choices. It is not as easy as it sounds. The author has selected some surprising and far-fetched devices: a tapeworm trap, an egg counter (it straps right on to the chicken and keeps a tally of her production), a beard grinder, and 42 others. The author's comments on the need for each invention plus his brief sketches of five inventors make this book a rich source of social history as well as a delight for the merely curious.

Sequel to
Weird & Wacky
Inventions

Murphy makes clear that we have been and continue to be a nation of inventors, that where individuals have seen a need, they have sought to satisfy it in inventive ways. Younger readers might enjoy drafting a creative design for an invention that solves some problem in their lives. Perhaps the teacher or librarian could pose a problem that needs an invention to eliminate it, encouraging children who work individually or in groups to see whose invention is most plausible. "The Olympics of the Mind," a program that many schools participate in, poses problems like this for students. For information about "Olympics of the Mind," write to OM Association Inc., P.O. Box 27, Glassboro, NJ 08028, or call (609) 881-1603.   H.M.

Science,
Social Studies
Intermediate
Middle School
Junior High School

453.   Oechsli, Helen and Kelly Oechsli. *In My Garden: A Child's Gardening Book*. Illustrated by Kelly Oechsli. Macmillan, 1985. ISBN 0-02-768510-1, $12.95. Ages 4-7.

This gardening book is a thorough presentation with entertaining illustrations. The information is geared toward gardeners with limited space and a minimum of tools, but it also has instructions for more ambitious projects. The subjects covered include outdoor plants, weeding and thinning, composting, indoor gardens, and helpful insects and animals. The directions are clear and encouraging to those who might otherwise be hesitant to begin a project of this sort.

Most younger children enjoy growing plants. Preschool and primary grade teachers can use this as a motivating and helpful introduction to a gardening activity, since the emphasis is on an actual

Science
Primary

garden rather than on raising a single plant indoors or out. An area the size of a window box to a good-sized garden plot set aside on the school grounds will suffice. Other books about gardening to share are Lois Ehlert's *Planting a Rainbow* (Harcourt Brace Jovanovich, 1988), Judy Taylor's *Sophie and Jack Help Out* (Putnam, 1984), Bruce McMillan's *Growing Colors* (Lothrop, Lee & Shepard, 1988), and Cynthia Rylant's *This Year's Garden* (Bradbury, 1984).   C.S.

Related Sources

454.   Parnall, Peter. *Winter Barn*. Illustrated by the author. Macmillan, 1986. ISBN 0-02-770170-0, $12.95. Ages 5-8.

Peter Parnall demonstrates in *Winter Barn* that he can write as well as he can draw: "At thirty below, with each icy breeze that darts through cracks and holes, wooden fibers wince and complain. They creak. They crackle. They play their own music, those great oak beams hewn two hundred years ago." Into this barn come all kinds of creatures—feathered, furry, scaly, and creepy! These are pictured in detailed, finely-textured drawings, which, though departing from the style of Parnall's collaborations with Byrd Baylor, still exhibit that sense of design and oneness of creatures to environment that is so characteristic of Parnall. This is another fine example, like Kathryn Lasky's *Sugaring Time* (Macmillan, 1983), of how well written and stimulating an informational book can be.

Related Source

Winter Barn could be used with Ronald M. Fisher's *Animals in Winter* (National Geographic, 1982) as part of a study of the changes this harsh season brings to wild creatures. Other resources, that would extend the study of winter are *Exploring Winter* by Sandra Markle (Atheneum, 1984), *Shivers and Goose Bumps: How We Keep Warm* by Franklyn Branley (Crowell, 1984), and *Snowy Day: Stories and Poems*, edited by Caroline Feller Bauer (Lippincott, 1986). Students may want to contrast these books by researching, writing, and illustrating their own "Summer Barn," "Animals in Summer," or "Exploring Summer."   M.A.C.

Science, Language Arts Primary

Related Sources

455.   Pellowski, Anne. *The Family Storytelling Handbook*. Illustrated by Lynn Sweat. Macmillan, 1987. ISBN 0-02-770610-9, $15.95. All ages.

This is another "must have" storytelling handbook by Anne Pellowski, the author of *The Story Vine* (Macmillan, 1984). Pellowski describes the whys, whens, whats, and hows of storytelling. She discusses it as a natural family activity, a useful and enriching entertainment for all kinds of situations. In doing so, she takes the "scaries" out of "performing" stories. As in *The Story Vine*, she also gives numerous stories that can be easily learned and successfully shared. Many involve props—handkerchiefs, fingers, sand trays, etc.— and their use is illustrated and explained alongside the story in a three column format. She even presents a simple finger story in ten languages written phonetically so that anyone can read them!

Related Source

Librarians may want to highlight this book in some way so that it will circulate among its intended audience: families. A workshop on family storytelling could even be given in the library setting using *The Family Storytelling Handbook* as a text. Each participant should come away with a small stock of stories and perhaps a new passion. Many libraries also offer babysitting courses for teens, which would be enriched by the addition of storytelling techniques for entertaining children. Teachers could use the book in a similar way with high school students studying child development and family living.   M.A.C.

456.   Pellowski, Anne. *The Story Vine*. Illustrated by Lynn Sweat. Macmillan, 1984. ISBN 0-02-770590-0, $14.95. Ages 12-up.

This is a varied and practical source book for storytellers. Included are stories that use realia in the telling: string stories, sand paintings, chalk drawings, nesting dolls, finger games, and other materials. Parents, teachers, baby sitters, grandparents and other storytellers will find a rapt audience when they tell these prop stories, just as have the storytellers in Africa who use the story vine from which the title comes.

These stories can delight and amaze children. They take practice, but they are worth it. Also look at Verna Aardema's *Tales From the Story Hat* (Coward-McCann, 1960). These stories, too, were told via realia, but this was in the form of objects kept on a big hat the storyteller wore. Either of these books could be used to make a bulletin board full of stories waiting to be told.   M.A.C.

457.   Reader's Digest. *Facts and Fallacies: Stories of the Strange and Unusual*. Illustrated with photographs and drawings. Reader's Digest, 1988. ISBN 0-89577-273-6, $23.95. Ages 12-up.

Unusual ideas and customs, footsteps into the unknown, and amazing feats of building and engineering are just a few of the sections in *Fact and Fallacies* that should grab the reader's attention and hold it fast. Each topic in this large format book receives one to two pages of coverage with photos included whenever possible. This book contains approximately 400 stories of uncommon and aberrant events and provides whatever information is known about each occurrence. There is something here for every taste and for all ages.

This is an excellent reference book to have in the classroom, especially in social studies, history, or the sciences. A routine lesson can be given a fresh and stimulating send–off when the teacher pulls an provocative, obscure fact and the story behind it from this wide ranging volume. An example is the section entitled "The Bone Wars" (page 22-23) which describes the facts upon which Kathryn Lasky based her novel of the same name, *The Bone Wars* (Morrow, 1988). *Facts & Fallacies* is an excellent contribution to the faculty library as well as to the school library.   L.A.B.

458.   Reit, Seymour. *Behind Rebel Lines*. Harcourt Brace Jovanovich, 1988. ISBN 0-15-200416-5, $12.95. Ages 9-12.

What an exciting and memorable way to learn about the Civil War!
Sarah Emmonds was a feminist long before the word became
popularized. She enlisted in the Union Army disguised as a man and
often acted as a spy for the North. Each chapter of this entertaining and
lively book tells of one of the many disguises she assumed and the
characters she played: a black slave, a bumbling young soldier, or a
middle aged rag picker. Sarah will amaze readers with her courage and
shrewdness. Reit brings this biography to life with writing that is
smooth and fast-paced. A guide to other stories about the Civil War and
the part women played in it is included for those who want to read more.

This book is an excellent accompaniment to the textbook study of
the Civil War. Each chapter tells a complete story and can be read,
studied, and discussed independently. Students can discuss how battles
were often won not solely because of military might, but also because of
help from spies and sympathetic citizens. Dorothy Sterling's classic
Captain of the Planter (Doubleday, 1958) is a tribute to ex-slave
Robert Smalls's heroism during the same conflict. These books and
others like Ann Rinaldi's *The Last Silk Dress* (Holiday House,
1988), a novel based upon the true story of a Confederate surveillance
balloon made of donated ladies' dresses, help focus students on the
importance of common people in the flow of history.   L.A.B.

U.S. History
Intermediate
Middle School
Junior High School

Related Source

459.   Richter, Elizabeth. *Losing Someone You Love: When A
Brother or Sister Dies*. Photographs by the author.
Putnam, 1986. ISBN 0-399-21243-4, $11.95. Ages 12-up.

Richter's book is not a standard "how to cope with death" book,
and it does not go through the steps of the grieving process. It simply
serves as a forum for sixteen young people to express how they felt
when a sibling died and, by doing so, help other young people in similar
situations. Each autobiographical story (about 600 words long),
accompanied by a photograph of the surviving brother or sister, tells
about events prior to the death, the impact on the family, as well as
reflections of the brother or sister about their loss. A myriad of problems
that a child might experience are discussed, such as guilt, fear of the loss
of parents, emotional outbursts, grieving parents, and the failure of
parents to adjust. The emotions expressed by these young people are
compelling, insightful, and worth reading.

Because of its very specific and sensitive topic, *Losing Someone
You Love* is probably best read independently by a student who can
bond with one of the young people telling his or her story. The student
and teacher might privately discuss the book or a particular story in it.
Teachers who do share this book with a class, however, might want to
do the unexpected: discuss the perspective that thinking about how
relatively short our time on earth is gives us a different perspective on
our daily family relationships.   J.F.A./M.A.C.

Social Studies,
Family Life
Junior High School
High School

460. Roy, Ron. *Whose Shoes Are These?* Photographs by Rosmarie Hausherr. Clarion, 1988. ISBN 0-89919-445-1, $13.95. Ages 4-7.

The photographs of small feet standing in adult footwear emphasize that this concept book is for a very young audience. Close up pictures of ballet shoes, ski boots, fluffy slippers, swim fins, snowshoes, and fifteen other items worn on the feet are explained with young children in mind. The question-answer format invites participation as youngsters learn about familiar things we put on our feet and the special circumstances for their use. The information is clear and at a level appropriate for young children. This is an excellent companion book to Roy and Hausherr's *Whose Hat Is That?* (Clarion, 1987).

Related Source

Here is a golden opportunity to plan some basic categorizing activities. The shoes pictured in *Whose Shoes Are These?* can be easily grouped in a number of different categories (e.g., by function, by where they are worn, etc.). Younger children can either add new examples to categories the teacher identifies, or they can create new categories for the items in the book. They can cut from magazines pictures of different shoes that belong to each category and paste them on a personal or class chart. The activity can be readily extended to categorizing other groups of objects, such as tools, toys, foods, clothing in general, etc. Be sure each time to discuss the common and distinguishing charac-teristics of each grouping or category. H.M.

Math, Science, Social Studies Primary

461. Samuels, Cynthia K. *It's a Free Country!: A Young Person's Guide to Politics and Elections.* Illustrated with photographs. Atheneum, 1988. ISBN 0-689-31416-7, $12.95. Ages 8-12.

Samuels outlines the nature of the political/electoral process through anecdotes, history, and a realistic view of how we do things in this country. Seeing politics from the inside, she says, is critical to being able to make the process work for the good of society and to under-standing what is happening at all levels of government. Why people run for office, organizing support and getting money, political parties, campaigning, the electoral process—these and other topics provide a sharp picture of election politics. This is a forthright and positive view that encourages young people to be informed about political events so that they can contribute to the political process, even at relatively young ages.

Every four years teachers and parents have the opportunity to involve young people in national elections. There is an overwhelming amount of information about candidates and campaigns from television and newspapers. Samuels's book can be the primer by which teachers can help young people understand the subtleties and complexities of political elections. The short sections of the book make it possible to read aloud for 7–10 minutes and discuss the concepts, providing additional information for the rest of the period, thereby completing a reading and discussion of the book over a two-week period. Take the

Government Intermediate Middle School

opportunity to point out any current campaigns that illustrate the concepts. The books listed in the bibliography can provide outside reading for those who want to go beyond.   H.M.

462.   Schwartz, David M. *How Much is a Million?* Illustrated by Steven Kellogg. Lothrop, Lee & Shepard, 1985. ISBN 0-688-04050-0, $15.00. Ages 7-up.

ALA Notable Book

How Much is a Million? is an effective and imaginative picture book that portrays the enormity of numbers. Kellogg has humorously conceptualized what a million, a billion, and a trillion might be. A million "all-star" kids standing on each other's shoulders would almost reach the moon. A tower of a trillion kids would stretch past Mars and Jupiter, too. And if you think this is just fancy, at the end of the book the author has included the mathematical computations in small print for older readers.

Math
Primary
Intermediate
Middle School

This is a book that can stretch from primary to even high school math classes. Older math students should find the illustrations fun and the computations silly but exacting. Small children may come away with the idea that a million is a lot, a billion is more, and a trillion is out-of-sight (but that puts them on a par with most of us). The computations are not terribly difficult, and even younger children could be encouraged to find novel ways to explain how much 50, 100, or even 200 is. Older students could use Schwartz's computational method for more intricate descriptions, like how many cars make a mile-long line.   C.S.

463.   Sender, Ruth Minsky. *The Cage.* Macmillan, 1986. ISBN 0-02-781830-6, $13.95. Ages 12-up.

This biography of a young teenage girl tells sadly familiar stories about the Holocaust: rejection by former gentile friends, the physical deprivations and uncertainty of everyday life in the ghetto, followed by the inevitable cattle car trips to the camps where each day is a struggle against indignities, suffering, and fear. The children had to act as adults to survive. Families were destroyed. Yet in this world without food or joy, the author acquired a great treasure: a pencil and a brown bag to write her poetry. Her poetry, as well as the kindness and brutality she experienced while ill, reveals deep insights into human nature,. though the book never veers from the sad and horrible truth of her story.

Holocaust Studies
Junior High School
High School

Related Sources

There is a growing number of biographies appropriate for older readers that a teacher could share to help students comprehend the enormity of inhumanity that was the Holocaust. Recent additions include Anne E. Neimark's biography *One Man's Valor: Leo Baeck and the Holocaust* (Lodestar, 1986) and Barbara Gehrts's autobiographical *Don't Say A Word* (Macmillan, 1986). These resources should help student groups better understand memorable moments in a history we wish we did not have.   J.F.A.

464. Seuling, Barbara. *Elephants Can't Jump and Other Freaky Facts about Animals*. Illustrated by the author. Lodestar, 1985. ISBN 0-525-67155-2, $9.95. Ages 9-12.

Trivia fans are in luck. Barbara Seuling has gathered a superb collection of unusual but truly odd facts about animal behavior. She has creatively placed humorous drawings between such surprising and fascinating facts as: cows give more milk when listening to music and moose are so nearsighted that some have mistaken automobiles for their mates! These intriguing and captivating bits of information should entertain a wide range of readers, especially those labelled "reluctant."

Elephants Can't Jump is a handy companion for teachers. To settle a restless class in the morning, after lunch, or at the start of a class period, teachers could present "Today's Freaky Fact." If students want to look up a fact about a specific animal, an index is provided. Trivia fans may also be interested in Seuling's *You Can't Sneeze with Your Eyes Open: And Other Freaky Facts About the Human Body* (Lodestar, 1986)   C.G.T.

Science Intermediate Middle School

Related Source

465. Seuling, Barbara. *It Is Illegal to Quack Like a Duck & Other Freaky Laws*. Illustrated by Gwenn Seuling. Lodestar, 1988. ISBN 0-525-67250-8, $11.95. Ages 10-up.

In twenty-two short chapters, Seuling explores yet another series of incredible laws, incredible because it is hard to believe such stupid—yes, stupid!—laws were ever written, let alone enforced. For example, "in Omaha, Nebraska, a person receiving an injury due to a defective pavement must advise the city clerk of the fact five days before the accident in order to receive compensation." Each brief chapter is organized around a theme and carries a clever title reflecting it, like "Shave and a Haircut, Two Bits," "Dollars and Sense," or "Isn't It Romantic?" In her introduction, Seuling assures us that "although the laws that appear in this book may no longer be on the books by the time you read this, they are—or were—for real." Another of Seuling's freaky facts books is *You Can't Sneeze with Your Eyes Open: And Other Freaky Facts About the Human Body* (Lodestar, 1986). Both books are entertaining enough to make a person want to dance a jig. Students in Purdy, Missouri, had better resist the temptation, however, for it is illegal to dance in the schools there!

Related Source

As they are reading through *It Is Illegal to Quack Like a Duck & Other Freaky Laws*, students may ask themselves how in the world these laws became law. This could result in an interesting activity in critical thinking. In small groups, the students could discuss why they think the laws might have been thought necessary at the time they were written. Students might, in some cases, want to do some research to substantiate their guesses. For example, "In Scotland, during Mary Stuart's reign, playacting was against the law" could lead students to reading more about that historical period. This background reading is likely to reveal plausible reasons for the law. The small groups could share their ideas with the class for further discussion.   M.A.C.

Social Studies Intermediate Middle School

466.   Shaffer, Carolyn and Erica Fielder. *City Safaris*. Drawings by Erica Fielder. Sierra Club, 1987. ISBN 0-87156-720-2, $9.95. All ages.

Through dozens of games, treasure hunts, and imaginative activities, Shaffer and Fielder prove that the city is a wonderful place for a safari. Both adults and young people will find out that a city holds many different types of nature and "wild" places if they only look closely enough. The inventive activities and worksheets may be used with a single child or a group, and range from sensory experiences of the environment to community projects that can be implemented by children. This book may be used in correlation with science, social studies, or ecology, and it outlines ideas about how to adapt activities for different age groups. No matter how the book is used, children and adults can learn to be more careful observers of their environment, as well as to better understand the city systems in which most of the population lives.

Local History,
Language Arts
Primary
Intermediate
Middle School

In addition to using the book for its intended purpose, teachers may also want to extend the activities into a writing experience. Students may want to imagine themselves as part of the city vegetation and tell how it feels to live there as opposed to in the country, or tell the advantages of living near the city dump from a rat's perspective. While students are "on safari," they could keep a notebook and record the new sounds, smells, and sights they encounter along the way. Students can then expand upon these notes, using them as they write either personal narratives or imaginative stories about their safari.   K.B.B.

467.   Shefelman, Janice. *Victoria House*. Illustrated by Tom Shefelman. Gulliver, 1988. ISBN 0-15-200630-3, $12.95. Ages 4-8.

Teaching children to have a reverence for the past should not be restricted to celebrating birthdays of national heroes. *Victoria House* tells of two architects and their son who find a deserted Queen Anne style house which is scheduled to be demolished. They buy it and have it transported to the city where it eventually becomes their home and office. Like Spier's lively *Tin Lizzie* (Doubleday, 1975), which ends happily with the restoration of a Model T, and von Tscharner's impressive *New Providence: A Changing Cityscape* (Harcourt Brace Jovanovich, 1987), which concludes with the successful preservation of a town square, *Victoria House* acknowledges the importance of enjoying that which was built in the past. These books and others like them are helpful for those who wish to make the study of history come alive to children.

Related Sources

Local History
Primary
Intermediate

As this book celebrates preservation, it should be available in any school located in or near an historic district to help children understand the passions of their neighbors and parents for old houses. It should also be included on the book table when the primary class is studying "shelters." Perhaps a more exciting activity would be to establish a class historical museum. Each child can contribute an old object, tell its age and origin, and why it is loved by his or her family. Old newspaper pictures, family photographs, boxes or bottles from former businesses, old city maps, etc. can be added over the year. Label the objects and display them for other classes, as well as for parent and community programs or exhibits.   J.F.A.

468.   Silverstein, Alvin and Virginia. *World of the Brain*. Illustrated by Warren Budd. Morrow, 1986. ISBN 0-688-05777-2, $11.75. Ages 12-up.

There is so much scientists are learning about the brain and brain behavior that this well organized and clearly-written book is a welcome addition to a middle school or high school library (many adults will find it fascinating as well). The Silversteins, who have written scores of excellent books for children and young adults, discuss in understandable terms brain research involving many animals, including humans; memory, intelligence, and emotions; left brain-right brain relationships; and the influence of various drugs on the mind. Equally important are questions of ethics and morality that new discoveries pose for society. For example, if research shows us how to control behavior through surgery or drugs, who shall decide what behavior is appropriate? This approach to presenting information about research and raising moral/social implications of new information is refreshing and deserves praise. Readers will be asked to do more than simply absorb facts.

The questions that are posed in the context of presenting information are significant and worthy of broad discussion among older students. Teachers and librarians (as well as parents, clergy, and other interested individuals) can review the text for the value questions posed, and the context in which they are raised. Discussions can focus on the urge to acquire new information versus using the power and responsibility the new information gives us. Though the issues are complex and value-laden, young people deserve the guidance of wise adults.   H.M.

Science
Junior High School
High School

469.   Simon, Seymour. *The Dinosaur is the Biggest Animal That Ever Lived and Other Wrong Ideas You Thought Were True*. Illustrated by Giulio Maestro. Lippincott, 1984. ISBN 0-397-32076-0, $10.89. Ages 7-10.

Simon's book is excellent. The title alone draws attention of the reader who wants to find out just what "wrong ideas" have been accepted as fact. Through his informative and entertaining selections, e.g., snakes are slimy, lightning never strikes twice, lemmings march to the sea to commit suicide, the sky is blue, Simon reminds us that we must not accept absurd ideas just because we lack knowledge or understanding. In fact, the tales we have all been exposed to are made to sound so absurd that we will wonder how we could ever have believed them.

This book should be in every science collection, but would also team up well with Jean Fritz's *Who's That Stepping on Plymouth*

Related Source

Rock? (Coward, McCann & Geoghegan, 1975) in which myths in social studies and the writing of history are brought to light, helping young readers better understand how tales of our past have, over time, been accepted as fact. Also of comparable interest is David and Marymae Klein's *How Do You Know It's True?* (Scribners, 1984), a very useful book for older readers that helps students sort out the truth from nonsense in what they read or hear.   J.R.W./E.A.H.

470.   Simon, Seymour. *Galaxies*. Illustrated with photographs. Morrow, 1988. ISBN 0-688-08004-9, $12.88. Ages 4-8.

As is true in the six earlier books in this series (*Mars, Saturn, Jupiter, Uranus, Stars, The Sun,* all published by Morrow) *Galaxies* displays page after page of brilliant color photographs, including computer-colored examples with large print explanations superimposed on top. The text contains comparisons with familiar objects such as: "An elliptical galaxy looks like a squashed ball," or "If a dozen tennis balls were spread out across the U.S., they would be more crowded than most of the stars in the (Milky Way) Galaxy." Because of the almost startling photographs from space, Simon's books succeed in whetting the appetite for more in-depth study using sources with more detailed information.

It is difficult for a child to grasp the enormity of space, but this book offers explanations in simple terms. Perhaps, unlike adults, children may better comprehend these startling facts since they are accustomed already to everyday wonders and have an unending capacity for discovery. Because the concept of infinity is difficult for children (and many adults), Ekker's book *What is Beyond the Hill* (Lippincott, 1985) is another book which may help describe this concept for a young child. The Milky Way is perhaps the most visible evidence of a galaxy. Encourage children to look at the night sky, particularly in dark rural areas where they may live, might visit, or merely drive through. Observing the skies with simple binoculars will greatly increase the detail and scope of what can be seen without sophisticated telescopes.   F.M.H.

471.   Simon, Seymour. *How to Talk to Your Computer*. Illustrated by Barbara and Ed Emberley. Crowell, 1985. ISBN 0-690-04449-6, $11.89. Ages 5-9.

Seymour Simon, former science teacher and author of many science books for the young reader, provides a rich and timely volume on computers for Crowell's "Let's Read-and-find-Out-Science Book" series. The text is simple to understand, with careful explanations on microcomputer use. Information is also clarified by Ed and Barbara Emberley's colorful drawings. Handicapped children are portrayed with their computers, as are boys and girls of different races. Girls, as well as boys, are shown as scientists and athletes. Funny robots, a turtle, and tiny mouse also grace the pages as both BASIC and Logo languages are introduced. A definition of programs follows with clear step-by-step directions for writing and running them.

As more and more of our school children are using computers at home and in the classroom, a simple book of this nature is a welcome addition. A teacher may wish to use the book with children who are being introduced to a computer for the very first time. A list of special computer vocabulary words could be prepared, as explained and illustrated in this book. In addition, some pages have exercises for rearranging steps in a program in correct order. Older children could write some simple programs of their own.   F.M.H.

472.   Simon, Seymour. *Turtle Talk: A Beginner's Book of Logo*. Illustrated by Barbara and Ed Emberley. Crowell, 1986. ISBN 0-690-04522-0, $11.89. Ages 5-9.

In this fifth in a series of books about computers, Seymour Simon introduces young children to the computer language "Logo." Logo is often the first computer language to which young children are exposed and *Turtle Talk* does an good job of teaching the basic programming skills. Colorful cartoon characters illustrate the step-by-step directions as students learn how to program their computer to move their turtle around the screen in different patterns. As children master the simple concepts of Logo, *Turtle Talk* will help guide them to more complex experiences.

Logo is a very satisfying computer language for children to learn and use. It offers exciting on-screen experiences with minimal programming skills. After mastering a few basic concepts of Logo, students may pre-plan their time with the computer by using graph paper to map out designs for their turtles to make. Programs can be written to make these patterns come alive on screen. Students can experiment with new commands to make their turtles perform as directed.   R.K.J.

473.   Stanley, Diane. *Peter the Great*. Illustrated by the author. Four Winds, 1986. ISBN 0-02-786790-0, $12.95. Ages 6-9.

Peter the Great is a fascinating biography of the tsar who introduced Russia to the ways of the modern world. Used to getting his own way, he set about modernizing Russia both humbly and high handedly. He was a man who could learn ship building as a lowly carpenter and yet order his subjects to build him a fabulous capital city in the middle of nowhere. Diane Stanley is doubly successful in her endeavor to bring Tsar Peter to life for children. Her writing is vivid and understandable even to her young audience, and her primitive-style paintings evoke Russia through detail in clothing and buildings.

Russia was never the same after the reign of Peter the Great. Students may enjoy documenting the changes he made by creating a chart with two columns, one headed "Before Peter" and the other "After Peter." An extension of this would be to make similar charts on other people who have made significant contributions to civilization in a variety of ways, people like Thomas Edison, Alexander Fleming, the Wright Brothers, Marco Polo, Elizabeth Cady Stanton and Marie Curie, to name a few. This may lead students into a thorough exploration of biography as a literary form and means to enjoy history.   M.A.C.

474.   Sufrin, Mark. *Focus on America: Profiles of Nine Photographers*. Scribner's, 1987. ISBN 0-684-18679-9, $13.95. Ages 11-up.

They shared a spirit of adventure, courage, and the drive to preserve for future generations the human and natural landscapes of this country. This was their greatness as people as well as artists. The informative and lively tributes to Brady, Jackson, Bourke-White, Lange, and other giants of American photography resound with the growth and development of our country from the Civil War to the present. Each brief chapter (25-30 pages) whets the appetite for more information about the people, the places, and the times described. Speaking of Matthew Brady, "Were it not for him, we would be ignorant of our past..." The same must be said of each.

There are selected samples of the works of each individual profiled by Sufrin. Students can and should find collections of the major works of each in a library. Both fiction and nonfiction books about the places or events represented in the photographs add further dimension to understanding history. For example, reading John Steinbeck's *Grapes of Wrath* helps illuminate many of Dorthea Lange's works; the same is true for stories about the Civil War (with Brady), about settling the Western frontier (with Curtis), and about the Great Depression (with Evans and Bourke-White). Photographic and literary images presented together enrich each other and help the reader better know the social history and photographer-historian.   H.M.

Art, U.S. History,
Literature
Middle School
Intermediate
Junior High School

Related Source

475.   Tapert, Annette, editor. *The Brothers' War: Civil War Letters to Their Loved Ones from the Blue and Gray*. Illustrated with photographs. Times Books, 1988. ISBN 0-8129-1634-4, $18.95. Ages 12-up.

The Brother's War is a collection of touching letters written by both Confederate and Union soldiers during the Civil War. Tapert attempts to present the war as it was felt by those who fought it and to dispel the glorious image that paradoxically was created, at least in part, by the veterans themselves. Photographs from that era, sometimes of the letter writers, enhance the reader's appreciation for the truths found in these heart-wrenching writings. Interestingly, beyond the predicted longings for home and family, gruesome descriptions of battles and their aftermath, and references to God and the rightness of both causes, there are those occasional references that show societal prejudices. One Union soldier writes, "Ask father if he would not like to have a darky to work for him when I come home. I presume I might bring one home. Some of them are keen. It is sport to have them around." There are also stories told to entertain loved ones that reflect both the distance between the two sides and some intermingling between them. The impact of this remarkable volume is impossible to gain from an historian's secondhand account.

These letters are recommended to teachers of history to read aloud when discussing the Civil War. Students may want to discuss how the letters reveal the social times in which they were set and how we today might view some of their contents with more enlightened eyes. What prejudices do we still cling to that might raise the eyebrows of future generations if they were to read our letters? Some library research for other people's letters or articles might expand and deepen this idea. Jack Lang's *Letters in American History: Words to Remember* (Crown, 1982) and Ingpen's *Women as Letter Writers* (Telegraph Books, 1981) might be good books to start with. A class might want to write "A Letter to the Future," their impressions of their own time and place to be read by a future generation. These could be saved in a time capsule or kept by each individual to share with their children or grandchildren.　　M.A.C.

*U.S. History, Literature
Language Arts
Junior High School
High School*

Related Sources

476.　Tchudi, Stephen. *Soda Poppery*. Illustrated with photographs. Scribner's, 1986. ISBN 0-684-18488-5, $13.95. Ages 12-up.

It is clear that, like millions of people here and throughout the world, Stephen Tchudi has had a lifelong fascination and love affair with soda pop. This "History of Soft Drinks in America" is part nostalgia, part social history, and filled to the brim with surprising bits of detail and information about the origins, the manufacture, and the selling of the major American soft drinks. The bubbly narrative is amply interspersed with old photographs and advertising art ("Drink a Bite to Eat" urges a World War II ad for Dr. Pepper). There are suggestions for 23 worthwhile research activities that will extend the interested reader's thinking.

Tchudi recalls when, as a youngster, he first tasted home brewed soda pop. That memory stayed with him so that now he is a "practicing soda popper." He shares recipes, necessary supplies, and techniques in a simple, step-by-step format. Not only is making home brewed soda pop legal, easy, and tasty, but it could be a lucrative source of fund raising for an individual or group throughout the year.　　H.M.

*Science
Middle School
Junior High School
High School*

477.　Tchudi, Stephen. *The Young Learner's Handbook: A Guide to Solving Problems, Mastering Skills, Thinking Creatively*. Scribner's, 1987. ISBN 0-684-18676-4, $14.95. Ages 12-up.

This is a great resource book for students who want to improve their thinking skills and for teachers who want to encourage such growth. Included are chapters on questing—the idea of independent learning; the art of questioning; gathering data; learning from people, places, and research; applying what is found; and sharing what is found. In other words, this book is a basic guide to the inquiry method of learning. Tchudi's writing is clear and interesting, and the book is sprinkled with projects to get readers started.

Tchudi ends by giving suggestions for starting a QUESTARS club. This would be something a school or public library or an individual teacher could easily sponsor. It is also recommended that all teachers take a look at Tchudi's book and consider giving over part of their teaching to this highly effective model of learning.   M.A.C.

All Subjects
Middle School
Junior High School
High School

478.   Tchudi, Susan and Stephen. *The Young Writer's Handbook*. Scribner's, 1984. ISBN 0-684-18090-1, $12.95. Ages 10-up.

ALA Notable Book

This is a very utilitarian book that is supportive of budding writers. The content is logically organized and would encourage any young penner. Two chapters are exceptional: Chapter 4, "What Shall I Write About?" and Chapter 8, "Write About Town." These are the heart of the book for upper elementary, middle, or junior high school age children.

Language Arts
Middle School
Junior High School
High School

The chapters that might prove to be most appealing for teachers are the third and fourth: "The Writer's Journal" and "What Shall I Write About?" In articles on writing, authors often encourage students to begin the process by keeping a journal. This is clearly spelled out in this book and makes a logical starting place for teacher and student. The fourth chapter is a marvelous display of what teachers might start with in terms of subject matter. This would be a worthwhile resource for every upper grade teacher's desk.   W.J.C.

479.   Terban, Marvin. *Too Hot to Hoot: Funny Palindrome Riddles*. Illustrated by Giulio Maestro. Clarion, 1985. ISBN 0-89919-319-6, $11.95. Ages 7-10.

"Able was I ere I saw Elba" and "Madam I'm Adam" are two famous palindromes—words or phrases which spell the same forward or backwards. *Too Hot to Hoot* is a richly illustrated "word play" book that encourages the young reader to guess palindromes from short definitions or questions. The first examples are simple ones: three letter words for mother, father and small child; several pages later there are more challenging puzzles (the answer pages are welcome). Palindrome sentences and palindromic numbers complete the volume. *Too Hot to Hoot* is an appealing introduction to this form of word game.

For the child who is looking for or needs special activities, for the Friday afternoon doldrums for the whole class, for those holiday times when a "game" is expected, this book has the kind of word puzzles that

Language Arts
Primary
Intermediate
Middle School

are both fun and stimulating. Students may enjoy creating their own palindromes with descriptions or questions similar to those in this book. Accompanying illustrations by the students might provide the necessary "hints." More experienced students may want to look through *Games Jr. Magazine* for more of these and other word games.   F.M.H.

480. Tison, Annette and Talus Taylor. *The Big Book of Animal Records*. Illustrated by the authors. Grosset & Dunlap, 1985 (1st Am. ed.). ISBN 0-448-18968-2, $8.95. Ages 7-11.

In a style similar *The Guinness Book of World Records* (published annually by Sterling), this book sets down scores of animal superlatives: the largest, smallest, fastest, slowest, longest neck, biggest eyes, most elastic tongue, and so on. The text is amply illustrated with colorful drawings, in which animals take on a kind of human mien. There is an index to the contents plus an index to the records themselves, making specific information easy to locate quickly.

Most scientific curricula include animal study on several grade levels. Elementary classes often lack sufficient reference volumes for their age group; this book offers a plethora of facts for reports. Individuals or small groups could take on the weekly responsibility of reporting a group of such "records" to the rest of the class or school through a weekly bulletin board display illustrating the information or a one-page newsletter for home circulation.   F.M.H.

Related Source

Science
Primary
Intermediate

481. Van Allsburg, Chris. *The Z Was Zapped*. Illustrated by the author. Houghton Mifflin, 1987. ISBN 0-395-44612-0, $15.95. All ages.

Not only did the Z get zapped, but the A was in an Avalanche, the B was badly Bitten, the C was Cut to ribbons, and so on through the end of this alphabetic drama in 26 acts. Not since the *Mysteries of Harris Burdick* (Houghton Mifflin, 1984) has Van Allsburg conjured up such an original and curiously strange string of events for all ages. Readers won't find a story line here, but the odd goings-on will hold the attention of preschoolers and older. The black and white drawings, detailed and humorous, complement perfectly the mood of this imaginative presentation.

Alphabet books were rarely created with the intention of teaching young children the names of the letters of the alphabet; the "Alphabet Song" usually took care of that. Rather, alphabet books have been vehicles for moral instruction ("In Adam's fall we sinned all"), for information (*From Ashanti to Zulu* [Dial, 1976]), for word play (*All About Arthur* [Watts, 1974]), or for some other purpose. Even younger students, individually or collaboratively, can search out words, images, objects, or events to organize around a particular theme for creating an alphabetical presentation in words and images. Finished products should be made into sturdy books and entered into the regular library collection of alphabet books.   H.M.

ALA Notable Book

Related Source

Related Sources

Language Arts
Primary
Intermediate

482. Ventura, Piero. *Great Painters*. Illustrated by the author. Putnam, 1984. ISBN 0-399-21115-2, $15.95. Ages 10-up.

From Giotto to Picasso, this lavish panorama of Western art is a unique approach to the history of painting. Ventura's own art, depicting events and people that were part of each painting's creation and various artists' lives, gives great art an immediacy not usually realized. Glowing reproductions of masterpieces are part of two-page spreads detailing the human and historic settings of each period. Caravaggio's plumed hat is flung on the frame of "The Martyrdom of St. Peter," while in the street outside his friends restrain him from dueling. Thus, Ventura's story-telling is both visual and narrative. The text is straightforward and easy to read, yet appropriately informative. Quality reproductions, glossy paper, and an intriguing format make this book a delight to hold and treasure.

Art
Intermediate
Middle School
Junior High School
High School

First, this is an excellent art reference book, particularly as an introduction to great painting. As the detail demands close observations, this book could be put into a child's hands for leisurely reading and viewing. Ventura's art is similar to Anno's: colorful, detailed village scenes with ordinary people engaged in everyday activities. It may stimulate students to investigate the social life of various historical periods. Even the development of artists' tools can be traced by studying illustrations of their workbenches.   B.B.

483.   Ventura, Piero. *There Once Was A Time*. Illustrated by the author. Putnam, 1987. ISBN 0-399-21356-2, $19.95. Ages 10-up.

There Once Was a Time is a visual delight that takes readers into a retelling of history through Ventura's colorful and lively water-color illustrations. Readers are treated to descriptions of people from different historical times: what they wore, what they did, where they lived. For each time period—from the ancient world to the turn of the twentieth century—there are nine aspects depicted on a two-page spread: society, homes, agriculture, crafts, trade, dress, transportation, inventions and warfare. With each picture there is a brief explanation as well as a caption. Its only weakness lies in its rather narrow depiction of children. Though they are sometimes portrayed, there is no text describing what children did or the games they played. This book would be an excellent supplement for any social studies textbook, as children may gain a better understanding of history not just through important figures and events, but through the people and their everyday lives.

History,
Social Studies
Intermediate
Middle School
Junior High School
High School

This book provides marvelous opportunities for creative writing. Let students choose a favorite era and write a fictitious account of someone living in that time by using the information given in the text and pictures, or the additional information in the back of the book. Intermediate students can write "A Day in the Life of..." and accompany their story with illustrations. They might, for example, choose to describe how cumbersome it was for a woman in the eighteenth century to get around wearing enormous hoop skirts, or maybe choose a knight from the thirteenth century and describe how it felt to wear a suit of armor and carry a twelve foot lance on a horse. The possibilities are nearly endless   K.B.B.

484. Vinke, Hermann. *The Short Life of Sophie Scholl.* Harper & Row, 1984. ISBN 0-06-026302-4, $10.95. Ages 12-up.

Sophie Scholl was a member of the anti-Hitler underground movement called "The White Rose." In 1943, at the age of 21 along with her older brother and a handful of others, she was executed for treason. Vinke's biography of this remarkable woman, translated from the German, draws heavily from Sophie's diaries and from interviews with those who remember her and the short-lived efforts of this group of anti-war activists. This biography also reveals a young person's transition from middle class roots and membership in the Hitler Youth to a principled, reflective freedom fighter during the early years of World War II.

Secondary history and social studies teachers will find invaluable the first-person sketches of German life during the rise of National Socialism and the early years of World War II. Materials on anti-Hitler efforts are relatively scarce and few have the immediacy of this biography. Literature teachers may want to explore such themes as war, personal integrity and responsibility, and courage in the face of insurmountable odds.   H.M.

Holocaust Studies,
Literature
Junior High School
High School

485. von Tscharner, Renata and Ronald Lee Fleming. *New Providence: A Changing Cityscape.* Illustrated by Denis Orloff. Harcourt Brace Jovanovich, 1987. ISBN 0-15-200540-4, $10.95. Ages 8-up.

The town square and distant views of the area surrounding an imaginary small city are shown in colorful, detailed bird's-eye views as the city might appear in 1910, 1935, 1980, and 1987. Each two-page spread is followed by a brief narrative which points out details in the illustrations that depict significant economic, social, and cultural aspects of the period. If the ultimate compliment a dinner guest can give is to ask for a second helping, the ultimate compliment a reviewer can give is to buy the book. I did.

Oral history, using cassette recorders to capture recollections about an individual's past experiences, is frequently being used by teachers to promote student interest in history. This book is recommended to potential interviewers of parents or senior citizens as it gives the students not only a sense of the change the subject has seen in the built environment, but also it provides background information and possible topics that a subject might wish to discuss.   J.F.A.

Local History
Primary
Intermediate
Middle School

486. Wilks, Mike. *The Ultimate Alphabet.* Illustrated by the author. Henry Holt, 1986. ISBN 0-8050-0160-3, $19.95 ($22.45 with workbook). Ages 12-up.

The dictionary associates *ultimate* with "definitive," "extreme," "conclusive," and/or "last." Though future alphabet books are inevitable, Wilks's masterpiece is certainly definitive and extreme: no other book of its kind has exceeded the 7,777 objects illustrated here. It may well become the basis for all alphabet book makers who are seeking subjects to illustrate. In an effort that spanned four years, Wilks has painted 26 beautifully surrealistic scenes that display the objects named in the workbook. The search through each brilliantly designed painting is a mind-trip through a visual dictionary. A prize of $15,000 was offered to the person or group who identified the most objects by April 1, 1988.

The workbook suggestions for strategies to search out the words painted into the pictures and the directions for entering the contest. In spite of the fact that the contest is officially over, schools and libraries might sponsor private contests following the official rules among grades, classes, or teams of students competing for local prizes. The answers can be found in Wilks's *The Annotated Ultimate Alphabet* (Henry Holt, 1988)   H.M.

Language Arts, Math, Art, Science
Middle School
Junior High School
High School

Related Source

487.   Wirths, Claudine G. and Mary Bowman-Kruhm. *I Hate School: How to Hang In and When to Drop Out*. Illustrated by Patti Stren. Crowell, 1987. ISBN 0-690-04558-1, $11.89. Ages 12-up.

ALA Best Book

Believe it or not, there is a book that does not insist that high school is for everybody. *I Hate School* admits classes may not always be peaches and cream and identifies what legitimate circumstances can get in the way of scholastic success. Authors Wirths and Bowman-Kruhm discuss choices teenagers face and some of the consequences of their decisions. Tips on homework, study skills, test taking, and reading are spelled out in easy-to-follow language. Pen–and–ink illustrations by Patti Stren are funny, funky, and far enough off-the-wall to be teenager approved. The authors deserve an "A" for this challenging and reliable resource book.

Family Life,
Social Studies
Junior High School
High School

As a personal book for a personal problem, *I Hate School* could be a lifesaver for individual teenagers. Because this volume offers help with homework as well as crisis hot line phone numbers, teachers' and librarians' familiarity with the scope of the material is important. Likewise, parents would benefit from much of the information offered to their children. Someone on the staff—the librarian, the guidance counselor, the principal, a teacher—can prepare a list of this and similar resources for the staff, parents, and community groups.   G.G.

488.   Yue, Charlotte. *The Pueblo*. Illustrated by David Yue. Houghton Mifflin, 1986. ISBN 0-395-38350-1, $12.95. Ages 9-12.

The author–illustrator team who created the award-winning *The Tipi: A Center of Native American Life* (Knopf, 1983) has continued to explore aspects of Native American culture in this well-written volume. Black and white pencil sketches clearly and simply show children how pueblos were constructed, while the concise, readable text explains both the dwellings and the people who constructed them at an introductory level. The author delineates clearly between Native American culture prior to European conquest and after European settlement began, but handles this issue without blaming either side for the drastic changes that ensued in Native American culture. Everyone who teaches about Native American cultures should welcome this book into the classroom.

People adapt the style and construction of their dwellings to accomodate geographic, economic, and cultural requirements. Among Native American homes the Pueblos of the Southwest are widely recognized, making this book a useful introduction to a unit on local Native American culture. A community historical society, a university professor (either history or anthropology) who specializes in local history, or an Urban Indian organization (found in many large cities) could provide some information on the Native American communities that once existed—or continue to thrive—in the area, especially the types and styles of housing.   J.J.S./H.M.

Native American Studies
Intermediate
Middle School

INDEXES

Author, Title, Page Number

Aardema, Verna   1
Abells, Chana Byers   201
Ackerman, Karen   1
An Actor's Life for Me!   228
Adler, David A.   205, 206
Adoff, Arnold   181
After the Rain   156
Ahlberg, Janet and Allan   2
Aiken, Joan   71
Ain't Gonna Study War No More   249
Airmail to the Moon   7
The Alamo   222
Alexander, Lloyd   72, 127, 128
Aliki   206
All God's Children Need Traveling Shoes   209
All of Our Noses are Here   110
Allard, Harry   2
Alphabatics   245
Amazing Animal Alphabet Book   217
The Amazing Voyage of Jackie Grace   16
Ames, Lee J.   207
Amy's Eyes   96
Anastasia has the Answers   100
And Condors Danced   143
Anderson, Gretchen   208
Anderson, Joan   128, 208, 209
Angell, Judie   129
Angelou, Maya   209
Anno, Mitsumasa   3, 210
Anno's Flea Market   3
Anno's Sundial   210
Anthony Burns: The Defeat and Triumph of a Fugitive Slave   229
Apple Pie and Onions   11
Apple Tree Christmas   47
Archer, Jules   210
Arkin, Alan   129
Armor, John and Peter Wright   211
Aruego, Jose and Ariane Dewey   4
Ashabranner, Brent and Melissa   211
Asimov, Isaac   212
Ask Me Tomorrow   130
Assignment: Sports   243
Aster Aardvark's Alphabet Adventure   236
At the Edge of the Pond   219
Atkinson, Linda   213
Aylesworth, Jim   4

Babushka   45
Back Home   155
Back to Class   186
Bad Man Ballad   167
Baehr, Patricia   130
Baker, Jeannie   5
Ba-Nam   35
Bang, Molly   6
The Baron on the Island of Cheese   45
Bates, Betty   130
Bauer, Caroline Feller   73, 182
Bauer, Marion Dane   73
Bayberry Bluff   36
Baylor, Byrd   74
Be Ever Hopeful, Hannalee   74
Beatty, Patricia   74, 131
Beauty and the Beast   14
Beethoven's Cat   102
The Beggar Queen   127
Behind Rebel Lines   256
Behn, Harry   183
Being Born   237
Bell, Ruth   213
Bellairs, John   75
Berger, Barbara   6

Best Friends   188
Beyond the Chocolate War   134
The Big Beast Book   214
The Big Book of Animal Records   267
The Big Sneeze   9
Birch, David   7
Birdseye, Tom   7
Birdsong   25
Birrer, Cynthia and William   8
Birthday Presents   52
Bjork, Christina   214
Blake, Quentin   8
Blume, Judy   75
Boat Song   119
The Bone Wars   151
Bonham, Frank   132
Booth, Jerry   214
The Boston Coffee Party   106
The Boy of the Three-Year Nap   53
Boyd, Candy Dawson   76
Branley, Franklyn M.   215, 216
Brats   190
Bravo, Minski   65
Breadsticks and Blessing Places   76
Bridger: The Story of a Mountain Man   149
Bridgers, Sue Ellen   132
Bring Back the Deer   49
British Folk Tales   135
Brittain, Bill   77
Brooks, Bruce   132, 133
The Brothers' War   264
A Brown Bird Singing   120
Brown, Ruth   9
Buffalo Woman   21
Bulla, Clyde Robert   78
Bunting, Eve   9, 10, 11, 78
The Butter Battle Book   19
Byers, Betsy   79

A Cache of Jewels   231
The Cage   258
The Candlemaker and Other Tales   85
The Cardboard Crown   78
Carrick, Carol   79
The Cartoonists' Thanksgiving Day Hunger Project   216
The Case of the Watching Boy   103
Casey at the Bat   201
Caseley, Judith   11
Cassedy, Sylvia   80
Celebrations   193
Chaiken, Miriam   80, 217
Changing Bodies, Changing Lives   213
Changing of the Guard   171
Charlie Pippin   76
Charley Skedaddle   131
Chester's Way   29
Child of War   169
Children of Appalachia   209
Children of Long Ago   192
Children of the Dust   152
Children of the Wolf   177
The Children We Remember   205
China Homecoming   225
China's Long March   225
The Chinese Mirror   20
Chouinard, Roger and Mariko   217
City Safaris   260
Clap Your Hands: Finger Rhymes   188
Claude and Sun   48
The Clearing   129
Cleary, Beverly   218
Cleaver, Elizabeth   12
Cleaver, Vera   81

Clements, Bruce   134
Climo, Shirley   12
Cohn, Janice   13
Cole, Brock   81
Come A Stranger   172
Come Sing, Jimmy Jo   104
Comic Relief   216
Coming—and—Going Men   138
Conover, Chris   13
Conly, Jane Leslie   82
Corcoran, Barbara   82
Cormier, Robert   134
Commander Toad and the Dis-Asteroid   121
Cracker Jackson   79
Crafty Chameleon   24
Crean, Patrick
The Cremation of Sam McGee   200
Cresswell, Helen   135
Crews, Donald   13, 218
Crickets and Bullfrogs and Whispers of Thunder   183
The Crossing   160
Crossley-Holland, Kevin   135
Crutches   141
The Curse of the Squirrel   121
The Cut-ups   41

Dahl, Roald   83
The Dallas Titans Get Ready For Bed   33
The Dawn Palace   145
Danzinger, Paula   83
Dear Baby   108
Death of the Iron Horse   21
de Beaumont, Mme. Leprince   14
Deford, Deborah H.   136
de Gerez, Toni   14
de Jenkins, Lyll Becerra   136
Dekkars, Midas   219
Demi   183
de Regniers, Beatrice Schenk   184
The Devil's Arithmetic   122
Dewey, Jennifer Owings   219
Dinosaurs, Dragonflies and Diamonds   227
The Dinosaur is the Biggest Animal That Ever Lived and Other Wrong Ideas You Thought Were True   261
Dinosaurs Walked Here and Other Stories Fossils Tell   240
The Disappearance of Sister Perfect   164
Does Anyone Know the Way to Thirteen?   95
Dogsong   161
Doherty, Berlie   137
Don't Care High   149
Dr. Dredd's Wagon of Wonders   77
The Drackenberg Adventure   127
Dragon Kites and Dragonflies   183
Dragon Steel   174
Dragons and Dreams   123
Dragonwagon, Crescent   15
Draw 50 Beasties and Yugglies and Turnover Uglies and Things that Go Bump in the Night   207
The Dream Keeper   137
The Duplicate   168

1812: The War Nobody Won   248
Edwards, Sally   84
Ehlert, Lois   220
The El Dorado Adventure   72
Elbert's Bad Word   62
Elephants Can't Jump and Other Freaky Facts About Animals   259
The Enchanted Caribou   12

The Enchanted Umbrella   44
An Enemy Among Them   136
Esbensen, Barbara Juster   15, 184
The Eternal Spring of Mr. Ito   86
Euvremer, Teryl   16
The Everlasting Hills   94
Evernden, Margery   137
Exploration—Great Lives   243
The Explorer of Barkham Street   115
Exploring Winter   247
Eye of Darkness   142
Eyes of the Dragon   35

Facts and Fallacies: Stories of the Strange and
        Unusual   255
The Facts and Fictions of Minna Pratt   101
Fahrmann, Willi   138
Falling Scales   130
Family Farm   38
The Family Storytelling Handbook   254
The Farmer and the Moon   39
Fat Man in a Fur Coat and Other
        Bear Stories   111
Faulkner, Matt   16
Favorite Folktales from Around the
        World   122
Feldbaum, Carl B. and Ronald J. Bee   220
Find Waldo Now   26
Fine, John Christopher   221
A Fine White Dust   109
The First Book of Football   245
First Flight   44
The First Thanksgiving Feast   208
Fisher, Aileen   185
Fisher, Leonard Everett   222
The Flame of Peace   34
The Flame-Colored Taffeta   116
Flanagan, Dennis   222
Flanagan's Version   222
Flash, Crash, Rumble, and Roll   215
Fleischman, Paul   17, 138, 185
Fleischman, Sid   85
Fleming, Alice   223
Focus on America   264
Follow the Drinking Gourd   61
The Forgetful Wishing Well   191
Forrester, Victoria   85, 186
Foster, Sally   224
Fox, Mem   17
Fox, Paula   86
Frederick's Fables   37
Free Fall   60
Free to Be...A Family   57
Freedman, Russell   224
The Friendship   117
Fritz, Jean   225, 226
The Fun of Cooking   238
Futuredays: A Ninteenth-Century Vision of the
        Year 2000   212

Galaxies   261
Galdone, Paul   18
Gardner, Beau   18
Garrigue, Sheila   86
Geisel, Theodore (Dr. Seuss)   19
George, Jean Craighead   139, 227
George Midgett's War   84
Gerstein, Mordicai   20
The Ghost-Eye Tree   42
Ghost's Hour, Spook's Hour   9
Ghosts Beneath Our Feet   120
Gibbons, Gail   227
Gilson, Jamie   87
Ginsburg, Mirra   20
A Girl From Yamhill: A Memoir   218
Gish, Lillian   228
Glenn, Mel   186
The Glow-in-the-Dark Night Sky Book   230

Go In and Out the Window   195
The Goats   81
Goble, Paul   21, 22
Goennel, Heidi   23
Goffstein, M.B.   24, 228
The Gold Cadillac   117
Goldilocks and the Three Bears   41
Goodall, John S.   229
Good-bye My Wishing Star   88
Grandfather Twilight   6
Grandparents: A Special Kind of Love   242
Granny Was a Buffer Girl   137
Great Painters   267
The Great Skinner Getaway   171
Greenfield, Eloise   187
Greens   181
Greer, Gery and Bob Ruddick   87
Greens   181
Grove, Vicki   88
Guess Again   253

Hadithi, Mwenye   24
Hadley, Irwin   88
Haley, Gail E.   25, 26
Half a Moon and One Whole Star   15
Hall, Mary Bowen
Hamilton, Virginia   89, 90, 139, 140, 229
Handforth, Martin   26
Hanna's Hog   4
Hannah's Farm: The Seasons on an Early
        American Homestead   249
The Happiest Ending   118
Happily May I Walk: American Indians and
        Alaska Natives Today   233
Harlan, Elizabeth   141
Harper's Index Book   239
Harris, Jonathan   230
Hartling, Peter   141
Hatchet   161
Hatchett, Clint   230
Hattie and the Fox   17
Haugaard, Erik Christian   27
Hayes, Sarah   188
Hear the Wind Blow (Pendergraft)   163
Hear the Wind Blow (Sanders)   109
Hearn, Michael Patrick   27
Heckedy Peg   63
Heidi, Florence Parry   91
Heller, Ruth   231, 232
Hello, My Name is Scrambled Eggs   87
Hendershot, Judith   28
Henkes, Kevin   29
Henry, Joanne Landers   232
Henry, Maeve   92
Henry's Quest   48
Her Own Song   93
Her Seven Brothers   22
The Hero and the Crown   156
Hest, Amy   29
Heuck, Sigrid   142
Hey, Al   66
Heyer, Marilee   29
The Hideout   142
Higgledy-Piggledy: Verses and Pictures   193
Highwater, Jamake   142, 143
Hilts, Len   92, 232
Hinton, S.E.   144
Hirschfelder, Arlene   233
Hoban, Tana   233, 234
Hodges, Margaret   30
Hoguet, Susan Ramsay   31
Home Free   151
Home in the Sky   5
Homecoming   164
The Honorable Prison   125
Hoover, H.M.   145
Hopkins, Lee Bennett   188, 189
Horwitz, Joshua   145

The House on Maple Street   50
How a Book is Made   206
How Many Days to America?   10
How Much is a Million?   258
How Sweetly Sings the Donkey   81
How to Be a Reasonably THIN Teenage
        Girl   244
How to Make Pop-Ups   234
How to Talk to Your Computer   262
How to Think Like a Scientist   238
Howard, Ellen   93
Howe, James   93
Howker, Janni   146
Hughes, Monica   146
The Hunger Road   221
Hunt, Irene   94
Hurd, Thatcher   31
Hurmence, Belinda   147

I Be Somebody   88
I Go With My Family to Grandma's   36
I Had a Friend Named Peter   13
I Hate School: How to Hang in and When to
        Drop Out   270
I Walk and Read   233
I Wear the Morning Star   143
Ike and Mama and The Seven Surprises   114
Iktomi and the Boulder: A Plains Indian
        Story   22
The Illyrian Adventure   127
I'm in Charge of Celebrations   74
In a Dark, Dark Room and Other Scary
        Stories   110
In Coal Country   28
In Kindling Flame   213
In My Garden: A Child's Gardening Book   253
In Shadowland   3
In the Beginning   89
In the Night, Still Dark   191
In the Year of the Boar and Jackie
        Robinson   99
Into a Strange Land   211
Irvine, Joan   234
Irwin, Hadley   147
The Inside-Outside Book of Washington,
        D.C.   252
Inside Turtle's Shell and Other Poems of the
        Field   199
Isaac Campion   146
Isaacson, Philip M.   235
The Island   162
It is Illegal to Quack Like a Duck & Other
        Freaky Laws   259
It's a Free Country!: A Young Person's Guide to
        Politics and Elections   257
The Ivory Lyre   157

Jack and the Bean Tree   25
Jack and the Fire Dragon   26
Jackaroo   172
Jacob Two-Two and the Dinosaur   107
Jacques, Brian   95
Jakes, John   235
Janeczko, Paul B.   189, 190
Johnson, Annabel and Edgar   148
Johnston, Ginny   236
Johnston, Norma   148
Johnston, Tony   32
The Jolly Postman and Other People's
        Letters   2
Jonas, Ann   32, 33
Joyful Noise: Poems for Two Voices   185
Junius Over Far   139
Just as Long as We're Together   75

Kaufman, Stephen   95
Kaye, Marilyn   96
Kellogg, Steven   33, 236

Kennedy, Richard   96
Kennedy, X.J.   190, 191
Kherdian, David   148
Kim/Kimi   147
King Bidgood's in the Bathtub   63
King of the Birds   12
*The King of Prussia and a Peanut Butter
    Sandwich*   223
The King's Chessboard   7
Kites Sail High   232
Kitzinger, Sheila   237
Koch, Kenneth and Kate Farrell   191
Kome, Penny   237
Konigsburg, E.L.   97
Korman, Gordon   149, 150
Kramer, Stephen P.   238
Krementz, Jill   238
Kuklin, Susan   239
Kuskin, Karla   33

Lanes, Selma   228
Lapham, Lewis, et al.   239
Lasky, Kathryn   151, 152, 240
The Last Silk Dress   165
A Latch Against the Wind   186
Lattimore, Deborah Nourse   34
Lauber, Patricia   240, 241
Lawrence, Louise   152, 153
Leaf, Margaret   35
Lee, Jeanne M.   35
Legend Days   143
L'Engle, Madeleine   154
Lent, Blair   36
LeShan, Eda   242
Lester, Julius   98
Levinson, Riki   36, 37
Levitin, Sonia   154
Levoy, Myron   99
Lewis, Richard   191
Lillian Gish: An Actor's Life for Me   228
Lincoln: A Photobiography   224
Linnea in Monet's Garden   214
Lionni, Leo   37
Lipsyte, Robert   243
Little, Lessie Jones   192
Livingston, Myra Cohn   193, 194
Lobel, Arnold   38
Locker, Thomas   38, 39
*Log Cabin in the Woods— A True Story About
    a Pioneer Boy*   232
Lomask, Milton   243
The Long Journey of Lukas B.   138
Look! Look! Look!   234
*The Look Again...and Again, and Again
    Book*   18
Looking the Tiger in the Eye   220
Lord, Bette Bao   99
*Losing Someone You Love: When a Brother or
    Sister Dies*   256
Louhi, Witch of North Farm   14
The Louisa May Alcott Cookbook   208
Lowry, Lois   100
Lukes, Bonnie L.   244
Lussert, Anneliese   39
Lyon, Georgia Ella   40

M.E. and Morton   80
Mac   155
MacDonald, Suse   245
MacLachlan, Patricia   101
MacLean, John   155
Madden, John   245
Maebelle's Suitcase   58
Maestro, Betsy   246
The Magic Hat of Mortimer Wintergreen   99
Magorian, Michelle   155
Mahy, Margaret   40
Make Way for Sam Houston   226

Mama Don't Allow   31
The Man Who Could Call Down Owls   11
Mansfield, Sue   246
Many Waters   154
Manzanar   211
Marguerite, Go Wash Your Feet   201
Mark, Michael   102
Markle, Sandra   247
Marrin, Albert   248
Marshall, James   41
Martin, Jr., Bill and John Archambault   42
Martin Luther King, Jr.: Free at Last   205
*Mary McLeod Bethune: Voice of Black
    Hope*   250
Matilda   83
Maudie in the Middle   103
Maus   168
Max and Me and the Wild West   87
Mayer, Mercer   42, 43
Mazer, Norma Fox   156
McCurdy, Michael   249
McHugh, Elisabet   102
McKinley, Robin   156, 157
McKissack, Patricia C.   43
McPhail, David   44
Meanwhile Back at The Ranch   47
Meltzer, Milton   249, 250, 251
A Memory of Dragons   148
Merriam, Eve   195
Metropolitan Museum of Art   195
Meyer, Carolyn   252
Meyers, Odette   44
Midnight Hour Encores   133
Mikolaycak, Charles   45
Miracle of Clements' Pond   105
Mirandy and Brother Wind   43
Miss Nelson Has a Field Day   2
Mitchell, Adrian   45
Mojave   200
Monkey and the White Bone Demon   67
Moondial   135
The Moon's Revenge   71
Moonwind   153
The Moosepire   105
*A More Perfect Union: The Story of Our
    Consitution*   246
More Tales of Uncle Remus   98
Mori, Tuyosi   46
Morrison, Lillian   196
Mountain Light   175
The Mountains of Tibet   20
The Moves Make the Man   132
Mrs. Armitage on Wheels   8
Mufaro's Beautiful Daughters   55
Munro, Roxie   252
Murphy, Jim   253
Murphy, Shirley Rousseau   157
Music, Music for Everyone   60
The Music of What Happens   189
My Parents Think I'm Sleeping   196
Myers, Walter Dean   158
The Mysteries of Harris Burdick   118
Mysteries of Outer Space   216
The Mystery of Drear House   89

Namovicz, Gene Inyart   159
The Napping House   64
Nate the Great Stalks Stupidweed   113
The Nature Book   219
Naylor, Phyllis Reynolds and Lura Schield
    Reynolds   103
Nell's Quilt   170
Nettie's Trip South   58
The New Kid on the Block   197
New Providence: A Changing Cityscape   269
Newman, Robert   103
Night in the Country   52
A Nightmare in History   217

Nighty-Nightmare   98
No Way Out   167
Noble, Trinka Hakes   47
Not Separate, Not Equal   174
Novak, Matt   48

Oakley, Graham   48
O'Dell, Scott   159, 160
Oechsli, Helen   253
Oh, Kojo! How Could You!   1
The Old Woman and the Willy Nilly Man   64
On My Honor   73
Once There Was A Tree   51
Once Upon a Time...   50
One Day in the Alpine Tundra   227
One-Eyed Cat   86
One-Way to Ansonia   129
Only Birds and Angels Fly   145
The Outlaws of Sherwood   157
Owl Lake   57
Owl Moon   65

Pageant   152
Pangur Ban   167
The Paper Crane   6
Park's Quest   104
Parnall, Peter   254
Past Eight O'Clock   71
Paterson, Katherine   104
Paulsen, Gary   160, 161, 162, 163
Peace: A Dream Unfolding   237
Pecos Bill   33
Pellowski, Anne   254, 255
Pendergraft, Patricia   163
The People Could Fly   90
Permanent Connections   132
Peter the Great   263
Phillips, Mildred   49
Phoebe   96
The Pied Piper of Hamelin   42
Pinkwater, Daniel   105
Pinkwater, Jill   164
Planting a Rainbow   220
Pocket Poems   190
Polar Express   59
Pollack, Pamela   106
The Porcelain Cat   27
Posell, Elsa   164
The Potter's Wheel   148
Prelutsky, Jack   196, 197, 198
Premonitions   132
Prince Boghole   27
Prusski, Jeffrey   49
Pryor, Bonnie   50
The Pueblo   270
Puppeteer   240
The Purple Coat   29

Quanah Parker   232
Quentin Corn   116
The Quilt   32

Rabble Starkey   100
Rainy Day: Stories and Poems   182
The Random House Book of Humor   106
Rappaport, Doreen   106, 107
Rasco and the Rats of NIMH   82
A Rat's Tale   111
Read-Aloud Rhymes for the Very Young   197
Reading is Fundamental   50
Reader's Digest   255
Redwall   95
Reflections   33
A Regular Rolling Noah   40
Reit, Seymour   256
The Relatives Came   53
The Reluctant God   112
Remember Me To Harold Square   83

Rescue: The Story of How Gentiles Saved Jews
    in the Holocaust   251
The Return   154
Return to Bitter Creek   114
Rhythm Road: Poems to Move To   196
Richler, Mordecai   107
Richter, Elizabeth   256
Ride a Purple Pelican   198
Rinaldi, Ann   165
The Road to Damietta   159
Roberts, Willo Davis   108
Rochman, Hazel   166
Rockabye Crocodile   4
Rocklin, Joanne   108
Rogasky, Barbara   51
Romanova, Natalia   51
Rondo in C   17
Round Buildings, Square Buildings, & Buildings
    That Wiggle Like a Fish   235
Roy, Ron   257
Ruckman, Ivy   167
Rumplestiltskin   66
The Runner   173
Rhythm Road: Poems to Move To   196
Ryder, Joanne   199
Rylant, Cynthia   52, 53, 109, 199

1787   128
17 Kings and 42 Elephants   40
Saint George and the Dragon   29
Samuels, Cynthia K.   257
Sanders, Scott R.   167
Sandwriter   146
Sarah, Plain and Tall   101
Scaly Babies: Reptiles Growing Up   236
School Bus   13
School of Names   24
Schwartz, Alvin   110, 111
Schwartz, David   258
Science Mini-Mysteries   247
Scorpions   158
The Sea is Calling Me   189
Seasons   23
Seidler, Tor   111
Sender, Ruth Minsky   258
A Sending of Dragons   177
The Serpent Never Sleeps   160
The Serpent's Children   176
Service, Pamela F.   112
Service, Robert   200
Siebert, Diane   200
Seuling, Barbara   259
Shaffer, Carolyn   260
Shannon, George   112
Sharmat, Marjorie Weiman   113
Shefelman, Janice   260
Shh! We're Writing the Constitution   226
The Short Life of Sophie Scholl   269
The Sign in Mendel's Window   49
Silverstein, Alvin and Virginia   261
Simon, Seymour   261, 262, 263
Sing a Song of Popcorn   184
Singer, Marilyn   113
Singularity   143
Sixth-Grade Sleepover   78
The Sky is Falling   82
Sky Songs   194
Sleator, William   168
The Sleeping Beauty   43
Smith, Doris Buchanan   114
Snyder, Carol   114
Snyder, Dianne   53
Snyder, Zilpha Keatley   143
Socrates and the Three Little Pigs   46
Soda Poppery   265
Solomon Grundy   31
Some Reasons for War   246

Somehow Tenderness Survives: Stories from
    Southern Africa   166
Son of Interflux   150
Song and Dance Man   1
Song to Demeter   8
Sons From Afar   173
Snowy Day: Stories and Poems   182
The Spell of the Sorcerer's Skull   75
Spiegelman, Art   168
Spinky Sulks   54
Sports Pages   181
Stanley, Diane   264
The Star Maiden   15
Starting from Home: A Writer's
    Beginnings   251
A Statue for America   230
Stay Away from Simon   79
Steig, William   54
Steptoe, John   55
Stevenson, James   55
Stolz, Mary   56, 115, 116, 169
Stories to Solve: From Around the World   112
The Story of a Main Street   229
The Story Vine   255
The Stranger   59
Street Talk   202
Stringbean's Trip to the Shining Sea   61
Sufrin, Mark   264
Sugar Isn't Everything   108
Sullivan, Mary Ann   169
Sun's Up   16
Susanna of the Alamo   235
Sutcliff, Rosemary   116
Szilagyi, Mary   56

Tales for the Perfect Child   91
Tales Mummies Tell   241
The Tales of Uncle Remus   98
Talking to the Sun   191
Taming the Star Runner   144
Tancy   147
Tapert, Annette   264
Taylor, Mildred   117
Tchudi, Stephen N.   265
Tchudi, Susan and Stephen   266
The Teeny-Tiny Woman   18
Tejima   57
Ten Black Dots   218
Terban, Marvin   266
Terris, Susan   170
Thayer, Ernest Lawrence   201
There Was a Place and Other Poems   194
There Once Was a Time   268
There's Nothing to Do   55
Thinking Big   239
Thomas Jefferson, Father of Democracy   206
Thomas, Karen   171
Thomas, Marlo   57
Thunderstorm   56
Time Enough for Dreams   165
Timmy O'Dowd and the Big Ditch   92
Tison, Annette and Talus Taylor   267
To Talk in Time   159
Toba   102
Tolan, Stephanie   171
The Tom Sawyer Fires   176
Too Hot to Hoot: Funny Palindrome
    Riddles   266
Tracker   163
The Treasure of Plunderell Manor   134
Tree By Leaf   119
Treehorn's Wish   91
Tripp, Wallace   201
Trouble at the Mines   107
The Turnaround Wind   38
Turner, Ann   58, 202
Turtle Talk: A Beginner's Book of Logo   263

Tusa, Tricia   58
Tyrannosaurus Was a Beast   198

Uchida, Yoshiko   118
The Ultimate Alphabet   269
Under the Sunday Tree   187
Up From Jericho Tel   97

Van Allsburg, Chris   59, 118, 267
Ventura, Piero   267, 268
Victoria House
Vinke, Hermann   269
Voices of Northern Ireland: Growing Up in a
    Troubled Land   252
Voigt, Cynthia   119, 172, 173,
Volcano: The Eruption and Healing of Mount St.
    Helens   241
von Tschamer, Renata and Ronald Lee
    Fleming   269

Waiting to Waltz: A Childhood   199
The War for Independence   248
The Warriors of Taan   153
Watch the Stars Come Out   37
The Water of Life   51
Water Sky   139
Watershed   141
The Weaving of a Dream   29
Weller, Frances Ward   119
When Grownups Drive You Crazy   242
When it Comes to Bugs   185
Where the Forest Meets the Sea   5
Where the River Begins   39
Where There's a Will There's a Wag   113
Where Time Stands Still   224
The Whipping Boy   85
A White Romance   140
Whose Shoes Are These?   257
Wiesner, David   60
Wilkinson, Brenda   174
Wilks, Mike   269
Williams, Vera B.   60, 61
A Williamsburg Household   209
Windy Days: Stories and Poems   73
Winners and Losers: How Elections Work
    in America   210
Winter, Jeannette   61
Winter Barn   254
Wirths, Claudine G. and Mary Bowman-
    Kruhm   270
The Witch King   92
The Wizard's Daughter   13
Womek, Frances   120
Wood, Audrey   62, 63, 64
Words with Wrinkled Knees   184
World of the Brain   261
Wright, Betty Ren   120
Wright, Jill   64
A Writer   228

Yep, Laurence   121, 174, 175, 176
Yolen, Jane   65, 121, 122, 123, 177,
Yonder   32
Yorinks, Arthur   65, 66
Yossi Asks the Angels for Help   80
You Be Good & I'll Be Night   195
The Young Learner's Handbook   265
The Young Writer's Handbook   266
You're Only Old Once!   19
Yue, Charlotte   270

The Z Was Zapped   267
Zekmet, the Stone Carver   56
Zelinsky, Paul O.   66
Zhang, Xiu Shi   67

Subject Area, Entry Number

All Subjects
477

Art
2, 4, 6, 9, 11, 14, 20, 22, 26, 29, 31, 33, 34, 36, 45, 51, 56, 58, 62, 63, 65, 67, 69, 73, 75, 86, 92, 102, 103, 105, 110, 112, 114, 116, 117, 126, 129, 209, 217, 246, 257, 320, 332, 335, 340, 343, 345, 348, 359, 360, 365, 366, 372, 379, 380, 383, 387, 389, 390, 400, 405, 408, 415, 416, 417, 418, 423, 428, 437, 474, 482, 486

Asian-American Studies
68, 157, 158, 169, 180, 265, 314, 315, 316, 374, 375

Author/Illustrator Studies
1, 14, 41, 79, 97, 156, 192, 226, 277, 317, 336, 356, 360, 386, 398, 449

Black Studies
111, 118, 135, 161, 163, 164, 177, 178, 214, 215, 251, 252, 264, 309, 313, 363, 370, 407, 447

Contemporary Affairs
250, 266, 278, 285, 289, 294, 299, 383, 392, 450

Drama/Speech/Reader's Theater
2, 6, 18, 22, 40, 76, 123, 154, 176, 208, 223, 224, 243, 263, 302, 326, 329, 348, 349, 354, 404, 428

Emerging Readers
34, 35, 121, 122

English/Language Arts
3, 15, 25, 26, 27, 29, 31, 32, 36, 38, 40, 45, 46, 47, 48, 51, 52, 53, 54, 55, 56, 57, 58, 60, 62, 64, 67, 72, 73, 74, 76, 77, 78, 81, 82, 84, 88, 91, 93, 96, 100, 101, 102, 103, 105, 106, 107, 110, 114, 115, 116, 117, 119, 120, 122, 124, 129, 132, 136, 137, 141, 142, 149, 150, 152, 154, 155, 159, 160, 165, 170, 172, 175, 176, 179, 181, 182, 183, 185, 189, 190, 191, 193, 198, 205, 206, 207, 211, 214, 217, 218, 221, 222, 227, 228, 229, 240, 242, 246, 260, 262, 267, 269, 270, 281, 283, 292, 301, 320, 321, 322, 323, 324, 325, 326, 327, 328, 333, 334, 335, 351, 352, 353, 354, 355, 357, 358, 359, 365, 380, 385, 387, 389, 390, 398, 405, 410, 411, 415, 416, 420, 421, 423, 428, 437, 441, 454, 466, 475, 478, 479, 481, 485, 486

Family Life
24, 137, 143, 150, 198, 234, 236, 253, 279, 307, 346, 378, 422, 425, 426, 432, 433, 436, 459, 487

Health/Drug/Physical Education
65, 197, 237, 261, 286, 312, 321, 378, 380, 434, 436, 438

History/Government/Local History
19, 21, 69, 96, 135, 152, 153, 159, 168, 174, 184, 194, 205, 230, 231, 235, 244, 245, 247, 248, 249, 265, 268, 271, 273, 280, 287, 288, 297, 298, 299, 301, 302, 309, 310, 311, 312, 316, 318, 346, 361, 364, 368, 369, 370, 373, 380, 384, 393, 395, 397, 400, 401, 407, 412, 413, 419, 423, 435, 439, 443, 444, 458, 461, 466, 467, 474, 475, 483, 485

Holocaust Studies
224, 254, 255, 296, 303, 362, 377, 384, 448, 463, 484

Jewish-American Studies
146, 210, 247, 296

Literature
4, 7, 8, 12, 31, 41, 42, 43, 44, 46, 47, 49, 52, 57, 63, 64, 80, 82, 83, 84, 87, 88, 94, 98, 114, 127, 130, 132, 148, 151, 155, 161, 162, 163, 164, 166, 167, 168, 170, 175, 177, 190, 193, 201, 203, 204, 212, 213, 218, 224, 225, 232, 233, 234, 235, 236, 238, 239, 240, 241, 243, 252, 259, 260, 261, 262, 268, 270, 277, 282, 284, 287, 288, 291, 292, 293, 314, 315, 324, 325, 326, 327, 328, 329, 330, 331, 332, 336, 337, 338, 339, 340, 341, 343, 344, 345, 347, 348, 349, 351, 352, 353, 356, 359, 362, 367, 377, 386, 397, 400, 409, 449, 473, 474, 475, 484

Math/Computers
13, 17, 89, 159, 166, 206, 209, 372, 380, 400, 424, 460, 462, 471, 472, 486

Multicultural Studies
19, 21, 59, 71, 128, 162, 173, 180, 216, 225, 231, 238, 278, 313, 363, 395, 396

Music
2, 12, 33, 60, 78, 84, 110, 118, 168, 189, 200, 208, 219, 228, 229, 239, 326, 348, 358, 423

Native American Studies
30, 41, 42, 43, 44, 95, 220, 250, 256, 257, 258, 290, 414, 487

Peace Studies
37, 66, 139, 227, 255, 274, 305, 391, 423, 440, 446

Science
10, 15, 16, 17, 20, 23, 31, 45, 89, 99, 108, 109, 126, 131, 132, 140, 168, 186, 206, 207, 228, 250, 271, 272, 275, 286, 300, 311, 319, 322, 323, 327, 328, 329, 330, 335, 342, 354, 355, 358, 376, 380, 381, 382, 388, 389, 390, 394, 402, 403, 409, 420, 422, 424, 429, 431, 441, 442, 445, 452, 453, 454, 457, 460, 464, 468, 469, 470, 476, 480, 485, 486

Social Studies
5, 10, 16, 18, 23, 24, 28, 38, 50, 54, 61, 65, 70, 74, 77, 81, 85, 90, 93, 100, 104, 110, 120, 121, 125, 131, 133, 134, 138, 140, 141, 143, 144, 145, 148, 154, 171, 174, 179, 181, 186, 187, 188, 189, 190, 195, 196, 199, 200, 201, 204, 211, 213, 215, 219, 221, 228, 229, 233, 251, 253, 294, 295, 297, 304, 308, 325, 340, 341, 342, 344, 345, 350, 355, 358, 367, 376, 391, 398, 399, 402, 404, 406, 408, 418, 425, 426, 427, 430, 432, 433, 445, 451, 452, 456, 459, 460, 465, 469, 473, 483, 487

Storytelling
28, 35, 39, 50, 98, 123, 164, 178, 202, 203, 225, 455, 456

Women's Studies
147, 258, 276, 282, 306, 371, 447

Publishers' Addresses and Toll Free Numbers

Andre Deutsch (See Dutton)

Atheneum (See Macmillan)

Bantam Doubleday Dell
666 Fifth Avenue, New York, NY 10103
(800-223-5780)

Bradbury (See Macmillan)

Clarion (See Houghton Mifflin)

Coward-McCann & Geoghegan (See Putnam)

Crowell (See Harper & Row)

Crown (See Random House)

Delacorte (See Bantam Doubleday Dell)

Dell (See Bantam Doubleday Dell)

Dial Books (See Dutton)

Doubleday (See Bantam Doubleday Dell)

E.P. Dutton
Dutton Order Department, Box 120,
Bergenfield, NJ 07621
(800-526-0275)

Farrar, Straus & Giroux
Sales Department, 19 Union Square West,
New York, NY 10003
(800-631-8571)

Four Winds (See Macmillan)

David Godine (See Harper & Row)

Greenwillow (See William Morrow)

Grosset & Dunlap (See Putnam)

Harcourt Brace Jovanovich
Trade Order Entry, Harcourt Brace Jovanovich, Pub.,
465 South Lincoln Drive, Troy, MO 63379
(800-543-1918)

Harmony (See Crown)

Harper & Row
Harper & Row, Inc., Keystone Industrial Park,
Scranton, PA 18512
(800-242-7737)

Holiday House
18 East 53rd Street, New York, NY 10022
(212-688-0085 [not toll free])

Henry Holt
Henry Holt Distribution Center,
P.O. Box 30135, Salt Lake City, UT 84130
(800-247-3912)

Holt, Rinehart & Winston (See Henry Holt)

Houghton Mifflin
Public Library: Trade Order Department,
Houghton Mifflin Co., Wayside Road,
Burlington, MA 01803
(800-225-3362)
School : School Division,
Houghton Mifflin, 1900 South Batavia Ave.
Geneva, IL 60134
(800-225-3362)

Joy Street (See Little, Brown)

Knopf (See Random House)

Lippincott (See Harper & Row)

Little, Brown and Co.
200 West Street, Waltham, MA 02254
(800-343-9204)

Lodestar (See Dutton)

Lothrop, Lee & Shepard (See William Morrow)

Macmillan Children's Book Group
Order Department, Macmillan Publishing Co.,
Front and Brown Streets, Riverside, NJ 08075
(800-257-5755)

McElderry Books (See Macmillan)

William Morrow & Co.
Wilmor/Order Department, 39 Plymouth Street,
Box 1219, Fairfield, NJ 07007
(800-631-1199)

Mulberry (See William Morrow)

North-South (See Henry Holt)

Orchard Books: (See Franklin Watts)

Pantheon (See Random House)

Philomel (See Putnam)

Platt & Munk (See Putnam)

Potter (See Random House)

Putnam Publishing Group
1 Grosset Drive, Kirkwood, NY 13795
(800-847-5515)

R & S Books (See Farrar, Straus & Giroux)

Random House, Inc.
400 Hahn Road, Westminster, MD 21157
(800-337-7000)

Reader's Digest (See Random House)

Scholastic, Inc.
2931 East McCarty St., Jefferson, MO 65102
(800-325-6149)

Scribner's (See Macmillan)

Sierra Club (See Random House)

Simon & Schuster
Order Department, Simon & Schuster, Inc.,
200 Old Tappan Road, Old Tappan, NJ 07675
(800-223-2336)

Times Books (See Random House)

Viking Penguin, Inc.
Viking Penguin Order Department, Box 120,
Bergenfield, NJ 07621
(800-526-0275)

Frederick Warne (See Viking Penguin)

Franklin Watts
Order Department, Franklin Watts, Inc.
387 Park Avenue South, New York, NY 10016
(800-843-3749)